Teaching
Environmental Education

Teaching Environmental Education

Trends and Practices in India

Chong Shimray

SSAGE | TEXTS
www.sagepublishing.com
Los Angeles | London | New Delhi | Singapore | Washington DC | Melbourne

First published in 2016 by

$\circledS$SAGE | TEXTS

SAGE Publications India Pvt Ltd
B1/I-1 Mohan Cooperative Industrial Area
Mathura Road, New Delhi 110 044, India
www.sagepub.in

SAGE Publications Inc
2455 Teller Road
Thousand Oaks, California 91320, USA

SAGE Publications Ltd
1 Oliver's Yard, 55 City Road
London EC1Y 1SP, United Kingdom

SAGE Publications Asia-Pacific Pte Ltd
3 Church Street
#10-04 Samsung Hub
Singapore 049483

Published by Vivek Mehra for SAGE Publications India Pvt Ltd, typeset in 10/12 pt ITC Stone Serif by Diligent Typesetter India Pvt Ltd, Delhi and printed at Saurabh Printers Pvt Ltd, Greater Noida.

Library of Congress Cataloging-in-Publication Data

Name: Shimray, Chong, author.
Title: Teaching environmental education : trends and practices in India / Chong Shimray.
Description: New Delhi; Thousand Oaks : Sage Publications, 2016. | Includes bibliographical references and index.
Identifiers: LCCN 2015041359 | ISBN 9789351507321 (pbk.)
Subjects: LCSH: Environmental education—India.
Classification: LCC GE90.I4 S55 2016 | DDC 333.7071054—dc23 LC record available at http://lccn.loc.gov/2015041359

ISBN: 978-93-515-0732-1 (PB)

The SAGE Team: Amit Kumar, Indrani Dutta, Sudeshna Nandy, Shobana Paul and Rajinder Kaur

Dedicated to

my parents…
Anem Shimray & A.V. Shimray
my mentors…
Martha C. Monroe & Jaishree Sharma
my soul mate…
Alana Golmei

Bulk Sales

SAGE India offers special discounts
for bulk institutional purchases.

*For queries/orders/inspection copy requests
write to* **textbooksales@sagepub.in**

Publishing

Would you like to publish a textbook with SAGE?

Please send your proposal to **publishtextbook@sagepub.in**

Get to know more about SAGE

Be invited to SAGE events, get on our mailing list.

Write today to **marketing@sagepub.in**

Contents

Foreword by Madhav Gadgil   xiii
Preface   xv
About the Author   xvii
Acknowledgments   xix
The Book at a Glance   xxi

1. Introduction to Environmental Education   **1**
    Chapter Overview   1
    Introduction   2
    1.1 The Paradox of Environmental Issues   5
    1.2 Emergence of Environmental Education Globally   9
    1.3 What Is Environmental Education?   9
    1.4 Roots of EE   12
    1.5 Evolution of EE in the Modern Era   15
    1.6 Initiatives by International Environmental Education Programme   17
       1.6.1 First Phase   17
       1.6.2 Second Phase   22
       1.6.3 Third Phase   23
    1.7 Environmental Education and Education for Sustainable Development   23
    1.8 Chronology of Important Events in EE   25
    Conclusion   27
    Summary   27
    Exercises   28
    References   28

2. Why Environmental Education?   **31**
    Chapter Overview   31
    Introduction   32
    2.1 Nature of Disciplinary Areas   32
    2.2 Nature of EE   34
    2.3 EE and Science–Technology–Society (STS) Education   38
    2.4 Converging EE with Science Education: Possibilities and Limitations   42
    2.5 Environmental Education–Environmental Science–Environmental Studies   45
    Conclusion   51
    Summary   52
    Exercises   52
    References   53

3. Environmental Education in the School Curriculum   56
Chapter Overview   56
Introduction   57
3.1 EE through the School Curriculum   57
3.2 Approaches in EE   61
    3.2.1 Separate Subject (Interdisciplinary) Approach   62
    3.2.2 Infusion (Multidisciplinary) Approach   66
3.3 Comparisons between Interdisciplinary and Multidisciplinary Approach   71
3.4 Examples of EE in Different Disciplines   73
    3.4.1 EE in Science   73
    3.4.2 EE in Social Science   74
    3.4.3 EE in Mathematics   76
    3.4.4 EE in Languages   76
    3.4.5 EE in Arts   77
3.5 Integration of Different Approaches   77
Conclusion   77
Summary   78
Exercises   79
References   79

4. Tracing Environmental Education in India   81
Chapter Overview   81
Introduction   81
4.1 Basic Education (1937)   82
4.2 Report of the Secondary Education Commission (1953)   83
4.3 Report of the Indian Education Commission (1966)—Education
    & National Development   84
4.4 National Policy on Education (1968)   84
4.5 Curriculum for the Ten-year School: A Framework (1975)   85
    4.5.1 Syllabi for Classes VI–VIII (1976)   87
4.6 Report of the Review Committee on the Curriculum for the Ten-year
    School (1977)   88
4.7 National Policy on Education (1986)   89
4.8 Science Education for First Ten Years of Schooling: Working Group
    Report (1987)   90
4.9 National Curriculum for Elementary and Secondary Education:
    A Framework (Revised Version) (1988)   90
    4.9.1 Guidelines and Syllabi for Upper Primary Stage (1988)   92
    4.9.2 Guidelines and Syllabi for Secondary Stage (1988)   92
4.10 Learning without Burden: Report of the National Advisory
    Committee (1993)   92
4.11 National Curriculum Framework for School Education 2000 (NCFSE-2000)   92
    4.11.1 Guidelines and Syllabi for Upper Primary Stage (2001)   95
    4.11.2 Guidelines and Syllabi for Secondary Stage (2001)   95
4.12 Curriculum Framework for Teacher Education (2004)   95
4.13 Environmental Education in Schools: Syllabus (2004)   96
4.14 National Curriculum Framework 2005 (NCF-2005)   97

4.14.1 Syllabus for Classes at the Elementary Level (2005) 100

4.14.2 Syllabus for Secondary and Higher Secondary Classes (2005) 100

4.15 National Curriculum Framework for Teacher Education (2009) 101

Conclusion 102

Summary 103

Exercises 104

References 104

Appendices 105

5. Global Trends in Environmental Education and Implementation in India **118**

Chapter Overview 118

Introduction 118

5.1 Trends in India vis-à-vis Global Initiatives 119

5.1.1 International Union for Conservation of Nature (IUCN) 119

5.1.2 The United Nations Conference on the Human Environment Organized in Stockholm in 1972 120

5.1.3 International Environmental Education Programme (IEEP) 121

5.1.4 IEEP Activities in India's Context 122

5.1.5 Brundtland Commission Report, Agenda 21, Decade of Education for Sustainable Development 123

5.2 Implementation of EE in India 128

5.2.1 Intervention of the Hon'ble Supreme Court of India 129

5.2.2 Chronology of Important Events in EE in India 130

5.2.3 Present Status of EE in India 130

5.2.3.1 Three-pronged Focus of EE 132

5.2.3.2 Curricular Materials in EE 132

5.2.3.3 Assessment-related Concerns 134

5.2.3.4 Monitoring Implementation of EE 135

5.2.3.5 Implementation in States and Union Territories 135

5.2.3.6 Barriers in Implementation 136

5.2.4 EE in Schools in India vis-à-vis USA 138

5.3 Practicability of Project-based Environmental Education in India 139

5.3.1 Project-based EE in India 140

5.3.2 Pilot Study on Project-based EE 143

5.3.3 Why Did It Work? 149

Conclusion 150

Summary 150

Exercises 151

References 151

Appendix 153

6. Responsible Environmental Behavior: Ultimate Goal of Environmental Education **163**

Chapter Overview 163

Introduction 164

6.1 The Context of Responsible Environmental Behavior (REB) 164

6.2   Traditional Thinking of REB   165
6.3   Responsible Environmental Behavior: What Decides?   166
6.4   Responsible Environmental Behavior Model   167
    6.4.1   Complexity of Responsible Environmental Behavior   169
    6.4.2   Categorization of Variables   170
    6.4.3   Other Factors/Variables   171
6.5   Different Levels of Activities for Behavioral Change   172
6.6   Significance of REB Model   173
Conclusion   174
Summary   175
Exercises   175
References   175

7.   **Multi-perspectives of Environmental Education**   **177**
Chapter Overview   177
Introduction   177
7.1   Three Perspectives of Environmental Education   180
    7.1.1   Environmental Education Is All-inclusive   180
    7.1.2   Environmental Education Is Moderately Ecocentric   181
    7.1.3   Environmental Education Is Purely Ecocentric   183
7.2   The Perspectives in India's Context   184
Conclusion   187
Summary   188
Exercises   188
References   189

8.   **Teacher Empowerment in Environmental Education: A Concern**   **191**
Chapter Overview   191
Introduction   192
8.1   Teacher Preparation in Environmental Education   193
    8.1.1   Barriers in the Popularization of EE in Teacher Preparation   195
    8.1.2   Course Content in EE for Teacher Preparation   197
8.2   Teacher Preparation in EE in India: Preservice   202
    8.2.1   Comparative Study of B.Ed. Syllabus   203
    8.2.2   Duration of Preservice Courses   206
8.3   Teacher Preparation in EE in India: In-service   207
    8.3.1   Possibilities for In-service Teacher Empowerment   210
    8.3.2   Some Systemic Issues   210
8.4   Teacher Preparation in EE in India: Teacher Educators   211
8.5   Changing Names   212
Conclusion   212
Summary   214
Exercises   215
References   215

**9. Education for Sustainable Development: Departure from
Environmental Education**   **217**
Chapter Overview   217
Introduction   218
9.1   Education for Sustainable Development (ESD)   218
      9.1.1   Genesis   218
              9.1.1.1   Education   219
              9.1.1.2   Sustainable Development   220
9.2   What Is Education for Sustainable Development?   224
      9.2.1   Key Characteristics of ESD   224
      9.2.2   Four Major Thrusts of ESD   224
      9.2.3   Dimensions of ESD   226
9.3   Decade of Education for Sustainable Development (DESD)—2005
      to 2014   226
      9.3.1   Relationship of DESD with Other International Initiatives   226
      9.3.2   Impact of DESD   228
9.4   Global Action Programme (GAP)   229
      9.4.1   Goals and Objectives   232
      9.4.2   Priority Areas of GAP   232
9.5   Types of Sustainability Education   232
9.6   Is EE Very Different from ESD?   236
9.7   Do Away with EE?   238
9.8   Ramifications of Implementation of ESD   239
Conclusion   241
Summary   242
Exercises   242
References   243

10. Way Forward   **245**
Chapter Overview   245
Introduction   246
10.1 Brief Description of the Roles and Contributions of Stakeholders   247
      10.1.1   Government Agencies   247
              10.1.1.1 Ministry of Environment and Forests (MoEF)
                        (Recently Renamed as Ministry of Environment,
                        Forests and Climate Change, i.e., MoEF&CC)   247
              10.1.1.2 Ministry of Human Resource Development (MHRD)   249
              10.1.1.3 National Council of Educational Research and Training
                        (NCERT), State Council of Educational Research and
                        Training (SCERT)/State Institute of Education (SIE)/
                        State Institute Educational Research and Training (SIERT),
                        National Council for Teacher Education (NCTE),
                        University Grants Commission (UGC)   250
              10.1.1.4 Central and State Boards and School Systems   251
      10.1.2   Non-governmental Organizations and Other Institutes   251
              10.1.2.1 Centre for Environment Education (CEE)   251

10.1.2.2 Centre for Science and Environment (CSE) 251
10.1.2.3 C.P.R. Environmental Education Centre (CPREEC) 252
10.1.2.4 Institute of Environment Education and Research,
Bharati Vidyapeeth University, Pune 252
10.1.2.5 The Energy and Resources Institute (TERI) 254
10.1.2.6 Toxics Link 254
10.1.2.7 Uttarakhand Seva Nidhi Paryavaran Shiksha Sansthan
(USNPSS) or Uttarakhand Environmental Education
Centre (UEEC) 254
10.1.2.8 World Wide Fund for Nature—India (WWF-India) 254
10.2 Road Map for Implementation of EE in India 257
10.2.1 Administrative and Academic Set-ups 259
10.2.2 Development of Curriculum and Curricular Materials 259
10.2.3 Training 260
10.2.4 Research 260
10.2.5 Monitoring 260
10.2.6 Evaluation 260
10.2.7 Networking 260
10.2.8 Implementation 261
10.2.9 Web Portal for EE 261
10.3 Areas for Research in Environmental Education in India 262
10.3.1 Trends and Practices 262
10.3.2 Policy Documents 263
10.3.3 Curricular Materials 263
10.3.4 Pedagogy 263
10.3.5 Information and Communications Technology (ICT) 264
10.3.6 Impact of Implementation 264
10.3.7 Functioning in States and UTs 264
10.3.8 Assessment and Evaluation 264
10.3.9 Professional Development 265
10.3.10 Roles of Institutions 265
10.3.11 Government Agencies 266
10.3.12 Non-governmental Organizations (NGOs) 266
Conclusion 266
Summary 267
Exercises 267
References 268

Afterword A-1
Index I-1

Foreword

I had the pleasure of getting to know Dr Chong Shimray, the author of this book, in 2006 while working on project-based environmental education resource materials in the light of the National Curriculum Framework 2005. As a young environmental educator on the faculty of NCERT, with an enquiring mind and a genuine dedication to the cause of environment, she provided excellent inputs and support to the work of our group. She has continued her quest for an ever-deeper understanding of the field over the last decade, and the result is this well-designed, comprehensive book for Indian environmental educators.

In this book, Dr Chong Shimray has successfully attempted to bring out Indian and world-wide practices and latest trends in the area of environmental education. I would like to point out that the last decade has witnessed revolutionary changes not only in the field of education but, more broadly, in the creation and dissemination of knowledge. An outstanding example of this is Wikipedia, a truly bottom-up enterprise in which common people are working, on an equal footing with the experts, to compile all the knowledge of the world in an open, transparent fashion and make it freely available to all, eventually in their own languages. The National Curriculum Framework 2005 had attempted to outline a similar approach, wherein the students and teachers all over India would, through projects, generate environment-related knowledge that would come to constitute a vital component of our understanding of the environmental issues and help us undertake informed positive actions. I fervently hope that this book would help us move forward in that direction, for I am convinced that therein lies the future.

Madhav Gadgil

Preface

During the initial years of my exposure to the area of environmental education, I remember going through a hard time, hunting for appropriate books on environmental education that would give me a comprehensive idea about environmental education, especially in the context of India. Almost 10 years have passed since then but, surprisingly, even today such books are hard to find. It was the struggles that I went through in search of such material that instilled in me the 'burden' to write this book, a burden because it would be a challenge to take up such a task which was going to be one of the first attempts in the country, if not the first. However, considering the fact that lack of appropriate material for reference could deter young students, who would want to become teachers, educators, and researchers in the field of environmental education, from pursuing environmental education, I deeply felt that not writing this book was not even an option. The book, therefore, primarily targets those neophytes in the area of environmental education.

Another purpose of this book is to cater to the needs of the bunch of teacher educators throughout the country who have not had much of experience in terms of training or practice in environmental education, yet are assigned the task of completing courses on environmental education or related courses. This book will do a world of good to these educators to empower and enrich them and help them understand the basics of environmental education to deliver the courses meaningfully. Educators who have already received basic training in environmental education and who are already associated with it for a while will also greatly benefit out of it. This book will give them some fresh ways of looking at the practices and the latest trends in the area of environmental education. The book also caters to the needs of those educators and educationists who contribute in policy-making. The discussions contained in the book will constitute a useful guide to take appropriate policy decisions.

Yet another pressing reason to come up with the idea of writing this book was because I had come across too many people, even those in the field of education, who, although had very limited understanding about environmental education could exalt it or write it off, just like that! All because environmental education is still such an unpopular discipline which people tend to associate only with 'pollution' and 'planting trees.' This book is an attempt to throw some light on the importance, the relevance and the expanse of environmental education so that learners in general and those in the field of education in particular are informed and are educated about it. If this book could induce some clarity on people's perception about environmental education, it would serve much of its purpose.

Readers will find that not a single chapter is complete in itself. It will probably leave them with more questions than answers. However, this is exactly how the book has been perceived to be. It throws open several new ideas and intends to provoke its readers to critically think and enquire about the situations and arguments provided in various chapters of the book. It is envisaged that the thoughts and ideas that emerge from such critical thinking will guide students to take up further research in their topic of interest or will be need-based and take the field forward in a country like ours where most of the areas in environmental education are yet to be explored. This aspect of the book, which encourages students to become researchers, also sets it apart from other conventional books on environmental education where the content is heavily theoretical and purely examination-based.

Writing the book for a specific course or audience would have restricted the topics to be covered and hence this book is not written around any specific syllabus or for any specific user. A book with limited content coverage would mean doing disservice to the readers as well as to the book itself. A major portion of the content, however, will still meet the requirements of all environment-related courses. This book is therefore unique in that its coverage is much beyond what would be found in a conventional book on environmental education.

In order to make the book reader-friendly, sincere efforts have been put in to make each chapter exclusive with necessary supporting illustrations, pictures, and tables. However, at certain places, cross-references have been given to chapters which are interlinked, which was unavoidable. Hence readers may be required to read the book in its entirety so as to understand the connections between the chapters. Efforts were put in to ensure that sufficient opinions and findings of various professionals, researchers, experts, practitioners, and so on, are reflected in the book, which will give the readers a balanced idea of the differing philosophies, concepts and opinions. Key references have been substantially cited and provided wherever necessary. Complete references have been provided at the end of every chapter so that readers can turn to the references for further detailed readings.

The book, in short, is a 'starter' for those who want to venture into the field of environmental education, especially those in India. And it is a 'booster' or an enrichment material for those who have already had exposure in the form of training or research in the area of environmental education. An attempt has been made to present the concepts and concerns related to environmental education in the most comprehensive and understandable way by tapping all possible resources at my disposal in the form of books, journals, websites, and so on, besides my personal experiences in India and abroad, and interactions with experts in the field.

During the process of writing this book, I was also able to form some ideas which could have possibly influenced the chapters to head in a certain direction. Such instances, wherever they might have occurred, were only to enhance the chapters and not to present any biased or prejudiced opinions. Readers might also at times find themselves struggling to juggle as they go through the chapters due to the somewhat lack of uniformity in the manner they have been presented—book-like as well as journal-like nature. However, in spite of all its limitations and failings, it is hoped that readers will be able to make the best use of the book and appreciate the humble endeavor to bring out a book of this nature which has not yet been attempted by many in the country.

About the Author

Chong Shimray is Assistant Professor in the Department of Education in Science and Mathematics, National Council of Educational Research and Training (NCERT), New Delhi. She completed her Master of Science in Life Sciences (Zoology) and Ph.D. on thrips biodiversity from the Department of Life Sciences, Manipur University. She has published several research papers in reputed journals and contributed chapters in books in the area of her research.

Dr Shimray began her career in the area of school education as Lecturer in Zoology at the Regional Institute of Education, a constituent of NCERT located in Mysore, Karnataka, where she taught a course for Bachelor of Science Education from 2004–2005. Thereafter, she joined the Department of Education in Science and Mathematics, NCERT, New Delhi in 2005 and continues to serve in the same department in the capacity of Assistant Professor till date. Dr Shimray is associated with various tasks related to school education, especially in environmental education and curricular subjects of science and biology. She has contributed in the development of various textbooks and other complementary and supplementary materials in science and biology. However, her most notable contributions are reflected in the area of environmental education where she coordinates the projects and programs undertaken by NCERT in the area, and networks with States, Union Territories, different school systems, non-governmental organizations and other stakeholders. Dr Shimray has coordinated and contributed in the development of several books on environmental education in the NCERT for the upper primary to the higher secondary stages. Apart from these, she has also been associated with several training programs in environmental education for in-service teachers and teacher educators conducted by NCERT and other agencies. Her contribution in the implementation of environmental education in India has been encouraging, even as she continues to do so.

Dr Shimray also has some notable achievements to her credit. She was awarded the Junior Research Fellowship in Life Sciences in the CSIR-UGC NET examination. She was also a recipient of the prestigious Fulbright–Nehru Fellowship in 2009 during which she was affiliated to the School of Forest Resources and Conservation, University of Florida, Gainesville, Florida, USA. As a Fulbright Fellow, Dr Shimray undertook a study to look into the implementation of environmental education in the schools in United States. This Fulbright experience was significant in shaping her outlook about the field of environmental education.

Acknowledgments

I would like to thank Professor Madhav Gadgil, a very eminent yet down-to-earth and internationally acclaimed environmentalist of India, to have readily agreed to write the Foreword of this book. His invaluable words have richly added value to the book. Professor Gadgil is an inspiration and is looked up to as a role model by many, including myself, which makes it all the more special.

Several individuals have contributed in different ways during the course of the writing of this book. A very special person, Professor Jaishree Sharma, had patiently gone through the manuscript and suggested ways for improvements. Besides, Professor Jaishree has always been a pillar of support academically as well as emotionally ever since she introduced me to the world of environmental education. And I cannot thank her enough for that. There are a few other names that deserve mention who might not even be aware that they had made a difference in the process of writing this book. They are those who have generously shared their valuable resources at various points of time—Martha C. Monroe, School of Forest Resources and Conservation, University of Florida; David Sobel, Antioch University, New England and Jennie Lane Farber, Educational Sciences, Faculty of Education, Bilkent University, Turkey. I specially appreciate Martha for being there to guide me every time I needed to clarify a doubt or simply to share her opinion or patiently hear me out and critically comment on my views. I have been able to organize my thoughts on important fundamental issues related to environmental education through such interactions.

Others, like Asanna, has worked tirelessly to go through the initial draft and give shape to the book. My brother, Alfred Shimray, has helped me out with the illustrations. I appreciate their significant contributions. Words cannot express the value of the 'you-can-do-it' boosters that I received day-in and day-out from family and friends, especially Alana Golmei. The fact that most people, including educationists, attest little importance to environmental education also gave me enormous strength and gumption to put this book together by any means. I sincerely thank this unclassified set of people who indirectly pushed me beyond my limits to get this book done.

Portions of the section 'Stakeholders for the implementation of environmental education in India,' in Chapter 10: Way Forward, were contributed by the concerned organizations such as Dr Shamita Kumar, Professor and Vice Principal, Bharati Vidyapeeth Institute of Environment Education and Research (BVIEER) and WWF-India. The concerned person at The Energy and Resources Institute (TERI) had given consent for the content provided on their activities in the chapter. Their valuable contributions in the form of text and pictures which have enriched the book are sincerely acknowledged. In this world of business, a reference book of this nature is seldom a priority for publication. I sincerely thank SAGE Publications India for publishing this book under their prestigious banner and tag. Such commitment shown toward quality education is highly appreciated. I am grateful to the subject-matter experts who have reviewed portions of the book and provided valuable suggestions, especially Dr M. Rajendran and Dr Yukti

Sharma, Department of Education (CIE), University of Delhi; Dr Magre Sunita Vithalrao, Department of Education, University of Mumbai and Dr Madhumala Sengupta, Department of Education, University of Calcutta.

The whole publishing team at SAGE who contributed at various stages of the publication of this book, especially Indrani Dutta and Amit Kumar with whom I was associated from the initial stage of submission of the book proposal and Sudeshna Nandy from the time of editing, till its publication in the form that you are holding, each one of them deserve much appreciation. Without them this book would not have seen the light of the day.

Above all, I thank God Almighty for the privilege and the favor He bestowed upon me to author this book. I could have never done it by myself. But His grace was indeed sufficient for me!

The Book at a Glance

Environmental education has been in practice for several decades now. Some countries have marched far ahead, as is evident from their curriculum of the primary, secondary and tertiary education, while other countries are slowly catching up. The sincerity with which it is implemented may vary. Nevertheless, every country has been doing their bit to incorporate environmental education in their curriculum.

The Context

Environmental education has become more relevant now than ever before. This is because while we are draining our exhaustible natural resources with all the technological advancements that we are making, at the same time we are filling our environment with all its ill-effects in the form of pollution, other forms of hazardous and toxic chemicals and the likes causing threat to our own survival. We have realized that laws and penalties imposed to tackle environmental issues is only topical treatment of the issues and is not sustainable. We know education will be instrumental in bringing about the change that we want to see, and hence the importance of environmental education. However, for this to materialize in the school systems, environmental education has to be done in a systematic manner, with clearly defined goals and pedagogy. This will require an understanding of the specific concerns related to environmental education in terms of implementation, such as curriculum for schools and to-be teachers, skills and competencies of the teachers and teacher educators, challenges and barriers in implementation, and so on.

This book is about understanding environmental education with a focus on formal school education in India. Other forms of environmental education, informal and non-formal, if mentioned, have been done only on specific contexts.

The Structure of the Book

The book has 10 chapters with an Afterword at the end. A very brief introduction as to how each chapter has been organized in the book is provided below.

The first chapter, 'Introduction to Environmental Education,' introduces the readers to the various benefits humanity has received as a result of development in science and technology. At the same time, it also discusses the various environmental issues brought about by the use of such technologies and the need to come up with newer technologies so as to tackle the issues brought about by the use of technologies. Examples have been cited to explain the paradox that is encountered in solving environmental problems. How such growing concerns about environmental issues world over has led to the introduction of environmental education have been discussed in detail in the chapter.

It then discusses how the concept of environmental education has evolved over the years. Some landmark events and selected definitions of environmental education have also been provided in the chapter. The goals, objectives and guiding principles of environmental education have also been discussed.

Why do we need environmental education when we are already learning about environmental issues in science is a question still asked by many. The second chapter, 'Why Environmental Education?', consolidates the status of environmental education as an indispensable area of study and therefore the need for its inclusion as an integral component in the school curriculum. The chapter explains the unique nature of environmental education and how it is different from other disciplinary subjects. For this purpose, the nature of environmental education and other disciplinary areas have been discussed. It goes on to explain the limitations to implement environmental education through Science–Technology–Society (STS) education. The possibilities and limits to implement environmental education through a science curriculum have also been discussed. At the end, the chapter discusses the relationships that exist between environmental education, environmental science and environmental studies.

The third chapter, 'Environmental Education in the School Curriculum,' is an extension of the second chapter which gives the readers some idea of the different ways environmental education is done and can be done through the curriculum. It explains how the goals of environmental education can be achieved through the school curriculum. The chapter then discusses the two common approaches of implementing environmental education—interdisciplinary (separate subject) approach and multidisciplinary (infusion) approach. The pros and cons of both the approaches are discussed in the chapter. It then provides numerous examples on how environmental education can be incorporated in the teaching–learning of different disciplines.

Environmental education has come a long way in India to be what it is today. As the title of the chapter suggests, the fourth chapter, 'Tracing Environmental Education in India,' traces the evolution of environmental education in India by looking at the various school education-related documents such as educational commission reports, national policy on education documents, national curriculum frameworks for schools and teacher education and other nationally important educational reports that were brought out in India since beginning the 1930s. How each document has reflected environmental education has been provided succinctly in the chapter.

Someone who has just been introduced to the area would be naturally curious to know whether the initiatives taken at the global level on environmental education have any effect on the implementation or decisions taken in India. This aspect is discussed in the fifth chapter, 'Global Trends in Environmental Education and Implementation in India.' The present status of implementation of environmental education in India, covering different aspects such as objectives, curricular materials, assessment, and implementation in different states and union territories, is then discussed in the chapter. This chapter also makes a special mention of how a public interest litigation (PIL) filed in the Hon'ble Supreme Court of India had an impact on the course of implementation of environmental education throughout the country. In view of the importance of project-based environmental education, as highlighted in the National Curriculum Framework 2005 and also in the affidavit submitted to the Hon'ble Supreme Court, the chapter incorporates a detailed pilot study undertaken to find out its practicability in schools. A special feature of this chapter is the inclusion of a comparative study of implementation of environmental education in schools in India and the United States of America.

The sixth chapter, 'Responsible Environmental Behavior—Ultimate Goal of Environmental Education,' discusses the importance of environmental responsible behavior through 'doing.' It elaborates on how, in spite of all the efforts that we put in, environmental education will not be meaningful unless we see some positive actions being taken, or observe some patterns of behavior (not inherited but learned) or, in other words, if only students display some kind of responsible environmental behavior (REB). It discusses several factors which contribute to REB. Several views on behavioral change are being discussed in the chapter while emphasis has been laid on a model of REB which illustrates the complexity of REB. The chapter also explains how it is impossible to get a perfect model to bring about REB while also bringing out the importance of understanding REB for practitioners and policy makers.

Environmental education could be the most misconceived discipline due to lack of consistencies in the presentation of what environmental education is. The seventh chapter, 'Multiperspectives of Environmental Education,' explores the different views or perspectives on what is included under environmental education. Three different perspectives have been presented in the chapter—environmental education is all-inclusive, environmental education is moderately ecocentric, and environmental education is purely ecocentric. It elaborates how these three perspectives can impact the implementation of environmental education. The chapter further delves into the trends and practices in India to find out which of the perspectives can be considered to be accepted or practiced in India.

The success of the implementation of environmental education totally depends on how prepared teachers are. The eighth chapter, 'Teacher Empowerment in Environmental Education—A Concern,' focuses on the concerns related to the various aspects of teacher empowerment. It discusses the status of teacher empowerment in the area of environmental education and provides the basic content that should be incorporated in all teacher education courses. Issues pertaining to both preservice and in-service courses are discussed comprehensively in the chapter. A comparison of selected Bachelor of Education courses provided across the country is done in the chapter to find out how well the objectives of environmental education can be achieved through such courses. Besides these, issues concerning teacher educators with respect to environmental education are also discussed. At the end, some suggestions toward improving the situation and empowering teachers in the area of environmental education are also provided.

More than three decades after environmental education have been put into practice globally and also the United Nations Decade of Education for Sustainable Development (UNDESD) having been concluded, there is still lack of clarity on the similarities or the differences between environmental education and Education for Sustainable Development (ESD). The ninth chapter, 'Education for Sustainable Development—A Departure from Environmental Education,' introduces the concept of sustainable development and thence the goals of Education for Sustainable Development. It also discusses the impact of UNDESD and the Global Action Programme developed by UNESCO as a follow up of UNDESD. The different types of sustainability education are then discussed. It also explains elaborately how ESD and EE can be considered similar and how they can also be considered different. The chapter also discusses the departure of ESD from environmental education and provides some of the possible implications and ramifications that such departure might bring about related to environmental issues.

The tenth chapter, 'Way Forward,' provides an implementation strategy for the implementation of environmental education in India. However, successful implementation of such efforts will only be possible with the collective efforts of different agencies—both governmental and non-governmental. While government bodies have put in much effort, the role of non-governmental organizations has also been commendable. The chapter discusses the roles these bodies have played in the past and their anticipated efforts in the implementation of environmental education. Emphasis has been given on the role of the Ministry of Human Resource Development (MHRD) and Ministry of Environment, Forests and Climate Change (MoEF&CC) along with some prominent NGOs and institutes working in the area of environmental education. The chapter also discusses the roles of other institutes and school systems which are indispensable. Lack of implementation strategies can be considered as one of the reasons why environmental education in India has not made much headway. The chapter, therefore, provides a roadmap which will help policy makers and implementers to come out with an appropriate plan of action for the implementation of environmental education in India. While these initiatives are undertaken, a component that necessitates special mention is that of research. Hardly any studies are available based on which strategic measures can be taken up for the implementation of environmental education. The chapter identifies the different areas where research can be undertaken. This will guide researchers to take up need-based research.

The book concludes with an Afterword where the author tries to share a piece of her mind highlighting the one reason why things are the way they are (referring to environmental issues) and why nothing is likely to change in spite of all the most brilliant heads and the Heads of all powerful countries coming together for a solution. The author attributes the cause of the issues as well as the solution to the issues to one factor—Attitude! The issue begins with attitude and the solution also begins with attitude, the only difference in the two being whether it is the right attitude or the wrong attitude. Degradation of the environment begins with a wrong attitude and nurturance of the environment begins with a right attitude. The author concludes by highlighting the role of educators in addressing this issue and makes a clarion call to all educators to act, not based on the prescribed syllabus, but in response to their conscience.

Introduction to Environmental Education

Worth a Thought!

A science teacher in a secondary school was asked if environmental education was part of their curriculum. Her prompt response was, "[Y]es, our science textbooks include air and water pollution. Our students also plant trees!" It is not uncommon to hear such response from teachers. Somehow environmental education is seen to be conveniently equated with simply providing information about pollution and planting trees.

Chapter Overview

The chapter broadly introduces the readers to the area of environmental education. It begins by elucidating the contributions of technological advancements which transformed our way of living and at the same time attributing such technologies as the cause of the present day environmental issues facing the world. It then brings out some of the pros and cons of such technological advancements, especially in terms of environment, equity in the society, and health. The complexity of addressing environmental issues is discussed and how often a well-thought of solution itself becomes an issue to be addressed is also elaborated. With the readers fairly exposed to concerns related to the environment, the chapter highlights the important role environmental education can play in tackling environmental issues. The roots and evolution of environmental education and the landmark events in its history is then discussed. It also discusses the various definitions of environmental education provided by various practitioners and professionals. It is envisaged that this chapter will facilitate the readers to:

- explain the importance of environmental education.
- justify that environmental issues are complex.
- define environmental education.
- describe the root and evolution of environmental education over the years and decades.
- identify the role of UNESCO and the United Nations Environmental Programme (UNEP) in the popularization of environmental education globally.
- explain the origin of education for sustainable development.

Introduction

Beginning the 19th century, significant development and changes have been taking place all across the globe. There have been remarkable advancements in science and technology which have led to speedy growth and expansion of industries, numerous innovations, and great inventions of machines and tools for various purposes. New technologies and inventions have enabled increase in farm and industrial productions, including dairy products, agricultural products, and other food products including genetically modified foods, lifesaving drugs, chemicals, household appliances, and electronic devices. Gone are the days when one has to struggle hard to survive or venture out in search of cooler clime and places or mechanically fan oneself to get some relief from the scorching summer heat or curl up around a fireplace to escape from the biting winter. Development and new technologies have enabled easier and comfortable life for humans to a great extent.

The world has changed so much due to technological inventions and innovations. And humans have 'evolved' with the changes taking place around them, rapidly working toward creating a more comfortable living and at the same time changing the environment around them. A lifestyle sustained by using simple limited resources has now transformed into a more sophisticated lifestyle which is tremendously resource intensive. Through this process which they call progress, human beings have been successful in making available almost all their every requirement. They have invented themselves papyrus which significantly contributed to know the past; papers and carbon papers, typewriters, pens for different purpose; photocopy machines, and 2D printers. The latest in this area being the invention of 3D printers using which anything available virtual can now be obtained in its real 3D form. One cannot even imagine what is up next. Advancements in science and technology has also enabled fast-paced new mode of transport and communication. This has made the world indeed smaller. Today, things that are available in any corner of the world can be made available in any part of the world. It is just the question of one's capacity to buy or afford. Destinations which took days and weeks, or even months to reach can now be reached in a matter of few hours or few minutes. Distance no more remains a reason to distance people. A person anywhere in the world can now be in contact with another person any day, anytime, anyplace, virtual of course.

With new developments and great possibilities at our disposal, life definitely appears better, easier, and improving. And much of our endeavors are toward developing newer technologies which would make our lives better and better. But little did we realize that the development and the great progress achieved so far and the changes taking place all over the world are at the cost of exploitation of our environment which is causing health hazards due to various toxic wastes released, deterioration of the environment, such as air, water and soil pollution, scarcity of water, desertification, loss of biodiversity, and so on, destructions due to increase in natural disasters such as floods and cyclones, and social injustice. Though it is true, rich or poor, ultimately no one can escape the hazards and disasters brought about by the downside of development, clearly there seem to be injustice in terms of bearing the brunt. The poor apparently end up paying more. While a set of people, or even nations for that matter, are enjoying the 'growth' and 'development,' another set is at the receiving end and are suffering the ill-effects brought about by the same. The ramifications of this in the lives of the people who suffer constitutes another set of issues that needs to be taken care of, such as health concerns, relocation, job, education, and so on. Should we be content with such forms of development, the benefit of which is not shared equally by people belonging to different economic strata? Development will take a different form if we are reminded of Mahatma Gandhi's *talisman* every time we try to invent or put into use new technologies or initiate developmental activities—"[R]ecall the face of the poorest and weakest man you may have seen and ask yourself if the step you contemplate to take is going to be of any use to him. Will he gain anything by it?" Cautioning about the advances in science and technology, decades back, Nash (1976 in Schoenfeld and Disinger 1978, 9) had opined that unless science takes into consideration the ethical and humanitarian influences, it could turn out to be "mankind's greatest problem rather than its greatest blessing." However, this finds no place in today's science and society unfortunately and hence the evident disparity and injustice prevailing everywhere. In short, man's progress has also resulted in bringing about serious threatening issues not only related to his biophysical environment but also to his social environment.

With the increasing disparity and injustice prevailing in the society, the world is seeing an ever-increasing number of different environmental groups and activists springing up to involve citizens in public environmental affairs which have resulted in the stalling or dropping of several developmental projects. While many would appreciate and support such initiatives, others launch attacks on such groups labeling them to be anti-development, ignorant about the need of such projects and often to fulfill their personal vendetta.

JUST A MOMENT

Of all the technological advances the world has made, what has intrigued you the most and what has disappointed you the most?

Another area of concern is that of human health vis-à-vis economic growth and development. How far do we take into account the 'health' component in our arithmetic of economic index? If economic growth and development represents the well-being of a nation, human health of its citizens should be considered as the most important index or indicator. And this is not just about human health and economic development. It has much to do with environment. We are aware of the fact that all development activities, directly or indirectly, affect the environment. Pollutions of different kinds are all caused by such developmental activities or are the result of such developmental activities. And needless to say, such pollutions cause several health related complications. In short, it reduces our lifespan and at the same time much of the earnings are spent in healthcare. It has become impossible to talk about health and not talk about environment and vice versa (Wenzel 1997). Recently, a popular newspaper quoted a study by economists from the University of Chicago, Harvard, and Yale that was published in *Economic and Political Weekly,* which says that:

Over half of India's population—660 million people—live in areas where fine particulate matter pollution is above India's standards for what is considered safe... If India reverses this trend to meet its air standards, those 660 million people would gain about 3.2 years onto their lives. (*The Hindu*, 21 February 2015)

If we really want to live healthier, longer, and be more productive, we need to look back and find ways to reduce pollution. This means that we need to revisit and rethink about our developmental activities and policies. We need to think beyond developmental activities for economic growth and also consider the impact on human health. If this is done seriously, the environment will also be automatically taken care significantly. However, doing this will not be as easy as it sounds. It is a complex issue which will require great and committed minds coming together to work out appropriate strategies. Besides such complex issues, there exist simple issues which we still struggle to get over. For example, indoor air pollution due to the use of traditional high soot and smoke releasing *chulhas* or stove by a large number of households in the country is one of the causes for respiratory-related health issues in the rural areas and also amongst the urban poor.

There is another very complicated issue when it comes to environmental degradation. How do we address our greed and crave for luxury? Mahatma Gandhi had said, "The earth provides enough to satisfy everyman's need but not for everyman's greed." The present day unprecedented rate of environmental deterioration can be, to a great extent, attributed to our greed and crave for luxury (Khoshoo and Moolakkattu 2009, 14). No

Photo 1.1   Huge Population of India Still Depend on Traditional *Chulha* for Cooking

doubt, with time our need has also been changing but it is becoming a serious concern only because of our greed. We want to have it all because 'possession' defines who we are in the society that we live in and to be at the top of the pyramid defined by such possessions, have become every person's dream. Besides, once thought of to be a luxury is now considered a necessity. And who does not want to lead a comfortable life? But the question now is, where do we draw the line between need and greed and also between comfort and luxury? For example, how many buildings or mansions do we need to own to lead a comfortable life or how many cars for that matter? How many trees do we need to fell to use as timber or firewood? How much food, water, energy, and so on, are we going to waste? Are we ready to act positively in this direction by taking some moral, social, and ethical responsibility? Our action could be as simple and trivial-sounding as restricting ourselves from buying that extra set of clothes if we do not need it or extending the use of that pair of dress before discarding it or holding on to our urge a little longer to replace our nicely working mobile phones or any gadget or appliances, or depending on local produce as far as possible, or making sure that the discarded items are put to reuse or they are recycled.

JUST A MOMENT

Reflect on your lifestyle and also ponder on your perspective about life. Has it been to meet your need or has it been to accumulate as much as possible?

1.1 The Paradox of Environmental Issues

We have seen that environmental concerns are deep and widespread. But we seem to be doing too little too less for too long to heal the damage that we had done and to prevent new ones from emerging. Lack of awareness and growing human activities are also adding to the problem each day. As a result, nothing much seems to have changed even decades after widespread global efforts were initiated and pressed forward to tackle environmental issues. It is also being realized that environmental issues are much more complex than it was thought to be and addressing the issues are more complicated and challenging than the issue itself.

Environmental issues range from exploitation of natural resources to all kinds of pollution—land, air, and water—to global warming, human rights to ecological justice to social justice to conflicts to issues of the 'commons' (any shared resources such as atmosphere, rivers, oceans, and so on.) and much more. To address each of these issues, numerous aspects have to be considered—broadly, social, economic, and environmental concerns. Hence often, if not always, addressing environmental issues is paradoxical. Even well-intended and well-thought out decisions often lead to another more complicated problem. It appears that only the form of environmental issue changes but the issue remains. For example, the onset of the Green Revolution reduced farmer's dependency on forest resources. For this, the state provided water, electricity, fertilizers, and machinery at highly subsidized rates. This greatly increased food production and the program was considered a great success. But, unfortunately, it also led to heavy destruction of forests with the building of large dams for irrigation and large power generation (Gadgil and Guha 2000, 222; Ramakrishnan 2001, 165–192). Therefore, it is not the development of new technology per se that is important but often to do with its appropriate use (Tortajada 2005, 12). Another example is of the invention of plastic shopping bags of the 1960s and 1970s which began to be used indiscriminately since the 1980s. Convenient as it is, it was not realized then that such a once-thought boon could someday turn out to be a bane and become such a serious environmental concern. Owing to its improper disposal, polythene bags are found to litter every possible place on earth—inhabited areas, soil, oceans, rivers, drains, mountains, and so on. Adding to the woes is the flouting of rules by manufacturers on the minimum thickness that has caused a major concern in terms of recycling. We now have to device another technology to address this issue. This cycle of solution-problem-solution brought about by invention of new technologies seem to have no end. Hirst (1977 cited in Schoenfeld and Disinger 1978, 9) holds such rampant technology responsible for environmental problems and blames engineers and scientists who are involved in the development of such technologies for the problems.

A huge chunk of population of the world continues to glorify science and technology and believes it to be a *deus ex machina*. That is, they believe that all the problems facing the world can be solved by technologies, though this notion seems to decrease as educational levels increase (Silvernail 1978 cited in Disinger and Lisowski 1986, xi).

Photo 1.2   Solar Concentrators Used for Heating Water

Photo 1.3   Solar Power Plant under Construction

Rightly so to some extent! For example, the latest innovations in negative emission technologies will do a world of good to tackle climate change. Similarly, inventions and innovations of new technologies to tap renewable sources of energy will drastically reduce our dependency on nonrenewable sources of energy. The Report of the World Commission on Environment and Development, *Our Common Future* (WCED 1987), also promotes management and improvement of technology to make way for a new era of economic growth. But the larger question that we must be asking is "can we in any way restrict our tendency to depend on technology completely" or "what are the practices that we can reinforce in our daily lives which will reduce our dependency on technology?" We need to be reminded that invariably all the technologies that humans have invented for their welfare have adverse effects in some way or the other on the environment.

Tremendous efforts are being made to improve the human development index (which include indicators such as life expectancy at birth, adult literacy rate, and GDP per capita) by catering to different aspects of life such as literacy, health care, immunization, safe drinking water, sanitation, and so on, especially in developing countries like India. And all these are directly or indirectly connected with the use of energy. It has never occurred in history that a country has improved its level of human development without corresponding increase in per capita use of energy (Ghosh 2010, 182). At present, due to the issues of global warming and climate change facing the world, countries world over have to reduce their energy consumption, irrespective of their present level of per capita energy consumption. In this scenario, developing countries like India are in a Catch-22 situation. While they want to improve their human development index, the same will require increase in energy consumption. While such a move to reduce energy consumption worldwide is the need of the hour, it will not be fair to ask developing countries like India to reduce their energy consumption.

Wenzel (1997) also discusses about such paradox wherein development brings about individual benefits while at the same time in the process of doing so brings about threat to their own lives collectively. He puts down the same in the following words:

> [D]eveloped societies in uncontrolled ways have gone so far that individual life can be extended to limits never experienced before but simultaneously threatening collective lives in pursuit of their economic prosperity by establishing modes of production, manufacturing, housing codes, environmental pollution, and living standards hazardous to the health of the population rather than to the health of particular individuals.

The paradox seems to apply to almost every activity that we are engaged in. We are associated with several activities such as land-clearing, agriculture, and forestry, for good intended results such as increase in food production, shelter, comfort, and so on. However, such activities also bring about the negative unintended results such as habitat destruction, deforestation, and desertification. (Fig. 1.1)

Figure 1.1   Effects of Human Activities

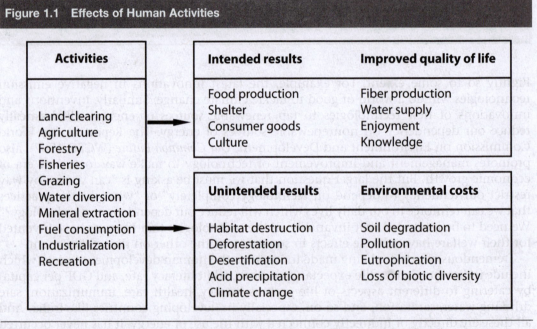

Activities	Intended results	Improved quality of life
Land-clearing Agriculture Forestry Fisheries Grazing Water diversion Mineral extraction Fuel consumption Industrialization Recreation	Food production Shelter Consumer goods Culture	Fiber production Water supply Enjoyment Knowledge

	Unintended results	Environmental costs
	Habitat destruction Deforestation Desertification Acid precipitation Climate change	Soil degradation Pollution Eutrophication Loss of biotic diversity

Source: Adopted from Lubchenco et al. (1991: *Ecology*, 72: 371–412 in Ramakrishnan 2001, 16)

JUST A MOMENT

Reflect on the complexity of dealing with environment issues. Try to relate it with a situation that you have come across in your locality or area or read about it in a newspaper, journal, magazine, or book.

1.2 Emergence of Environmental Education Globally

It is being noted that, since the 1970s, humanity has become increasingly aware and concerned about the deteriorating environment and the changing climatic conditions the world over. Environmental concerns are no longer restricted to a country or few countries, but have become global issues that call for serious attention. It was realized that such environmental problems posed a threat to man's own existence. With this, there dawned a realization among world leaders that the issues are to be addressed with the concerted efforts of all nations. The realization spread among all people and all communities in the world. Nations came together and they agreed to collectively work toward nurturing the environment more evidently, beginning the United Nations Conference on the Human Environment held at Stockholm in 1972. During this conference, the need of education on environment to address the issues was strongly felt and highlighted. This was followed by the International Environmental Education Workshop held in Belgrade (formerly in Yugoslavia, now in Serbia) which brought out the Belgrade Charter of 1975 (discussed in more detail later) and the International Conference on Environmental Education held in Tbilisi, Republic of Georgia which came up with the Tbilisi Declaration of 1977. Subsequent to these, several other global initiatives have been undertaken and many are being carried out toward the same end.

Environmental education (EE) thus has been considered an important component of education the world over since the Stockholm conference. It is envisaged that environmental education will provide "the much needed foundation for a new international order which will guarantee the conservation and improvement of the environment" (NCERT 1981). However, as we have seen in the above discussion, it is important to note that environmental education developed due to man's perceived threat for its own survival and not out of concern or fascination for nature per se (Disinger and Howe 1990, 1; Lahiry et al. 1988, 20; Schoenfeld 1971, 41; Tilbury 1997). This could bring about, in fact it has brought about, selectively biased conservation practices which are purely anthropocentric as we shall discuss in other sections of the book, especially in Chapter 9.

1.3 What Is Environmental Education?

Today, environment-related studies are being increasingly emphasized and promoted in school and college education throughout the world. In formal school education system, environmental education takes different forms as 'environment studies' depending on the environmental settings (not just the physical environment but the facilities in schools and the priorities and flexibilities in the curriculum). It is not uncommon to see practitioners 'do EE' through a wide range of activities: observation of environmentally important days; planting of trees; painting; slogan or essay writing competitions on environment-related themes; preparation of models of environmentally friendly technologies and structures; holding rallies to create awareness and encourage public to take certain environmental responsible actions or to promote certain environmentally sound practices; visits to biodiversity parks, national parks, botanical and zoological gardens, and museums; nature trails, and so on.

Photo 1.4   Animal Mask-Making by Students on Earth Day

Photo Courtesy: WWF-India

Photo 1.5   Maintaining School Campus (at Remote Part of Tripura)

Photo 1.6   Animal Museum, Camp Crystal Lake, Florida

However, every curricular area has its own unique way of approach (Carter and Simmons 2010, 11) and definition. Hence, the question that arises at this point is—What is environmental education? Is environmental education limited to the activities mentioned above, or is there more to it? How did environmental education take its present form? How do we define environmental education and what are its goals? These questions will be asked by a person who has just been introduced to the field of environmental education. We will focus our discussions on these questions based on various studies by several researchers and leading professionals in the field.

Following studies and views of experts, environmental education can be variously placed within the framework of education. The multiplicity of the meaning of the term environmental education by different people, including environmental educators, was clearly pointed out by Disinger (1986). It means many things to many people, including those who profess to be "environmental educators" (Disinger and Wilson 1986, 3). It can be considered an approach to education, a philosophy, a tool and a discipline (Monroe et al. 2007), and a perspective—a way of looking at things, of analyzing, of evaluating (Sarabhai et al. 1998). Tilbury (1997) calls it 'a new concept in education.' It is also considered a new approach in education which "not only gives a few pieces of information on environmental concerns but also brings about a new personal and individualized behaviour based on a 'global ethic'" (Lahiry et al. 1988, 17). The National Council of Educational Research and Training (NCERT 1981) opines that environmental education can make a powerful contribution to the renovation of the educational process due to its very nature of being interdisciplinary and holistic. It has also been observed that practitioners and professionals have defined environmental education according to the goal(s) they want to attain. Some limit it to the study of nature and natural resources, while others stretch it wide open to include the total environment (biophysical as well as social). Besides the variations in the definition of environmental education, there exist issues due to lack of clarity as Lucas (1980) cited Wheeler (1975) as follows, "[I]t is clear that different people mean different things by it, and also that some who use it are not really certain what they mean." The literature has also revealed that there exists cynical use of the term 'environmental' as a prefix to make a subject a better competitor in the academic marketplace such as using the title 'Environmental Physics' for a physics course which discusses topics such as work, energy, and the thermodynamic laws which has little to do with the concept of environmental education (Lucas 1980). However, the most widely accepted definition of environmental education seems to be that which was proposed in the Belgrade Charter:

> Environmental education is a process aimed at developing a world population that is aware of and concerned about the total environment and its associated problems, and which has the knowledge, motivations, commitments, and skills to work individually and collectively toward solutions of current problems and the prevention of new ones. (UNESCO-UNEP 1976; UNESCO 1984).

While some more definitions will be part of the discussion that follows, few others are provided in Box 1.1. As varied as the definitions may appear, all converge to one essence: environmental education is all about well-living and well-being of humankind.

1.4 Roots of EE

The term 'environmental education' is considered to have been first used in 1948 by Thomas Pritchard, the then Deputy Director of The Nature Conservancy in Wales, during the meeting of the International Union for the Conservation of Nature and Natural Resources (IUCN) held in Paris. It was used to suggest an educational approach to the synthesis of the natural and social sciences (Disinger 1983).

However, over the years, different views and approaches of different philosophers, professionals, educationists, and practitioners have largely contributed and shaped environmental education to its understanding today. The pedagogy of environmental education was influenced by the following: educational philosopher Jean-Jacques Rousseau (1712–1778) who maintained through his writings that education should include a study on environment that we should return to nature and discover nature as it is, rather than memorize scientific facts (Biedenweg et al. 2013; McCrea 2006); Sir Patrick Geddes (1854–1932), an advocate of nature conservation; and John Dewey (1859–1952), who was a strong proponent of experiential education that included opportunities to explore, reflect upon, and apply newly learned concepts (Biedenweg et al. 2013). Another renowned scientist, Louis Agassiz, strongly advocated learning directly from nature and not books (Disinger and Monroe 1994).

BOX

Definitions of Environmental Education

Environmental management education is the process of developing a citizenry that is:

1. knowledgeable of the interrelated biophysical and sociocultural environments of which man is a part;
2. aware of the associated environmental problems and management alternatives of use in solving these problems; and
3. motivated to work toward the maintenance and further development of diverse environments that are optimum for living.

— Robert E. Roth (1970)

Environmental education is that education which develops in man a recognition of his interdependence with all of life and a recognition of his responsibility to maintain the environment in a manner fit for life and fit for living—an environment of beauty and bounty, in which man lives in harmony. The first part of environmental education involves development of understanding; the second, development of attitudes—a 'conservation ethic.'

— Matthew J. Brennan (1970)

For the purpose of this act, the term 'environmental education' means the educational process dealing with man's relationship with his natural and manmade surroundings, and includes the relation of population, conservation, transportation, technology, and urban and regional planning to the total human environment.

— Environmental Quality Education Act (1970)

From nature study, environmental education draws an emphasis on an understanding of our ecological system—man, culture, natural environment. From conservation education, environmental education draws a concern for the husbandry of the system. From outdoor education, environmental education borrows the concept that such issues should cut across the entire curriculum. From citizenship education, environmental education draws social dimensions and a commitment to action. From resource management education, environmental education draws a technological point of entry to public policy change.

— Clay Schoenfeld (1971)

Environmental education is a way of implementing the goals of environmental protection. Environmental education is not a separate branch of science or subject of study. It should be carried out according to the principle of lifelong integral education.

— Finnish National Commission for UNESCO,
Report of the Seminar on Environmental Education, Jammi, Finland, 1974

Environmental education is an interdisciplinary, integrated process concerned with resolution of values conflicts related to the man-environment relationship, through development of a citizenry

(Continued)

(Continued)

with awareness and understanding of the environment, both natural and man-altered. Further, this citizenry will be able and willing to apply enquiry skills, and implement decision-making, problem-solving, and action strategies toward achieving/maintaining homeostasis between quality of life and quality of environment.

— Gary D. Harvey (1977)

To create an awareness and an understanding of the evolving social and physical environment as a whole, its natural, man-made, cultural, spiritual resources, together with the rational use and conservation of these resources for development.

— Report of a Conference of African Educators, EDC and CREDO,
Nairobi, African Social Studies Programme, 1986

The process of identifying an issue of concern, of researching and choosing the most appropriate solution, and of implementing a plan to make their idea a reality is environmental education.

— Martha Monroe (1991)

Environmental education is a learning process that increases people's knowledge and awareness about the environment and associated challenges, develops the necessary skills and expertise to address these challenges, and fosters attitudes, motivations, and commitments to make informed decisions and take responsible action.

— National Environmental Education Advisory Council, U.S. EPA EE Division (1996)

Environmental education is essentially an education involving the head (knowledge), heart (responsibility) and hand (skills).

— Daniella Tilbury (1997)

The primary antecedents of environmental education were nature study, outdoor education, and conservation education. The nature study movement in formal education, which took students outdoors to explore an indivisible environment with an integrated academic approach, began as early as 1891 with Wilbur Jackman's *Nature Study for the Common Schools*. Outdoor education has historically been defined as an educational method or approach—"the use of resources outside the classroom for educational purposes" (Swan 1975 cited in Disinger 1983). It has a very similar purpose as nature study. However, it differs in that, outdoor education encouraged teachers to go outdoors for lessons in every subject area, not just science, and aimed to advance not only an appreciation for the natural world, but also outdoor knowledge and skills. Its focus is in the place for learning—outside the school building, rather than a content area. Hence, it has been described as a potential vehicle for all subjects of the curriculum, including science, mathematics, English, art, and music.

Unlike nature study and outdoor education, conservation education was started in the United States by governmental agencies following the Dust Bowl of the 1930s which resulted from irresponsible use of natural resources. Conservation education was initiated to spread awareness about conservation issues, espouse the importance of wise use of natural resources, and encourage the public to understand and comply with environmental laws (Disinger and Monroe 1994). In 1949, the Commission on Education of the IUCN was established (Cook and Weider cited in Lahiry et al. 1988, 5) with a focus on environmental conservation education. But it was Rachel Carson's *Silent Spring* published in 1962 that triggered the environmental movement in America during the 1960s and 1970s. Although the book is exclusively about chemical pesticides and its impacts, it conveyed a larger message about the complexity of nature as Linda Lear (1998) wrote in the Afterword of the book "that everything in nature is related to everything else" and that "nature is not easily moulded."

1.5 Evolution of EE in the Modern Era

The first discussion on environmental education at a global platform took place in 1968 at the UNESCO Biosphere Reserve Conference held in Paris. A call was made at the meeting for developing curricula for all grade levels, promoting technical training and increasing awareness of global environmental problems. A subsequent meeting cosponsored by UNESCO and IUCN in Nevada in 1970 set forth the following definition of EE:

[T]he process of recognizing values and clarifying concepts in order to develop skills and attitudes necessary to understand and appreciate the interrelatedness among man, his culture, and his biophysical surroundings. Environmental education also entails practice in decision-making and self-formulation of a code of behaviour about issues concerning environmental quality.

In 1969, William B. Stapp and his students at the University of Michigan formally developed and published a definition of 'environmental education' in the first issue of *The Journal of Environmental Education* as: "Environmental education is aimed at producing a citizenry that is knowledgeable concerning the biophysical environment and its associated problems, aware of how to help solve these problems, and motivated to work toward their solution" (Stapp et al. 1969 cited in Disinger 1997).

Dr William Bill Stapp, Professor Emeritus at the University of Michigan, Ann Arbor, Michigan, was one among a handful of individuals who had shaped the field of environmental education. He was the first Director of the International Environmental Education Programme (IEEP) at UNESCO. Bill spearheaded the first international conference on environmental education held in Tbilisi, Georgia, in 1977. His environmental education program was the first to be unanimously accepted by all 135 UNESCO member nations. Bill was a true champion for environmental education. His contribution in the field is recognized worldwide and for which he earned numerous international, national and regional awards.

Lucas (1972) had characterized the perspectives of environmental education based on detailed analysis of early literature. He argued that:

> [U]ses of the term environmental education can be classified into education *about* the environment, education *for* (the preservation of) the environment, education *in* the environment, and the classes formed by the combinations *about* and *for*, *about* and *in* and *about*, *for* and *in*. Education *about* the environment, which is concerned with providing cognitive understanding including the development of skills necessary to obtain this understanding, and education *for* the environment, which is directed environmental preservation or preservation for particular purposes, are characterized by their aims; education *in* the environment...is characterized by a technique of instruction. In the *in* case, environment usually means the world outside the classroom, and in the other usages it usually refers to the biophysical and/or social context in which groups of people...exist. (1980, 1980–81; Disinger 1997)

JUST A MOMENT

What do you think has been the focus in our education? Try to recollect some moments in your school or college where you thought education *about*, *for* and *in* was actually practiced.

In 1972, the United Nations Conference on the Human Environment was held in Stockholm, Sweden. This conference is considered one such landmark event in the history of environmental education. Its Recommendation 96 made a call for the introduction of environmental education as a means to address environmental concerns worldwide. The gist of the Stockholm Declaration (Declaration of the United Nations Conference on the Human Environment) is provided in Box 1.2. The conference also identified the need of "creating citizenries not merely aware of the crisis of overpopulation, mismanagement of the quality of human life, but also able to focus intelligently on the means of coping with them." Further, the Declaration of the conference proclaimed: "To defend and improve the environment for present and future generations has become an imperative goal for mankind." It led to the creation of the IEEP, jointly funded by the UNESCO and the UNEP. The IEEP aims to promote reflection and action, as well as international cooperation in this field. Its principal long-term objectives were: (a) facilitating the coordination, planning, and programing of activities essential to the development of an international program in environmental education; (b) promoting the international exchange of ideas and information pertaining to environmental education; (c) coordinating research to understand better the various phenomena involved in environmental teaching and learning; (d) designing and evaluating new methods, curricula, materials, and programs (both in-school and out-of-school; youth and adult) in environmental education; (e) training and retraining personnel to adequately staff environmental education programs; and (f) providing advisory services to Member States in environmental education (UNESCO 1984).

Declaration of the United Nations Conference on the Human Environment

The United Nations Conference on the Human Environment, having met at Stockholm from 5 to 16 June 1972, *having considered* the need for a common outlook and for common principles to inspire and guide the peoples of the world in the preservation and enhancement of the human environment, proclaims that:

1. Man is both creature and moulder of his environment, which gives him physical sustenance and affords him the opportunity for intellectual, moral, social and spiritual growth...Both aspects of man's environment, the natural and the man-made, are essential to his well-being and to the enjoyment of basic human rights-even the right to life itself.

2. The protection and improvement of the human environment is a major issue which affects the well-being of peoples and economic development throughout the world; it is the urgent desire of the peoples of the whole world and the duty of all Governments.

3. Man has constantly to sum up experience and go on discovering, inventing, creating, and advancing. In our time, man's capability to transform his surroundings, if used wisely, can bring to all peoples the benefits of development and the opportunity to enhance the quality of life. Wrongly or heedlessly applied, the same power can do incalculable harm to human beings and the human environment.

4. In the developing countries most of the environmental problems are caused by under-development...the developing countries must direct their efforts to development, bearing in mind their priorities and the need to safeguard and improve the environment. For the same purpose, the industrialized countries should make efforts to reduce the gap themselves and the developing countries.

5. The natural growth of population continuously presents problems for the preservation of the environment, and adequate policies and measures should be adopted, as appropriate, to face these problems. Of all things in the world, people are the most precious... Along with social progress and the advance of production, science, and technology, the capability of man to improve the environment increases with each passing day.

6. For the purpose of attaining freedom in the world of nature, man must use knowledge to build, in collaboration with nature, a better environment. To defend and improve the human environment for present and future generations has become an imperative goal for mankind's goal to be pursued together with, and in harmony with, the established and fundamental goals of peace and of worldwide economic and social development.

7. To achieve this environmental goal will demand the acceptance of responsibility by citizens and communities and by enterprises and institutions at every level, all sharing equitably in common efforts...The Conference calls upon Governments and peoples to exert common efforts for the preservation and improvement of the human environment, for the benefit of all the people and for their posterity.

1.6 Initiatives by International Environmental Education Programme

1.6.1 First Phase

The action of IEEP in the period 1975–1983 was conducted in three phases, centering successively on: (a) Development of general awareness of the necessity of environmental education; (b) Development of concepts and methodological approaches in this field; and (c) Efforts for incorporating an environmental dimension into the educational process of UNESCO Member States (UNESCO 1984).

In its first phase (1975–1977), the IEEP organized a series of regional workshops for education practitioners represented by governmental delegations toward creating environmental education policy. These workshops culminated in the final practitioner workshop held in Belgrade (formerly in Yugoslavia, now in Serbia) in 1975, which resulted in the Belgrade Charter of 1975 (Box 1.3). The goal as mentioned in this charter is considered to be the most accepted definition of environmental education.

BOX

The Belgrade Charter

The Belgrade Charter
A Global Framework for Environmental Education

Adopted unanimously at the close of the 10-day workshop at Belgrade was a statement, subject to modification by subsequent regional meetings, of the framework and guiding principles for global environmental education, which became known as the Belgrade Charter.

It follows:

A Environmental Situation

Our generation has witnessed unprecedented economic growth and technological progress which, while bringing benefits to many people, have also caused severe social and environmental consequences. Inequality between the poor and the rich among nations and within nations is growing; there is evidence of increasing deterioration of the physical environment in some form on a world-wide scale. This condition, although primarily caused by a relatively small number of nations, affects all of humanity.

The recent United Nations Declaration for a New International Economic Order calls for a new concept of development—one which takes into account the satisfaction of the needs and wants of every citizen of the earth, of the pluralism of societies, and of the balance and harmony between humanity and the environment. What is being called for is the eradication of the basic causes of poverty, hunger, illiteracy, pollution, exploitation, and domination. The previous pattern of dealing with these crucial problems on a fragmentary basis is no longer workable.

It is absolutely vital that the world's citizens insist upon measures that will support the kind of economic growth which will not have harmful repercussions on people and that will not in any way diminish their environment and their living conditions. It is necessary to find ways to ensure that no nation should grow or develop at the expense of another nation and that the consumption of no individual should be increased at the expense of other individuals. The resources of the world should be developed in ways which will benefit all of humanity and provide the potential for raising the quality of life for everyone.

We need nothing short of a new global ethic—an ethic which espouses attitudes and behavior for individuals and societies which are consonant with humanity's place within the biosphere, and which recognizes and sensitively responds to the complex and ever-changing relationships between humanity and nature, and between people. Significant changes must occur in all of the world's nations to assure the kind of rational development which will be guided by this new

---

(Continued)

(Continued)

global ideal—changes which will be directed toward an equitable distribution of the world's resources and more fairly satisfy the needs of all peoples. This kind of development will also require the maximum reduction in harmful effects on the environment, the utilization of waste materials for productive purposes, and the design of technologies which will enable such objectives to be achieved. Above all, it will demand the assurance of perpetual peace through coexistence and cooperation among nations with different social systems. Substantial resources for reallocation to meet human needs can be gained through restricting military budgets and reducing competition in the manufacture of arms. Disarmament should be the ultimate goal.

These new approaches to the development and improvement of the environment call for a reordering of national and regional priorities. Those policies aimed at maximizing economic output without regard to its consequences on society and on the resources available for improving the quality of life must be questioned. Before this changing of priorities can be achieved, millions of individuals will themselves need to adjust their own priorities and assume a personal and individualized global ethic, and reflect in all of their behavior a commitment to the improvement of the quality of the environment and of life for the world's people.

The reform of educational processes and systems is central to the building of this new development ethic and world economic order. Governments and policy makers can order changes, and new development approaches can begin to improve the world's condition—but all of these are no more than short-term solutions, unless the youth of the world receives a new kind of education. This will require new and productive relationships between students and teachers, between schools and communities, and between the education system and society at large.

Recommendation 96 of the Stockholm Conference on the Human Environment called for the development of environmental education as one of the most critical elements of an all-out attack on the world's environmental crisis. This new environmental education must be broad based and strongly related to the basic principles outlined in the United Nations Declaration on the New International Economic Order.

It is within this context that the foundations must be laid for a world-wide environmental education program that will make it possible to develop new knowledge and skills, values, and attitudes, in a drive toward a better quality of environment and, indeed, toward a higher quality of life for present and future generations living within that environment.

B Environmental Goal

The goal of environmental action is:

To improve all ecological relationships, including the relationship of humanity with nature and people with each other.

There are, thus, two preliminary objectives:

1. For each nation, according to its culture, to clarify for itself the meaning of such basic concepts as "quality of life" and "human happiness" in the context of the total environment, with an extension of the clarification and appreciation to other cultures, beyond one's own national boundaries.
2. To identify which actions will ensure the preservation and improvement of humanity's potentials and develop social and individual well-being in harmony with the biophysical and man-made environment.

(Continued)

(Continued)

C Environmental Education Goal

The goal of environmental education is:

To develop a world population that is aware of, and concerned about, the environment and its associated problems, and which has the knowledge, skills, attitudes, motivations and commitment to work individually and collectively toward solutions of current problems and the prevention of new ones.

D Environmental Education Objectives

The objectives of environmental education are:

1. Awareness: to help individuals and social groups acquire an awareness of and sensitivity to the total environment and its allied problems.
2. Knowledge: to help individuals and social groups acquire basic understanding of the total environment, its associated problems, and humanity's critically responsible presence and role in it.
3. Attitude: to help individuals and social groups acquire social values, strong feelings of concern for the environment, and the motivation for actively participating in its protection and improvement.
4. Skills: to help individuals and social groups acquire the skills for solving environmental problems.
5. Evaluation ability: to help individuals and social groups evaluate environmental measures and education programs in terms of ecological, political, economic, social, aesthetic, and educational factors.
6. Participation: to help individuals and social groups develop a sense of responsibility and urgency regarding environmental problems to ensure appropriate action to solve those problems.

E Audiences

The principal audience of environmental education is the general public. Within this global frame, the major categories are:

1. The formal education sector: including preschool, primary, secondary, and higher education students as well as teachers and environmental professionals in training and retraining;
2. The nonformal education sector: including youth and adults, individually or collectively from all segments of the population, such as the family, workers, managers, and decision makers, in environmental as well as non-environmental fields.

F Guiding Principles of Environmental Education Programmes

The guiding principles of environmental education are:

1. Environmental education should consider the environment in its totality—natural and man-made, ecological, political, economic, technological, social, legislative, cultural, and aesthetic.
2. Environmental education should be a continuous life-long process, both in-school and out-of-school.
3. Environmental education should be interdisciplinary in its approach.
4. Environmental education should emphasize active participation in preventing and solving environmental problems.

(Continued)

(Continued)

> 5. Environmental education should examine major environmental issues from a world point of view, while paying due regard to regional differences.
> 6. Environmental education should focus on current and future environmental situations.
> 7. Environmental education should examine all development and growth from an environmental perspective.
> 8. Environmental education should promote the value and necessity of local, national, and international cooperation in the solution of environmental problems.

In 1977, the UNESCO together with the UNEP held the Intergovernmental Conference on Environmental Education in Tbilisi, Republic of Georgia. Sixty-six UNESCO Member States and several NGO representatives took part. Delegates adopted the Belgrade statement and prepared the Tbilisi final report (The Tbilisi Declaration) that characterizes environmental education as a lifelong process; as interdisciplinary[1] and holistic in nature and application; as an approach to education as a whole, rather than a subject; and about the interrelationship and interconnectedness between human and natural systems. The report also formalized the following goals, objectives, and guiding principles to guide UNESCO Member States in the development of environmental education policies, which are reproduced here in its entirety (UNESCO-UNEP 1978).

Environmental Education Goals

- **to foster** clear awareness of and concern about economic, social, political, and ecological interdependence in urban and rural areas;
- **to provide** every person with opportunities to acquire the knowledge, values, attitudes, commitment, and skills needed to protect and improve the environment;
- **to create** new patterns of behavior of individuals, groups, and society as a whole toward the environment.

Environmental Education Objectives

- **Awareness**: to help social groups and individuals acquire an awareness of and sensitivity to the total environment and its allied problems.
- **Knowledge**: to help social groups and individuals gain various experience in, and acquire a basic understanding of the environment and its related problems.

---

[1] The term 'Interdisciplinary' here simply means that environmental education should consider different disciplinary areas and hence it should not be confused with the 'interdisciplinary or separate subject approach' which is being discussed in Chapter 3. The term here, indicates the nature of environmental education and not the method. Therefore, it does not exclude the 'multidisciplinary or infusion approach,' which is mentioned in Chapter 3.

- **Attitudes**: to help social groups and individuals acquire a set of values and feelings of concern for the environment, and the motivation for actively participating in environmental improvement and protection.
- **Skills:** to help social groups and individuals acquire the skills for identifying and solving environmental problems.
- **Participation:** to provide social groups and individuals with an opportunity to be actively involved at all levels in working toward resolution of environmental problems.

Some Guiding Principles for Environmental Education

- consider the environment in its totality—natural and built, technological, and social (economic, political, technological, cultural–historical, moral, aesthetic);
- be a continuous lifelong process, beginning at the preschool level and continuing through all formal and nonformal stages;
- be interdisciplinary in its approach, drawing on the specific content of each discipline in making possible a holistic and balanced perspective;
- examine major environmental issues from local, national, regional, and international viewpoints so that students receive insights into environmental conditions in other geographical areas;
- focus on current and potential environmental situations, while taking into account the historical perspective;
- promote the value and necessity of local, national, and international cooperation in the prevention and solution of environmental problems;
- explicitly consider environmental aspects in plans for development and growth;
- enable learners to have a role in planning their learning experiences and provide an opportunity for making decisions and accepting their consequences;
- relate environmental sensitivity, knowledge, problem-solving skills, and values clarification to every age, but with special emphasis on environmental sensitivity to the learner's own community in early years;
- help learners discover the symptoms and real causes of environmental problems;
- emphasize the complexity of environmental problems and thus the need to develop critical thinking and problem-solving skills;
- utilize diverse learning environments and a broad array of educational approaches to teaching/learning about and from the environment with due stress on practical activities and first-hand experience.

Once environmental education objectives were set in place, nations across the world began to introduce and promote environmental education through the development of curricula, courses, and training programs (Biedenweg et al. 2013, 16). The Tbilisi Declaration became 'the document' for implementers and practitioners all over the world.

1.6.2 Second Phase

The IEEP initiated several programs as part of its second phase (1978–1980) actions. This phase was primarily devoted to the conceptual and methodological development of environmental education with the view to providing Member States with useful references for the incorporation of an environmental dimension into general educational practice. In this regard, the IEEP introduced a series of studies and activities concerning different pedagogical aspects of environmental education, launched a series of pilot projects in different countries of various regions of the world, and initiated a series of training workshops and seminars at the national, sub-regional, and international levels. Publication of a newsletter, Connect, and books such as *Trends in Environmental Education* (1977) and *Environmental Education in the Light of the Tbilisi Conference* (1980) were also the highlight of IEEP's activities in this phase (UNECSO-UNEP 1989).

1.6.3 Third Phase

In the third phase of the IEEP (1981–1983), emphasis was placed on the development of content, methods and materials for environmental education practices and training activities; experimental and pilot projects were intensified, with a view to facilitating Member States' efforts concerning practical incorporation of environmental education into school and out-of-school education. As for educational contents, methods, and materials relating to environmental education, the IEEP developed a series of studies, research activities and projects leading to the preparation of methodological guides concerning approaches for the inclusion of an environmental dimension into educational practice (UNESCO 1984).

1.7 Environmental Education and Education for Sustainable Development

After numerous initiatives at every level, it was felt that environmental education has finally come of age. It was expected that such initiatives would soon bring about the much anticipated change that we wanted to see in around us. However, with time, inconsistency began to be seen in the actual nature of environmental education and the way it was formulated and practiced. One of the main reasons for this was that the approaches and priorities pursued through environmental education were strongly influenced by political power, existing environmental issues, social priorities, and trends in educational policy (Biedenweg et al. 2013). At times it was ecologically biased, while at other times advocacy was the priority. It was felt that environmental education did not address social and economic issues such as poverty, excessive consumption, under-development, and so on, adequately. These compelled the world to think of a more holistic, all-encompassing approach on environmental education which will help tackle serious environmental concerns and which is, at the same time, socially viable.

It was in 1987 that the World Commission on Environment and Development first drew global attention in its report *Our Common Future* (Brundtland Report) on the concept of sustainable development. It highlighted how social and economic factors contribute to environmental problems. This concept was received well by all the nations during the Earth Summit held in Rio de Janeiro in 1992 and the Agenda 21 was drafted which consist of 40 chapters (Box 1.4). Chapter 36 of the Agenda focused on "reorienting education toward sustainable development; increasing public awareness; and promoting

BOX 1.4

Agenda 21–40 Chapters of Sustainability

Chapter 1: Preamble
Section One: Social and Economic Dimensions
Chapter 2: International Cooperation
Chapter 3: Combating Poverty
Chapter 4: Changing Consumption Patterns
Chapter 5: Population and Sustainable Development
Chapter 6: Protecting and Promoting Human Health
Chapter 7: Sustainable Human Settlements
Chapter 8: Making Decisions for Sustainable Development
Section Two: Conservation and Management of Resources
Chapter 9: Protecting the Atmosphere
Chapter 10: Managing Land Sustainably
Chapter 11: Combating Deforestation
Chapter 12: Combating Desertification and Drought
Chapter 13: Sustainable Mountain Development
Chapter 14: Sustainable Agriculture and Rural Development
Chapter 15: Conservation of Biological Diversity
Chapter 16: Environmentally Sound Management of Biotechnology
Chapter 17: Protecting and Managing the Oceans
Chapter 18: Protecting and Managing Fresh Water
Chapter 19: Safer Use of Toxic Chemicals
Chapter 20: Managing Hazardous Wastes
Chapter 21: Managing Solid Wastes and Sewage
Chapter 22: Managing Radioactive Wastes
Section Three: Strengthening the Role of Major Groups
Chapter 23: Preamble to Strengthening the Role of Major Groups
Chapter 24: Women in Sustainable Development
Chapter 25: Children and Youth in Sustainable Development
Chapter 26: Strengthening the Role of Indigenous People
Chapter 27: Partnerships with NGOs
Chapter 28: Local Authorities
Chapter 29: Workers and Trade Unions
Chapter 30: Business and Industry
Chapter 31: Scientists and Technologists
Section Four: Means of Implementation
Chapter 32: Strengthening the Role of Farmers
Chapter 33: Financing Sustainable Development
Chapter 34: Technology Transfer
Chapter 35: Science for Sustainable Development
Chapter 36: Education, Training and Public Awareness
Chapter 37: Creating the Capacity for Sustainable Development
Chapter 38: Organizing for Sustainable Development
Chapter 39: International Law
Chapter 40: Information for Decision-Making

training." In addition, each of the forty chapters included education as a component in the implementation strategy.

Following the World Summit on Sustainable Development (WSSD) held in 2002 in Johannesburg, the United Nations General Assembly in its meeting held in December 2002 proclaimed the period 2005–2014 as the UN Decade of Education for Sustainable Development (UNDESD). It designated the UNESCO as the lead agency to promote and implement the Decade. With this, there has been a transition in environmental education and it took the form of Education for Sustainable Development (ESD) in many countries. Is this transition merely putting a new label on an old bottle as some believed in the case of transition from old conservation practices such as conservation education, outdoor education, citizenship education, or resource management education to environmental education (Schoenfeld 1971, 40)? Or is there significant difference between the two? How different or similar is environmental education from ESD in philosophy and effect is still being debated amongst professionals. This aspect is discussed in more detail in Chapter 9. Nevertheless, whatever form environmental education has taken, what is important to be recognized and acknowledged is that it remains an indispensable component of education which cannot be compromised or replaced. This is because, as mentioned earlier, environmental education is all about well-living and well-being of humankind. As a matter of fact, environmental education has become more relevant than ever before.

1.8 Chronology of Important Events in EE

A chronology of important events which shaped environmental education is provided in Table 1.1.

Table 1.1	Chronology of Important Events in EE
Year	**Event**
1762	Jean-Jacques Rousseau published *Emile*, an educational philosophy written in the form of a novel wherein he maintains that education should include a focus on environment.
1807	Louis Agassiz was born. He grew up to become a renowned scientist who urged his students to learn directly from nature.
1891	Wilbur Jackman wrote the *Nature Study for the Common School*, which defined the nature study movement.
1930s	The "Dust Bowl" in the American heartland gave rise to the conservation education movement supported by state and federal natural resource agencies as well as many nongovernment organizations.
	John Dewey promoted a more student-centered and holistic approach to education by providing opportunities to explore, reflect upon, and apply newly learned concepts.

(Continued)

(Continued)

Year	Event
1948	Thomas Pritchard, Deputy Director of the Nature Conservancy in Wales used the term "environmental education" at a meeting in Paris of the International Union for the Conservation of Nature.
1949	The Commission on Education of the International Union for Conservation of Nature and Natural Resources (IUCN) was established to promote environmental conservation education.
1968	The first discussion on environmental education at a global platform took place at the UNESCO Biosphere Reserve Conference held in Paris.
1969	Dr William Bill Stapp and his students at the University of Michigan formally developed and published a definition of "environmental education."
1972	Arthur M. Lucas classified environmental education as education 'about' the environment, education 'in' the environment, and education 'for' the environment.
	The United Nations Conference on the Human Environment in Stockholm, Sweden, was held. Recommendation 96 called for the provision of environmental education as a means to address environmental issues worldwide.
	The IEEP, jointly funded by UNESCO and UNEP, was created to promote reflection and action, as well as international cooperation in this field.
1975	The International Environmental Education Workshop was held in Belgrade (which was then in undivided Yugoslavia, now in Serbia). The delegates ratified the Belgrade Charter which outlines the basic structure of environmental education.
1977	The International Conference on Environmental Education was held in Tbilisi, Republic of Georgia. The conference laid out the goals, objectives, and guiding principles of environmental education.
1987	The World Commission on Environment and Development published the Brundtland Report (*Our Common Future*) which introduced the idea of sustainable development.
1992	The United Nations organized the Conference on Environment and Development in Rio de Janeiro, Brazil. The Agenda 21 was prepared in which Chapter 36 focuses on "reorienting education toward sustainable development; increasing public awareness; and promoting training."
2002	The WSSD was held in Johannesburg. It proposed that the United Nations should consider adopting a decade of education for sustainable development, starting 2005.
	The United Nations General Assembly proclaimed 2005–2014 as the UN Decade of Education for Sustainable Development (UNDESD).
2014	World Conference on Education for Sustainable Development was held in Aichi-Nagoya, Japan in November which not only marked the end of UNDESD but an important milestone for pointing the way ahead.

Conclusion

Dealing with environmental issues is indeed the most important concern for humanity today since our existence itself will be at stake if our ignorance continues. And rightly so, the world recognized that education would be an important tool for a sustainable solution to deal with the issues facing us. Environmental education thus became accepted in the curricula. However, given the fact that environmental issues are very complex in nature, as we had discussed in the chapter, environmental education must be looked at with much seriousness. It has been, and will remain a challenge for practitioners to implement environmental education in such a way that it actually leads to resolution of environmental issues.

As much as it was important for different countries of the world to come together to collectively press the need for introducing environmental education in the education system, how effectively it can be implemented will also largely depend on the commitment and cooperation of these countries. While some countries are abound with experts in different areas of environmental education, such as development of resource material, capacity building, advocacy, and so on, many other countries are still struggling to prepare experts in these areas. In this situation, it can only be hoped that there is sharing of resources and expertise between nations so that every country will be able to contribute meaningfully in the world's collective initiative to improve the environment.

SUMMARY

- A general understanding about EE—what it is, how and why it came about, and how the world responded to it through education were provided.
- Many changes have taken place since the past two centuries which have impacted life and the environment.
- The role of science and technology in apparently improving life has also brought about other complications in life.
- There exists a paradox surrounding the impact of technologies as well as those concerning environmental issues.
- Environmental issues are complex and even well intended efforts results into several other environmental issues.
- Environmental concern became a global issue due to the realization of the enormity of adverse effect of development on environment and brought the world together to collectively

- work toward addressing all environment-related issues facing humanity.
- The necessity and importance of education on environment to address the issues was highlighted at the United Nations Conference on the Human Environment held at Stockholm in 1972.
- Significant realization about the importance of education in addressing environmental issues led to the introduction of environmental education as an important component in the education system, in schools and colleges.
- The contributions of different pioneers in the field of environmental education as well as the important events that have happened over the decades gave shape to environmental education to be what it is today.
- There are definitely issues related to defining environmental education itself.
- The Belgrade Charter and the Tbilisi Declaration guided nations for effective

implementation of environmental education by clearly defining its goals, objectives, and guiding principles.

- UNESCO and the UNEP were instrumental in setting up the IEEP which strengthened different countries in carrying out environmental education.
- It was felt that environmental education could not effectively address prevailing environmental

issues and hence this largely resulted in the introduction of the concept of "education for sustainable development."

- Due to the challenges facing the world in general and practitioners in particular there is ever increasing need for the nations of the world to share its resources and expertise between each other.

Exercises

1. Do you think environmental education should be considered an integral part of the curriculum? Justify your answer.
2. Give an example of an actual situation to explain the complexities of addressing environmental issues.
3. How do you think can we strike a balance between development and conservation?
4. Why did environmental education catch global attention? Explain.
5. Mention some common ways through which environmental education is practiced in schools. Do you think such practices are enough for schools to take up? Justify your answer.
6. Environmental education is all about well-living and well-being of humankind. Justify the statement.
7. Environmental education is commonly known as education *about* the environment, education *for* (the preservation of) the environment, education *in* the environment. Explain this with an example.
8. Name the five components which environmental education tries to address to achieve its objectives.
9. List some of the activities initiated by International Environmental Education Programme.
10. Do you think environmental education and education for sustainable development are drastically different? Justify your answer.

References

Biedenweg, K., M.C. Monroe, and D.J. Wojcik. 2013. "Foundations of Environmental Education." In *Across the Spectrum: Resources for Environmental Educators,* edited by Martha C. Monroe and Marianne E. Krasny, 9–28. Washington, DC: North American Association for Environmental Education (NAAEE).

Carson, Rachel. 1962. *Silent Spring.* London: Penguin Books.

Carter, R.L. and Bora Simmons. 2010. "The History and Philosophy of Environmental Education." In *The Inclusion of Environmental Education in Science Teacher Education,* edited by Alec M. Bodzin, Beth Shiner Klein, and Starlin Weaver, 3–16. New York: Springer. Available at: https://books.google.co.in/books?id=NrrnM5M HT3UC&pg=PR15&dq=Environmental+Education:+What+is+it,+For+whom,+For+what+purpose,+and+How? &hl=en&sa=X&ei=3gsdVePaF8W8uAT24YKgAg&ved=0CDYQ6AEwBQ#v=onepage&q=Environmental%20 Education%3A%20What%20is%20it%2C%20For%20whom%2C%20For%20what%20purpose%2C%20 and%20How%3F&f=false (Accessed on 3 April 2015).

Disinger, J.F. 1983. *Environmental Education's Definitional Problem.* ERIC Information Bulletin No. 2, Columbus, OH: ERIC Clearinghouse Science, Mathematics, and Environmental Education. Available at: http://

globalenvironmentaleducation.wikispaces.com/file/view/EE_Definitional_Problem.pdf. (Accessed on 5 April 2015).

——— 1986. *Current Practices in Science/Society/Technology/Environment Education: A Survey of the State Education Agencies*. Columbus, OH: ERIC Clearinghouse for Science/Mathematics, and Environmental Education, Ohio State University. Available at: http://files.eric.ed.gov/fulltext/ED81709.pdf (Accessed on 14 April 2015).

——— 1997. Environmental Education's Definitional Problem. Reprinted from: *ERIC Clearinghouse for Science, Mathematics and Environmental Education Information* Bulletin No. 2, 1983. An Epilogue EE's Definitional Problem: 1997 Update. Columbus, OH: RIC/SMEAC. Available at: http://globalenvironmentaleducation. wikispaces.com/file/view/EE_Definitional_Problem.pdf (Accessed on 2 August 2014).

Disinger, J.F. and R.W. Howe. 1990. *Trends and Issues Related to the Preparation of Teachers for Environmental Education*. Environmental Education Information Report No. ED335233. ERIC Clearinghouse for Science, Mathematics, and Environmental Education Information Report. Columbus, OH: ERIC/SMEAC. Available at: http://files.eric.ed.gov/fulltext/ED335233.pdf (Accessed on 15 April 2015).

Disinger, J.F. and M. Lisowski. 1986. *Teaching Activities in S/Society/Technology/Environment*. Columbus, OH: ERIC Clearinghouse for Science, Mathematics, and Environmental Education. Available at: http://files.eric. ed.gov/fulltext/ED282711.pdf (Accessed on 16 April 2015).

Disinger, J.F. and M.C. Monroe. 1994. *EE Toolbox—Workshop Resource Manual, Defining Environmental Education*. Ann Arbor, MI: University of Michigan, National Consortium for Environmental Education and Training.

Disinger, J.F. and Terry L. Wilson. 1986. *Locating the "E" in S/T/S*. ERIC/SMEAC Information Bulletin No. 3. Available at: http://files.eric.ed.gov/fulltext/ED277547.pdf (Accessed on 15 April 2015).

Gadgil, M. and R. Guha. 2000. *The Use and Abuse of Nature*. New Delhi: Oxford University Press.

Ghosh, Prodipto. 2010. "The Climate Change Debate: View from India." In *Dealing with Climate Change–Setting a Global Agenda for Mitigation and Adaptation*, edited by R.K. Pachauri. New Delhi: TERI.

Hadzigeorgiou Yannis and Michael Skoumios. 2013. "The Development of Environmental Awareness through School Science: Problems and Possibilities." *International Journal of Environmental and Science Education* 8: 405–426.

Khoshoo, T.N. and J.S. Moolakkattu. 2009. *Mahatma Gandhi and the Environment—Analysing Gandhian Environmental Thought*. New Delhi: TERI.

Lahiry, D., Savita Sinha, J.S. Gill, U. Mallik, and A.K. Mishra. 1988. *Environmental Education: A Process for Pre-service Teacher Training Curriculum Development*. UNESCO-UNEP International Environmental Education Programme Environmental Education Series No. 26, edited by Patricia R. Simpson, Harold Hungerford, and Trudi L. Volk. Paris: UNESCO.

Lucas, A.M. 1972. *Environment and Environmental Education: Conceptual Issues and Curriculum Implications*, PhD Dissertation, Ohio State University. Available at: https://www.researchgate.net/profile/Arthur_Lucas/public ations?sorting=newest&page=4 (Accessed on 28 September 2014).

——— 1980. "Science and Environmental Education: Pious Hopes, Self Praise and Disciplinary Chauvinism." *Studies in Science Education* 7: 1–26.

——— 1980–1981. "The Role of Science Education in Education for the Environment." *Journal of Environmental Education* 12(2): 33–37.

McCrea, E.J. 2006. *The Roots of Environmental Education: How the Past Supports the Present*. Environmental Education and Training Partnership (EETAP). Available at: http://cms.eetap.org/repository/moderncms_ documents/History.Final.20060315.1.1.pdf (Accessed on 19 July 2015).

Monroe, M.C., E. Andrews, and K. Biedenweg. 2007. "A Framework for Environmental Education Strategies." *Applied Environmental Education and Communication* 6: 205–216.

NCERT, National Council of Educational Research and Training. 1981. *Environmental Education at the School Level: A Lead Paper*. New Delhi: NCERT.

Ramakrishnan, P.S. 2001. *Ecology and Sustainable Development—Working with Knowledge Systems*. New Delhi: National Book Trust.

Sarabhai, K.V., K. Kandula, and M. Raghunath. 1998. *Greening Formal Education—Concerns, Efforts and Future Directions*, Ministry of Environment and Forests, Government of India, Centre for Environment Education.

Schoenfeld, Clay. 1971. "Defining Environmental Education." In *Outlines of Environmental Education*, edited by Clay Shoenfeld, 40–41. Madison, WI: Dembar Educational Research Services. Available at: http://files.eric. ed.gov/fulltext/ED050973.pdf. (Accessed on 16 April 2016).

Schoenfeld, Clay and J.F. Disinger. (1978). *Environmental Education in Action—II: Case Studies of Environmental Studies Programs in Colleges and Universities Today*. Columbus, OH: ERIC Information Analysis Center for

Science, Mathematics, and Environmental Education. Available at: http://files.eric.ed.gov/fulltext/ED152557.pdf (Accessed on 16 April 2015).

Tilbury, D. 1997. "A Head, Heart and Hand Approach to Learning about Environmental Problems." *New Horizons in Education* 38: 13–30.

Tortajada, Cecilia. 2005. "A Critical Assessment." In *Appraising Sustainable Development—Water management and Environmental Challenges,* edited by Asit K. Biswas and Cecilia Tortajada, 1–17. New Delhi: Oxford University Press.

UNESCO, United Nations Educational, Scientific and Cultural Organization. 1984. *Activities of the UNESCO-UNEP International Environmental Education Programme (1975–1983)*. Paris: UNESCO.

UNESCO-UNEP, United Nations Educational, Scientific and Cultural Organization-United Nations Environment Programme. 1976. "The Belgrade Charter." *Connect, UNESCO-UNEP Environmental Education Newsletter* I(1): 1–2.

——— 1978. "Tbilisi Declaration." *Connect, UNESCO-UNEP Environmental Education Newsletter* III(1): 1–8.

——— 1989. "Publications of the IEEP." *Connect, UNESCO-UNEP Environmental Education Newsletter* 14(4): 7–8.

WCED, World Commission on Environment and Development. 1987. *The Report of the World Commission on Environment and Development: Our Common Future*. New York: United Nations.

Wenzel, Eberhard. 1997. "Environment, Development and Health: Ideological Metaphors of Post-traditional Societies?" *Health Education Research—Theory & Practice* 12(4): 403–418. Available at: https://www.researchgate.net/publication/249278804_Health_environment_and_education (Accessed on 11 July 2015).

Why Environmental Education?

"We don't need environmental education. All environment-related topics are taught in science."

There is a widespread believe that environmental education is about teaching certain environmental facts and phenomena which can be conveniently incorporated as part of science curriculum. The fact that environmental education is interdisciplinary in nature and that any particular discipline cannot comprehensively integrate environmental education is yet to be understood and appreciated by many in the teaching community.

Chapter Overview

This chapter delves into the nature of different disciplinary subjects so as to bring out the uniqueness of environmental education. It further explains the limitations of other disciplinary subjects to address environmental concerns and hence the need to have environmental education which is interdisciplinary and holistic in nature. The addition of another subject in the school curriculum in the name of environmental education will not be appreciated at the present situation where there is competition for time slots for different disciplines. To address this, this section of the book also delves into the possibilities of converging environmental education with other subjects. After going through the chapter it is envisaged that readers will gather sufficient understanding to:

- differentiate the nature of different disciplinary subjects.
- describe the uniqueness of environmental education.
- justify the importance of environmental education.
- relate/differentiate between environmental education, environmental science, and environmental studies.
- explain the limitations of other disciplinary subjects to address environmental concerns.
- describe the possibilities of converging environmental education with other subjects.

Introduction

Today, as we have seen in the previous chapter, environmental concerns no longer remain a local issue, but have become one big global issue. The world agrees in unison the necessity and the urgency to address the related environmental issues facing every country of the world and the ever-increasing environmental disasters, if not the impending doom. The urgency in the need to spread awareness and educate the entire world on environment protection and how to contain the already existing problems facing humanity was strongly felt, beginning from 1970. In the light of these considerations, environmental education was introduced and it gradually became an essential part of formal education. As a matter of fact, many countries, including India, have made it mandatory to include environmental education in its curriculum throughout the different stages and levels of education. However, questions still arise in the minds of many about the nature of environmental education vis-à-vis other disciplinary subjects. Some of the questions most often asked include: "Why should we have environmental education?" "Is it not possible to address environmental concerns through the existing disciplinary subjects?" "Does it mean that we should have another school subject by the name 'environmental education' to add to the burden of the students?" "Is environmental education different from environmental science or environmental studies for that matter?" The same questions will haunt those neophytes in the field of environmental education. These questions are not only relevant, but are very important because one can only begin to value and appreciate environmental education when one is convinced of the answers to these questions. This section attempts to frame some plausible discussions toward answering the questions. Much of the discussion in relation to other disciplinary areas will be on science education in view of the fact that science has been seen to take the dominant role to deliver environmental education.

2.1 Nature of Disciplinary Areas

It is expected that all disciplinary areas, including mathematics, arts, and languages, should incorporate environmental components in their curriculum which is the essence of environmental education. However, Disinger and Howe (1990, 5) reported that in nearly all instances, in both elementary and secondary schools, science courses were found to be 'hosts' for the infusion of environmental topics with social studies courses listed less frequently, and other subjects only occasionally. While acknowledging that biology and geography are the subject areas that most are able to identify with environmental education, Fensham (1978a cited in Lucas 1980) argued that:

> [S]ubjects like literature, social studies, commercial subjects, physical sciences, and mathematics are much more likely to be the real bases that will get at the social values, political organizations, economic policies and structures, technological control and development, and national and international patterns of distribution that determine the environmental situation.

What is being argued here is that biology and geography may introduce environmental education at its best, however, such efforts will hardly be reflected when it comes to actual practices and priorities in the society or when it comes to taking economic or developmental policies and decisions. Environmental education is most likely to be effective when emphasis is given in 'other subjects,' referring to subjects other than biology and geography. This suggests the need to seriously consider integrating environmental education in the teaching–learning of subjects other than those 'traditional environmental education subjects' of biology and geography. However, it is not to be confused with the unique nature every disciplinary area carries with it and also that of environmental education (Carter and Simmons 2010, 11). To understand this better, we need to first look at the nature of the disciplinary areas. Let us consider some of the areas for the purpose of our discussion.

We know that science/scientific inquiry is based on the following:

1. Truth (until otherwise proven) for example, scientific laws and principles
2. Conclusions must be rationally justified by empirical evidence—observation and experiment
3. Objective (i.e., based on facts and not feelings or opinions)
4. Equality (there is no bias)

Speculation and conjecture may have a place in science or more specifically in natural science (biological or physical sciences), but ultimately, a scientific theory, to be acceptable, must be verified by relevant observations and/or experiments. However, the methodology of science and its demarcation from other fields continue to be a matter of philosophical debate. Its professed value-neutrality and objectivity have been subject to critical sociological analyses. Moreover, while science is at its best in understanding simple linear systems of nature, its predictive or explanatory power is limited when it comes to dealing with nonlinear complex systems of nature. This clearly shows the limitations of science in dealing with complex issues, such as those related to the environment. Yet, with all its limitations and failings, science is unquestionably the most reliable and powerful knowledge system about the physical world known to humans (NCERT 2006a). This nature of science is what forms a very important aspect of environmental education which cannot be compromised with.

Similarly, other disciplinary subjects in humanities, such as language, literature, philosophy, religion, and so on, have its unique nature. It tries to answer to questions related to:

1. Meaning
2. Purpose
3. Value
4. Beauty
5. Moral/ethical
6. Equity

Unlike in natural science, answers to these questions are invariably not scientifically verifiable.

Social science, which generally includes economics, history, political science, human geography, psychology, and sociology, is a systematic study of society and its institutions, and of the behavior of people as individuals and in groups within a society and their relationships. It carries a normative responsibility to create and widen the popular base for human values, namely freedom, trust, mutual respect, and respect for diversity. It aims at investing in children a critical moral and mental energy to make them alert to the social forces that threaten these values (NCERT 2006b). Although social sciences are considered to be 'scientific' as they involve a systematic and disciplined method of acquiring knowledge which is verifiable, unlike scientific enquiry in natural sciences where 'truth' is obtained, scientific enquiry in social sciences in many instances is able to provide only a factual base or a more general answer instead of a clear and precise answer as in natural sciences.

The above discussion makes it clear that each discipline has its boundaries. How strong or weak, how flexible or rigid, is not in the purview of our discussion here. By nature, every discipline does not attempt or seek to answer every question. Science tries to answer a few things which are related to physical phenomena and natural processes; humanities and social sciences also have their limitations. Nevertheless, curricula of different disciplines go beyond their disciplinary boundary to make teaching–learning effective. But again this happens only to a certain limit and is practiced only by few teachers, which could be due to expertise in only a specific subject or simply because the teacher does not feel the need. If any subject or discipline was meant to address everything related to the topic, then there would not be what we called disciplines or subjects. For example, if science, as a subject, was to address every detail and concerns related to water, such as properties of water, availability of water in different places, water cycle, water disputes, injustice on women as they walk miles to get water, pollution of water due to industries as well as traditional and religious practices, laws on water, and constitutional rights and duties related to water, then geography and political science would not be subjects. But, as we know, this does not happen due to the disciplinary nature of science. And therefore, all that a science curriculum includes is the scientific facts and knowledge about water such as properties of water, availability of water, water cycle or water pollution, while geography takes care of some other aspects and so also does political science.

JUST A MOMENT

Can you recall some topics which were taught across different subjects in your school? Did you learn different aspects of the topic in different subjects? Or do you think it was a mere repetition in different subjects?

2.2 Nature of EE

In the previous chapter we have seen that the Tbilisi Declaration emphasized the need to create awareness about the economic, social, political, and ecological interdependence through EE. The Declaration also characterized environmental education as a lifelong process; as interdisciplinary and holistic in nature and application; as an approach to education as a whole, rather than a subject; and about the interrelationship and interconnectedness between human and natural systems. It also identified five components to be addressed as part of its objectives—awareness, knowledge, attitude, skill, and participation. Environmental education being interdisciplinary draws upon the specific content of each discipline (Carter and Simmons 2010, 12) so as to make possible a holistic and balanced perspective. This interdisciplinary nature of environmental education makes teaching components of environmental education possible through science, history, language, and so on (Lahiry et al. 1988, 19). As this is done, an attempt is also made to integrate the inputs from different disciplinary subjects so that the learner is able to view the issue from a holistic perspective.

Often environmental problems are presented to students as the issue of depletion of natural resources which needs protection since it serves human interests, while the intrinsic value of nature (including all species) is not reflected (Kopnina 2014). Environmental education overrides such lapses as it addresses value education concerning ethical, social, or aesthetic values (NCERT 1981). This is especially important in the context of decision-making. While science may provide information related to the decision, it does not help in taking value choices (Holsman 2001). Environmental education puts the emphasis on developing environmental values such as inculcating a concern for the environment, a sense of ownership and responsibility, commitment and motivation to participate in improving the environment, and some even going to the extent of prescribing environmental 'morals,' a code of socially desirable behavior (Sauvé 2005). However, conventionally, it does not mean prescribing or teaching any particular set of values but about all of the values (Disinger 2009; Holsman 2001).

In situations where values or ethics are concerned, purely empirical treatment cannot be applied to EE. Whether clarifying positions or debating prospective solutions to moral dilemmas, environmental education activities give students an opportunity to develop their ideas of right and wrong and to accept the many 'gray' areas created by different viewpoints (Disinger and Monroe 1994). For example, while discussing about government's proposal to construct a dam in a location which is inhabited by an indigenous population in a classroom, an issue springs up. A set of students who hold the view 'development at all cost' is most probably likely to respond promptly in favor of the construction. While there could be another set of students who understand the possible impacts on the local inhabitants in terms of their livelihood, rehabilitation, and occupation. The latter set of students in most probability is not likely going to take a stand or decision immediately but would like to be more convinced about the steps taken to avoid emergence of social issues as a consequence of such proposal by the government. There could be yet another set of students who are concerned about the impacts on the natural resources, ecosystem, and wildlife. As students share their views and justify their stands, it will help other students clarify their positions and enhance their understanding of other groups' opinions and values. Often the eventual choice may result from a compromise between conflicting positions and values, as in this case, the construction of dam and the displacement of the inhabitants to an unfamiliar place. Environmental education provides such opportunity to explore various value perspectives which will help students understand that often issues are controversial because of different, not right or wrong ways of looking at information (Monroe 1991).

Another conflicting position most commonly seen or most certainly to be seen is regarding setting up of factories close to human inhabited locality. While factories definitely provide job opportunities, it is also a source of pollution which could be that of air, water or soil. Taking positions in such a situation is not always easy and it eventually leads to compromise (Disinger 1986, 1987; Patrick and Remi 1985 cited in Disinger 1986). However, it is not always about positions which are mutually exclusive (here as in this example, a choice between a pollution-free environment and factories) where one has to take a position either to have a pollution-free environment or have pollution causing factories which also create jobs. There are ways to work out in most cases. Factories and pollution-free environment are not necessarily mutually exclusive. Although it is a fact that most factories always turn out to be polluters, that need not be the rule. There are possibilities that we can have factories with controlled or reduced emission technologies in place and have all the 'goods' (Kibert et al. 2012, 56). Thus factories can be set up, jobs can be created, and pollution can be controlled without causing pollution-related impact on the lives of the local populace. These are the skills that environmental education teaches in decision-making about environmental issues.

JUST A MOMENT

Make a list of some environmental issues which are locally relevant to you and which are yet to be settled due to controversial views. What do you think needs to be done for such issues?

Although environmental education does not always practice prescribing a value or a set of value or behavior, there are times when advocacy seems to be the best alternative. Such situation is encountered in those cases where conflicts are irreconcilable as Caldwell (1980, 198–199) states in the following words:

> There are major policy areas involving, among others, questions of land use, transportation, energy, and species preservation, where no amount of joint problem-solving, mediation, or compromise can resolve differences...Where confirmed evidence points unmistakably to outcomes that would maintain or enlarge future options, or where the degradation of the biosphere is threatened, environmental education may appropriately assume an advocacy role. I cannot regard advocacy as inappropriate to environmental education when the destruction of the biosphere is clearly at stake.

Indeed, a fair understanding of social studies, mathematics, and the laws of science is essential to be able to comprehend environmental issues (Sarabhai et al. 1998). And certainly, science is an indispensable component of environmental education since all environmental issues are invariably related to scientific concepts. But science by nature does not deal with such value clarification or taking positions as discussed above. Therefore, Disinger and Monroe (1994) maintained that "science is just one part of EE." While noting that a firm grounding in scientific information was critical to understanding the problems and potential solutions of many environmental issues, it was also noted that the answers to these problems must encompass other disciplines as well. They added that the challenge with environmental education "is to help non-science teachers tackle environmental subjects while helping science teachers cross disciplinary lines." This clearly signifies that, like science, humanities, and social sciences, environmental education has its unique nature—majorly composed of elements from all three, yet different from all three. Therefore, environmental education cannot be isolated from science, humanities, or social sciences, and vice-versa. An isolated approach to environmental education will not bring out its holistic perspective since the 'whole' in environmental education is more than the sum of the parts (Sarabhai et al. 1998). This holistic approach of environmental education sets it apart from other approaches used in the teaching–learning of disciplinary subjects and makes learning more meaningful, connects learners to their environment, and helps them in taking appropriate actions regarding environmental issues. Environmental education is therefore often said to be 'good education' (Athman and Monroe 2004; Disinger and Monroe 1994; NAAEE 2004, 1; Sarabhai et al. 1998). A few simple examples to explain how an environmental education classroom could be different from a traditional classroom are provided in Box 2.1.

BOX

Examples to Illustrate How EE Is Different

Following is an excerpt from a science textbook (Class VII Science, NCERT, 212–213):

"Tibu told them that the forest is not just home to plants and animals. Many people also live in the forest. Some of them may belong to different tribes. Tibu explained that these people depend mostly on the forests. The forest provides them with food, shelter, water and medicines. They have traditional knowledge about many medicinal plants in the forest."

In a traditional science class, the above mentioned lines may be simply read out by the teacher or one of the students and they must have moved on to the next topic. However, if the same is to be converted into an environmental education classroom, the teacher would take into consideration the following points:

1. Discuss with students about the rights of people living in the forests.
2. Discuss the concerns of people living in forests and the problems they would face if they are forced to move away from the forests. This will help students change their attitude toward forest dwellers.
3. Help students appreciate the self-sufficiency of forest dwellers and the implications brought about by developmental activities in and around the forests and the people living there.

Let us consider another passage:

"A very large fraction of our people defecates in the open, on dry riverbeds, on railway tracks, near fields and many a time directly in water. Untreated human excreta is a health hazard. It may cause water pollution and soil pollution. Both the surface water and groundwater get polluted. Groundwater is a source of water for wells, tube wells, springs and many rivers as you learnt... Thus, it becomes the most common route for water borne diseases. They include cholera, typhoid, polio, meningitis, hepatitis, and dysentery."

It is such a regular practice to teach students about the impacts of open defecation, just as it is given in the above passage. We conclude the topic by giving only scientific facts, which the students easily 'learn' and move on. However, in environmental education, such topics are discussed holistically. Various other concerns related to such practices are also discussed such as poverty, ignorance, lack of awareness, social and traditional practices, and so on. Discussions may even include manual scavenging and sensitivity toward fellow citizens who take up such professions. Through such holistic discussions students will not only learn but also become more sensitive to the issues.

Unlike other disciplinary subjects, at the heart of environmental education is behavioral and attitudinal change. This feature also contributes to the uniqueness of environmental education. It envisages that the knowledge gained, skills developed, or values imbibed should translate into behavioral change or environmentally responsible behavior, that is, it should lead to certain positive actions. Without this, our attempt to protect and conserve our deteriorating environment can never be achieved. However, such behavioral change does not occur easily or naturally. It involves a complex array of factors which contribute to such behavioral change. The detail about environmentally responsible behavior is discussed in Chapter 6.

Finally, the million dollar question—are we going to have another subject as EE? Is environmental education adding burden to the already existing disciplinary subjects in schools? Several approaches on how environmental education can be implemented have been worked out by professionals. Environmental education can be framed as a separate subject by incorporating inputs from different subjects or along with science, humanities, and social sciences or a combination of both. This option is left to the curriculum developers and practitioners. As we shall see in detail in the next chapter, each approach has its pros and cons. However, given the present situation where there is so much competition for time and space in the school time-frame, besides the already loaded curriculum, incorporating inputs into different disciplinary subjects might well be more acceptable to the stakeholders. But keeping in view the escalating environmental problems and issues emerging everywhere today, the choice should be based on what ought to be done and not on convenience. However, it is clear that having a separate environmental education subject is not the only option.

2.3 EE and Science–Technology–Society (STS) Education

The interactions of science and society are often implicitly or explicitly reflected in science and social studies education. Lucas (1980; 1980–1981), in his review of literature related to science education, found that many science education programs carried an implicit view that science needs to be taught in a way that reflects the social issues that arise from the application of science, or which can be considered as candidates for an application of science. During the same time, due to the accelerating development and use of new technologies at the science–society interface, the problems of human society had exacerbated. This resulted in the STS movement which has been drawing attention since the 1970s. One of the earliest mentions of STS appears to be in 1971 by Jim Gallagher in *Science Education,* wherein he had predicted that in a democratic society it would be important to understand the interrelationships of science, technology, and society, as much as it would be important to understand the concepts and processes of science (Pedretti and Nazir 2011). STS education was proposed following the rationale that "understanding of the interactions of science and society, is of central importance to citizens individually and collectively, and that schooling can and should, perhaps must, address this concern squarely" (National Commission on Excellence in Education 1983 cited in Disinger 1986), and through which attempts were also made to raise environmental awareness by way of science and social studies education (Disinger 1986).

There is no denying that much of the goals of environmental education and STS approach are common or at least some direct crossover exists between environmental education and STS education as Rubba (1987) puts in the following words:

> [A]ll science and technology-related societal issues impact the biosphere. Still, we tend to differentiate between "environmental" and "STS" issues. Those science and technology-related societal issues for which we recognize direct or overt ecological connections (e.g., energy consumption, land use, waste management, water quality) are referred to as "environmental" issues. These so-called environmental issues have been the primary focus of environmental education over the past two decades. Science and technology-related societal issues for which the ecological connections are of a more extended and covert nature, and for which the science–technology aspects are more easily recognized (e.g., sexually transmitted diseases, the right to life/death, technology in the workplace, organ transplantation) we tend to refer to as "STS" issues. Societal issues with a strong STS flavor typically have not been dealt with in environmental education programs.

In fact, characterization of environmental education clearly indicates that it foreshadows STS emphases with its explicit and necessary interconnections with science and technology and the issues and problems of society (Disinger and Wilson 1986). Further, Volk (1984, cited in Disinger 1986) finds that environmental education and STS are identical in many respects and notes that much of the experience that educational community has had with STS education has been accomplished under the rubric of EE. As environmental educators practice serious issue-oriented education the goals of STS can be achieved (Volk 1984 cited in Disinger and Howe 1990).

However, gaps that exist between theory and practice, which is described by some to be as wide as between 'science' and 'humanities' (Snow 1963 cited in Disinger 1986), is what makes it practically unsound to address environmental education through STS approach (as part of science education). For example, though the theory of STS existed, teachers had not been prepared toward that end accordingly so that it can be practiced. Thus it was difficult for 'practice' to catch up with 'theory.' According to Harms (1981 cited in Disinger 1986), statistics indicated that:

> Ninety percent of practicing science teachers emphasize goals directed toward preparing students for further formal study of science, that 99 percent of science teachers have a philosophical orientation only toward a specific science discipline, and that more than 90 percent of all science teachers use a textbook 95 percent of the time, so that the textbook in effect sets the course outline, the framework, the parameters for student experience, testing, and their worldview of science.

Such facts revealed that teachers were neither equipped nor inclined to incorporate environmental issues or its inherent social issues through science curriculum. Besides, other factors such as use of purely science textbook and testing based on science knowledge alone, acted as additional barriers to consider STS approach in the curriculum. As a result of these, actual implementation of STS programs has been found to be minimal (Yager 1984, 35–37 cited in Disinger, 1986). Social studies educators also note a disparity between 'what should be' and 'what is' with respect to theory and practice, similar to that identified by the science education community (Disinger and Wilson 1986). The limitations of STS in achieving the goals of environmental education is also evident from the fact that science teachers use traditional instructional procedures such as discussions, lectures, audio-visual media, and labs which are limited to knowledge and awareness components only and do not empower students to take appropriate action, which is the ultimate goal of environmental education (Rubba 1987).

Pedretti and Nazir (2011) pointed out the fact that there exist widely differing discourses on science–technology–society–environment (STSE) education and diverse ways of practicing that have led to an array of distinct pedagogical approaches, programs, and methods. They revisited the orientation of STSE education in science education over the course of four decades of its implementation in *Currents in STSE Education*: *Mapping a Complex Field, 40 Years On* and identified six currents (used as a metaphor to represent ideas, principles, and practices) in STSE education namely:

1. application/design (wherein it focuses on students on solving utilitarian problems through designing new technology or modifying technology),
2. historical (wherein it focuses on extending students' understanding of the historical and socio-cultural embeddedness of scientific ideas and scientists' work),
3. logical reasoning (wherein students are introduced to risk/benefit analysis, stakeholder analysis, and use of argumentation and decision-making models),
4. value-centered (wherein it focuses on enhancing student understanding and/or decision-making about socio-scientific issues through explicit consideration of ethics and moral reasoning),
5. socio-cultural (wherein it focuses on enhancing student understanding of science and technology as existing within a broader socio-cultural context, sometimes interacting with, but at other times, existing collaterally with other forms of knowledge), and
6. socio-ecojustice (wherein the focus is not simply on understanding the impacts of science and technology on society and environments, but on critiquing and solving these problems through human agency and action) currents.

While currents such as value-centered, socio-cultural, and socio-ecojustice could very well mirror the concerns of EE, currents such as application/design (which could also encourage students to become solely reliant on technological solutions to all problems) and logical reasoning (which fail to address non-logical factors such as feelings, values, spirituality, cultural norms, and politics which are critical in issue-based education) could help little in achieving the goals of EE. Moreover, their focus of STSE education was in science education alone, as if STSE education was the subject-matter of science curriculum only. How competent the science teachers are in the area of socio-cultural dimensions so as to be able to practice STSE education meaningfully is another question that demands serious attention.

More recently, the possibilities of raising environmental awareness through science education have been acknowledged especially with the introduction of the science–technology–society (STS) approach and inclusion of socio-scientific issues (SSI). SSI is a field with similar principles as STS which "focuses on empowering students to consider how science-based issues reflect, in part, moral principles and elements of virtue that encompass their own lives, as well as the physical and social world around them"

(Zeidler et al. 2005, 358 cited in Pedretti and Nazir 2011). However, in spite of such attempts, limitations that are inherent to science education remains to be an issue. Hadzigeorgiou and Skoumios (2013) also strongly raised their apprehension regarding the associated problems owing to the nature of science itself. They pointed out that science education fails to answer the 'significance' or 'purpose' or 'why should we know?' component, which is fundamental to raising environmental awareness. They argued that students might have studied science but they were not aware what they had learned. In other words, students are not able to place what they have learned in the context of their life or reality. For example, students may know the detailed process of photosynthesis but they are not aware of the connection of the process with their life or in the sustenance and maintenance of life on earth. They seem to fail to recognize that as much as photosynthesis is important for the plant for their survival, it is also a life support for other organisms which depend on the oxygen and the food it produces. Students are unable to visualize the 'big picture.' There are also other concerns and drawbacks pointed out by Hadzigeorgiou and Skoumios (2013) regarding science education. For example, ethical/moral discourse and aesthetic appreciation of nature are not seriously considered in science education, which otherwise are indispensable to environmental education. They argued that such discourses and practices are very crucial since it help students become aware of the wider significance of environmental issue as well as mold their outlook toward such issues.

Environmental education, on the other hand, envisages letting students think 'differently' and more holistically. For example, when a child sees a tree, she does not merely understand it as a carbon dioxide-taking, oxygen-giving entity or does not merely visualize the cells and stomata present on the leaves, but also sees the shade it provides, the birds that perch on the branches and the nests they build, the insects that crawl on the trunks, the roots that holds the soil together, the water it absorbs from the soil, the water it releases from its leaves through the stomata in the form of water vapor by the process called transpiration, which contributes in water cycle and so on. Similarly, when a child uses a computer, she understands that many resources such as water, chemicals, metals, have been utilized to manufacture it, many of which can be recycled, and most importantly, it requires energy (mostly obtained from burning of fossil fuels which produces greenhouse gases during the process) to run it. She also understands that electronic wastes have become a major environmental concern, releasing hazardous chemicals such as mercury, lead, cadmium, and polyvinyl chloride (PVC), which impact our health, especially those of rag pickers, sorters, recyclers, and so on. She understands the scientific concepts along with the other concerns—social, environmental, or economic—associated with it. Such broader understanding is not brought out through the STS approach in science education or social science education.

The above discussions suggest that though it has been difficult to achieve the goals of environmental education by way of STS approach through science education, the issue is not with the nature of STS as such. The reasons include lack of implementation strategies such as preparation of teachers to integrate STS approach in science education and the nature of science itself which does not naturally accommodate social and economic concerns or value aspects in its discourses. Similar issues will be met in social studies education. Besides, it will not be the best consideration to encourage STS through science and social studies education at the expense of EE.

However, it is also a fact that the content to be provided through environmental education is to a significant extent subsumed in the STS education. Due to this, it has been argued that the inclusion of the term 'environment' in the title of the S/T/S (Disinger 1986; Lubbers 1986 cited in Disinger and Wilson 1986) such as S/T/S/E, S/S/T/E, and S/E/T/S, would make more sense (Disinger and Wilson 1986). Indeed, STS education gradually evolved to include the environment (E) component and subsequently came to be known with the acronym STSE (Pedretti and Nazir 2011).

JUST A MOMENT

Do you think science has been able to raise enough environmental awareness amongst students? What do you think are the reasons?

2.4 Converging EE with Science Education: Possibilities and Limitations

As has been discussed, science education provides a favorable platform to implement environmental education since all environmental issues are invariably related to scientific concepts. And topics such as resource management, biodiversity, and other related topics have traditionally been addressed within science education (Feinstein and Kirchgasler 2015). But we are also aware of the fact that implementation of environmental education through science education, however, has been found to be limited to providing scientific information and content knowledge on environmental issues. This information-based transmission of environmental contents and facts is not environmental education at all.

In spite of the above facts and practices, converging environmental education with science education is not only a possibility but it has become a necessity. However, this convergence should not impede or interfere with the possible convergence of environmental education with other disciplinary areas. Instead, other disciplinary areas should follow the same. There are several reasons for the need to converge environmental education with science education—(a) since environmental education is interdisciplinary in nature, it cannot be left out of science education, (b) to avoid introducing environmental education as a separate curriculum subject, and (c) the introduction of an infusion approach of environmental education. In fact, the long association of environmental education with science education is well known and science has been the dominant subject for infusion (Gough 2013, 10). Studies suggests that such infusion benefits science education, surprisingly to an extent not thought of, though the underlying purpose of such infusion is to promote environmental education. The reason being, science education in itself is not able to draw students' attention anymore (Gough 2008). The World Conference on Science and Technology-2007 pointed out a widespread lack of student's interest in school science and technology education and of its relevance to them. But we have reasons to cheer about. Numerous surveys and research studies have shown that students are interested in the environment. Some of the topics that students are keen to learn about include the ozone layer and how it might be affected by humans, what can be done to ensure clean air and safe drinking water, the possible radiation dangers of mobile phones and computers, and how to protect endangered species (Gough 2008). Such environment-related topics find place in science curriculum and careful planning of pedagogy and applying an appropriate approach can bring about meaningful environmental education and at the same time increase students' interest in the subject—in this case, science (Feinstein and Kirchgasler 2015). Thus, science education can play an important part in the implementation of environmental education and the two can complement each other very well.

However, there are several questions that arise as we converge environmental education with science education. Can we really achieve the goals of environmental education through such initiatives as simply incorporating environment topics in science transacted by untrained teachers? Are we going to use environmental education to enhance learning in science? Are we going to make science course only 'environmental' as Lucas (1980–1981) mentioned, in the sense of using current environmental concerns as a vehicle for promoting the study of science or for developing themes 'about' science, particularly as a method of demonstrating or discussing the social relevance of science or the social responsibility of scientists? Or are we looking to achieve the goals of environmental education through science? These are the questions to be considered more deeply by science educators. Unless science educators are sure of what they want to achieve, convergence of environmental education in science education in its true sense can never be expected. For this to happen, as Gough (2008) pointed out, it will require a major reconstruction of science education.

In "Science and Environmental Education: Pious Hopes, Self-praise and Disciplinary Chauvinism," Lucas (1980) presented a thorough review of literature relating to science and environmental education where he concentrated on material written by science educators or scientists and published in journals, books, and pamphlets likely to be read by science educators. His review was based on his classification, or rather, definition of environmental education as mentioned in Chapter 1 as education 'about,' 'in,' and 'for' the environment. In spite of science taking on the dominant role in environmental education, he found little evidence that science education had made any successful contribution to the goal of enhancing the preservation of man's environment. This, he said, was because science educators were fully not aware of the complete definition of environmental education and hence their narrow focus was on the 'about' and 'in' components while ignoring the most important component, 'for.' In his review, he found that some literatures presented the view that science teachers are able to teach the content of the other subject areas which is a sheer act of labeling science educators superior. The most extreme statement of this position that he came across was in McMichael and Strom's (1975) suggestion that high school 'science' courses should include topics on society; aesthetics; cultural heritage; freedom, justice, and responsibility; and economic systems. Lucas also found that science educators themselves feel that they are superior and hence do not need to draw upon literature available in other disciplines which focuses on the aims of, and issues in, environmental education. These educators seem to believe that science is 'the' vehicle for environmental education through which they can achieve all that environmental education looks to achieve. Lucas called this unjustified glorification of science by science educators as 'omnipotent disciplinary chauvinism.' Such glorification of science and science educators is unjustified because without any competence in the area of environmental education it is doubtful that these science teachers will be able to handle environmental issues appropriately. To substantiate this view, Lucas cited Arnsdorf who commented as follows: "[A]s a result, if social, political, geographical, economical and historical dimensions of environmental issues are taught, they are often under the tutelage of faculty with inadequate preparation." This indicates the dangers of resting environmental education entirely in the hands of science educators. Thus sticking the field of environmental education just to science would also mean a disservice to a generation to develop the ability to critically evaluate issues and to apply skills in citizen action to resolve those issues (Holsman 2001).

However, his review also indicated that many science education programs and projects that were taken up in different countries showed some relevance to environmental education but in different ways which he grouped under three categories—(a) such courses which is only 'environmental' in the sense of using current concerns as a vehicle for promoting the study of science and hence environmental education is subsidiary, (b) those where science courses use an environmental organizing theme, and (c) those which has strong environmental education component (illustrating the impact of science on society and its interaction with other aspects of human life and hence most relevant). Lucas also maintained that the remarkable success of achieving the goals of environmental education through science education as claimed in many literatures is without any supporting or evaluative evidence. He found little evidence to show that science education can help achieve the goals of environmental education, especially the goals of educating 'for' the environment. The only evidence Lucas found were typically self-reports by teachers who describe their programs or a very small-scale study of the effects of particular teaching techniques. Hence, he labels the effectiveness of such environmental education programs as nothing more than 'self-praise' and 'pious hopes.' He also found very few science educators or scientists like Baer (cited in Lucas 1980) suggesting the need to include values such as play, festivity, beauty, wonder and praise in the understanding of and treatment of nature, an area which is not naturally reflected in the science curriculum, which otherwise is a very important aspect of environmental education.

The literature review of those pertaining to environmental education as well as science for environmental education revealed that development of attitudes have been given too much emphasis when it, without action, will not produce the desired environmental conditions (Lucas 1980–1981). Therefore, it is important that environmental practices and researches should also focus on the appropriate behavior or actions. Toward resolution of the impending issues on how education 'for' the environment can be best implemented, Lucas cited the view of Fensham and May (1979) who suggested the concept of a core curriculum wherein environmental education forms one of the prime concerns with education 'for' the environment clearly elaborated.

More recently, Feinstein and Kirchgasler (2015) conducted a study to find out how the Next Generation Science Standards (NGSS) in science education approach sustainability, wherein they concluded that there are three major concerns on how sustainability has been projected in the NGSS. They are—(a) Universalism, wherein, sustainability issues are projected to be universal, the benefits and harms are equally shared by all. The fact however is, some humans are more responsible for existing sustainability challenges while others suffer the consequences more severely. (b) Scientism, wherein, most questions related to sustainability issues can be answered by science. The fact however is, sustainability is a complex problem requiring multiple sources of knowledge. (c) Technocentrism, wherein, sustainability issues are portrayed as a set of problems to be addressed with technical knowledge and technological solutions. The fact however is, sustainability issues have much to do with ethics, values, and decision-making. It is therefore important that science education looks into these concerns more seriously.

In spite of the many issues surrounding the convergence of environmental education with science education, the idea of convergence makes a lot of sense in the school curriculum. Such convergence will result in a win-win situation for both environmental education and science education as Gough (2008) puts it in the following words:

> By bringing science education and environmental education together in the school curriculum, science content is appropriate to a wider range of students and more culturally and socially relevant. The convergence is also important for environmental education, because it needs science education to underpin the achievement of its objectives and to provide it with a legitimate space in the curriculum to meet its goals, which are very unlikely to be achieved from the margins. Adopting an environmental education approach might be just what science education needs. However, the task is to convince those who control the school curriculum and those who teach science in classrooms that science education needs to change.

JUST A MOMENT

Do you consider the approaches of environmental education and science education to be different? Do you think they complement each other?

2.5 Environmental Education–Environmental Science–Environmental Studies

We have discussed elaborately about the nature of environmental education and how it can be integrated in different disciplinary subjects. But there is another confusion that remains to be resolved, the confusion being, whether environmental education, environmental science and environmental studies, are one and the same. Concerns related to the lack of clarity of the terms have been pointed out by many (Filho and O'Loan 1996, 29 cited in Monde 2011; Harde 1982) and have been considered to be barriers in the successful implementation of environmental education (Monde 2011). It is seen that, more often than not, the terms environmental education, environmental science and environmental studies, are used synonymously. While it is true that environmental education cannot make sense without having the basic understanding of the environment which is the concern of environmental science, the objectives of the two are different. Davis (1978a cited in Harde 1984) argues that "Environmental Science largely is a disciplinary or multidisciplinary approach to the scientific and technical aspects of manipulating, modifying, or preserving our natural environment. Emphasis is generally placed on the physical sciences, on the ecologically-oriented biological sciences, on engineering and on statistical and computer modeling." In an attempt to bring out the relationship between environmental education and environmental science, Carter and Simmons (2010, 12–13) assert the following:

> A major contributor to the EE knowledge base is environmental science. Environmental science is the engine of data collection and knowledge creation, while EE is the vehicle for dissemination and application of that knowledge with environmental literacy as the ultimate goal...There can be no argument that EE and environmental science are very closely intertwined and interdependent, but to say that they are one and the same is to say that science and education are the same.

Further, the objectives of environmental science is restricted to focusing on the awareness and knowledge components of the environment, while environmental education includes the dimensions of attitudes, value, skills (Monroe 1991), and opportunities for participation in the issue resolution.

Similarly, environmental studies has its own objective. Nash (cited in Harde 1984) argues that the basic concept in environmental studies is the study of humans as they affect and are affected by their environments and further identifies the most distinguishing characteristic of environmental studies as its recognition that the welfare of the total environment may require a subordination of the parochial interests of humankind. As defined by Harde (1984), environmental studies is the interdisciplinary search for knowledge about and understanding of natural (physical and biotic) systems and of the dynamic interactions between these systems and humankind's social and cultural systems. In order to characterize environmental studies, the following factors or criteria seem to be implicit:

1. Concern with the environment of humankind: the concept in environmental studies is the study of humans as they affect and are affected by their environments;
2. Concern with the total environment: its social, cultural, economic, and aesthetic, as well as its physical and biological aspects;
3. Concern with interdisciplinarity: contributions which can and must be made individually and collectively by all the arts, sciences, and professions;
4. Concern with problem-solving and the clarification of open-ended options, as opposed to 'ivory tower' studies (separated from real life problems); and
5. Concern with configurations that transcend traditional lines of endeavor, with central focus on the relationships between humankind and the total environment. (Disinger and Schoenfeld 1988; Schoenfeld 1971, 111–112; Schoenfeld and Disinger 1978, 8–9).

Recognizing the importance of environmental sciences in environmental studies, Schoenfeld and Disinger (1978) label the former as the biophysical 'hard ware' of environmental studies in contradistinction to the social science and humanities 'software.' Fields such as meteorology, climatology, plant and animal ecology, oceanography, agriculture, geochemistry, soil engineering, civil engineering, and many more are included under environmental science (Harde 1984; Lapedes 1974 in Schoenfeld and Disinger 1978). On the other hand, environmental studies seek to bring perspective to both the sciences and the arts (Schoenfeld and Disinger 1978) and it is "a new way of looking at a variety of old disciplines, their relationships, and their potential contributions" (Schoenfeld 1971, 112). Hence, though environmental sciences play a major role in environmental studies program, its contribution is only partial (Nash 1974 cited in Harde 1984).

Often, environmental science is deemed to be merely a subset of environmental studies and is considered to treat only the symptoms of man's dysfunction with his physical environment. It is also believed that the ultimate solution to environmental problems is to deal with those areas related to human values, attitudes, and policy which are in the purview of environmental studies. However, due to the accelerating environmental problems arising from uncontrolled technology and lifestyles such as air and water pollution, solid waste accumulation, wasted energy, and multiple pressures on the land, Frey (1978 cited in Harde 1984) argues that such are precisely the kinds of problems which can best be solved through the application of the principles found in the biological, physical, and engineering sciences; that is, programs in environmental science. He goes on to say that "Rather than to dwell on the differences between the concerns of environmental studies and environmental science, and perhaps unnecessarily develop internecine warfare, let me simply say we need both approaches."

Although environmental education, in its broadest sense, is the designation used to refer to all forms and levels of facilitating learning and disseminating knowledge about the environment and humanity's impact upon it, the terms 'environmental studies' and 'environmental education' have been often used interchangeable. Those which differentiate between the two consider environmental education as the process of acquiring, and applying, the content of environmental studies (Schoenfeld and Disinger 1978). It is also commonly observed that in many universities environmental education is the province of the school or department of education, while environmental studies is found to be associated with any or all other schools or colleges (Schoenfeld and Disinger 1978, 10). While schools and colleges of education developed courses in environmental education pedagogy and research, universities themselves tended to adopt the rubric 'environmental studies' as their umbrella term (Schoenfeld and Disinger 1978, 12). In spite of this segregation being adopted in the universities, environmental education or environmental studies has a basic message—interdependence—implying that everything is connected to everything else (Schoenfeld and Disinger 1978, 13).

It has also been argued that environmental education does not give importance to the content but emphasis is placed on developing effective methods and vehicles for presenting the content to school students and the general public. Hence it is considered to be 'delivery-oriented' (Davis 1978 cited in Harde 1984).

While in the broadest use of the term environmental education, environmental studies is enclosed under its umbrella, in the narrower sense of the term, environmental education is a distinct professional specialization that falls outside the field of generalized environmental studies. In that usage, environmental education is not synonymous with environmental studies, although courses from the curriculum of environmental education and environmental studies contribute to the curriculum of the other (Harde 1984).

In contradistinction to the predominant thrust of EE, Craig B. Davis (1978 cited in Harde 1984) points out that:

[E]nvironmental studies is more than a series of instructional programs for training undergraduate and graduate students. It is also a field of scholarly pursuit. Faculty members engaged in environmental studies are, for the most part, keenly interested in examining the body of knowledge, sifting it, resorting it, and examining it again with the hope and expectation that their efforts will shed some light on the interrelationship of man, culture, society and the environment. It is this pursuit of knowledge that is the true raison d'etre for the field of environmental studies.

Notwithstanding its distinction from environmental science and EE, environmental studies is 'virtually synonymous' with Human Ecology, it being an effort to merge human sociology and ecology, and dealing with the interaction of human culture and the environment, drawing on the social and natural sciences, as well as on the humanities, to present a broad view of the phenomena of human culture. But it is not synonymous with Ecology which is a systems approach to various specializations of the biological sciences. As such, Ecology does not draw sufficiently upon the other disciplines to achieve a total approach to the complex of activities defined as environmental studies (Harde 1984).

While environmental studies is offered as a course consisting of several areas/papers in general, in India, environmental studies (EVS) at the primary education is introduced as a composite area of study with insights drawn from sciences, social sciences, and environmental education and visualized as 'child-centered' (NCTE 2009, 2015).

The following table (see Table 2.1) will provide a better picture of the relationship amongst the three. As we can see, clear-cut differences are not seen in some of the points clearly indicating that the three cannot be completely isolated from each other.

Further, when it comes to actual implementation or practice or in the teaching–learning process, the dividing lines amongst the three may not remain and tend to become insignificant. They can overlap so much so that one may not be able to make out whether teaching–learning in environmental education or environmental science

Table 2.1 Relationship of Environmental Education—Environmental Science—Environmental Studies

	Environmental Education	*Environmental Science*	*Environmental Studies*
1.	In preservice courses, deals with designing effective educational methodologies/pedagogies and communication strategies to transact environmental concerns. That is, 'how to teach' is given emphasis.	In preservice courses, designing educational methodologies/pedagogies is not part of the curriculum.	In preservice courses, designing educational methodologies/ pedagogies is not part of the curriculum.

(Continued)

(Continued)

	Environmental Education	Environmental Science	Environmental Studies
2.	Addresses questions which are not scientifically verifiable such as those related to values and ethics. Not restricted to scientific enquiry method.	Restricted to scientific enquiry method. Addresses questions which are rationally justified by empirical evidence.	Addresses questions which are not scientifically verifiable such as those related to values and ethics. Not restricted to scientific enquiry method.
3.	Process-oriented. It is an educational process aimed at building awareness, knowledge, attitudes, skills, and participation to tackle environmental concerns. It is holistic taking into account the social, environmental, and economic aspects.	Content-oriented. Its objective is to teach specified topics related to the environment through dissemination of scientific information and knowledge.	Content-oriented. Its objective is to teach specified topics related to the environment holistically by taking into account the social, environmental, and economic aspects.
4.	Participatory.	Often one-way mode of transaction.	May be participatory.
5.	Interdisciplinary and integrated in disciplinary subjects such as science, social science, earth science, environmental science, languages, mathematics, psychology, economics, and arts, or as a separate subject as environmental education.	Partially interdisciplinary and integrated in disciplinary subjects such as biological science, earth science, physical geography or as a separate subject as environmental science.	Interdisciplinary with contents drawn from science and social science. Taught as a separate subject.
6.	As an approach, it is as much as interdisciplinary as it is multidisciplinary. This is because it can be integrated in any subject and it can also be taught as a separate subject taking inputs from each.	As an approach, it is more interdisciplinary than it is multidisciplinary. This is because it can be integrated only in few subjects but can be easily taught as a separate subject.	As an approach, it is interdisciplinary.
7.	Broad objective covering different components such as awareness, knowledge, attitude, skill and participation to address environmental issues more effectively.	Deals with environmental facts about environmental processes and phenomena. Hence it limits its discussion to spreading awareness and providing knowledge about the environment.	Deals with the natural environment and its associated social and economic issues.

(Continued)

(Continued)

	Environmental Education	Environmental Science	Environmental Studies
8.	Environmental education helps understand environmental issues and work toward resolution of such controversial issues.	Issues related to environmental problems are considered secondary. For example, cremation on river banks pollutes the water. Issue emerging from such practices as whether such practices should be permitted or not is not the concern of environmental science.	Environmental issues are discussed but resolution of such issues may be or may not be part of its objectives.
9.	Focuses on developing process skills for issue resolution such as critical thinking, conducting survey, analytical skill, communication, value clarification, evaluating, and decision-making. For example, employs various skills to identify how such contamination by industrial waste is affecting the health of the people and how the same can be addressed holistically.	Uses established protocol for environmental problem resolution. That is, for issue resolution only scientifically verifiable answers are taken into consideration. For example, uses protocol to treat contaminated ground water due to industrial waste.	Problem resolution is flexible and can take any form.
10.	Values are indispensable in decision-making.	Values—ethical, moral, social or aesthetic—have little place.	Values are given emphasis.
11.	Appreciates the differences of opinions about environmental issues, which brings about value clarification and encourage attitudinal change toward the environment and its issue.	Limits the discussion to scientific facts.	Discussions are democratic and open, encouraging value clarification and attitudinal change toward the environment and its issues.
12.	Ultimate aim is to bring about environmentally responsible behavior.	Restricted to imparting environmental knowledge. Environmentally responsible behavior is not the concern.	Encourages environmentally responsible behavior but not necessarily the ultimate aim.

(Continued)

(Continued)

	Environmental Education	**Environmental Science**	**Environmental Studies**
13.	Involves actions to protect the environment which sets it apart from environmental science and environmental studies.	Does not necessarily involve actions to protect the environment.	Does not necessarily involve actions to protect the environment.
14.	Generally finds itself accommodated in the school or department of education.	Finds place in any other department related to science.	Finds place in any other department.

or environmental studies is in progress. This suggests that, though the three may apparently be different, it all depends on how the practitioner takes up the topic since the teaching–learning process as such has no rigid boundary. A passionate environmental educator will deliberately make efforts to convert an environmental science classroom into an environmental education classroom by incorporating the concerns of environmental education in the teaching–learning process. The reverse is also true in that a practitioner can turn an environmental education classroom into an environmental science classroom by focusing only on imparting environmental facts. For example, a practitioner can emphasize value or behavioral change in an environmental science classroom. It may also so happen that a practitioner in environmental education for some reason may fail to address the value or attitude component in the teaching–learning process.

Conclusion

Environmental education has now been established as an area of education that cannot be left out from the school curriculum. Yet, questions are still raised as to why we need to introduce another area of study to the already loaded curriculum. From the elaborate discussions that we had in the chapter, we can now conclude that environmental education is indeed important because no other subjects will be able to address all the concerns which it addresses or attempts to address.

With the deteriorating environment that we are increasingly witnessing, environmental education must receive equal and corresponding attention, if not more, in the curriculum. The hurdles en route its implementation will be many but that should not diminish or marginalize its importance. As we have seen in the chapter, persistent and sincere efforts should be made so that environmental education is reflected in the curriculum, as a separate subject or through the curriculum of different subjects. Which approach should be adopted or which subject is most appropriate to transact environmental concerns should hardly be a matter of dispute. A motivated teacher or a teacher who feels a moral responsibility to take care of the environment will always find a way out wherever relevant to incorporate environmental concerns in her teaching–learning process and prepare environmentally responsible students.

SUMMARY

- The uniqueness of environmental education necessitates its inclusion in the curriculum.
- The nature of different disciplinary areas are different which makes it clear that different disciplines have their own limitations in addressing different topics of learning. Science can best bring out the 'truth' of the physical phenomena and processes while social science, 'factual base.'
- Environmental education is holistic in nature as it takes into consideration the concerns of both science and social sciences. This aspect is important to address environmental issues which are trans-disciplinary.
- Environmental education is also unique in nature in terms of value clarification.
- Environmental education concerns values–ethical, social or aesthetic, which is missing in the discourse of disciplinary subjects such as science.
- Environmental education provides opportunity to explore various value perspectives which help students understand controversial environmental issues better.
- It is not necessary to have a separate subject by the name Environmental Education to implement environmental education in the curriculum.
- STS education has been used as a tool by many to achieve the goals of environmental education.
- Limitations of STS education to achieve the goals of environmental education are: Science teachers prepare students for further formal study of science; philosophical orientation of science teachers only toward a specific science

discipline; use of single textbook with limited an narrow worldview of science; it does not address the 'significance' or 'purpose' or 'why should we know?' component; science education does not give importance to moral/ethical discourse and aesthetic appreciation of nature.
- There exist possibilities and limitations of converging environmental education in science education. Convergence will be meaningful only if science educators have clarity on the goals of environmental education and are equipped to do it.
- Science educators have been acknowledged to be 'superior' and 'all-able' and they are expected to know the contents of other disciplines. This harms the implementation of EE by these teachers.
- There is little evidence to show that science education had made any successful contribution to achieve the goal of EE.
- The emphasis need to shift toward education *for* the environment if we want to achieve the goal of preserving our environment.
- There is a lot of confusion in the understanding of the terms environmental education, environmental science, and environmental studies. However, the terms do not restrict or limit their implementation.
- Teachers who are motivated or passionate about environmental education can make a difference in their classroom transaction whether they are in their environmental education class or environmental science class or environmental studies for that matter.

Exercises

1. Is environmental education different from other disciplinary areas? Justify.
2. Do you think environmental education is necessary when we already have other disciplinary subjects which also discuss environmental concerns? Explain.
3. What sets apart environmental education from other disciplinary subjects? Give two points to justify your answer.

4. Do you think there is a need to include environmental education as a separate disciplinary subject? Explain.
5. Explain the limitations of addressing environmental concerns through science.
6. Environmental education lets students think differently. Elaborate your answer by giving a suitable example.
7. Why do you think STS approach was not successful to address environmental concerns?
8. Converging environmental education with science education is not only a possibility but a necessity. Justify the statement.
9. Do you think we can actually integrate environmental education in all disciplinary subjects?
10. Give an example to differentiate environmental education from environmental science.

References

Athman, Julie and M.C. Monroe. 2004. "The Effects of Environment-based Education on Students' Achievement Motivation." *Journal of Interpretation Research* 9(1): 9–25.

Caldwell, L.K. 1980. "Environmental Activism, Phase III: The Burdens of Responsibility." In *Current Issues VI: The Yearbook of Environmental Education and Environmental Studies*, edited by Arthur Sacks, (Selected Papers from the 9th Annual Conference of the National Association for Environmental Education), Columbus, OH and Troy: ERIC Clearinghouse for Science, Mathematics, and Environmental Education, and National Association for Environmental Education. Available at: http://files.eric.ed.gov/fulltext/ED197947.pdf (Accessed on 16 April 2015).

Carter, R.L. and B. Simmons. 2010. "The History and Philosophy of Environmental Education." In *The Inclusion of Environmental Education in Science Teacher Education*, edited by Alec M. Bodzin, Beth Shiner Klein, and Starlin Weaver, 3–16. New York: Springer. Available at: https://books.google.co.in/books?id=NrrnM5MHT3UC&pg=PR15&dq=Environmental+Education:+What+is+it,+For+whom,+For+what+purpose,+and+How?&hl=en&sa=X&ei=3gsdVePaF8W8uAT24YKgAg&ved=0CDYQ6AEwBQ#v=onepage&q=Environmental%20Education%3A%20What%20is%20it%2C%20For%20whom%2C%20For%20what%20purpose%2C%20and%20How%3F&f=false (Accessed on 3 April 2015).

Disinger, J.F. 1986. *Current Practices in Science/Society/Technology/Environment Education: A Survey of the State Education Agencies*. Columbus, OH: ERIC Clearinghouse for Science/Mathematics, and Environmental Education, Ohio State University

——— 1987. "Environmental Education Research News." *The Environmentalist* 7(2): 85–89.

——— 2009. "The Purposes of Environmental Education: Perspectives of Teachers, Governmental Agencies, NGOs, Professional Societies, and Advocacy Groups." In *Environmental Education and Advocacy: Changing Perspectives of Ecology and Education*, edited by Edward A. Johnson and Michael J. Mappin, 137–158. Cambridge: Cambridge University Press. Available at: http://books.google.co.in/books?id=ac2M9upsf54C&pg=PA154&lpg=PA154&dq=should+schools+have+specific+roles+in+teaching+values?+john+f+disinger&source=bl&ots=_jJykxLhG9&sig=DWdL16A5XOedV68GQaogETaVmYc&hl=en&sa=X&ei=kY8iVPThLcjluQTk6YKoCQ&ved=0CB4Q6AEwAA#v=onepage&q=should%20schools%20have%20specific%20roles%20in%20teaching%20values%3F%20john%20f%20disinger&f=true (Accessed on 25 September 2014).

Disinger, J.F. and R.W. Howe. 1990 *Trends and Issues Related to the Preparation of Teachers for Environmental Education*. Environmental Education Information Report No. ED335233. ERIC Clearinghouse for Science, Mathematics, and Environmental Education Information Report. Columbus, OH: ERIC/SMEAC. Available at: http://files.eric.ed.gov/fulltext/ED335233.pdf. (Accessed on 15 April 2015).

Disinger, J.F. and M.C. Monroe. 1994. *EE Toolbox—Workshop Resource Manual, Defining Environmental Education*. Ann Arbor, MI: University of Michigan, National Consortium for Environmental Education and Training.

Disinger, J.F. and C. Schoenfeld. 1988. "Environmental Education Research News." *The Environmentalist* 8(4): 245–248.

Disinger, J.F. and T.F. Wilson. 1986. *Locating the "E" in S/T/S*. (ERIC/SMEAC Information Bulletin No. 3), Columbus, OH: ERIC Clearinghouse for Science, Mathematics, and Environmental Education. Available at: http://files.eric.ed.gov/fulltext/ED277547.pdf (Accessed on 16 April 2015).

Feinstein, N.W. and Kathryn L. Kirchgasler. 2015. "Sustainability in Science Education? How the Next Generation Science Standards Approach Sustainability, and Why it Matters." *Science Education* 99(1): 121–144.

Gough, Annette. 2008. "Towards More Effective Learning for Sustainability: Reconceptualising Science Education." *Transnational Curriculum Inquiry* 5(1): 32–50. Available at: http://nitinat.library.ubc.ca/ojs/index.php/tci (Accessed on 5 June 2014).

Gough, Annette. 2013. "Historical, Contextual, and Theoretical Orientations That Have Shaped Environmental Education Research: Introduction." In *International Handbook of Research on Environmental Education,* edited by Robert B. Stevenson, Michael Brody, Justin Dillon, and Arjen E.J. Wals, 9–12. New York: Routledge, Available at: https://books.google.co.in/books?id=efMxqII6FtwC&pg=PA9&dq=Historical,+Contextual,+and+Theoretical+Orientations+that+have+shaped+Environmental+Education+Research:+Introduction&hl=en&sa=X&ved=0CBwQ6AEwAGoVChMIrIPHlML-xgIV0HOOCh1HkQ7u#v=onepage&q=Historical%2C%20Contextual%2C%20and%20Theoretical%20Orientations%20that%20have%20shaped%20Environmental%20Education%20Research%3A%20Introduction&f=false (Accessed on 13 November 2015).

Hadzigeorgiou, Yannis and Michael Skoumios. 2013. "The Development of Environmental Awareness Through School Science: Problems and Possibilities." *International Journal of Environmental & Science Education* 8: 405–426.

Harde, R.B. 1984. "'Environmental Studies': Towards a Definition." In *Monographs in Environmental Education and Environmental Studies*. Vol. I, edited by Arthur Sacks, 31–54. Columbus, OH: ERIC Clearinghouse for Science, Mathematics, and Environmental Education; Troy, OH: North American Association for Environmental Education. Available at: http://files.eric.ed.gov/fulltext/ED251293.pdf (Accessed on 16 April 2015).

Holsman, R.H. 2001. "Viewpoint: The Politics of Environmental Education." *The Journal of Environmental Education* 32(2): 4–7.

Kibert, C.J., M.C Monroe, A.L. Peterson, R.R. Plate, and L.P. Thiele. 2012. *Working Toward Sustainability—Ethical Decision Making in a Technological World*. Hoboken, NJ: John Wiley & Sons, Inc.

Kopnina, H. 2014. "Future Scenarios and Environmental Education." *The Journal of Environmental Education* 45(4): 217–231.

Lahiry, D., Savita Sinha, J.S. Gill, U. Mallik, and A.K. Mishra. 1988. *Environmental Education: A Process for Pre-service Teacher Training Curriculum Development*. UNESCO-UNEP International Environmental Education Programme Environmental Education Series No. 26. Edited by Patricia R. Simpson, Harold Hungerford, and Trudi L. Volk. Paris: UNESCO.

Lucas, A.M. 1980. "Science and Environmental Education: Pious Hopes, Self Praise and Disciplinary Chauvinism." *Studies in Science Education* 7(1): 1–26.

Lucas, A.M. 1980–1981. "The Role of Science Education in Education for the Environment." *Journal of Environmental Education* 12(2): 33–37.

Monde, P.N. 2011. *Barriers to Successful Implementation of Environmental Education in Zambian High Schools: A Case Study of Selected High Schools of Central Province*, PhD thesis. University of Zambia. Available at: http://dspace.unza.zm:8080/xmlui/bitstream/handle/123456789/809/Monde.pdf?sequence=1 (Accessed on 15 April 2015).

Monroe, M. 1991. "Meeting the Mandate: Integrating Environmental Education." *Clearing* 71: 8–9.

NAAEE, North American Association for Environmental Education. 2004. *Environmental Education Materials: Guidelines for Excellence*. Washington D.C.: NAAEE.

NCERT, National Council of Educational Research and Training. 1981. *Environmental Education at the School Level: A Lead Paper*. New Delhi: NCERT.

——— 2006a. *Position Paper of the National Focus Group on Teaching of Science*, No. 1.1. New Delhi: NCERT.

——— 2006b. *Position Paper of the National Focus Group on Teaching of Social Sciences*, No. 1.5. New Delhi: NCERT.

NCTE, National Council for Teacher Education. 2009. *National Curriculum Framework for Teacher Education 2009*. New Delhi: NCTE.

——— 2015. *Curriculum Framework of Diploma in Elementary Teacher Education (D.El.Ed.) Programme*. New Delhi: NCTE.

Pedretti, E. and J. Nazir. 2011. "Currents in STSE Education: Mapping a Complex Field, 40 Years On." *Science Education* 95(4): 601–626.

Rubba, P.A. 1987. "An STS Perspective on Environmental Education in the School Curriculum." In *Trends and Issues Environmental Education: EE in School Curricula—Reports of a Symposium and a Survey*, Environmental

Education Information Reports No ED292608, edited by John F. Disinger, 63–71. Columbus, OH: ERIC Clearinghouse for Science, Mathematics, and Environmental Education in cooperation with NAAEE. Available at: http://files.eric.ed.gov/fulltext/ED292608.pdf (Accessed on 16 April 2015).

Sarabhai, K.V., K. Kandula, and M. Raghunath. 1998. *Greening Formal Education—Concerns, Efforts and Future Directions.* Ministry of Environment and Forests, Government of India, Centre for Environment Education.

Sauvé, Lucie. 2005. "Currents in Environmental Education: Mapping a Complex and Evolving Pedagogical Field." *Canadian Journal of Environmental Education* 10(Spring): 11–37.

Schoenfeld, Clay. 1971. "Environmental Studies Come to the Campus." In *Outlines of Environmental Education*, edited by Clay Shoenfeld, 111–112. Madison, WI: Dembar Educational Research Services. Available at: http://files.eric.ed.gov/fulltext/ED050973.pdf (Accessed on 16 April 2015).

Schoenfeld, Clay and J.F. Disinger. 1978. *Environmental Education in Action—II: Case Studies of Environmental Studies Programs in Colleges and Universities Today.* Columbus: OH: ERIC Information Analysis Center for Science, Mathematics, an Environmental Education. Available at: http://files.eric.ed.gov/fulltext/ED152557. pdf (Accessed on 16 April 2015).

Environmental Education in the School Curriculum

Worth a Thought!

"How can we practice infusion model of environmental education when we have not even studied or heard about it?"

This is the question that is raised by every teacher who is attending a training or orientation program on environmental education for the first time. This raises a serious concern since infusion model of environmental education is what is being prescribed to be practiced in the schools across India.

Chapter Overview

Inclusion of environmental education in the school curriculum is welcome by all. However, there has been no consensus on how it should be reflected or implemented in schools. This chapter discusses the various ways in which environmental education can be implemented in the existing school curriculum so as to achieve its objectives. It also provides the different approaches that can be adopted to achieve them. Examples of how environmental education can be integrated in different subject areas are also discussed. It is envisaged that this chapter will be insightful to the readers and will assist them to:

- **explain how the objectives of environmental education can be achieved.**
- **explain and justify the importance of education 'about' the environment.**
- **explain and justify the importance of education 'in' the environment.**
- **explain and justify the importance of education 'for' the environment.**
- **describe the different approaches to implement environmental education through the curriculum.**
- **distinguish between the separate subject and infusion approach or model.**
- **demonstrate the practice of infusion model.**
- **integrate environmental education in the teaching–learning of different curricular areas.**

Introduction

In the previous chapters we have discussed the objectives of environmental education, which are to help students acquire awareness, knowledge, attitude, and skills and to provide opportunities to participate in the solving of environment problems. However, how such objectives can be achieved by way of the school curriculum depends on the methods and strategies adopted in the teaching–learning process. It is no secret that, in the name of environmental education, only content and information are being added in the curriculum without any serious efforts being put in to accomplish its objectives. This section of the book will look into the possibilities to meaningfully integrate environmental education in the school curriculum and also discuss the issues related to meeting the objectives of environmental education. It will elucidate the importance of addressing all the three dimensions of environmental education, that is, education 'about,' 'in,' and 'for' the environment to successfully achieve its objectives.

Further, the discussions will also comprise of how best environmental education can be implemented and which approach should be adopted, a concern which has been haunting practitioners ever since environmental education began to be considered a part of the educational curriculum. Some of the popular approaches adopted world-over will be discussed elaborately. Besides, ample examples of how environmental education can be integrated in different curricular areas will also be provided in the discussions that will follow.

3.1 EE through the School Curriculum

In the light of the Tbilisi Declaration, the objectives of environmental education through the school curriculum is to help students acquire 'awareness' (of and sensitivity to the total environment), 'knowledge' (a basic understanding of the environment and its related problems), 'attitudes' (a set of values and feelings of concern for the environment, the motivation to actively participate in environmental improvement and protection, and so on), 'skills' (for identifying and solving environmental problems) and provide students with an opportunity for 'participation' (to be actively involved at all levels in working toward resolution of environmental problems).

Although all the components are essential for a meaningful environmental education, Engleson (1987, 46) suggests that, due to the intellectual and moral developmental characteristics of children, some kinds of objectives should be emphasized more than others at certain levels and therefore suggests specific emphases for different levels (Table 3.1).

Environmental education, today, has established itself in the formal school systems as an important component of the curriculum. However, when it comes to implementation, unfortunately, it seems to be more accepted than actuated in the schools (Lahiry et al. 1988, 1). In other words, environmental education has a presence in the curriculum, but remains marginalized in practice. In most cases, it is found that the curriculum addresses only part of the whole of environmental education. This is largely attributed to lack of

Table 3.1	Grade-Level Emphases on Environmental Education Objective Categories	
Level	**Major Emphasis**	**Minor Emphasis**
K–3	Awareness, Attitudes	Knowledge, Skills, Participation
3–6	Knowledge, Attitudes	Awareness, Skills, Participation
6–9	Knowledge, Skills, Attitudes	Awareness, Participation
9–12	Skills, Participation, Attitudes	Awareness, Knowledge

Source: David C. Engleson (1987)

understanding of the philosophy or concept of environmental education by the teachers (Lahiry et al. 1988, 16; Lucas 1980). As a result of this, nothing much has changed in the ground. In the name of environmental education, additional scientific facts and information is provided about the natural environment through the curriculum, most commonly in science and geography curricula. This traditional way of handling environmental education is the easiest and most non-controversial way and continues to be practiced even today in most classrooms. Through this practice, students gain adequate environmental knowledge and become quite aware of environmental issues facing the world but it is never solution-oriented (Lahiry et al. 1988, 16). For example, students are taught about government decision-making in civic or social studies classes, but they fail to use such knowledge effectively as citizens in environmental problem-solving, all because they were never taught how to use the knowledge in their daily lives (Hungerford and Peyton, 1994 11). If we recall Lucas' (1972) classification of environmental education as mentioned in chapter 1, we can group such practices in schools as 'education about the environment' which focuses on providing cognitive understanding including the development of skills necessary to obtain this understanding. Tilbury (1997) calls it a 'head' approach to environmental education. Students learn about the theories of how natural systems function, man–nature interactions, various environmental issues—their causes, impacts, and so on. They also learn some of the skills in the classrooms or laboratories to tackle such issues—some process skills and technical skills. These skills could be related to methods of collection of information or data and its analysis, investigation of environmental issues, problem-solving, and use of information and communication technology (ICT)—all in theory learned in the classroom. By addressing this dimension of environmental education, that is, education about the environment, at the most, students are able to acquire the 'awareness,' 'knowledge,' and 'skill' components of the objectives of environmental education. However, studies have revealed that this increase in cognitive understanding of the students about the environment does not, in any way, lead to attitudinal change nor does it encourage students to act on environmental issues. Moreover, it is also not uncommon to find that local environmental issues do not find place in such discourses. No connection between what is being learned about the environment and what is actually happening in their environment is reflected in the teaching–learning in schools. Therefore, such education 'about' the environment in itself is not complete and cannot achieve the objectives of environmental education.

> ## JUST A MOMENT
>
> Can you recall some classes in your school days where your teacher discussed the local environmental issues which were not necessarily part of your school curriculum?

What then needs to be done so that students can acquire a set of values and feelings of concern for the environment and the motivation for actively participating in environmental improvement and protection? In short, how can they acquire environmental 'attitudes'? Going back to Lucas' (1972) classification of environmental education, the second dimension of environmental education is 'education in the environment.' This refers to education that takes place in a situation that best reflects what is being learned. Such education favors student-centered and inquiry-based learning facilitated by more open-ended and flexible teaching styles and often takes the form of outdoor education and experiential learning (Tilbury 1997). By way of doing environmental education 'in' the environment, students are able to link their curriculum with their environment which ultimately increases not only their awareness level but also their concern for the issue and their personal value toward the environment. It is through such experiences students acquire environmental attitudes—a set of values, concern, a sense of responsibility, commitment, and motivation to participate in improving the environment. For example, learning about a degrading lake and its impact by taking the students to one such location will help them acquire attitudes toward the issue. Tilbury (1997) considers such attempts as a 'heart' approach to environmental education since it involves building of personal values and concern. However, the linear causality between educational experience (in the above example, visiting a degrading lake) and pro-environmental behavior has also been disputed with critics arguing that "people's environmental behaviors are too complex and contextually dependent to be captured by a simple casual model" (Kopnina 2014). This aspect of environmental behaviors is discussed elaborately in Chapter 6. Though such learning 'in' the environment may not always bring about pro-environmental behavior, it will definitely enhance the tendency toward such behavior. However, such practices hardly seem to be happening in the schools. What is being observed is, instead of doing environmental education 'in' the environment, most of the activities go on within the four walls of the classroom. It is found that there is still very inadequate exposure of the students to their 'habitat' and there is little active learning from the natural and social worlds around them (NCERT 2006, 4; Shimray et al. 2013). Schools make do with potted plants, mini-aquariums, movies, photographs, slide shows on environmental degradation, and so on, to replace outside classroom activities and experiences. Such alternatives are not likely to help students develop environmental attitudes. Though development of environmental attitudes is important to achieve the goals of environmental education, Lucas (1980) warned that too much emphasis is given to it without focusing on the appropriate behavior or actions. He added that without action, attitude will not produce the desired environmental conditions that we strive to achieve through environmental education.

Education 'about' the environment and education 'in' the environment together still cannot achieve the objectives of environmental education. This is because education 'about' and 'in' the environment is mostly theoretical and not real situation-based. To bring about improvement in the environment, environmental education has to be action-oriented and participatory in real environmental issues. That is, it has to address certain environmental issues through action. This forms the third dimension of environmental education as proposed by Lucas (1972), that is, 'education for the environment.' It is about improving or protecting the environment. While addressing this dimension of environmental education, students are provided opportunities for 'participation' so that they can be actively involved in the resolution of environmental problems. This is necessary to achieve one of the goals of environmental education, that is, environmental education must develop problem solvers and thus should itself utilize a problem-solving approach (UNESCO 1980, p.i). Tilbury (1997) considers it as a 'hand' approach to environmental education since it involves action. Through such activities, students feel empowered and believe that they themselves can be instrumental in bringing about change. Thus it conveys the message that environmental issues can be resolved, it has been resolved due to involvement of committed people, and each one can participate in the resolution (Monroe 1991). Hence, this dimension of environmental education can be considered the most important, though it is dependent upon education 'about' and 'in' the environment to provide the skill, rationale, and knowledge to support its transformative intentions (Fien 1993 cited in Tilbury 1997). By ignoring the 'for' component of environmental education, the expected end result of environmental education, that is, resolution of environmental issues, cannot be realized and the whole educational purpose of environmental education will be defeated. Chawla and Cushing (2007) went a step further by suggesting that it is not enough to promote action for the environment but the most strategic actions need to be emphasized. Yet, unfortunately, many researchers have found that education 'for' the environment has always received least coverage and support in the classroom. One of the reasons could be that since education 'for' the environment focuses on actual environmental issues, which are often controversial and action-oriented and many teachers either feel unconfident with handling such controversial issue or they fear of being accused of bias or indoctrination (Tilbury, 1997). Spork (1992 cited in Fien and Ferreira 1997) attributes the dilution of environmental education due to lack of emphasis on the 'for' dimension of environmental education as a result of which the focus to nurture students to inculcate the appropriate environmental attitudes, such as values, ethics, morals, motivations, and behaviors, receives little importance. Also, students are not helped to develop skills necessary to act constructively for the environment. All that is done is to pass on information about the environment to build cognitive knowledge and increase awareness about environmental issues.

JUST A MOMENT

Do you think your education so far has in any way brought about some kind of attitudinal or behavioral change in you toward the environment?

As important as it is to address the 'for' component of environmental education, it is equally important to identify the 'actions' students could be involved in. It is felt that issue analysis and action may be appropriate to be taken up from the high school level (Lane 2006, 161). Nevertheless, there are actions that can be taken up by students at the primary level too. For example, for a kid in the primary stage, it could be as simple as closing taps properly, using water judiciously, turning off fans and lights when not in use, not littering, using paper judiciously, nurturing a sapling, spreading awareness to friends in the locality to avoid using firecrackers. From the secondary stage onward, students may be engaged in resolving actual environmental concerns and issues in their locality. For example, they can look into the health and hygiene issues in slums, plights of rag pickers, waste disposal, scarcity of water, and lack of space for recreation. Once students have identified the issue of their concern, they can look for alternative solutions, choose the most appropriate, and apply it and see if it works.

As we have seen, unless all the three dimensions of environmental education, that is, education 'about,' 'in,' and 'for' the environment are addressed, the objectives of environmental education which fall under the five categories such as 'awareness,' 'knowledge,' 'attitude,' 'skills,' and participation cannot be achieved. However, the issues that exist in the implementation of environmental education are not new to us. Besides many other reasons, lack of professional development stands out prominently in the list, the details of which are discussed in Chapter 8.

JUST A MOMENT

Reflect on our present education system and analyze the space and opportunities it provides to achieve the objectives of environmental education.

3.2 Approaches in EE

So far we have discussed the possibilities of implementation of environmental education in school curriculum in general. As mentioned earlier, which approach should be adopted in its implementation has been a matter of debate amongst professionals and practitioners. Professional environmental educators have suggested several approaches or models, which include separate subject approach, infusion, insertion, and integration approaches. Some educators maintain the ambiguity in the latter three approaches keeping in view the lack of clear demarcation in the three as is practiced by teachers (Lane 2006, 167), while others treat them as distinct from each other in that environmental education is integrated into the curriculum by way of infusion (the incorporation of environmental concepts, activities, and examples into existing curricular goals) and insertion (the addition of an environmental unit or course to the class or curriculum; usually something else is removed) (Monroe and Cappaert 1994, 11). Much of the following discussions will focus on the two broad approaches or models that have been most commonly in use in environmental education curriculum development and implementation globally: Separate subject or 'Interdisciplinary' approach and Infusion or 'Multidisciplinary' approach. We will look into these two approaches as have been put forward by many experts in the field. Besides, a third approach, which propagates the inclusion of both the infusion and separate subject approach in the curriculum, will also be discussed in brief.

3.2.1 Separate Subject (Interdisciplinary) Approach

We had clarified in Chapter 1, the term 'interdisciplinary' (indicating the nature of EE) as used in the guiding principles in the Tbilisi Declaration and as it is being used here (as a method or approach to implement EE). As the name suggests, separate subject or interdisciplinary approach is about teaching environmental education as a separate discipline. This approach reflects an important feature of the Tbilisi Declaration which states that environmental education should be provided to all ages and at all grade levels and be interdisciplinary in its approach, drawing on the specific content of each discipline in making possible a holistic and balanced perspective (UNESCO-UNEP 1978). In this approach, environmental concerns are addressed by taking into consideration all possible perspectives from different subject areas (see Fig. 3.1). In other words, a systems perspective or systems thinking (where the environment is visualized as a set of connected, interdependent objects that forms a complex unity, that is, as a whole and not in compartments) (NCERT 2011) is employed while looking at environment-related topics, concerns and issues which helps to understand the complex relationships within and between issues.

As shown in Figure 3.1, owing to its holistic approach, students using the interdisciplinary approach may show better understanding of environmental concerns and issues,

Figure 3.1   Interdisciplinary Model

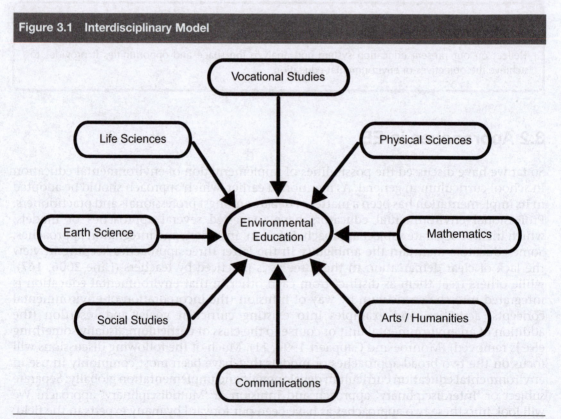

Source: Hungerford and Peyton (1994a)

compared to other students adopting different approaches. The approach, however, has several disadvantages as well. Braus and Wood (1993, 35) provided a set of advantages and disadvantages of the approach which is given in Table 3.2.

Several others have written in support of this approach while others have been critical. Views expressed by Feng (2012) show support of the approach. He maintains that interdisciplinarity enables learners to create links between individual disciplinary areas. They are able to have a holistic perspective of the concepts and hence make learning more meaningful and interesting. This, in turn, enables learners to understand the complexity of the world better. This is especially important for learners at the lower stage of school education where they find it difficult to create links by themselves of the concepts they learn in different disciplinary areas (Sarabhai et al. 1998, 5). Interdisciplinary approach can help remove or reduce such gaps. For example, concepts related to water can be studied in different disciplinary areas. Properties of water, stomata and transpiration, evaporation, condensation, precipitation, water cycle, and rain water harvesting, will be invariably part of the science curriculum. Water table, sources of water, rainfall, and so on, will most probably be studied in geography. Water crisis in a society and acts and laws related to water are within the purview of another subject, that is, social

Table 3.2   Interdisciplinary (Separate Subject) Approach

Sl. No.	PROS	CONS
1.	Easier to implement as a single subject	Hard to get schools to 'buy' it (difficult to cull out time slot for environmental education in the already congested schedule)
2.	Allows teacher to present concepts that build throughout the course	Needs trained environmental education teachers (requires more in-depth knowledge of different subjects)
3.	Teacher training is somewhat easier, although it requires teachers to have a more in-depth background of different subjects	Takes time from other standard topics (hard to squeeze in with other curriculum demands)
4.	Easier to evaluate as a separate course	Might imply that the environment is its own subject and not interdisciplinary
5.	Pulls everything together for students and can achieve greater depth and comprehension	Hard to find qualified teachers to design and teach courses
6.	Puts a priority on the subject	Not as easy to see the connections with other subjects
7.	Students' experience with interdisciplinary environmental education will go a long way	May limit the number of students exposed (especially if it is made optional)
8.	The concerned teacher will be equipped enough to do justice to environmental education.	May cause some teachers to assume environmental education 'is not my responsibility'

Source: Adapted from Braus and Wood (1993)

science. Unless these concepts are linked together, learning will never be meaningful. Learners will not be able to view each issue from a holistic point of view. An interdisciplinary approach certainly helps to present the concepts holistically.

The key to interdisciplinarity is an open attitude, a willingness to learn, and an ability to engage with different ways of thinking on common issues faced. Such an approach exposes learners to the plurality of thinking and the limitations of particular perspectives. It will be especially useful in terms of taking positions on values and ethics. As a result, such learners are able to seize opportunities to disagree, to explore, to reflect, and to develop their own perspectives (Jickling 2003 cited in Feng 2012). It may be noted that learning does not take place in isolation but in connection with other disciplines and, hence, interdisciplinary courses provide students with 'a valuable model of lifelong holistic learning' (Stolpa 2004 cited in Feng 2012).

We have discussed above in detail the most common way to practice the interdisciplinary approach which is by way of a separate subject wherein an individual teacher draws perspectives from different subject areas. In such cases, it is expected that the teacher must have a fair knowledge of different disciplines. However, this is not the only way to achieve the purpose of the interdisciplinary approach. There are several other different ways of employing this approach. Such strategies are most advantageous when an individual teacher does not have sufficient knowledge of different disciplines. We will discuss a few of those here. One predominant way of doing it is by having two or three courses taught separately yet ensuring that the contents are carefully designed by all the teachers to highlight significant connections among the disciplines. The success of such a practice lies in presenting a holistic picture to the learners in spite of the topics being taught at different times and space. Another way of doing it is by team-teaching. Two or three classes can be team-taught in a learning-community format where all the instructors who specialize in different disciplines are present at the time (Stolpa 2004 cited in Feng 2012). Learners are likely to understand complex issues better through this practice. And this practice seems to be more effective compared to the former. A possible drawback could be the difference in the style, language, and terms used by instructors from different disciplines which might affect learners in their process of learning.

Whatever be the model of interdisciplinary teaching and learning adopted, what is aimed for is to bring about systemic, relational thinking which emphasizes seeing contexts, connections, and developing integrative approaches. Systemic thinking enables a learner to build up whole pictures of phenomena without breaking them into parts. Flood (2001, 133 cited in Feng 2012) qualifies such learning as 'valid knowledge and meaningful understanding.' It also helps "learners shift focus and attention from 'things' to processes, from analysis to synthesis, from detail to pattern, from static states to dynamics, and from 'parts' to 'wholes'" (Feng 2012). Sterling (2005) also presents a view that systemic thinking offers a 'holistic approach through recognizing the complex interconnected nature of all aspects of the world around us from an individual to a global level' (cited in Feng 2012).

The merits of interdisciplinarity are also clearly visible when it comes to real world situations. We know that environmental and societal challenges are not defined by academic disciplines and, hence, when problematic situations arise—which is defined as a situation in which habitual responses to an environment are experienced as inadequate for continuing some activity that is aimed to fulfil needs and desires—the resolution of such a situation is initiated with inputs from a diversity of disciplines (Frodeman et al. 2007 cited in Feng 2012).

Although interdisciplinary approach is ideal and desirable, it will not be practically easy to achieve it. Disinger (1997) in *Environmental Education's Definitional Problem* writes:

[T]hough environmental education is ideally interdisciplinary—an eclectic assemblage of interacting disciplines, its practitioners typically approach it as if it were multidisciplinary—an eclectic assemblage of discrete disciplines. Because environmental education practitioners typically are grounded in no more than one of the multiplicity of disciplines involved, logic leads them to approach environmental education through the intellectual filters of their own disciplines.

As a result, they are unable to present environmental issues holistically. But instead of making efforts to fill this gap by discussing or collaborating with practitioners from other disciplines, Disinger (1997) adds:

[T]hese practitioners in environmental education typically continue to talk past one another, rather than with one another; all say things approximating 'the right thing', but they apparently do not recognize the generally subtle, sometimes glaring, differences in meaning between their utterances and those of their colleagues. (Disinger 1997)

Besides being grounded in only one subject, it has also been observed that teachers teaching a certain specific subject tend to think that they are superior to the others. Many science teachers are, in Lucas' (1980) terms, 'disciplinary chauvinists' who place a higher priority on teaching content from their own disciplinary specialization rather than engage the interdisciplinary or cross-disciplinary demands of environmental education. Such an attitude of teachers is a setback in the implementation of the interdisciplinary approach. Liu et al. (2007 cited in Feng 2012) further points out the challenges brought forth by the existing system of knowledge production fortified by disciplinary boundaries. Such practices do not prepare us to be adaptive or responsive to the real world challenges and hence are a setback for the implementation of environmental education.

Besides the disadvantages of the interdisciplinary separate subject approach in terms of practicability as discussed above, there is yet another reason that makes this approach undesirable in the school curriculum and this needs to be highlighted here. We are aware that the existing school curriculum is already loaded in terms of disciplinary subjects to be learned, vast content to be covered, and numerous curricular activities to be fulfilled, and even in terms of the time allotted to complete the course. Given this situation, adding another subject would be too much of a burden, not only for the students but for the whole system, and the implementation of a separate subject under such circumstances would turn out to be only routine, lacking seriousness and without any meaningful impact.

JUST A MOMENT

Do you think disciplinary chauvinism exist in our education system? Are science and mathematics treated to be superior to other subjects? Do you think such treatment has any impact on our education?

3.2.2 Infusion (Multidisciplinary) Approach

In education, infusion refers to the incorporation of a particular content of study in a different established course, with the focus on the new content, without affecting the unique nature of the course itself.

Infusion in environmental education is about incorporating environmental education into the curriculum of different existing subjects (multiple disciplines) rather than teaching environmental education as a separate discipline. In other words, in infusion approach, a single topic permeates many other disciplines (Fig. 3.2). Though environmental education has been traditionally infused mainly into science, history, and social studies classes, it can also be infused into all subject matters, including reading, writing, languages, mathematics, music, physical education, art, and other courses (Braus and Wood 1993). However, care is taken in such a way that the infusion process does not isolate the objectives of environmental education so extensively that the meaningful synthesis of experiences in the context of the discipline in which it has been infused is not possible (UNESCO 1980, 45). According to Hungerford et al. (1994, 11):

> Infusion refers to the integration of content and skills into existing courses in a manner as to focus on the content (and/or skills) without jeopardizing the integrity of the courses themselves. In the case of environmental education, the professional educator carefully analyzes traditional courses for content and/or skills which could be "environmentalized."

Figure 3.2   Multidisciplinary Model

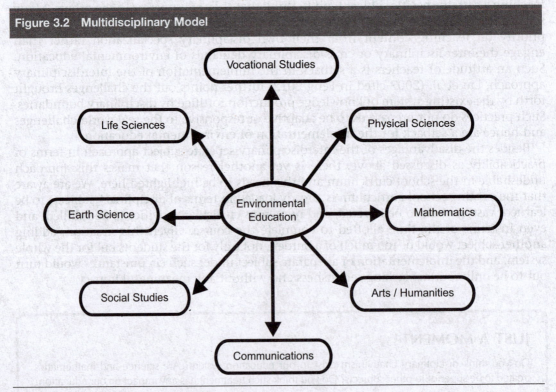

Source: Hungerford and Peyton (1994, 9)

While Monroe and Cappaert (1994, 11) equate infusion with thematic teaching, incorporating "environmental concepts, activities, and examples into existing curricular goals." However, in spite of the addition of content, the standard or the nature of the existing course/concept is not affected in any way. Ideally, the inclusion of a new content and skills in the process of infusion could enrich or enhance the existing courses or curriculum (Fellows 1980 cited in Lane 2006).

This approach is supported by professional environmental educators who believe that incorporating environmental education throughout the total curriculum at every grade level will bring about a more comprehensive treatment of environmental concerns (Simmons 1989 cited in Lane 2006, 12). It is also argued that "[S]uch an approach also recognizes that environmental issues cut across traditional disciplinary lines and that developing an environmentally responsible citizen involves acquiring knowledge, attitudes, and skills beyond that of a simple understanding of scientific or ecological principles." (15)

As discussed above, infusion is not merely adding certain environmental facts into the curriculum. But through infusion, different disciplines attempt to achieve the objectives of environmental education, that is, awareness, knowledge, attitude, skills, and participation, without jeopardizing the integrity of the concerned subject. Monroe (1991, 9) recommends the following four activities to turn environmental facts into environmental education and notes that each can be accomplished within existing subject areas and grade levels:

1. Include issues by extending the facts—the "often controversial edge between people and the environment" and solutions to these issues.
2. Carry out problem-solving skills with students: communications, group skills, leadership, creative thinking, and decision-making.
3. Find out suitable environmental feelings, attitudes, and values. Students may learn to appreciate and be responsible for others and the environment and compare their values to their ways of living.
4. Allow students to take part in the resolution of real issues.

Other professionals in the field have created certain steps that may be considered during infusion. For example, in *A Guide to Curriculum Development in Environmental Education*, Engleson (1985 cited in Lane 2006, 17) provides the following steps:

Step 1. Select the environmental topic to be infused into an existing subject area instructional unit...
Step 2. Identify the subject area units which relate to, or support the investigation of, the chosen environmental topic...
Step 3. Develop one or more environmental objectives for the subject-matter unit...
Step 4. Specify the environmental content to be added to the unit...
Step 5. Develop new instructional procedures as needed...
Step 6. Identify new process skills which might be used or developed in achieving the new environmental objectives...
Step 7. Identify new resources to be used in achieving the environmental objectives...
Step 8. Identify related activities and new topics for investigation which may be suggested by teaching the new infused unit. (51–52).

However, the above steps may not be applicable in India as it is. Practitioners will have to adapt to make the steps relevant in the context of their curriculum. In India, following the recommendation of the National Curriculum Framework 2005, environmental concepts and concerns have already been infused in the textbooks for different subjects and other textual materials, as in the case of materials developed by the National Council of Educational Research and Training (NCERT) as well as by states and union territories. In other words, contents on environmental issues and concerns have been added in the materials. However, in most instances, the content provided in subject textbooks is not sufficient to indicate environmental education objectives. In such cases, the subject teacher will have to identify the environmental concepts and concerns that have been incorporated in the textbooks and proceed from there.

Drawing from the suggestions of Monroe (1991) and Engleson (1985 cited in Lane 2006), let us illustrate infusion approach by giving an example which will be relevant to schools in India. For this, we will consider a passage from a Class VIII science textbook developed by NCERT:

> You know that coal and petroleum are fossil fuels. It required the dead organisms millions of years to get converted into these fuels. On the other hand, the known reserves of these will last, at most, a few hundred years. Moreover, burning of these fuels is a major cause of air pollution. Their use is also linked to global warming. It is therefore necessary that we use these fuels only when absolutely necessary. This will result in better environment, smaller risk of global warming and their availability for a longer period of time.

> In India, the Petroleum Conservation Research Association (PCRA) advises people how to save petrol/diesel while driving. Their tips are:

> Drive at a constant and moderate speed as far as possible,

> Switch off the engine at traffic lights or at a place where you have to wait,

> Ensure correct tyre pressure, and

> Ensure regular maintenance of the vehicle.

In the above passage a lot of information and environmental facts have been provided, such as 'fossil fuels are exhaustible,' 'burning of fuels causes air pollution which also causes global warming,' 'important tips to save petrol/diesel while driving.' A teacher in a science classroom may follow the following steps so as to practice infusion approach of environmental education while engaging in such topics:

1. Explain how fast we are using fossil fuels compared to the rate that they are produced naturally.
2. Explain some of the air pollutants from burning of fuels.
3. Correlate air pollution with global warming convincingly while keeping in mind that it is Class VIII students who are in the classroom. Hence the concept should be simplified but not trivialized.
4. Identify some issues associated with the topics which could be (a) people do not want to commute by public transport, (b) the public in general are not concerned about reducing air pollution, and (c) the steps undertaken by the government are not effective to reduce burning of fossil fuels or reduce air pollution.

5. Once the issues are identified the practitioners may choose appropriate steps to address the issues depending upon the skills that they want the students to learn. The following are some suggestions:

    (i) A debate can be initiated so that different perspectives of the students could be shared. Doing this will help students widen their perspective of the issue and introspect on their views.

    (ii) Group discussion may be conducted wherein different groups can discuss can come up with their suggestive measures.

    (iii) Students can also take up projects in their locality related to the issue such as investigate why people do not want to commute by public transport or conduct a survey on how often people give their vehicles for servicing, and so on. Based on their study they can come up with solutions from which they can choose the most appropriate option and act toward it. This will not only help students experience real issues surrounding them but also make them feel empowered to tackle such issues as responsible citizens.

JUST A MOMENT

Can you recall your teachers in school employing the above mentioned steps in their teaching–learning process? If so, did it enhance your learning?

The strategies presented above seem to suggest infusion approach as a sound practice to achieve the goals of environmental education. This multidisciplinary or infusion approach will allow students to apply environmental education concepts and problem-solving skills in a great variety of situations over a long period of time (UNESCO 1980, 15). For example, when students learn about how government functions in their civic or social studies classes, they can also learn how they can use such knowledge in solving environmental problems. Similarly, students can also learn to apply and connect the knowledge they obtain in different disciplines. If students learn long enough, year after year, to consider environmental consequences through different disciplines, it will do a world of good and bring about some attitudinal change in them at the end of their schooling.

However, in spite of its many advantages, the approach also has its disadvantages, as identified by Braus and Wood (1993, 35) which are shown in Table 3.3. One of the biggest concerns of the infusion approach as presented in the table is that, as a result of infusion the message that is intended to be sent across may not be done so. For example, while discussing qualities of polluted water of different rivers and water bodies, the focus could be so much on the physical properties of the polluted water that the teacher might not be able to bring in the issues related to health hazards and other concerns, especially of those who are not able to afford pure drinking water and other social issues related to it. This could occur because of the 'it-is-not-my-concern' attitude of the teachers or due to disciplinary chauvinism as we had mentioned earlier. While in some cases the issue may be discussed, but if the teacher fails to make a deliberate effort to put forward the message clearly, the students will not grasp the message that is being attempted to be conveyed. In such a situation the whole purpose of infusion approach will be defeated.

	Table 3.3 Multidisciplinary (Infusion) Approach	
Sl. No.	**PROS**	**CONS**
1.	Fewer resources are needed (do not need an environmental education specialist or a separate textbook).	Is difficult to infuse environmental education and it requires extensive teacher training and effort.
2.	Does not compete with other standard subjects; does not compete for a slot in the curriculum.	Often relies on motivated teachers for efforts to succeed.
3.	Can be done immediately, without core curriculum development.	EE message can be so diluted to fit the objectives of a course that it can get lost/ students might not "get it."
4.	Many supplementary resources exist.	Leaves too much to chance.
5.	Encourages transfer of learning and integrated problem-solving across the curriculum.	Difficult to evaluate success.
6.	Appropriate for all age levels, although may be more difficult at upper grades.	Subject specificity at upper grades seldom provides space for infusion.
7.	Allows all students at all levels an opportunity to get exposure.	Exposure is often superficial.
8.	When done on a large scale, can continually reinforce and build upon key environmental concepts.	Often brings about environmentally aware citizens but not environmentally committed warriors.

Source: Adapted from Braus and Wood (1993)

There are many others who are critical about the effectiveness of the infusion approach to achieve the goals of environmental education. For example, Feng (2012) writes: "In multidisciplinarity, learners may have studied, simultaneously or in sequence, more than one area of knowledge, without making connections between them or without collaborating as learners." The issue with this approach is that learners are unable to make connections or links between what they have studied in different disciplinary areas (Sarabhai et al. 1998). This will have serious implications on the implementation of environmental education since holistic understanding of environmental issues is fundamental to environmental education. In the absence of this, all other efforts related to environmental education will make little sense. Therefore, teachers must ensure that while they adopt the multidisciplinary approach, their attempt should be to make it as much interdisciplinary as possible in the process which is the true nature of environmental education.

The concerns related to multidisciplinarity are not limited to the teaching–learning process alone, but it is also seen in the area of research. Godeman (2006 cited in Feng 2012) argues that in multidisciplinary teams, researchers are likely to carry out their analyzes separately, working on "different aspects with their respective methods." The final result will tend to be a series of reports pasted together, without integrating synthesis (Max-Neef

2005 and Miller et al. 2008 cited in Feng 2012). For example, the impact of contamination of lake water can be studied by different researchers as a multidisciplinary team. One may study the impact on the economy of local people, another on the impact on the aquatic animals and plants, another on analysis of contaminants, and yet another on the health implications of people consuming fish and vegetables from the lake. If there is no synergy between the studies, the results obtained will not be meaningful and the report cannot be presented holistically.

Issues related to the infusion approach in India were already pointed out by Krishna Kumar (Kumar 1996; Sonowal 2009, 16). However, if the curriculum ensures that apart from the required knowledge of the discipline, other issues and concerns related to the topic also receive equal importance, it would be the perfect way of approaching environmental topics. This is what is expected out of the infusion approach in the school curriculum. And given the curriculum load in the present education system where there is competition for space in the curriculum, this is a pragmatic approach to find room for environmental education (Disinger 1993, 39).

3.3 Comparisons between Interdisciplinary and Multidisciplinary Approach

We have discussed separately about the pros and cons of interdisciplinary and multidisciplinary approach. Table 3.4 gives the comparison of the two on some specific considerations as mentioned by Hungerford and Peyton (1994, 10) and Hungerford et al. (1994, 11–15).

Table 3.4	Interdisciplinary (Separate subject) vs. Multidisciplinary (Infusion)		
Sl. No.	Considerations	Interdisciplinary (Single Subject) Characteristics	Multidisciplinary (Infusion) Characteristics
1.	Ease of implementation	Easier to implement as a single subject if time permits in the curriculum; teacher training is less of a problem.	Requires that more teachers be trained; greater coordination of curriculum necessary; requires less time/content in the existing curriculum.
2.	Teacher competencies	May require fewer teachers, but with more in-depth training in EE; thus teacher training is less demanding in terms of teacher numbers but more demanding in terms of level of competencies required.	Requires that teachers of all disciplines be competent to adapt and/or use environmental education materials, although perhaps not to the same depth as in single subject approaches.

(Continued)

(Continued)

Sl. No.	Considerations	Interdisciplinary (Single Subject) Characteristics	Multidisciplinary (Infusion) Characteristics
3.	Demand on curriculum load	Requires addition of this discipline to an already crowded curriculum.	May be effectively implemented with minimal demands on existing curricular load.
4.	Ease of curriculum development	Components easier to identify and sequence.	Components must be effectively identified, sequenced, and accommodated by the existing curriculum.
5.	Evaluation	A comprehensive evaluation is much easier to accomplish in single subject curriculum.	Comprehensive evaluation difficult due to the number of variables involved.
6.	Age-level appropriateness	For simple holistic approach, it will be more appropriate for lower age. But will be more appropriate at secondary level and above where greater depth of comprehension is required.	Appropriate at all age levels.
7.	Effectiveness in teaching for transfer	More difficult to use in effectively teaching for transfer of learning. Requires special efforts to do so.	Teaching for transfer of learning is inherent in this approach when properly used. Infusion permits decision-making to take place in other disciplines in an environmental context.
8.	Ability to provide in-depth coverage of environmental issues	Budget considerations entirely depend on the nature of the course being developed. A highly sophisticated course demanding many field excursions or laboratory equipment could prove costly.	Monetary considerations vary dependent on the nature of the curriculum being developed. Monies required could be greater than in single subject curriculum due to the number of learners involved across numerous grade (age) levels.
9.	Cooperation and collaboration amongst teachers	Does not necessarily require	Very much required for successful integration of different disciplines
10.	Level of learning in students	Students are expected to learn better because issues are presented to them holistically	Largely depends on how well teachers of different discipline connect with the rest

Source: Adapted from Hungerford and Peyton (1994) and Hungerford et al. (1994)

In spite of the several pros and cons inherent in both the models, multidisciplinary (infusion) model seem to have an edge over the interdisciplinary (separate subject) model because the former allows students to apply environmental education concepts and problem-solving skills in a great variety of situations over a long period of time. For example, if students consider ecological consequences of issues in a variety of situations, such as in economics, social studies, languages, or any other disciplines throughout their formal education, there is greater reason to expect them to use this knowledge in their own non academic lives as well (Hungerford and Peyton 1994, 12). However this does not mean discounting the many advantages that interdisciplinary model provides. For effective environmental education, all that is required is a sound educational procedure in either of the formats so that environmental education goals are achieved.

3.4 Examples of EE in Different Disciplines

Although environmental education comes naturally in the teaching–learning of science, it should not be a concern of science alone. It is but a challenge to the whole conventional subject-based curriculum and pedagogy since it requires a holistic accommodation of the personal, the social, and the economic, along with the scientific components (Jenkins and Pell 2006 cited in Gough 2008). This suggests that environmental education should be considered beyond disciplinary boundaries. Further, various studies have revealed that using the approach of environmental education in different subjects enhances learning and hence improves scores (Ernst and Monroe 2004; NEETF 2000).

In this chapter, as well as in the previous chapter, we had discussed some examples to incorporate environmental education in the curriculum. Provided later are some more examples which have been presented rather crudely to illustrate how environmental education can make a difference in the teaching–learning process in different subjects. The examples represent only some of the ways environmental education can be done in every classroom, that is, all the examples provided here are not prescriptive but suggestive of how, through discussions, debates, and sharing of experiences, a disciplinary teaching–learning can be extended or transformed to a more interdisciplinary and holistic approach as envisaged in environmental education. However, the approach to environmental education is not limited and should not be restricted to what is being presented in the following sections.

3.4.1 EE in Science

A science teacher prepares a slide of stomata of different plants—monocots and dicots—and tells his/her students about the structure, shape, number, and so on and explains its function in photosynthesis or the concept of transpiration. An environmental educator[1]

---

[1] An environmental educator, as mentioned here and also at several places elsewhere in the chapter or book, represents a teacher or educator (in elementary, secondary, or higher education) who deliberately uses environment, to the extent possible, as a context or incorporates environmental themes in her teaching–learning process, irrespective of whether she is a science, mathematics, social science, language, or arts teacher. In doing so, the teacher increases the students' awareness of the environment, leading them to adopt environmentally conscious attitudes and behaviors, and teaching them the knowledge and skills to make environmentally responsible choices (Bones 1994, 12).

takes it further to explain its role in water cycle and rainfall and how it is linked to conservation principles or how oxygen which sustains life is released by plants through these small pores called stomata. In short, the teacher provides the larger picture which makes learning more meaningful and, at the same time, helps them understand the environmental problems that may arise due to deforestation.

A science teacher tells about the properties of mercury and its uses in blood pressure measuring instrument (Mercury sphygmomanometers) or clinical thermometer. An environmental educator links its use in Compact Fluorescent Lamps (CFLs) and the dangers of improper disposal of broken instruments or fused CFLs and how such carelessness can be hazardous, especially to rag pickers and sorters. An environmental educator can also narrate the incident that resulted in Minamata disease due to improper disposal of industrial mercury in the water bodies. Consumption of fish and other aquatic organisms from such water bodies led to the death of hundreds of people due to the disease. Hundreds are still suffering from the disease.

A science teacher discusses about the types of trees, animals, shrubs, and the many services they provide in the form of timber, firewood, medicines, honey, and meat. An environmental educator purposely stretches the discussion to issues faced by forests dweller due to exploitation of forests and its products, developmental activities and its implications to their livelihood. An environmental educator can form groups in the class and ask each group to discuss whether forests dwellers should be rehabilitated to another place in the name of conservation of forests. Each group can then be asked to share the opinion of the group. The teacher can act as a facilitator of the discussion and intervene only when necessary. This will give opportunities to the students to hear differing views and understand other's point of view and help them rethink about their opinion.

A science teacher explains how technology in the area of communication, health care, transportation, and agriculture has improved life. An environmental educator adds how much resources are used in the invention and production of such technology and how the same can cause and has caused negative impacts such as pollution of air water and soil, health issues, and so on. For example, manufacturing industries for machine, tools, and chemicals, or thermal plants for production of energy are major sources of pollution causing not only health hazards but also degrading the quality of environment. An environmental educator emphasizes the practice of reduce, reuse and recycle.

A science teacher explains how food production can be increased to feed the ever-increasing population of the world by the use of Genetically Modified (GM) crops or fertilizers and pesticides. An environmental educator extends the discussion to the issues of farmers' inability to purchase seed for the next cropping season or how chemical fertilizers affect productivity, soil quality as well as health of the farmers owing to exposure to chemicals. The well-known harmful effects of chemicals are discussed.

3.4.2 EE in Social Science

A social science teacher talks of industrial growth. An environmental educator takes the discussion further and takes into account issues related to environmental justice to people who are most affected because of industrial developments. Industries are generally located in the outskirts of cities where in most cases, people with low-income group live.

They are the most affected owing to pollution of air, water and soil, but they hardly get any benefit out of such industries. An environmental educator brings out such discussions in the classroom and gives opportunities to students to analyze such situations and share their views.

A social science teacher talks of demand–supply in terms of economic growth and development. An environmental educator also discusses that with demand, supply also increases, and, in turn, increases the burden on the environment. This is because for every kind of production natural resources are used in the form of raw materials, energy, water, and so on. Hence, emphasizing on the maximum use of commodities and minimum extravagant purchase to check the increase in demand as a result of which supply will also decrease and production at the source will also decrease which would ultimately reduce the exploitation of natural resources. Besides, an environmental educator also makes students aware about the possible adverse impact on reduction in job opportunities thus introducing the larger picture of the situation to the students.

A social science teacher talks about how development has made it easy for us to get anything from anywhere at anytime of the year. For example, we get every kind of imported food items. An environmental educator adds to the discussion on how such food stuff travel—the cost of transportation of such food items, how much carbon dioxide is released during the transportation, and so on—taking the discussion to encourage the use of local products which will not only reduce harm to the environment but also improve the local economy. Such education helps students become aware of the choices they can make as consumers, and makes them realize that the choices they make can have many impacts on the environment.

A social science teacher discusses where mines are located in different parts of the country. An environmental educator takes the discussion further to its implications for local people at the time of mining, and after. A social science teacher talks of the importance of the transport systems, while an environmental educator takes the discussion beyond to include the measures to be undertaken to avoid or reduce deterioration of the environment owing to such activities. For example, hundreds of hectares of forests are being cleared to make way for rails or vast stretches of lands are inundated under water due to construction of dams, displacing people and destroying their habitats, and disturbing the whole ecosystem.

A social science teacher discusses the GDP of the country. An environmental educator discusses the contribution of women to the society and how it can be improved if women are empowered. Besides, discussions also include the unpaid care work that women are engaged in and how such sacrificial contributions are not paid due recognition, or appreciated, or accounted for.

A social science teacher discusses migration and other social issues associated with it. An environmental educator takes it further to include the environmental impacts associated with it, such as stress on the local resources which could be land, water, and food, which lead to scarcity, pollution, and other associated social issues such as reduction in job opportunities, social crimes, and conflicts.

Resolving environmental issues is at the heart of environmental education for which an individual has to be prepared, not only intellectually but more importantly psychologically (Ernst and Monroe 2004; NEETF 2000). An environmental educator in psychology discusses the factors that influence the human mind to take certain environment-friendly decisions or behave in a particular manner that is pro-environment. For example, while discussing the principles of how the human mind can be influenced, an environmental educator deliberately uses an environment-related theme as a context for such deliberations such as use of energy-efficient lighting system, equipment, or vehicle, construction of green building, use of solar energy, and so on. Such experiences will encourage students to have the right attitude toward the environment and also equip them to influence others in taking environmentally appropriate decisions.

3.4.3 EE in Mathematics

A mathematics teacher gives random data for analysis and plotting graphs. An environmental educator uses the real world or local environmental problems or issues as a context of teaching such topics. For example, while teaching topics such as data handling an environmental educator asks students to collect data such as daily weather report, or temperature in different towns and cities and use it for plotting a graph, which could be a single bar or double bar graph depending upon the data collected. The same can be used to study frequency distribution. While teaching topics related to comparing quantities an environmental educator can use actual examples of percent increase in population or petrol consumption, or loss of biodiversity over the years. Similarly, for calculation of direct proportion, an environmental educator can use the actual data of the current amount of carbon dioxide to calculate the expected amount in five years. Similarly, for calculation of indirect proportion, an environmental educator can use an example of rate of carbon dioxide emission with that of increase use of public transport or use of bicycle. Such teaching–learning experiences increase the awareness of the students about environmental problems and issues and at the same time connect the classroom with real life experiences. It will also remind the students that the state of affairs of the environment is understood clearly only when it is represented mathematically. And these mathematical representations make sense when students are able to relate it with their real life experiences.

3.4.4 EE in Languages

A language teacher often selects curricular material based on popularity or personal choice of authors/poets while an environmental educator purposely chooses environment-related topics—stories and poems based on nature, such as rivers, clouds, snow, forests, and wildlife in the teaching–learning of language. As part of their letter writing skills, an environmental educator asks the students to write a letter to the municipal authorities putting forward the grievances about the waste issue in their locality. Similar letters can also be written to the editors of newspapers. An environmental educator can even take students out into the nature or into natural surroundings, let them experience the beauty of nature, make them hear the chirping of the birds, and use such experiences to improve their writing skills in the form of prose or poetry. This will not only improve the skills necessary to be learned as part of the curriculum, but it will also make students aware about the environmental issues in their locality and learn to appreciate the beauty of nature. This could also bring about some attitudinal change in the students.

3.4.5 EE in Arts

An environmental educator in an arts class can meaningfully depict various environmental issues or degradations that they have seen in their environment over the years in different art form such as skits, paintings, songs, plays, making models, and so on. He/she can also encourage the students to come out with their own ideas and experiences in different art forms. Paintings can be displayed in the school while songs, skits, and plays can be performed on occasions in the school or even in the locality. Through such activities every student can be engaged to bring out their aesthetic sense as well as their creativity, including students with any form of special needs. Such activities form an important means to spread awareness about environment and its issues.

JUST A MOMENT

Did your teachers make deliberate efforts to incorporate environment-related concerns in the teaching–learning process? Based on the examples provided above, do you think you will be able to incorporate environmental issues meaningfully in your teaching–learning process if you were a teacher?.

3.5 Integration of Different Approaches

Keeping in view the limitations of the interdisciplinary (separate subject) approach and the multidisciplinary (infusion) approach, Sarabhai et al. (1998) suggested a third approach, a three-pronged approach, which is an integration of the separate subject approach, the infusion approach, and the nonformal (outdoor, extra and, cocurricular) methods. Meticulously implemented, this approach would be most appropriate to achieve the goals of environmental education. However, as in the case of the infusion and separate subject approach, this approach too is not without challenges. For example, the challenges could include identifying the objectives for each of the three components, how synergy can be brought about, and how to accommodate them in the existing system (Sarabhai et al. 1998).

Conclusion

Although the objectives of environmental education were identified which include awareness, knowledge, attitude, skills, and participation, the bigger concern has always been about how to achieve these objectives. All the five categories could be addressed if education 'about,' 'in,' and 'for' the environment is provided. A matter of debate has also been related to which approach will best suit to achieve these objectives. As discussed in the chapter, several approaches have been suggested and each approach has its pros and cons. While one approach might work well in a particular setting, the other might work better in another setting. The third may work better still in yet another setting. Therefore, it is not as much about which approach to adopt but about adopting any approach which works and working with it the best possible way.

However, there definitely exist gaps in the actual implementation. The fact that education 'for' the environment has been neglected by practitioners is doing little good to achieve the objectives of environmental education. It is therefore important to seriously address this aspect if we are to see our environment actually being healed. For this, the concerns of the practitioners as to what the barriers are which hinder them to implement environmental education in toto need to be first identified. Based on this, appropriate measures need to be taken so that practitioners are equipped in every aspect to address all the components of environmental education. While all teachers teaching any subject for that matter will be able to incorporate environmental education, there will be times when they would feel that in certain topics environmental education can be highlighted more strongly as compared to other topics. What is important is they need to grab all such opportunities.

SUMMARY

- Equal emphasis to the different components of environmental education such as 'about,' 'in,' and 'for' the environment during actual practice will help achieve the objectives of environmental education which include awareness, knowledge, attitude, skills, and participation.
- The most common and safest way of doing environmental education is by focusing on the 'about' component of environmental education and to some extent, the 'in' component. With this students become aware, acquire knowledge, and develop necessary skills and environmental attitudes.
- Environmental education cannot be implemented meaningfully because of the ignorance of the 'for' component by practitioners.
- For successful implementation of environmental education in the curriculum, a practitioner has to address all the five categories that defines environmental education—awareness, knowledge, attitude, skills, and participation. And this can be achieved only when all the components such as 'about,' 'in,' and 'for' the environment are given equal importance.

- Two major ways of approaching environmental education have been put forward by experts in the field: Interdisciplinary and multidisciplinary approach.
- Interdisciplinary approach appears to be appropriate to achieve the goals and objectives of environmental education, but there exist an issue of curriculum overload.
- Multidisciplinary infusion approach appears to be convenient to accommodate in the existing overloaded curriculum, but there exist an issue of linking what is learned in different disciplines.
- While a certain approach could work for a certain topic and in a particular setting, the same might not work in a different environmental setting.
- There is a third approach, wherein it is proposed to include both the interdisciplinary and multidisciplinary approaches in the implementation of environmental education.
- Educational planners, policy makers, curriculum developers, or practitioners will have to decide on the approach which will best suit different environmental settings.

Exercises

1. What does environmental education want to achieve through school education?
2. Do you think 'participation' component is so important to achieve the goal of environmental education? Explain.
3. What is 'education about the environment' all about?
4. What do you understand by 'education in the environment'?
5. Why do we say that environmental education cannot be complete without 'education for the environment'?
6. How do you think environmental education should be implemented at different stages in school?
7. What according to you is the biggest challenge in the implementation of infusion approach? Elaborate.
8. What according to you is the most important advantage of a separate subject approach?
9. Which approach of environmental education do you think will work best in the existing education system? Elaborate your answer.
10. Can environmental education actually improve teaching–learning of different subjects? Why?

References

Bones, David. 1994. *EE Toolbox: Getting Started—A Guide to Bringing Environmental Education Into Your Classroom.* Ann Arbor, MI: University of Michigan.

Braus, J.A. and D. Wood. 1993. *Environmental Education in the Schools: Creating a Programme That Works!* Manual M0044, Washington, D.C.: Peace Corps Information Collection and Exchange.

Chawla, Louise and D.F. Cushing. 2007. "Education for Strategic Environmental Behavior." *Environmental Education Research* 13(4): 437–452.

Disinger, J.F. 1993. "Environment in the K–12 Curriculum: An Overview." In *Environmental Education – Teacher Resource Handbook*, edited by Richard J. Wilke, 23–43. New York: Kraus International Publications.

——— 1997. *Environmental Education's Definitional Problem*, Reprinted from: ERIC Clearinghouse for Science, Mathematics and Environmental Education Information Bulletin No. 2, 1983; An Epilogue EE's Definitional Problem: 1997 Update. Columbus, OH: ERIC/CSMEE. Available at: http://globalenvironmentaleducation. wikispaces.com/file/view/EE_Definitional_Problem.pdf (Accessed on 2 August 2014).

Engleson, D.C. 1987. "Environmental Education in the Curriculum: It's Already There!" In *Trends and Issues Environmental Education: EE in School Curricula—Reports of a Symposium and a Survey*, edited by John F. Disinger, 43–50. Environmental Education Information Reports. Columbus, OH: ERIC Clearinghouse for Science, Mathematics, and Environmental Education, NAAEE. Available at: http://files.eric.ed.gov/fulltext/ ED292608.pdf (Accessed on 16 April 2015).

Ernst, J. and M. Monroe. 2004. The Effects of Environment-based Education on Students' Critical Thinking Skills and Disposition Toward Critical Thinking, *Environmental Education Research* 10(4): 507–522.

Feng, Ling. 2012. "Teacher and Student Responses to Interdisciplinary Aspects of Sustainability Education: What do we Really Know?" *Environmental Education Research* 18(1): 31–43.

Fien, John and Jo-Anne Ferreira. 1997. "Environmental Education in Australia—A Review." *International Research in Geographical and Environmental Education* 6(3): 234–259, Channel View Books/Multi-Lingual Matters Ltd.

Gough, Annette. 2008. "Towards More Effective Learning for Sustainability: Reconceptualising Science Education." *Transnational Curriculum Inquiry* 5(1): 32–50. Available at: http://nitinat.library.ubc.ca/ojs/ index.php/tci (Accessed on 5 June 2014).

Hungerford, H.R. and R.B. Peyton. 1994. *UNESCO–UNEP International Environmental Education Programme Environmental Education, Series 22, Procedures for the Development of Environmental Education Curriculum (Revised).* A Discussion Guide for UNESCO Training Seminars on Environmental Education. Paris: UNESCO.

Hungerford, H.R., T.L Volk, W.J. Bluhm, B.G. Dixon, T.J. Marcinkowski, and A.P.C. Sia. 1994. *UNESCO–UNEP International Environmental Education Programme, Environmental Education Series 27, An Environmental*

Education Approach to the Training of Elementary Teachers: A Teacher Education Programme (Revised). A Discussion Guide for UNESCO Training Seminars on Environmental Education. Paris: UNESCO.

Kopnina, H. 2014. "Future Scenarios and Environmental Education." *The Journal of Environmental Education* 45(4): 217–231.

Kumar, K. 1996. "An Agenda of Incoherence." *Down to Earth* 4(17): 32–34.

Lahiry, D., Savita Sinha, J.S. Gill, U. Mallik, and A.K. Mishra. 1988. *Environmental Education: A Process for Pre-service Teacher Training Curriculum Development*. UNESCO-UNEP International Environmental Education Programme Environmental Education Series No. 26. Edited by Patricia R. Simpson, Harold Hungerford, and Trudi L. Volk. Paris: UNESCO.

Lane, J.F. 2006. *Environmental Education Implementation in Wisconsin: Conceptualizations and Practices*, Unpublished PhD Thesis: Department of Philosphy, University of Wisconsin–Madison. Available at: http://www.uwsp.edu/cnr-ap/wcee/Documents/JennieLaneDissertation.pdf (Accessed on 23 May 2014).

Lucas, A.M. 1972. *Environment and Environmental Education: Conceptual Issues and Curriculum Implications*, PhD Dissertation, Ohio State University. Available at: https://www.researchgate.net/profile/Arthur_Lucas/publications?sorting=newest&page=4 (Accessed on 28 September 2014).

Lucas, A.M. 1980. "Science and Environmental Education: Pious Hopes, Self Praise and Disciplinary Chauvinism." *Studies in Science Education* 7(1):1–26.

Monroe, M. 1991. "Meeting the Mandate: Integrating Environmental Education." *Clearing* 71: 8–9.

Monroe, M. and D. Cappaert. 1994. *EE Toolbox: Integrating Environmental Education into the School Curriculum*. Ann Arbor, MI: Regents of the University of Michigan.

NCERT, National Council of Educational Research and Training. 2006. *Position Paper of the National Focus Group on Habitat and Learning*, No. 1.6. New Delhi: NCERT.

——— 2011. *Teachers' Handbook on Environmental Education for the Higher Secondary Stage*. New Delhi: NCERT.

NEETF, National Environmental Education and Training Foundation. 2000. *Environment-based Education: Creating High Performance Schools and Students*. Washington, DC: NEETF.

Sarabhai, K.V., M. Raghunathan, and K. Kandula. 1998. *Greening Formal Education—Concerns, Efforts and Future Directions*. Ministry of Environment and Forests, Government of India, Centre for Environment Education.

Shimray, C.V., S. Farkya, and S.L. Varte. 2013. *Study of Biology Curriculum at the Higher Secondary Stage: A Report (Unpublished)*. New Delhi: NCERT.

Sonowal, C.J. 2009. "Environmental Education in Schools: The Indian Scenario." *Journal of Human Ecology* 28(1): 15–36.

Tilbury, D. 1997. "Environmental Education: A Head, Heart and Hand Approach to Learning About Environmental Problems." *New Horizons in Education* 38: 1–11.

UNESCO, United Nations Educational, Scientific and Cultural Organization. 1980. *Strategies for Developing an Environmental Education Curriculum: A Discussion Guide for UNESCO Training Workshops on Environmental Education*. Paris: UNESCO.

UNESCO-UNEP, United Nations Educational, Scientific and Cultural Organization-United Nations Environment Programme. 1978. "The Tbilisi Declaration." *Connect, UNESCO-UNEP Environmental Education Newsletter* III(1): 1–8.

Tracing Environmental Education in India

Chapter Overview

Environmental education is thought to be a very recent development in India. However, the literature reveals that it is not so. It has always been there since ancient times. It is just that it is now receiving much attention due to the urgency felt to take care of the environment. This portion of the book introduces the readers to the various documents brought out in the area of education beginning the 20th century and presents the elements of environmental education reflected in such documents. It is envisaged that at the end of the chapter, readers will obtain sufficient clarity to:

- appreciate how environmental education has evolved in India
- describe the ideas reflected in different documents related to environmental education
- suggest how environmental education can be reflected ideally in a document

Introduction

India has come a long way in the field of environmental education in the modern era, beginning with the Basic Education Movement started by Mahatma Gandhi in 1937 (Gandhi 1951). The country saw the first environmental movement, the Chipko Movement, in the early 1970s in the remote villages of Uttarakhand (then, Uttar Pradesh). It is also important to note that basic tenets of ecology and environmental ethics were practiced even in the ancient periods. In the various texts of the Vedic period, man is exhorted to conserve the five elements such as air, water, fire, sky, and earth for his welfare and prosperity by scrupulously performing his duties prescribed in the texts (NCERT 2004b, 2). In fact, the earliest codified law traces back to the 2300 BCE when King Ashoka made a law in the matter of preservation of wild life and environment wherein killing of certain species of animals such as parrots, gees, rhinoceros, and so on, were prohibited (NCERT 2011).

We have learned in the previous three chapters about the roots of environmental education, its objectives and goals, how it is different from other subjects, its need in view of the developing world, the approaches for practitioners, and their prospects and limitations. Following its widespread promotion across the world in the changing global scenario and an increasing awareness on conservation of nature and protection of environment, environmental education has made a visible and formal entry into the Indian education system. Even after being recognized as an indispensable element in the educational process, environmental education in India continues to evolve in the wake of the rapid development taking place in the country. Hence, in this chapter, we shall trace the roots of environmental education and its evolution in India. The chapter will focus specifically on how environmental education has been reflected in various educational documents such as educational commission reports, national policy on education documents, national curriculum frameworks, and other nationally important educational reports. Some important documents have been identified for this purpose and the same are discussed in the chapter.

4.1 Basic Education (1937)

As mentioned, Mahatma Gandhi started the Basic Education Movement in India in 1937. It was an earnest attempt at providing education in schools to meet local environmental needs. The essential elements of Basic Education were: productive activity in education; correlation of the curriculum with productive activity and the social environment; and a close contact between the school and the local community (NCERT 2006). In short, it was a holistic approach to life and education. This was in essence environmental and sustainability education, which remains the core principles of most school educational curriculum. For example, in an effort to connect the education system with the surrounding environment, Gandhi emphasized the activity of spinning thread as a basic and serious activity to be taught in a proper and scientific manner in schools. It was the best supplement to agriculture as it could be practiced by all, unlike other professions such as barber, carpentry, or shoemaking. He maintained that it should not only be taught mechanically, but also scientifically so that the child understood every step of spinning. This would be beneficial in many ways. It would help the child in understanding the functioning of the wheels, which essentially is the scientific aspect, and improving the wheels, the economic benefits of the skill, enhance respect for manual labor and benefit the society at large. The importance of the laws of hygiene and sanitation was also envisioned, including waste management, such as proper disposal of food, excreta, and other wastes (Gandhi 1951).

JUST A MOMENT

Try to relate the ideas reflected in Basic Education with the objectives of environmental education.

4.2 Report of the Secondary Education Commission (1953)

This report was brought out by the Secondary Education Commission (1952–53) (GoI 1953), the first commission on education appointed after the country's independence by the union government. It was set up to examine the prevailing system of secondary education in the country and recommend measures for its reorganization and improvement. The report of the commission is discussed below in relation to environmental education.

The commission recommended a step beyond Gandhi's ideas of 'dignity of labor' and 'self-reliance' to 'self-fulfillment' and 'national prosperity.' It stated the need to focus on enhancing the productivity or technical and vocational efficiency of students not only to appreciate the dignity of all work, but also for self-fulfillment and national prosperity. It emphasized the proper utilization of the country's natural resources to add to the national wealth. For this, it suggested practical courses which would lead to equipping educated young men, psychologically and practically, to undertake technical professions and raise the general standard of efficiency, thereby helping to increase national wealth and ultimately to improve the general standards of living.

The commission felt that the existing secondary school curriculum was bookish and lacked provision for practical and other kinds of activities, for which it should reasonably find room for holistic education and proper development of the child's growth and personality. To shift from a narrowly conceived bookish curriculum to a more sustainable one, the Commission suggested that students needed to take part in various kinds of intellectual and physical activities, practical occupations, and social experiences which is not possible through the mere study of books. It pointed out the importance of practical training in the art of living and showing students through actual experience how community life is organized and sustained. It maintained that the entire school life became the curriculum which could touch the life of the students at all levels and help in the evolution of a balanced personality.

The commission also pointed out the importance of holistic teaching of botany, climatology, and the nature of soils and seed and pests that affect agricultural plants. It suggested vocational education at the end of secondary education.

As far as social studies was concerned, the commission suggested a curriculum which viewed all subjects as a compact whole, whose object was to adjust the students to their social environment—which included the family, community, state, and nation—so that they might be able to understand how society has come to its present form and intelligently interpret the matrix of social forces and movements in the midst of which they were living.

In general science, the commission advocated that special emphasis be placed on demonstrations, field trips, and practical projects which could link school science with actual life problems and situations, such as poor local sanitation, short water supply, elimination of pests, and so on. The classroom, the home, the city and the village, the fields, woods and streams, all offer rich resources and opportunities for science teaching that must be fully utilized by every science teacher. The teacher should aim at awakening in the students a lively curiosity about the natural phenomena around them, at developing their capacity for the practical application of their knowledge, and at appreciating the tremendous impact of modern science on all aspects of life. For this, the commission suggested the activity or project method as the basis of teaching, which would create opportunities for self-activity on the part of students and help them understand the relationship between their life and their lessons.

Overall, the Secondary Education Commission report reflected elements of environmental education such as learning by taking up locally-relevant activity or project. It also brought out the importance of linking community life with the curriculum and economy.

4.3 Report of the Indian Education Commission (1966)—Education & National Development

The union government appointed the Indian Education Commission (1964–1966) by a resolution, dated 14 July 1964, to advise the government on the national pattern of education and on the general principles and policies for the development of education at all stages and in all aspects.

The Education Commission Report in 1966, popularly called the Kothari Commission Report (GoI 1966), recommended the conception of education as an instrument of social transformation with a view to bringing education and national development together in a mutually supportive and interdependent relationship. It incorporated the best that basic education had to offer so as to relate it to the life, needs, and aspirations of the nation. For the primary stage, the report recommended that "the aim of teaching science in primary school should be to develop proper understanding of the main facts, concepts, principles, and processes in the physical and biological environment" (NCERT 2006).

The report also made a strong case for introducing 'work-experience,' which included manual work and production experience, and social service as integral parts of general education at almost all educational levels. It stressed on moral education and inculcation of a sense of social responsibility, and the role of schools to recognize their responsibility in facilitating the transition of youth from the world of school to the world of work and life. The commission recommended making secondary education vocational oriented which conformed broadly to the requirements of the developing economy and real employment opportunities. Introduction of work-experience and vocational education were significant in terms of environmental education.

With the aim of making a scientific outlook become part of everyday life and culture, the commission pointed out that, besides merely deepening the understanding of basic principles, science education should develop problem-solving and analytical skills and the ability to apply them to the problems of the material environment and social living and to promote the spirit of exploration, research, and experimentation. However, instead of moving toward interdisciplinary approach, the commission recommended that science from the post-primary stage should be taught as separate disciplines of physics, chemistry, and biology (NCERT 1970).

4.4 National Policy on Education (1968)

The Indian Government took strong cognizance of the Education Commission's recommendations of 1964 and the same were reflected in this first National Policy on Education document (GoI 1968). Some of the recommendations, which is of significance in the context of the present discourse/discussion, are: to relate education more closely to life of the people; a continuous effort to expand educational opportunity; a sustained and intensive effort to raise the quality of education at all stages; an emphasis on the development of science and technology; and the cultivation of moral and social values. In short, the policy envisaged an education system that would produce young men and women of character and ability, committed to national service and development which would ultimately promote national progress, create a sense of common citizenship and culture, and strengthen national integration.

As recommended by the Education Commission of 1964, 'work-experience' and 'national service' was strongly emphasized in the document. It reiterated that the school and the community should be brought closer through suitable programs of mutual service and support. Work-experience and national service, including participation in meaningful and challenging programs of community service and national reconstruction, should accordingly become an integral part of education. Emphasis in these programs should be on self-help, character formation, and developing a sense of social commitment. With a view to accelerating the growth of the national economy, science education and research should be given high priority.

As pointed out by the Education Commission, the document also reiterated the need to increase facilities for technical and vocational education at the secondary stage. Provision of facilities for secondary and vocational education should conform broadly to requirements of the developing economy and real employment opportunities. This should cover a large number of fields, such as agriculture, industry, trade and commerce, medicine and public health, home management, arts and crafts, secretarial training, and so on.

However, in all these documents, environmental concerns or issues were not specifically mentioned. During the time the documents were being written, the nation was in a phase when its sole focus was national development. The physical environment and the natural resources were largely unexploited. However, a closer look reveals that the inherent nature of environmental education is clearly visible in the programs it promoted such as 'work-experience' and other educational activities and projects. In addition, environmental concerns such as air and water pollution, pesticides, conservation of natural resources, and so on, found place in the syllabi (Appendix 4.1) and the textbooks developed during the time.

4.5 Curriculum for the Ten-year School: A Framework (1975)

It was the first national curriculum framework for school education of the country which was developed in the light of the National Policy on Education, 1968 (NCERT 1975). The document visualized a common curriculum with acceptable principles and values at the core which are in consonance with those enunciated in the Indian Constitution. This curriculum gave a thrust to curricular inputs related to social sensitivity which are fundamental to effective environmental education. It highlighted concerns such as social justice, national consciousness, national integration, and democratic values with the aim of including these issues in the discourse on curriculum construction (Yadav and Nikalje 2009).

The interdisciplinary nature of knowledge was also highlighted in the document. It reiterated the importance of the clustering of course content and its presentation through the teaching–learning method. It called for organizing course content in terms of 'units' rather than 'subjects.' This made a case for introducing students to the importance of seeing knowledge in an interdisciplinary way and appreciating its manifestation through specific situations as the document mentioned:

> By this approach the many-sided nature of knowledge will become self-evident to the learner, which is something that he completely misses while examining problems and situations from the narrow angle of a single 'discipline'. Another advantage is that areas such as health, sanitation, nutrition, population studies, pollution, water resources, elements of psychology, and culture, which have to find a place in the modern curriculum and which are multi-disciplinary, would be dealt with more easily through a unit approach.

This approach is aimed at better equipping students with abilities such as critical thinking, problem-solving skills, application of varied knowledge components, including skills and other competencies, and synthesis (Yadav and Nikalje 2009). This interdisciplinary approach provided immense scope for promoting environmental education.

The document recommended that physical and life sciences should be introduced in science subjects. Also, environmental education, nutrition, health, and population education should be given adequate attention so that science was related meaningfully to life and living. This was the first time that the term 'environmental education' appeared in a national educational document. It also made deliberate attempts to emphasize environmental education by stating that through science the child:

> [S]hould be able to contribute meaningfully to environmental conservation, the reduction of pollution, and the development of proper nutrition and health and hygiene in the community. He should be able to help in the development of proper habits and attitudes in childcare and in the improvement of the home.

In primary classes, sciences should be taught as environmental studies; in Classes I and II, as a composite course, including both the natural and the social environment, and later as two subjects, namely, environmental studies I (natural science) and environmental studies II (social science). The purpose is to sharpen the senses of the students, to enable them to observe their environment, and to enrich their experience. The activities provided in the school should be based on the experience drawn from the child's environment. The fact that this document suggested a two-subject approach for environmental studies is quite contradictory to the interdisciplinary approach it attempted to proclaim.

This document reiterated the recommendations of the Kothari Commission Report, 1964–66 and that of the National Policy on Education, 1968, on the importance of work-experience. It pointed out:

> For harmonious development of the child's personality, it is necessary not only to expose him to scholastic areas for intellectual development but also to put him in situations where he may get opportunities to work with his hands and develop proper attitudes towards manual labour.

It suggested that work-experience should permeate the entire curriculum and proposed work experience as one of the curricular subjects in school.

Work-experience provides the basis for the development of knowledge, skills, and attitudes, which are useful for later participation in productive work. It should cover production, maintenance, and the technological processes, as well as human relations, organization, and management and marketing. The areas of work chosen should have local significance and should be able to develop a sense of competency in the students. It is not just learning to do work, it is work education. This local specificity and 'activity'-based education provided a setting that was conducive for environmental education.

The document outlined the major objective of the study of social sciences in an attempt "to acquaint the child with his past and present geographical and social environment." It mentioned that teaching of social sciences should inculcate right attitudes and impart the knowledge necessary for the achievement of the principal values of a just world order, maximization of economic and social welfare, minimization of violence, and maximization of ecological stability. It suggested an integrated syllabus for social sciences wherein all the components of social sciences—history, geography, civics, and economics—can be integrated in the teaching in a way that students develop a proper understanding of the facts and problems in the right perspective without causing any damage to the totality of the individual disciplines. The document stressed the importance of relating the growing population to the available natural resources and the need for conservation.

For living well in a developing society where socio-economic changes are taking place at a fast pace, the curriculum suggested that it would be helpful if some rudimentary understanding of the economic forces that influence the citizens' daily life was provided even at the middle stage of education. Following this viewpoint, the need to introduce some elementary knowledge of consumer economics, such as earning and spending, controls, price rise, and the effects of increasing population, in a simplified form was felt. The document mentioned that the approach of the teaching of economics at the lower secondary stage should emphasize not so much the principles of economics as the current problems and issues that affect the everyday life of the common man, such as poverty, rising prices, agricultural stagnation, and so on. The course would throw some light on the future economic prospects of the country on the basis of its potential resources and the performance shown so far.

JUST A MOMENT

In this first national curriculum framework for schools, work experience was highlighted. How would you relate this with environmental education?

4.5.1 Syllabi for Classes VI–VIII (1976)

These syllabi provide ample scopes to address environmental concerns through different subject areas, including work experience (NCERT 1976). Some relevant topics under different subject areas for different classes are provided in Appendix 4.2.

4.6 Report of the Review Committee on the Curriculum for the Ten-year School (1977)

The union government set up the Review Committee on the Curriculum for the Ten-Year School (Ishwarbhai Patel Committee Report) in 1977 to scrutinize the NCERT syllabus and textbooks, in the light of the review of the stage-wise and subject-wise objectives identified in the NCERT document: "The Curriculum for the Ten-Year School." It brought out a document: "Report of the Review Committee on the Curriculum for the Ten-Year School" (GoI 1977).

A major criticism of the committee was that work experience, which was intended to be an integral feature of the curriculum at all stages did not find a proper place in the teaching–learning process that followed the introduction of the new pattern, hence giving the impression that curriculum and the syllabuses developed by NCERT would perpetuate the same old system of 'bookish-education.' Programs of work experience were introduced following the Kothari Commission Report recommendations with the objectives of relating education to productivity. These programs, however, lacked the component of social usefulness and, in practice, were not even casually correlated to other subject areas. Work experience was thus assigned a much wider concept in the document to include social and cultural aspects and it was renamed Socially Useful Productive Work (SUPW) (Yadav and Nikalje 2009).

The document maintained that SUPW must, therefore, be given a central place in the curriculum at all stages of school education and the content of the academic subjects should be related to it, as much as possible. The purpose of demarcating a distinct curricular area as SUPW was to emphasize the principle that education should be centered around work, as the concept of SUPW is to be developed in the light of the Gandhian philosophy of basic education, in and through work, the document added. It maintained that such work must not be performed mechanically, but must include practical planning, analysis, and detailed preparation at every stage so that it is educational in essence. It elucidated its view by providing the following examples: When children take part in an environmental cleanliness program by way of social service, they can prepare compost pits for manure. Similarly, if children conduct surveys of population, habitations or cattle, they can use the information for planning programs for childcare and sanitation. During the harvesting season when the entire village is under pressure of intensive work, the schools, instead of remaining in isolation, can render valuable help to farmers.

The document expressed optimism that such work-based education would bring about at least some reduction in traditional book-knowledge and acceptance of the applied sciences taught through field experience, such as agriculture, accountancy, and soil science, with equal importance to fundamental sciences.

According to the document, the criterion for selection of activities should, thus, be that the work involved was productive, educative, and socially useful. It was felt that if SUPW was given a central and dominant place in the curriculum the gap between work and education would be reduced, the school would not remain isolated from the community, and the gulf that divided the affluent from the weaker and poorer sections of the community would be bridged. It expressed that such a scheme would provide equality of opportunity for working and learning to all children irrespective of caste, creed, sex, and economic status. To ensure that the educational objectives of this program are achieved, the document suggested that it was necessary to follow the problem-solving approach. These suppositions clearly indicated that the document was environmental education-friendly. The syllabus frames suggested by the committee for different subjects that are mentioned later substantiate and validate the view.

Some of the SUPW activities suggested by the committee for different classes include cleaning school campus or surrounding, gardening, maintaining compost pit, planting and care of shade trees, soil conservation, growing medicinal plants, soil conservation, desert control, bee keeping, poultry farming, and so on.

The committee also provided syllabus frames for different classes. It recommended no textbook for Classes I–II in EVS and one textbook for EVS for Classes III–IV/V. The concepts were spirally woven. Some of the chapters suggested in science that directly relates to the environment are: Food and health; man's dependence on plants and animals and the balance in nature; environment: adaptation to and manipulation of water; energy; oxygen; water; population; pollution; electric energy and power; atomic nucleus and nuclear energy; materials (metals, alloys, plastics, and glasses); agriculture; agriculture practices and implements; man's problems in agriculture; improvement and protection of crops; useful plants and animals, animal husbandry; conservation of natural resources; science in human welfare; agricultural practices and animal husbandry; combustion and fuels; chemistry in industry; man and his environment.

Some of the chapters that can be directly related to environmental education in Social Science include the following: trade, transport, and population (internal and external, land, water and air, population—distribution and density), social and economic challenges before our country, water and nuclear power, and industries production and output.

4.7 National Policy on Education (1986)

The major thrust of the National Policy on Education, 1986 (NPE-1986) (GoI 1986) was to relate education to 'development' and 'social change' in general (Yadav and Nikalje 2009). The policy document stated:

> The National System of Education will be based on a national curricular framework which contains a common core along with other components that are flexible. The common core will include the history of India's freedom movement, the constitutional obligations, and other content essential to nurture national identity. These elements will cut across subject areas and will be designed to promote values such as India's common cultural heritage, egalitarianism, democracy and secularism, equality of the sexes, protection of the environment, removal of social barriers, observance of the small family norm, inculcation of the scientific temper.

The document clearly stressed the need to highlight environmental concerns in education wherein it stated:

> There is a paramount need to create a consciousness of the environment. It must permeate all ages and all sections of society, beginning with the child. Environmental consciousness should inform teaching in schools and colleges. This aspect will be integrated in the entire educational process.

The document also emphasized the need to highlight population growth and its related issues in educational programs.

Regarding work experience, the document laid down the following:

Work experience, viewed as purposive and meaningful manual work, organised as an integral part of the learning process, and resulting in either goods or services useful to the community, is considered as an essential component at all stages of education, to be provided through well-structured and graded programmes. It would comprise activities in accord with the interests, abilities, and needs of students, the level of skills and knowledge to be upgraded with the stages of education.

With its clear perspective on the environment, the NPE-1986 document is a major departure from the rest of the earlier documents and policies in terms of environmental education.

JUST A MOMENT

It is interesting to find that the concerns laid down in Article 51-A of Part IV-A of the Indian Constitution which talks about India's common cultural heritage, egalitarianism, democracy and secularism, equality of the sexes, protection of the environment, removal of social barriers, observance of the small-family norm, inculcation of the scientific temper found place in this document.

4.8 Science Education for First Ten Years of Schooling: Working Group Report (1987)

The Working Group was set up in 1987 by NCERT comprising distinguished scientists, science educators as its members and Professor Yash Pal as its Chairman to work out a viable action program for science education which will nurture and develop manpower for different levels of the economy (NCERT 1987).

Of the 20 points under "What is to be done?" laid down by the working group, those that need special mention in the context of environmental education include: "[a]bility to understand and appreciate the joint enterprise of science/technology and society," "science curriculum in general education must be directed toward the development of concern about consequences and about people," and "certain thrust areas like energy, environment, social forestry, wildlife management, industry, which need immediate attention to avoid environmental crisis, should be highlighted."

4.9 National Curriculum for Elementary and Secondary Education: A Framework (Revised Version) (1988)

This curriculum framework was developed in the light of the NPE-1986 (NCERT 1988c). The importance of environmental consciousness, which was highlighted in the NPE-1986, is reflected in this document. Hence, environmental concerns received equal importance in this curriculum framework, as much as the social, economic, and political aspects.

The document clearly spelt out the urgency to tackle environmental problems and how a school curriculum can address them. Following is an excerpt from the document in this context:

Protection of the Environment and Conservation of Natural Resources: The indiscriminate destruction of the environment and the use of the environmental resources, especially the non-renewable resources in nature by man have been upsetting the earth's ecological balance. Unfortunately, even some ambitious national developmental programmes, when not based on careful consideration of their consequences in terms of the ecology in the long run, may become sources of serious hazards for the ecological balance. There is urgent need of tapping new alternative sources of energy and development of new technology aimed at the protection of environment.

The document clearly points out the dangers that lie in developmental activities and the need to take precautionary measures. Toward this, the document highlights the utmost need to create consciousness of the environment among all sections of the society. It also identified the important role school education has in bringing about such consciousness as it states:

The school curriculum, therefore, should attempt to create a commitment on the part of pupils to protect the environment and conserve nature and its resources so that the ecological balances, especially the balance between man and nature, could be maintained and preserved...promote an awareness of the need of counter pollution, whether caused by affluence or poverty, and of the impending energy crisis due to the ever increasing consumption of fuels available in nature and the exhaustion of these fuels at an alarmingly rapid rate...highlight the measures for protection and care of the environment, prevention of pollution and conservation of energy...highlight the inter-dependence between the material environment and the plant and animal (including human) life for survival, growth and development.

The document also stresses that the significance of renewable and nonconventional energy resources should also form an important component of the curriculum.

It is seen that the document emphasized school curriculum to help promote in the learner "understanding of the environment and its limited resources and the need for conservation of natural resources and energy."

The document also highlighted the need to take into account the interconnectivity among different areas. For example, the document suggested that environmental education, energy management, and population education are to be seen as complementary to one another and they should be adequately reflected in the curriculum.

According to this document, school curriculum, on the whole, should aim at enabling the learners to acquire knowledge, develop concepts, and inculcate skills, attitudes, values, and habits conducive to the all-round development of their personality and commensurate with the social, cultural, economic, and environmental realities at the national and international levels. The document reiterated the perspective of the NPE-1986 on work experience.

4.9.1 Guidelines and Syllabi for Upper Primary Stage (1988)

Some of the relevant topics on environment for different subject areas and classes mentioned in the syllabi are provided in Appendix 4.3.

The syllabi clearly mentioned the importance of work experience to develop attitudes and values in an effort to "develop a deeper concern for the environment and a sense of responsibility and commitment to the community" (NCERT 1988b). The syllabi also suggested a list of activities for this stage which is provided in Appendix 4.4. These activities are largely environmental in nature.

4.9.2 Guidelines and Syllabi for Secondary Stage (1988)

Appendix 4.5 provides a list of environmentally relevant topics in different subject areas and classes.

As in the syllabi for the upper primary stage, the syllabus for secondary stage also clearly mentions that the importance of work experience is to develop attitudes and values to "develop a deeper concern for the environment and a sense of responsibility and commitment to the community" (NCERT 1988a). The syllabus also provided a suggested list of essential activities which are essentially 'environmental' in nature. The list is provided in Appendix 4.6.

4.10 Learning without Burden: Report of the National Advisory Committee (1993)

The Ishwarbhai Patel Review Committee (1977), the NCERT Working Group (1984) and the National Policy on Education Review Committees (1990) made several recommendations to reduce the academic burden on students, to ease learning. But instead of being mitigated, the problem became more acute and hence the Ministry of Human Resource Development set up a National Advisory Committee in 1992 to look into the issue of increasing academic burden on the students (GoI 1993). Its objectives included: "To suggest ways and means to reduce the load on school students at all levels, particularly young students, while improving quality of learning, including the capability for life-long self-learning and skill formulation." The committee came out with a report—"Learning without burden." This assumes significance in terms of environmental education as the decisions on environmental education curriculum subsequent to this report was guided by it to a great extent, especially in terms of the introduction of the infusion approach of environmental education in order to avoid addition of load by adopting a separate subject approach.

4.11 National Curriculum Framework for School Education 2000 (NCFSE-2000)

Responding to the phenomenon of globalization was considered to be one of the curricular concerns in this curriculum framework which would require the introduction of education toward active citizenship and human rights, environmental issues, and the promotion of consensus on a common core of universal values (NCERT 2000).

Keeping in view the diverse curricular concerns such as 'literacy,' 'family system,' 'neighborhood education,' 'environmental education,' 'human rights education,' 'tourism education,' 'AIDS education,' 'legal literacy,' 'peace education,' 'population education,' 'migration education,' 'global education,' and 'safety education,' which were making a case for separate place in the school curriculum, the NCFSE-2000 suggested that the best approach would be to integrate these ideas and concepts into the existing areas of learning in the curricula of different subjects.

Energy and environment was included in the "Frontline Curriculum" along with other areas, such as communication systems, space technology, biotechnology, genetic engineering, recent health issues, world geography, multinationals, archaeological findings, and the like.

This curriculum framework reaffirmed that the common core components mentioned in the NPE-1986 as well as the fundamental duties as laid down in the Article 51-A of Part IV-A of the Indian Constitution, such as the history of India's freedom movement; the constitutional obligations; the content essential to nurture national identity; India's common cultural heritage; egalitarianism, democracy and secularism; equality of sexes; protection of the environment; removal of social barriers; observance of the small-family norm; and inculcation of scientific temper, should be integrated in school curriculum in a suitable manner.

In addition, "to help to generate and promote among the learners understanding of the environment in its totality both natural and social, and their interactive processes, the environmental problems and the ways and means to preserve the environment" was laid down in this document as one of the general objectives of education.

Relating education to the 'world of work' was another curricular concern of the NCFSE-2000. The document stressed on work education and vocational education being integral components of the school education system. Work education, it envisaged, would develop the understanding of facts and principles involved in various forms of work and to create a positive attitude toward work in line with Gandhi's philosophy of 'work-centered' education. A very important and interesting point made in this curriculum framework was that "All vocational education programmes and activities must stress the concept of sustainable development with a focus on fostering the awareness of the key environmental concerns and the rights of all to a decent standard of living."

The following points discuss in brief how the curriculum framework envisaged integration of environmental education in different subject areas.

Mathematics: The application of mathematics is an inherent part of every functioning and operation of daily life. Hence lies the importance of its study and its study is related to the immediate environment of the child at different stages and the world at large.

Class I–II: Content of mathematics to be built around the immediate environment of the child.

Class III–V: The child should gain familiarity with geometrical forms and figures and be able to appreciate patterns and symmetry in the environment.

Upper primary: Should be confined mostly to the study of essentials of mathematics for day-to-day life.

Secondary stage: Emphasis is to be laid on wider applications of mathematics by way of making data-based problems pertaining to actual data on population, agriculture, environment, industry, physical and biological sciences, engineering, defence, and so on. While developing the instructional material, the content and language of problems included in the textbooks should highlight core components like gender equality, protection of environment, removal of social barriers, observance of small-family norm, and so on.

Science and technology: Science must cut across traditional subject boundaries and open itself to issues such as gender, culture, language, poverty, impairment, future occupation, environment, and observance of small-family norm.

Class I–II: Essentially, it has to be learned mainly through concrete situations related to immediate environment.

Class III–V: Environmental studies (science) is introduced. The focus would, however, remains on objects, events, natural phenomenal, and the learner's environment. Children would continue to learn to observe, explore, and identify occurrences in their environment.

Upper primary: The environment should continue to be a major source of learning and students should try to understand the changes taking place all around. They would also gain an understanding of the living world, balance of nature, and the role of air, water, and energy. Due emphasis should be given to protection and conservation of natural resources.

Secondary stage: Learning of science would continue to be built around natural and social elements of environment. Science, technology, society, and environment would coalesce in teaching and learning of science at this stage. Teachers could help the learners devise appropriate experimentation and activities within the school and outside school, involving immediate environment, such as farming, factories, industries, and community.

Social sciences: It helps the learners in understanding the human environment in its totality and developing a broader perspective and an empirical, reasonable, and humane outlook. Food security, population growth, poverty, water scarcity, climatic changes, and cultural preservation are some of the major issues of the 21th century which have relevance for the social sciences curriculum. Hence, 'environment, resources, and sustainable development' and 'man-environment interaction' would be drawing their content mainly from geography, economics, sociology, and other related areas.

Class I–II: Children are introduced to the environment in its totality. No clear cut distinction between natural and social environment has to be made.

Class III–V: Environmental Studies (Social Science) introduced. Starting from the surroundings of the children—home, school, and neighborhood—they may be familiarized with their state and country in a gradual manner. Schools will be given full autonomy at this stage to use locally developed curriculum and locally available resources for teaching of environmental studies.

Upper primary: For example, students may be motivated to raise questions pertaining to various physical and man-made features, phenomena, and events; recognize simple patterns, such as rainfall distribution in the country and patterns of agriculture and urban land uses.

Secondary stage: It may include the processes and patterns of man-environment interaction and issues related to environment, its resources, and development.

4.11.1 Guidelines and Syllabi for Upper Primary Stage (2001)

Environment-related topics, concerns, problems, and issues have been included exhaustively throughout the document (NCERT 2001b). Hence, it is felt that no further detail on this is needed to be provided.

4.11.2 Guidelines and Syllabi for Secondary Stage (2001)

Environment-related topics, concerns, problems, and issues have been included exhaustively throughout the document (NCERT 2001a). Hence it is felt that no further detail on this is needed to be provided.

4.12 Curriculum Framework for Teacher Education (2004)

This teacher-education curriculum framework was developed in keeping with the spirit of the NCFSE-2000 (NCERT 2004a). Protection and conservation of environment was considered an important concern of this curriculum framework in the document. It also highlighted the importance of teacher education in order to bring about change in the general attitude toward the treatment of the environment. The document pointed out: "The content and processes of teacher-education programs will have to equip teachers with a proper understanding of love for the nature around and the skill of inculcating these among their students," which will not only result in a healthier society, both physically and mentally, but also bring about the much needed replenishment and sustenance of natural resources affected by the unprecedented industrial development. Developing among teachers, awareness and sensitivity toward environmental concerns was included as one of the thrust areas of teacher education.

At the pre-primary stage the curriculum framework included: "Enabling teachers to inculcate among children a desire to know and understand their immediate natural environment, to love and respect it" and "preparing student teachers to use local resources and local contexts" as its objectives. The following curriculum content and transaction is envisioned by the document:

> Teacher-education curriculum at this stage need to develop awareness about literacy programmes, community dynamics, national and local customs, fairs and festivals and community mode of social living. It may also develop awareness of forces affecting environment, including pollution, appreciation of places of historical and cultural significance and special educational features and developmental tasks contained in policies and programmes.

At the elementary stage, the objectives included the following: "Developing among student teachers skills for teaching integrated environmental studies, integrated social sciences and integrated science and technology" and "enabling student teachers to inculcate among children a desire to know their immediate natural environment, to love and respect it."

As a part of the curriculum content and transaction for preservice teacher education, the document pointed out the need to sensitize teachers to the need for reducing curriculum load, organize appropriate learning experiences which are joyful in nature and related to immediate environment of the learner and help them develop and imbibe desirable values. It further stated that teacher-education programs at this stage needed to provide subject-based orientation. It added:

> Teaching and learning of mathematics would be woven around the environment of the learners so that environmental concerns are properly integrated. The activities would focus on local culture and environment using the local specific contexts and resources. Student teachers shall have to be provided with experiences to help children develop socio-emotional and cultural aspects. A realistic awareness and perspective of the phenomena occurring in the environment will have to be linked with social or scientific events. This may be accomplished by emphasizing observation, classification, comparison and drawing of inferences, conducted within and outside the classroom.

"Developing among student teachers awareness and sensitivity toward environment concern and promoting skills for meeting environmental challenges" was included as one of the objectives at the secondary as well as at the higher secondary stage of school education. In addition, concerns, such as ecological imbalances and environmental degradation also have to be studied in their socio-cultural-economic context in the academic stream.

This curriculum framework included "[E]nabling teachers to be sensitive to gender and environment-related issues" as one of the objectives for the in-service education of teachers (NCERT 2004a, 110–112).

4.13 Environmental Education in Schools: Syllabus (2004)

The syllabus for environmental education in schools was developed by the NCERT in pursuance of the Hon'ble Supreme Court of India order dated 18 December 2003 (NCERT 2004b). In response to the writ petition No. 860/1990 by M.C. Mehta, the Supreme Court stated in its order dated 22 November 1991: "We accept on principle that through the medium of education, awareness of the environment and its problems related to pollution should be taught as a compulsory subject." On 18 December 2003, the Hon'ble Supreme Court ordered, "We also direct the NCERT...to prepare a module (model) syllabus" and on 13 July 2004, the court directed that "the syllabus prepared by the NCERT for Class I–XII shall be adopted by every state in their respective schools." The Hon'ble Court also directed that "the NCERT be appointed as a nodal agency to supervise the implementation of the court's order."

Apart from its focus on bio-physical environmental concerns, the document visualized "EE as an instrument for inculcating healthy personal and social attitudes toward environment and development." It envisaged that a focus on the social environment would lead to better and healthier human relationships, which are vital for human survival and development.

This is a major departure from the earlier documents which largely focused on bio-physical environmental concerns. A comprehensive syllabus for Class I-XII is provided in this document. The document discussed in detail the expected learning outcomes for every stage and listed the topics and concepts to be covered for every class. Exemplar activities to be considered during transaction of such topics, teaching–learning strategies, and evaluation methods were also provided in the document. The syllabus is, therefore, not just a syllabus but is in itself a curriculum.

The document suggested that the teaching–learning strategies

[A]re to be designed in keeping with the local environmental conditions, both natural and social. At the same time, it should aim at helping learners to develop a global perspective of the environment and problems related to it. The most important parameter, however, to be considered while designing teaching-learning situations would be to provide adequate emphasis on the development of positive attitude as well as love and respect for the environment.

As for the evaluation methods, the document suggested: "The assessment of learners' achievement in environmental education would encompass all the three aspects of development, that is, cognitive, affective, and conative. Both process and product evaluation techniques will need to be used."

JUST A MOMENT

Reflect on the intervention of the Hon'ble Supreme Court regarding implementation of environmental education. Has it been very effective?

4.14 National Curriculum Framework 2005 (NCF-2005)

This curriculum framework (NCF-2005) incorporated the views presented in the position paper of the National Focus Group on Habitat and Learning, which is about environmental education. The NCF-2005 elaborately discussed concerns related to the environment all throughout the document, keeping in view the unprecedented environmental degradation witnessed in the recent past owing to the emergence of new technological choices and lifestyles (NCERT 2005a). The document stated: "Humankind must, therefore, make an attempt to comprehend its roots, to reestablish links with its habitat, and to understand and take good care of it."

Reiterating the NPE-1986 recommendations, this curriculum framework considered making children sensitive to the environment and making the need for its protection an important curricular concern. It believed that education can provide a necessary perspective on how human life can be reconciled with environmental crisis so that survival, growth, and development remain possible. Hence, the document stated that concerns and issues pertaining to the environment should be included in every subject and through a wide range of activities involving outdoor project work.

Like any other subject, environmental concerns can be best addressed in the school curriculum by linking knowledge to life outside the school, which is the first guiding principle of this document. The document stated that only when the living world becomes available for critical reflection within the school will the children come alive to the issues of the environment and nurture their concern for it. For example, apart from acquiring bookish knowledge, the children should examine water bodies and sources to know about water pollution.

However, the document did not limit environmental education to 'protection of the environment.' It stated:

> The main focus of EE should be to expose students to the real-life world, natural and social, in which they live; to enable them to analyse, evaluate, and draw inferences about problems and concerns related to the environment; to add, where possible, to our understanding of environmental issues; and to promote positive environmental actions to facilitate the move towards sustainable development. To achieve these goals, the curriculum may be based on: (i) Learning about the environment (ii) Learning through the environment, and (iii) Learning for the environment.

Holistic environmental perspective (which includes the physical, natural, and socio-cultural world) in terms of both their content and pedagogy, and which encourage flexibility to bring in locale specificities, are at the core of the curriculum. This curriculum framework emphasized the importance of working with hands and the need to encourage heritage craft traditions, which uses raw materials that are all indigenously available and are also environment friendly. The document mentioned that students should also be encouraged to learn local-knowledge traditions such as harvesting and storing water, or of practicing sustainable agriculture through projects, and so on.

The NCF-2005 also stressed that projects and activities would be the backbone of any scheme aimed at effective implementation of environmental education in schools. This would engage the young minds in the excitement of first-hand observation of nature and of understanding patterns and processes in the natural and social worlds. It suggested that, for successful implementation, a separate time needs to be carved out for projects and fieldwork from the existing periods of SUPW, science, and other subjects. It pointed out that some of the information and understanding flowing from such projects could contribute to the elaboration of a publicly accessible, transparent database on India's environment, which would in turn become the most valuable educational resource.

The document maintained that, if well planned, many of these student projects could lead to knowledge generation. Various school-based programs and projects pertaining to the environment could help create the knowledge base for the *Panchayati Raj* institutions to better manage and regenerate local environmental resources. The document stated that such projects and activities would not only enrich the curriculum so that it goes beyond textbooks, but would also ensure that learning is shifted away from rote methods.

Although the Hon'ble Supreme Court emphasized the need to teach environmental concerns as a compulsory subject at all stages of school education (details about the Supreme Court order is discussed in the next chapter), the document recommended that these significant concerns are best realized by infusing the components of environmental education as a part of different disciplines. This would also help fulfill one of the concerns of the NCF-2005—reducing the curriculum load.

The document mentioned:

This approach can be meaningfully employed in the treatment of content in Physics, Mathematics, Chemistry, Biology, Geography, History, Political Science, Health and Physical Education, Art, Music etc. Activities constructed for life situations become a meaningful means for the engagement of learners. Rainfall, for instance, exhibits intricate variations over space and time. Data on such variations are available and can be used to promote many interesting activities in Physics and Mathematics.

The document added that similar examples, such as effluents from sewage treatment plants in chemistry, biodiversity resources, medicinal plants, endangered fish, diets of tribal people, preparation of maps, water disputes, and so on, could form the raw data in different subjects.

The curriculum recommended by the NCF-2005 in Science and Social Science for different stages is discussed next.

Science Curriculum

At the 'primary stage,' the objectives should be to nurture the curiosity of the child about the world (natural environment, artifacts, and people). Science and social science should be integrated as 'environmental studies.' At the 'upper primary stage,' the child should continue to learn more about the environment and health, including reproductive and sexual health, through activities and surveys. Group activities, discussions with peers and teachers, surveys, organization of data, and their display through exhibitions, and so on, in schools and the neighborhood should be important components of pedagogy. At the 'secondary stage,' students should be engaged in activities and analyses on issues concerning the environment and health, including reproduction and sexual health. They should work on locally significant projects involving science and technology.

Social Science Curriculum

For the 'primary stage,' the natural and the social environment will be explained as integral parts of languages and mathematics. Children should be engaged in activities to understand the environment through illustrations from the physical, biological, social, and cultural spheres. For 'Classes III–V,' the subject EVS should be introduced. In the study of the natural environment, the emphasis would be on its preservation and the urgency of saving it from degradation. Children would also begin to be sensitized to social issues such as poverty, child labor, illiteracy, and caste and class inequalities in rural and urban areas. The content should reflect the daily experiences of children and their different worlds.

At the 'upper primary stage,' social studies would draw its content from history, geography, political science, and economics. The curriculum should take into account developments in different parts of India and the world; balanced perspective related to issues concerning the environment, resources, and development at different levels, from local to global; democratic processes of participation; and observe economic institutions like the family, the market and the state. There would also be a section that will indicate a multidisciplinary approach to these themes.

At the 'secondary stage,' the curriculum would focus on understanding the social and economic challenges facing the nation and concerns of scheduled castes (SC) and scheduled tribes (ST) and disenfranchised populations. It would enable students to understand their world better and also understand how their own identities came into being as shaped by a rich and varied past; inculcate in the child a critical appreciation for conservation and environmental concerns along with developmental issues; and engage in-depth discussion on equality, liberty, justice, fraternity, secularism, dignity, plurality, and freedom from exploitation.

Work and Education

The NCF-2005 elaborately discussed the meaning of 'work' in terms of productive activity and fulfillng their needs, contribution to the good of the society, an activity through which a person gains identity, and construction of knowledge. However, unlike the earlier curriculum framework where work-related education/work experience/SUPW was treated as a separate curricular subject, this curriculum framework recommended that work should form an integral part of the curriculum, not as a separate subject but as a pedagogical tool; that is, work-centered education, similar to the Gandhian philosophy and concept of work, and not just the completion of work. This is also because work is an interdisciplinary activity and it could be well-covered in all disciplines.

Work involves interaction with materials or people (mostly both), hence creating a deeper and wider comprehension and increased practical knowledge of natural substances and social relationships. The NCF-2005 believed that when academic learning and work are simultaneously collocated, there is a chance of greater creativity in academic pursuits and in the methods and approaches of working. At the same time, disciplinary boundaries that are normally drawn traditionally also diminish or disappear. The rich work-knowledge base and skills of marginalized children can be turned into a source of dignity as well as of learning for other children through work-centered pedagogy.

4.14.1 Syllabus for Classes at the Elementary Level (2005)

Environment-related topics, concerns, problems, and issues have been included exhaustively throughout the document (NCERT 2005b). Hence, it is felt that no further detail on this needs to be provided.

4.14.2 Syllabus for Secondary and Higher Secondary Classes (2005)

Environment-related topics, concerns, problems, and issues have been included exhaustively throughout the document (NCERT 2005c). Hence it is felt that no further detail on this needs to be provided.

4.15 National Curriculum Framework for Teacher Education (2009)

The NCFTE-2009 was prepared "towards preparing professional and humane teacher" (NCTE 2009).

The document elaborately discussed the context, concerns, and vision for teacher's education. It reflected upon the concerns related to environmental education.

The document observed:

> In order to develop future citizens who promote equitable and sustainable development for all sections of society and respect for all, it is necessary that they be educated through perspectives of gender equity, the perspectives that develop values for peace, respect the rights of all, and respect and value work. In the present ecological crisis, promoted by extremely commercialised and competitive lifestyles, teachers and children need to be educated to change their consumption patterns and the way they look at natural resources.

It is encouraging to see environmental education discussed as part of contemporary studies under the foundations of education in the light of its critical perspective in sustaining a democratic social order.

The document also highlighted the importance of connecting community knowledge in education with formal school knowledge and inclusion of locally relevant content in the curriculum as well as pedagogy, conditions fundamental to environmental education.

As a part of its vision for 'teacher and teacher education,' the document stated that teacher-education programs should broaden the curriculum (both school and teacher education) to include different traditions of knowledge; educate teachers to connect school knowledge with community knowledge and life outside the school; reconceptualize citizenship training in terms of human rights and approaches of critical pedagogy; emphasize environment and its protection, live in harmony within oneself and with natural and social environment; and promote peace, democratic way of life, constitutional values of equality, justice, liberty, fraternity and secularism, and caring values.

The curriculum framework also suggested that environmental hygiene should form an important component of teacher-education curricula. As for pedagogic studies, this document suggested a departure from conventional teacher education which focused on a pure disciplinary approach of teaching individual school subjects such as physics, chemistry, biology, history, and geography to a more integrated approach of sciences and social sciences. All theory courses will need to be 'interdisciplinary' in structure and have 'field-based units of study' it maintained, which is a necessity in terms of environmental education.

It suggested that a pedagogy course on EVS should include the following: philosophical and epistemological basis of EVS as a composite area of study that draws upon sciences, social sciences, and environmental education; acquainting student-teachers with children's ideas of their physical and social world so that these can later be interpreted for classroom instruction; and helping student-teachers develop the ability to plan comprehensive units that do not compartmentalize knowledge but view it holistically. It also suggested that elementary school teachers needed to engage in research relating to different aspects of young children's learning in different areas, including environmental education in an effort to develop sound pedagogic understanding. The document added that: "A 'critical examination of and engagement with teaching methods' such as concept formation, enquiry-based teaching, problem-solving, discovery, and activity-based learning and related terms can go along way in making him/her a reflective teacher." Practical activities, such as workshops and course work, also form an integral part of the curriculum.

Many concerns related to environmental education have been addressed in the document. However, there still appears to be a sort of disconnect between this document and what the National Curriculum Framework 2005 for school education recommends for environmental education. For example, there is no mention of infusion approach of environmental education in the curriculum or the pedagogy component. It is felt that an explicit and clearer picture of environmental education would have been more appropriate instead of reflecting the concerns in patches.

Conclusion

Although the root of modern environmental education in India can be traced back to 1937, beginning with Gandhi's concept of 'basic education,' it was only since beginning the 1970s that its relevance is more evident in the education system. An interesting and important observation made in NCERT (1981, 21–22) regarding noninclusion of environmental education as an integral part of school education prior to 1975 is provided below verbatim.

1. Lack of comprehensive awareness of the importance of the earthly environment and the impact of its distortion and mutilation on man's present and future existence on earth along with other living beings from whom man is continuously deriving some form of benefit, directly or indirectly.
2. Inheritance of an old-fashioned and tradition education as a legacy of British rule over India, which was considerably divorced from the country's own environment.
3. Lack of expertise in developing an environment-related curriculum.
4. Traditional outlook toward education and societal unpreparedness to accept a new content of education, that is, environmental education.

Subsequently, the National Policy on Education-1986 provided a strong base to incorporate environmental education in the curriculum. This document can be considered a landmark for environmental education since all the programs and projects related to environmental education till today have in some way emerged and are being implemented based on this document. All the curriculum frameworks brought out after this highlighted environmental concerns more evidently. Having seen the impact that a policy document can have, it becomes the more important that such documents contain a more specific, yet comprehensive content on concerns related to environmental education. This is necessary to prevent misinterpretation of the ideas and philosophies reflected in the document when different stakeholders begin 'deciphering' and 'decoding' the document during the process of implementation.

The Hon'ble Supreme Court's order of 1991, to make environmental education a compulsory subject in schools, to a great extent, promoted environmental education in the country and shaped environmental education into its present status. As we saw in all the documents that we have discussed in the chapter, elements of environmental education are found implicitly or explicitly. However, for better and effective implementation of environmental education, we need a policy document which explicitly and strongly advocates environmental education. If such documents could accommodate a separate section purely for environmental education, it will make a world of difference in its implementation. The recent renaming of the Ministry of Environment and Forests to the Ministry of Environment, Forests, and Climate Change (MoEF&CC) suggest the Government's concern for the environment. Education, being an important tool to address environmental issues, it is expected that such concerns will also be reflected in the activities initiated by the Ministry of Human Resource Development. As India is in the process of drafting a new education policy, it is hoped that environmental education will receive more attention in the document. The fate of environmental education hangs on how well it is reflected in the 'Bible' for education which is being prepared.

SUMMARY

- Root of modern environmental education in India can be traced as far back as 1937 with Mahatma Gandhi's concept of 'Basic Education' where the focus was learning by/ and doing. Education was not only for the sake of learning but the resultant product was also to add to the nation's wealth.

- After independence, the focus was shifted to building the nation and how to make the maximum use of the natural resources available which could have resulted in a lot of exploitation of the environment.

- Beginning the seventies, environmental concerns received more recognition and relevance in the education system which was reflected in the national curriculum framework developed in 1975.

- The National Policy on Education-1986 (NPE-1986) provided a strong base to incorporate environmental education in the curriculum and can be considered a landmark for environmental education since all the

programs and projects related to environmental education till today have in some way emerged and are being implemented based on this document.

- All the curriculum frameworks brought out subsequent to NPE-1986 highlighted environmental concerns more evidently.

- Increasing environmental pollution and degradation brought about the Supreme Court's order of 1991 to make environmental education a compulsory subject in schools. This order, to a great extent, promoted environmental education in the country and shaped environmental education into its present status.

- There appears to be a sort of disconnect between teacher-education curriculum framework and what the curriculum framework for school education recommends for environmental education.

Exercises

1. Do you think environmental education has been adequately reflected in our national educational documents? Justify your answer.
2. What difference do you see in the documents before and after the Hon'ble Supreme Court's order? Elaborate your answer.
3. Is there any coherence between the curriculum framework for schools and curriculum framework for teachers in terms of environmental education? Explain.
4. Based on the discussions about different documents in the chapter, which document do you think best reflects the concerns of environmental education? Elaborate your answer.
5. The National Policy on Education 1986 is considered a landmark document for environmental education in India. Do you agree with the statement? Justify your answer.
6. Do you see any difference in the documents in terms of environmental education before and after the National Policy on Education 1986 was brought out? Elucidate your answer.
7. How has the document 'Learning without burden' impacted the implementation of environmental education in schools?
8. Do the documents suggest that environmental education is getting increasing attention over the years and decades? Justify your answer with example.
9. Do you think environmental education has been reflected adequately in the documents discussed in the chapter?
10. Which document according to you stands out compared to other documents in terms of environmental education? Explain.

References

Gandhi, M.K. 1951. *Basic Education*, edited by Bharatan Kumarappa. Ahmedabad: Navajivan Publishing House.

GoI, Government of India. 1953. *Report of the Secondary Education Commission (1952–1953)*, Ministry of Education, Government of India.

——— 1966. *Report of the Indian Education Commission (1964–66)—Education & National Development*, Ministry of Education, Government of India.

——— 1968. *National Policy on Education—1968*, Ministry of Education, Government of India.

——— 1977. *Report of the Review Committee on the Curriculum for the Ten-Year School*, Ministry of Education and Social Welfare (Ishwarbhai Patel Committee Report), Government of India.

——— 1986. *National Policy on Education—1986*, Ministry of Human Resource Development, Government of India.

——— 1993. *Learning without Burden—Report of the National Advisory Committee appointed by the Ministry of Human Resource Development*, Government of India.

NCERT, National Council of Educational Research and Training. 1970. *Syllabus of Science and Mathematics for the Middle School Level*. New Delhi: NCERT.

——— 1975. *The Curriculum for the Ten-year School: A Framework*. New Delhi: NCERT.

——— 1976. *Syllabi for Classes VI-VIII*. New Delhi: NCERT.

——— 1981. *Environmental Education at the School Level: A Lead Paper*. New Delhi: NCERT.

——— 1987. *Science Education for the First Ten Years of Schooling—Report of the Working Group*. New Delhi: NCERT.

——— 1988a. *Guidelines and Syllabi for Secondary Stage*. New Delhi: NCERT.

——— 1988b. *Guidelines and Syllabi for Upper Primary Stage*. New Delhi: NCERT.

——— 1988c. *National Curriculum for Elementary and Secondary Education—A Framework (Revised Version)*. New Delhi: NCERT.

——— 2000. *National Curriculum Framework for School Education 2000*. New Delhi: NCERT.

——— 2001a. *Guidelines and Syllabi for Secondary Stage*. New Delhi: NCERT.

——— 2001b. *Guidelines and Syllabi for Upper Primary Stage*. New Delhi: NCERT.

——— 2004a. *Curriculum Framework for Teacher Education*. New Delhi: NCERT.

—— 2004b. *Environmental Education in Schools—Syllabus for Environmental Education in Schools Submitted to the Hon'ble Supreme Court of India in Pursuance of its Order Dated 18th December 2003*. New Delhi: NCERT.

—— 2005a. *National Curriculum Framework-2005*. New Delhi: NCERT.

—— 2005b. *Syllabus for Classes at the Elementary Level*. New Delhi: NCERT.

—— 2005c. *Syllabus for Secondary and Higher Secondary Classes*, New Delhi: NCERT.

—— 2006. *Position Paper of the National Focus Group on Habitat and Learning*. New Delhi: NCERT.

—— 2011. *Teachers' Handbook on Environmental Education for the Higher Secondary Stage*. New Delhi: NCERT.

NCTE, National Council for Teacher Education. 2009. *National Curriculum Framework for Teacher Education—Towards Preparing Professional and Humane Teacher 2009*. New Delhi: NCTE.

Yadav, M.S. and V.M. Nikalje. 2009. *National Curriculum Framework—A Historical Perspective*. New Delhi: NCERT.

Appendices

Appendix 4.1: Syllabus of Science and Mathematics for the Middle School Level (1970)

Biology First Year (Part I i.e. class VI)
Part I – Section VIII: Plant as Living Organism—Conditions necessary for plant life—air, water, and light; role of soil; Importance of green plants in nature, an idea of conservation of plants—"Vana Mahotsava"

Biology Third Year (Part III i.e. class VIII)
Topic-wise Part IV: Man and his Environment—includes topics such as

1. Interdependence of the living and nonliving: Food chains, exchange of chemicals between living and nonliving, water, and other cycles
2. An agricultural field: Sun as energy source, environment in the field, daily and seasonal changes, drought and flood, animals and plants of the field, adaptations of animals for living in soil and litter layers, role of insect and other invertebrates—food chains, potential pests, aids to farmers as pollinators, nutrition of soil, and so on. Brief consideration of the chemical cycles (water, oxygen and carbon and nitrogen) in the field. Dangers of disturbing the cycles by total removal of crop etc. Roles of fertilizers, rotation of crops, contour ploughing, fallow periods, proper crop and herd arrangement.
3. Man and the conservation of nature: the need to conserve biological resources—soil, plants and wildlife, methods of conservation, methods of preventing polluting of air and water, dangers of careless use of pesticides in disturbing the balance of nature, responsibilities of every citizen to practice conservation.

Appendix 4.2: Syllabi for Classes VI–VIII (1976)

Classes I and II
Environmental Studies (Social Studies and General Science)

- Integrated curriculum in environmental education

Work Experience and the Arts

Classes III, IV and V
Environmental Studies I (Social Studies)

- A separate subject where he/she would get an understanding of the geographical setting in which he/she lives and that of his/her social and cultural environment. In this course, the pupil would be gradually introduced to the life in his home and family, school, neighborhood, the State, the country, and the world at large.

Environmental Studies II (General Science)
Work Experience and the Arts

Class VI, VII and VIII
Social Science (elements of history, geography, civics and economics)

- Elements drawn primarily from history, geography, civics, economics and sociology
- Taught as separate subjects as history, geography and civics (economics and sociology to be integrated in these three subjects).
- Focus would be on interaction between man and his physical and social environment, and the relationship between man and his social and cultural heritage, and the community of which he is a part, which will help the pupil to understand various aspects of the contemporary problems in their totality.
- To develop an understanding of the economic forces that influence the everyday life of citizens.

Geography syllabus

Class VI
Unit 1: The Earth as a Globe—The earth and the solar system; rotation and revolution of the earth; latitude and longitude; globe & world map

Unit 2: Africa—Land and Peoples—land, climate, vegetation, wild life, gift of nature, peoples, and so on

Unit 3: Asia—Land and Peoples—land, climate, vegetation, wild life, gift of nature, peoples, and so on

Unit 4: Practical work—ideas of map

Class VII
Unit 1: Atmosphere and Hydrosphere—Composition and layers of atmosphere; air and its changing temperature; pressure and winds; humidity and precipitation; ocean waters and their circulation

Unit 2: Australasia—Land and People—land, climate, vegetation, wild life, gift of nature, peoples, and so on

Unit 3: South America—Land and Peoples—land, climate, vegetation, wild life, gift of nature, peoples, and so on

Unit 4: North America—Land and Peoples—land, climate, vegetation, wild life, gift of nature, peoples, and so on

Unit 5: The Soviet Union—Land and Peoples—land, climate, vegetation, wild life, gift of nature, peoples, and so on

Unit 6: Practical work—night and day

Class VIII
Unit 1: Lithosphere and Landforms—crust, rocks, earthquakes, volcanoes, process of gradation and its agents – weathering, soil formation, running water, ground water, moving ice, winds, sea waves

Unit 2: Europe—Land and Peoples—land, climate, vegetation, wild life, gift of nature, peoples, etc.

Unit 3: India—Physical Setting—relief features; climate, vegetation and wild life

Unit 4: India—Its Agricultural Resources—soils, irrigation, crops, methods of farming

Unit 5: India—Minerals and Industries—mineral resources; industries

Unit 6: India—Trade, Transport and Population—trade, transport and population structure, distribution and density

Unit 7: Practical work—weather study

Science (elements of the physical sciences and the life sciences)
Integrated Science

Class VI
Unit 11: Man's dependence on plants and animals and the balance of nature—dependence of man on plants and animals; interdependence of plants and animals; dependence of plants and animals on environment; different uses of plants and animals to man; interactions of organisms with other organisms; interactions of organisms with physical environment.

Unit 12: How do living species cope with the environment—changes in the environment; living organism can sense the change of environment; living organisms cope with the environment.

Unit 13: Water—Sources; purification of water for drinking; importance of water to living forms; some special properties of water like low melting point, high boiling point, density of ice, and good solvent and their importance of daily life.

Unit 14: Energy—Energy sources in nature—sun, water, wind, coal, petrol, etc. Relationship between work and energy; energy problems—social significance; various forms of energy; mechanical energy; chemical energy; transformation of energy from one form to another; use of energy in living systems.

Class VII
Unit 27: Population and pollution

Sub-Unit 27.1: Population—Definition; characteristics of population; external factors affecting the population; population explosion and its problems

Sub-unit 27.2: Pollution—Definition; environmental pollution—air, water, noise pollution; causes of pollution and its preventions; pollution and balance in nature

Class VIII
Unit 37: Agriculture

Sub-unit 37.1: Agriculture practices and implements—tilling leveling, manuring, sowing, transplanting, watering harvesting, water pump, spray pump

Sub-unit 37.2: Our Problems in agriculture—our problems in production and storage

Sub-unit 37.3: Improvement and protection of crops—nature and types of soil, treatment of soil; nutrient deficiency in soil; fertilizers (K, N and Phosphate), mixed fertilizers, and their composition; crop protection, use of insecticides, pesticides and weed killers; precautions in the use of fertilizers, pesticides, and weed killers; different types of crops—their growth patterns, climate and season; selection of seeds, water and irrigation, importance of crop rotation; hybridization, and crop breeding

Unit 40: Conservation of natural resources—what are natural resources—why conservation is necessary—how steps of conservation are taken for soil, water, air, forest, and wild life

Unit 42: Science in Human Welfare—what made developments possible (with reference to industrial development in modern India)

Class IX and X
Social Sciences (history, geography, civics, economics, psychology)
Science (the physical sciences and the life sciences)

Work Experience
No detailed syllabi are visualized for work experience. **No 'syllabus' is really necessary in connection with work experience but ideas for implementing this aspect of education will be available through separate books**.

Appendix 4.3: Guidelines and Syllabi for Upper Primary Stage (1988)

Science
Class VI
Unit I: Science in Everyday Life
Content: Role of Science in solving many basic problems in our every day life; misuse of science; scientific methods help us in making decisions, acquiring knowledge, and solving problems; contribution of scientists in the progress of science.

Unit 9: Air
Content: An envelope of air all around us; air—a mixture of various components; composition of air; oxygen—a supporter of combustion and life; necessity of air for sustenance of life; various uses of air to human beings.

Unit 10: Water
Content: Importance of water for living beings; need of water for various purposes; sources of water; purification of water for drinking; some special physical properties of water; different forms of water; change of one form into another; water cycle in nature; hard and soft water; uses of water in day-to-day life; need of conservation of water.

Unit 11: Energy
Content: Energy, relationship between work and energy; different forms of energy—mechanical energy, heat energy, light energy, sound energy; renewable and nonrenewable sources of energy; electric energy from coal; solar energy, wind energy, energy from water, energy from biomass.

Unit 12: Balance in Nature
Content: Living and nonliving components of environment; interdependence; food and energy relations; balance in nature; essential for survival; Indiscriminate human interferences are often harmful.

Class VII

Unit 5: Sound
Content: Various types of sound; modes of production of sound; formation of echo; noise and its hazards; human ear.

Unit 7: Energy
Content: Mechanical energy; potential and kinetic energies; transformation of energy; renewable and non-renewable sources of energy; judicious uses of energy.

Unit 9: Water
Content: Composition of water; electrolysis of water; some common physical properties of water, electrical attraction of water, some chemical properties of water; dissolution of various minerals and salts in sea water; hard and soft water; removal of hardness; water pollution.

Unit 10: Air
Content: Various constituents of air; oxygen—an important constituent of air, air pollution; acid rain; uses of various constituents of air.

Unit 12: Food, Health, and Diseases
Content: Food essential for human life; basic constituents, their main functions including water and roughage; different foods are rich in different constituents; balanced diet in relation to age and work; judicious choice of food; avoidance of fads; malnutrition; deficiency diseases; food preservation; contamination/spoilage; healthy living depends on hygiene, sanitation, and habits; diseases; disorders; role and spread of disease causing micro-organism; personal hygiene and environmental sanitation; non communicable diseases; smoking, alcohol, and drug addiction as health hazards.

Unit 13: Soils
Content: Composition of soils—gravel, clay, organic matter; humus and living organisms in top soil, soil formed by weathering; soil as important natural resource; soil erosion and conservation; soil pollution.

Unit 14: Agricultural practices and implements
Content: Management of plants and animals; usefulness, general methods; improved agricultural practices for increased food production; basic practices; sequencing; variation from crop to crop; practices common to gardening; agricultural implements and their uses and care; qualitative and quantitative improvement of crop yields; necessity and methods, improved practices and varieties; judicious use of soil, fertilizers and pesticides; animal management; need for keeping animals; general needs and maintenance of domestic animals with special reference to cattle, sheep, poultry; bee and fish rearing.

Class VIII

Unit 2: Alternative sources of energy
Content: Source of energy; fossil fuels; hydro-energy; bio-energy, wind-energy as renewable sources of energy; energy needs; development of alternative sources of energy; judicious use of energy.

Unit 4: Man made materials
Content: Various types of materials and their applications; synthetic fibres; plastics and its uses in daily life; glass and its formation; ceramics; soaps and detergents; fertilizers; pesticides.

Unit 8: The Microbial World
Content: Micro-organisms have divers forms; fungi, protozoa, bacteria, viruses, and certain algae; causes of disease in man and animal bacteria (cholera, typhoid, TB); virus (cold, measles, polio, chickenpox), protozoan and fungi (malaria, dysentery, etc.); animal diseases (anthrax and foot and mouth), plant diseases (rust, bacterial wilt, leaf curl, mosaic); modes of transmission of diseases; vectors; control of microbial diseases; proper storage and preservation to prevent microbial damage to clothing, timber and food.

Unit 10: Adaptation and Organic Evolution
Content: Meaning of adaptation; adaptation caused by structural changes; adaptation of aquatic, terrestrial, and Volant organisms; organisms have undergone continuous and gradual change since their evolution; origin of life from simple substances; origin of complex forms from simpler forms; slow process; evidence of evolution—external and internal structures; fossils; organic evolution through the process of natural selection.

Unit 11: Useful Plants and Animals
Content: Plants and animals affect human life in many ways, harmful and useful plants of economic importance—wild and cultivated; useful animals; animals; animals products from wild and domesticated animals—(ivory, lac, horn, lime, pearls, leather, and honey.)

Unit 12: Conservation of Natural Resources
Content: Necessity of natural resources of life; Matter or material from earth; energy from sun; living organisms get all requirements from nature; energy directly or indirectly from the sun; man requires more resources than other living organisms; proper distribution of resources; various types of natural resources; renewable and nonrenewable; depletion of resources and their causes; conservation of natural resources for human survival; conservation efforts at individual/community/governmental/international level is necessary.

Geography

Class VIII
Unit IV India—Natural Resources
Major natural resources their distribution and utilization (a) soil; (b) minerals—iron, coal, petroleum, bauxite and manganese; (c) forest and wild life; (d) water
Conservation of natural resources

Unit V India—Human Resources
Population: density, distribution, growth rate and structure of population—sex composition, literacy, rural–urban ratio, employment, age–structure
Quality of life—economic and social development, health and nutrition

Unit VI India—Economic Development
Economic Development (a) Agriculture: predominance of monsoon, irrigation projects, food production, green revolution. (b) Industries: heavy small-scale and cottage; few important industries—iron and steel textiles, sugar, oil refineries, heavy machinery and chemicals. (c) Trade: internal and external. (d) transport and communications: land, water, and air transport; means of communications: land, water and air transport; means of communication and their development.

Civics

Class VIII
Unit IV: Our Economic Problems—poverty and unemployment, population growth; production and productivity in agricultural, industrial, and household sectors

Unit VIII: World Problems—human rights; arms race; disparities between the developing and developed countries; environmental pollution (human activities and environmental pollution, types of environmental pollution, pollution of air, water, and land. Factors responsible for environmental pollution, impact of environmental problems on society, and the quality of life; ways and means to reduce environmental pollution at the local, national, and international levels).

Appendix 4.4: Guidelines and Syllabi for Upper Primary Stage (1988)

Work Experience: Essential Activities

1. Maintaining cleanliness at home.
2. Cleanliness of the classroom and school premises.
3. Keeping sources of water in the community safe and clean.
4. Looking after sanitary disposal of waste material during festivals.
5. Taking care of school dress.
6. Helping in the cleaning of poultry house cattleshed in rural area.
7. House/school decoration on special occasions such as festivals, marriages, birthdays.
8. Organizing community service programs for road repairs, tree plantation, and cleaning of surroundings in a village slum area.

9. Helping parents in looking after younger children in the family.
10. Maintenance of personal and household accounts, payment of household bills (electricity, water, newspapers, etc.).
11. Making small purchases for self and family.
12. Coaching primary school children including younger brothers and sisters who are weak in studies.
13. Monitoring the weight of babies in the neighborhood to detect malnutrition.
14. Preparation of charts and posters indicating causes, symptoms, and prevention of common diseases.
15. Carrying out environmental sanitation and tree plantation.

Appendix 4.5: Guidelines and Syllabi for Secondary Stage (1988)

Science

Class IX
Unit 3: Ways of Living
Habitat and organisms: Habitat, types of habitat; classification of organisms based on habitats, habitat and organisms, interdependence including man. Conservation of habitats.

   Adaptation: Structural and functional potentialities of organisms, structural adaptation with reference to internal and external factors. Functional adaptation refers to life processors.

Unit 4: Human Beings
Continuous efforts of man to reshape the natural environment. Necessity and inventions. Manipulation of environment to overcome limitations, for physical, biological and cultural needs. Regulation of environment; use and exploration of needs; control and use of fire regulation of micro and macro levels, Advantages and disadvantages of regulation.

Unit 5: World of Work
Technology—meaning and application; evolution of technology and human society; development of new and improved technology—need, acceptance by the society, time gap between development and application; role of technology in harnessing energy.

   Impact of technology on society—influence of technology on individual needs, energy requirements of the individual and the society, energy crisis, impact of technology on physical, social and cultural environment.

   Technology and science—interrelation between science and technology, application of technology in development of science, one technology creates need for another.

Class X
Unit 6: Energy
Sun as a source of energy—absorption of solar energy by earth, photosynthesis, solar heaters, solar cells.

   Wind—wind mills; hydroelectric generation, electricity from sea waves; bio-energy – bio-mass, bio-mass as fuel, biogas.

Fossil fuels—sources of fossil fuels, coal; natu-fuels—conditions for combustion, heat produced during combustion, combustion of food in living organism.

Types of fuels—energy from fuels, solid, liquid and gaseous fuels, characteristics of fuels-conditions for combustion, heat product during combustion, combustion, food in living organisms.

Nuclear energy—nuclear fission, energy released during fission, atomic power plants, radiation hazards. Energy crisis—causes of energy crisis, trends in energy consumption of individuals; industry and agriculture, depletion in known stocks of fossil fuels, inefficient use of energy, industrialization and urbanization; possible solutions for overcoming energy crisis—population control, exploration of renewable sources of energy and emphasis on their use, reducing wastage of energy, use of energy efficient machines, judicious use of nonrenewable sources of energy.

Unit 7: Food and Health

Necessity of balanced diet: Diet and nature of work, Need and functions of nutrients, Vitamins, minerals. Sources of dietary proteins, carbohydrates and fats, vitamins, minerals. Deficiency diseases and their symptoms. Protein energy malnutrition, mineral malnutrition. Symptoms of diseases, factors of insufficiency control, Harmful effects of over intake; obesity, and other complications, cardiovascular disorder, mottling of teeth and fluorosis, hypervitaminosis.

Wasteful Food Practices: Type of wastage, defective practices—post harvesting, mode of storage and distribution, traditional systems, faulty methods of preservation, cooking, pre-marketing.

Food yield: Different practices—use of fertilizers and manures, proper irrigation, nitrogen fixation, crop rotation mixed cropping, use of good hybrids, protection of plants against diseases, animal husbandry, artificial insemination, care and management.

Food spoilage: Internal and external factors, control factors effecting human health: factors—use of spoiled food, organic failure, metabolic malfunctions, genetically transmitted diseases, malignancies of different organs.

Environmental pollutants, contaminated water, causes, and transmission by physical contract or vectors.

Disorders caused by addiction to alcohol, smoking, and drugs.

Essentials for good health—hygienic habits and control of environmental pollution.

Unit 8: Environment

Biosphere: Sources of energy, food chain, food web, flow of energy.

Mineral Cycles: Carbon cycle, role of carbon and its compounds, nitrogen cycle, nitrogen fixation, oxygen cycle, oxidation processes, water cycle, role of energy in different cycles.

Ecological balance: man's role in disturbing the balance, efforts for maintenance of ecological balance.

Unit 9: Natural Resources

Water: Water as a natural resource, origin of life in water, water as medium for the activity of the living, water as a solvent, saturated and unsaturated solutions, sea water as habitat of organism, salts from sea, use of water.

Air: Role of atmosphere in protection from radiation, composition of atmosphere, water and, particulate matter in atmosphere, carbon dioxide and its adverse effects on living organisms, role of trees, release of carbon dioxide from fossil fuels and automobiles, corrosion of metals, damage of historical monuments from acidic gases, effect of metallic particles, asbestos, etc. on living organism, carbon monoxide and its ill effects, smog, air pollution, radioactivity, noise pollution and its effects on human beings.

Dependence of man on natural resources: minerals from earth metals and nonmetals, use of metals.

Carbon and its compounds: Properties of carbon and hydrocarbons, petroleum products.

Extraction of metals: Properties of metals and some alloys; uses of metals, nonmetals and some alloys at home and in industry.

Living resources: Renewable and nonrenewable resources, exploitation of resources, ecological crises due to deforestation, need for proper replenishment and management of living resources, means of replenishment through silviculture, Conservation and monitoring of wild life parks and sanctuaries, wild life conservation, legislative measures for protection of living resources.

Unit 10: Universe
Earth—physical and biological components, atmosphere, changes since its origin, evolution of life, role of solar energy in origin and sustenance of life.

Space exploration—history of space exploration, applications of space science—satellite communication, weather monitoring, collection of information about other planets and outer space.

Solar system—planets and satellites, structure of the solar system, age of planets including earth.

Universe—solar system and Milky Way galaxy, universe, comprising galaxies, expanding universe, origin of universe—big bang theory.

Recycling of waste material: Waste materials, biodegradable and non-biodegradable waste materials and their recycling, preparation of compost, proper disposal of nuclear and radioactive wastes, harmful effects of exposure to radioactive waste, technique for proper storage of radioactive wastes.

Geography
Class IX: Man and Environment
Unit 2: Natural Environment (the totality of the environment; special place of human beings in the environment)

Unit 3: Natural Resources and their utilization

1. Resources and their classification; renewable and nonrenewable; potential and developed; classification of resources based on their source, for example, land and water.
2. Land resources—land use patterns, soil-formation, utilization, forest and wild life resources, animal resources, fisheries, mineral and power resources, water resources.
3. Depletion and degradation of resources and their conservation.

Unit 4: Human interaction with the environment

1. Human population—distribution, growth of population, density of population, man and ecosystem, and food supply.

2. Human occupation—primary occupations—food gathering, hunting, fishing, animal rearing and mining; secondary occupations—industries; tertiary occupations—trade, transport, communication and other service.
3. Environmental degradation—nature of human intervention causing environmental degradation, depletion of resources, environmental pollution, environmental problems at local, regional, national and global levels; Need and efforts to improve the quality of environment.
4. The natural regions—concept of natural region, major natural regions of the world, how natural regions help in the study of World Geography.
5. Geography and area development—few case studies each of development from agricultural and industrial regions representing both developed and developing regions.

Class X: Geography of India
Unit I: India—physical features, climate, natural vegetation and wild life (natural vegetation, wild life, conservation of wild life)

Unit 2: Natural Resources

a. Water resources—uneven and undependable nature of rainfall, the twin problem of floods and famine, flood control, irrigation and drainage, water budget, sources of irrigation, river valley and multipurpose projects.
b. Mineral and power resources—minerals—metallic and nonmetallic mineral fuels, hydroelectricity, their exploration, distribution and extraction, power development, wise use and conservation of mineral and power resources.
c. Land use—forest lands, pasture, and farmlands, settlement and other uses, soil, forest and cattle wealth, fisheries.
d. Agriculture—problems of Indian agriculture, post-independence development, major food, fibre and cash crops, food budget, yield per unit area.

Unit 3: Developing our Resources

a. Manufacturing Industries—agro-based and mineral-based industries, iron and steel, heavy industries, large scale, small scale, and cottage industries, the need to step up industrial production and productivity.
b. Transport and communications—road, railways, waterways and airways, major ports, development of communication.
c. International trade—major exports and imports, major trading partners, recent trends.
d. People—the greatest resource of the country—population, size, distribution and density, composition in terms of age, sex and dependency, rural and urban, growth of population, quantitative vs. qualitative aspects of human population; need and efforts toward planned development of human resources in terms of education, health, occupational and vocational skills, productivity and employment opportunities, need and efforts to stabilize population growth.
e. Area development—case studies from India
   i.   Plantations in Assam
   ii. Tribal area development—Tribals in Andamans and Nicobar

    iii. Agriculture—Suratgarh Farm

    iv. Mineral—Neyveli

    v. Industrial development—Jamshedpur

Unit 4: Field Study Project Work

Any topic of local/regional importance such as irrigation problem in and arid region; deforestation, soil erosion, and afforestation programs in hilly and mountainous areas, effect of cyclones in coastal areas, environmental degradation in an industrial/mining region, and so on.

Civics

List of Projects (Study of some major developments in the national life, for example, role of the nationalized banks in the development of the society, nuclear arms race, food, population, health and sanitation problem, environmental pollution and preservation, and so on.

Economics

Unit I: Understanding an Economy (efficient use of Resources)

Unit II: An Overview of the Indian Economy (population situation in India: poverty, unemployment, consumer education)

Unit IV: Toward Economic Development (inputs in agriculture, new technology in agriculture, food problem in India, future outlook for agriculture, balanced industrial structure, future outlook for industrial development, foreign trade—exports & imports)

Appendix 4.6: Guidelines and Syllabi for Secondary Stage (1988)

Work Experience: Essential Activities

1. Use of bus and railway time-tables.
2. Milking of dairy animals.
3. Reception work in school.
4. Preparation and distribution of mid-day meal/snacks in composite schools.
5. Preparation of teaching aids and equipment for self and lower classes.
6. Helping school authorities in organizing exhibitions, picnics, tours and excursions.
7. First aid activities like counting of pulse, taking of temperature, and bandaging of wounds after cleaning them.
8. Helping traffic police in the regulation of traffic.
9. Plantation of shady/fuel/ornamental/avenue trees.
10. Preparation of family budget and maintenance of daily household accounts.
11. Acquaintance with common fertilizers and pesticides and their application with appropriate equipment.
12. Acquaintance with common pests and plant diseases and use of simple chemical and plant protection equipment.

13. Handling farm animals for feeding, washing or general examination.
14. Preparation of soak-pit for collecting liquid refuse from the cattle shed.
15. Studying the nutrition and health status of people in a village/city/slum/tribal area.
16. Helping community health programs for enhancing the nutrition, health, and environmental status of the community through door-to-door contact programs.
17. Digging trench latrines during festivals and maintaining them hygienically.
18. Participation in adult literacy program.
19. Helping in child-care in crèches.
20. Volunteer work in hospitals and fairs, during floods and famines, and in accidents.

Chapter

5

Global Trends in Environmental Education and Implementation in India

---

> **Worth a Thought!**
>
>
>
> Since the mid 20th century environment-related education began to receive global attention. Has environmental education in India followed similar trends? It would be interesting to dig this out.

Chapter Overview

The chapter attempts to bring out whether the global trends in environmental education have any semblance or corresponding impact on the trends in India. Besides, the details of implementation of environmental education in India highlighting the role of judiciary in the process of implementation are also discussed. Project-based environmental education has been specifically discussed keeping in view its importance which is highlighted in the latest national curriculum framework and as pointed out by various studies. It is envisaged that the chapter will be able to facilitate the readers to:

- correlate the global trends in environmental education with that of India.
- correlate the global initiatives and the enactment of various legislations related to the environment in India.
- explain the nature of implementation of environmental education in India.
- appreciate the intervention of the Hon'ble Supreme court in the implementation of environmental education in India.
- identify the barriers in the implementation of environmental education in India.
- justify the importance of project-based environmental education.
- design appropriate projects for project-based environmental education.
- apply project-based environmental education in the teaching–learning practices.

Introduction

In the preceding chapters, we learnt about the developments in environmental education and its evolution at the international as well as at the national level. Here, we shall try to find out whether there is any correlation between the two and how India has adapted to the changes at the international scenario. We shall learn about environmental education trends, the changes and its present status in India. For a clear understanding of it all, discussions will be broadly in three sections. The first part will look into how the trends and approaches in the field of environmental education in India have changed in tune with the developments and changes that have taken place at the international scenario.

The second section will focus on the status of the implementation of environmental education in India. Here, the discussion will include the intervention of the Hon'ble Supreme Court of India in the implementation of environmental education, its present nature of implementation, different areas of focus, and barriers in implementation. This section of the book also presents the result of a comparative study of the implementation of environmental education in schools in India and in the USA, in brief.

The last part of our discussions is devoted to project-based environmental education keeping in view its importance as envisaged in the National Curriculum Framework 2005 and, thereafter, as mentioned in the affidavit submitted to the Hon'ble Supreme Court. This section looks into how far project-based environmental education, as envisaged in these documents, is practicable in actual situations in schools.

5.1 Trends in India vis-à-vis Global Initiatives

To begin with, there is a need to understand how environmental education trends in India have changed (or appear to have changed) in the wake of the changes and developments that have taken place at the international level in the past few decades. For this purpose, we shall discuss, in brief, a few selected programs and projects that have been initiated at the global level and have influenced the Indian scenario. However, it is not claimed that the changes taking place in India, as will be discussed later, is purely the result of the developments taking place globally. In most instances it presents the possible impact of global developments in India, while in some the actual impact leading to the changes in India is presented.

5.1.1 International Union for Conservation of Nature (IUCN)

Founded in 1948, IUCN is the world's oldest and largest global environmental organization. At the time of its foundation, it was named International Union for the Protection of Nature (IUPN), the main focus being the protection and conservation of nature and natural resources. Later, in 1956, the name was changed to International Union for Conservation of Nature and Natural Resources. Again in 1990, the organization was renamed World Conservation Union though it continued to use IUCN as its abbreviation. In 2008, the name was reverted back to IUCN. The focus has now expanded to equitable use of natural resources and ecological sustainability.

The ideas promoted by IUCN appear to have influenced curriculum developers in India till the early 1970s. Although conservation of nature and natural resources did not appear in the Secondary Education Commission Report (1952–1953), or the Kothari Commission Report (1964–1966) and not even in the National Policy on Education 1968 (GoI 1968), some aspects of conservation were reflected in the documents, such as local sanitation, water supply, concepts, principles, and processes in the physical and biological environment. However, the curricular materials developed subsequent to NPE-1968 were more explicit, in that environmental concerns such as air and water pollution, pesticides, conservation of natural resources, and so on, found place in the curriculum.

5.1.2 The United Nations Conference on the Human Environment Organized in Stockholm in 1972

This conference marked a milestone for environmental education. Recommendation 96 of the conference called for the development of environmental education as one of the most critical elements of an all-out attack on the world's environmental crisis.

The outcome of the Stockholm Conference seems to have a significant impact on the development of India's first national curriculum framework for school education. Not only were the concerns and concepts added noticeably, but also, for the first time, the term 'environmental education' appeared in the national document related to education. Soon after this international conference on environment, the Water Pollution Control Act of 1974 came on the statute book in India. Interestingly, during the leadership of Indira Gandhi, in the 42nd amendment of the Constitution in 1976, Articles 48-A and 51-A (g) were inserted. Article 48-A states "The State shall endeavour to protect and improve the environment and to safeguard the forests and wild life of the country" and Article 51-A (g) requires every citizen to protect and improve the natural environment including forests, lakes, rivers, and wild life, and to have compassion for living creatures. These amendments could well be considered the positive outcomes of the Stockholm Conference which was attended by the then Prime Minister Indira Gandhi wherein she had strongly advocated the need to ensure protection of the environment without ignoring social issues such as poverty. These laid the foundation for the creation of Department of Environment in 1980, later renamed as the Ministry of Environment and Forests in 1985 and the Ministry of Environment, Forests, and Climate Change in 2014. Therefore, subsequent to the conference, many new Acts came into being while several others were amended such as:

- Water (Prevention and Control of Pollution) Act, 1974, Amended in 1988
- Air (Prevention and Control of Pollution) Act, 1981, Amended in 1987
- Wild Life (Protection) Act, 1972, Amendment in 1982, 1986, 1991, 1993, 2002, 2006, 2013
- Forest (Conservation) Act, 1980, Amendment in 1988
- Environment (Protection) Act, 1986
- Biodiversity Act, 2000

Amongst these, special mention may be made of the Environment (Protection) Act, 1986 which was passed by the Parliament based on Article 253[1] of the Constitution of India as a result of the Stockholm Conference.

---

[1] Article 253 of the Constitution of India (1949): "*Legislation for giving effect to international agreements*— Notwithstanding anything in the foregoing provisions of this chapter, Parliament has power to make any law for the whole or any part of the territory of India for implementing any treaty, agreement, or convention with any other country or countries or any decision made at any international conference, association, or other body."

The National Green Tribunal Act, 2009 was enacted,

[T]o provide for the establishment of a National Green Tribunal for the effective and expeditious disposal of cases relating to environmental protection and conservation of forests and other natural resources including enforcement of any legal right relating to environment and giving relief and compensation for damages to persons and property and for matters connected therewith or incidental thereto.

The enactment of this Act mentioned India being party to the decisions taken at the United Nations Conference on the Human Environment, Stockholm in June 1972 and the UN Conference on Environment and Development held at Rio de Janeiro in June 1992 and also the Article 21 of the Constitution (GoI 2009).

JUST A MOMENT

Recall news items that appear in the newspaper, TV, and so on, every now and then regarding violation of environmental laws by industries, builders, etc. Do you think our existing laws are strong enough to stop offenders from repeating the offence?

5.1.3 International Environmental Education Programme (IEEP)

As mentioned in Chapter 1, in response to Recommendation 96 of the Stockholm Conference, UNESCO and UNEP initiated the IEEP in 1975 to promote reflection and action, as well as international cooperation in this field. IEEP carried out numerous activities from 1975 to 1983 during which it organized several meetings at the international and regional levels. Lasting for twenty years (1975–1995), the IEEP provided technical, advisory, and financial support to governments, civil society groups and institutions of learning (UNEP 2005, 41). The International Environmental Education Workshop held at Belgrade (formerly in Yugoslavia, now in Serbia) on 13–22 October 1975 was one of the initiatives. The Belgrade Charter was the culmination of the workshop. Under the IEEP, the first intergovernmental conference on environmental education was held in Tbilisi, USSR (now in Georgia), on 14–26 October 1977. The Tbilisi Conference laid the basis for the development of environmental education at the international level as well as strategies for the advancement of environmental education at the national level and the promotion of international cooperation. The challenges that environmental problems pose to the society and the role that education can and must play in solving such problems was highlighted more than ever. The conference laid down the goals, objectives, and guiding principles of environmental education.

Following the Belgrade Charter and the Tbilisi Conference, environmental education in India came to be raised to another level. For example, the National Policy on Education 1986 (NPE-1986) more explicitly mentioned concerns related to the environment by reiterating and highlighting the 'fundamental duties' as laid down in the Indian Constitution, protection of the environment being one. It also stressed on the "paramount need to create a consciousness of the environment" and the need to integrate this aspect in the entire educational process (GoI 1986). The concerns laid down in this document was important because being a national policy document, such concerns were subsequently reflected in all the national curriculum frameworks brought out by India such as the National Curriculum for Elementary and Secondary Education—A Framework (Revised Version) (NCERT 1988), the National Curriculum Framework for School Education (NCERT 2000), the National Curriculum Framework (NCERT 2005) and the National Curriculum Framework for Teacher Education—Towards Preparing Professional and Humane Teacher 2009. It is seen that the NPE-1986 will continue to have an influence over future documents as well till a new policy document overriding the NPE-1986 is brought out. Hence, as of now, the NPE-1986 can be considered the most important guiding document with regard to environmental education in India.

5.1.4 IEEP Activities in India's Context

The significant role played by the twenty-three pilot projects undertaken by the IEEP is irrefutable. These initiatives have greatly contributed to the incorporation of environmental education into the national educational processes by facilitating the training of teachers and educators by developing educational and informational materials suitable to local environmental situations end conditions, and by sensitizing the population in general (UNESCO 1984). Out of the twenty-three projects, two were specific to India which are:

- **Pilot Project for Primary Schools, India (1979–1980):** This project was developed by the National Council of Education Research (NCERT) of India. The project's main objective was preparation and experimentation of the implementation of environmental education modules in primary schools of several Indian states, including Assam, Punjab, Karnataka, and Tamil Nadu. In this connection, the pilot project organized workshops for teachers of the areas involved. During these workshops, teachers and specialists refined the modules prepared and provided appropriate guidelines for their use. The modules were implemented and evaluated on a national scale.
- **Pilot Project on Environmental Problems of Urban Marginal Areas, India (1981–1983):** This project aimed at developing multimedia educational materials related to major environmental problems of marginal urban settlements (hygiene, nutrition, pollution, and other aspects), the training of community leaders, and the experimental development of actions-oriented toward improvement of the environmental quality of the community concerned in India.

IEEP also conducted several training of environmental education professionals and activists. Participants/experts from India who attended it benefited from the following programs implemented through different periods:

- International Training Course in Environmental Education organized on 1–28 September 1982 in Prague and other towns of the Czechoslovak Socialist Republic.
- Regional Training Workshop for Asia. This training workshop for Asia and Oceania was organized in September 1980 in Bangkok, Thailand. The workshop reviewed environmental education progress in the region and established concrete steps that

may be taken to enhance environmental education for both in-school and out-of-school populations.

- Sub-regional Workshop on Teacher Training in Environmental Education for Asia was organized in March 1983 in New Delhi, India. The objectives of the workshop were to familiarize educators with the contents of the series of EE teacher training modules prepared by the International EE Program; explore ways for their local adaptation and use; and exchange information and experience on EE material development in the sub-region.

JUST A MOMENT

A good number of initiatives seem to have been undertaken in India to improve the implementation of environmental education in schools. Do you think such initiatives have made visible impact on the ground?

5.1.5 Brundtland Commission Report, Agenda 21, Decade of Education for Sustainable Development

It may be noted that social and economic issues were inherent in all the initiatives undertaken to tackle environmental issues facing the world at large. The initiatives, however, focused largely on addressing only the ecological impact of the ever-increasing unrestricted development. A need was, therefore, felt to formalize a broader strategy to comprehensively address both the needs of the society and the environment. After an intense exercise which was initiated in the mid-1980s, the United Nations in 1987 brought out the Report of the World Commission on Environment and Development: Our Common Future, popularly known as the Brundtland Commission Report, wherein sustainable development was endorsed as an overarching framework or construct for future development policy at all levels of government.

Soon after the Brundtland Commission Report, from 1987 to 1992, the 40 chapters of the Agenda 21 on sustainability (Refer to Chapter 1, Box 1.4) were written by different committees. The Agenda 21 was adopted by over 178 nations as the official policy at the UN Conference on Environment and Development, popularly known as the Earth Summit held in Rio de Janeiro, Brazil, on 3–14 June 1992 (UN 1993). One of the most important documents in the conference, the Rio Declaration on Environment and Development, set out 27 principles (Box 5.1) that aim to guide international actions on the basis of environmental and economic responsibility toward SD. Chapter 36 of the Agenda, "Promoting Education, Public Awareness, and Training," underlines global concerns related to education and sustainability. In addition, each of the forty chapters includes education as a component in the implementation strategy.

The Johannesburg World Summit on Sustainable Development in 2002 deepened the commitments toward sustainable development, especially by proposing that the United Nations should consider adopting a decade of education for sustainable development beginning 2005. The UN General Assembly subsequently proclaimed the period 2005–2014 as the UN Decade of Education for Sustainable Development (UNDESD).

BOX

Rio Declaration on Environment and Development

REPORT OF THE UNITED NATIONS CONFERENCE ON ENVIRONMENT AND
DEVELOPMENT
(Rio de Janeiro, 3-14 June 1992)

RIO DECLARATION ON ENVIRONMENT AND DEVELOPMENT

The United Nations Conference on Environment and Development,

Having met at Rio de Janeiro from 3 to 14 June 1992,

Reaffirming the Declaration of the United Nations Conference on the Human Environment, adopted at Stockholm on 16 June 1972, a/ and seeking to build upon it,

With the goal of establishing a new and equitable global partnership through the creation of new levels of cooperation among States, key sectors of societies and people,

Working toward international agreements which respect the interests of all and protect the integrity of the global environmental and developmental system,

Recognizing the integral and interdependent nature of the Earth, our home,

Proclaims that:

Principle

Human beings are at the centre of concerns for sustainable development. They are entitled to a healthy and productive life in harmony with nature.

Principle

States have, in accordance with the Charter of the United Nations and the principles of international law, the sovereign right to exploit their own resources pursuant to their own environmental and developmental policies, and the responsibility to ensure that activities within their jurisdiction or control do not cause damage to the environment of other States or of areas beyond the limits of national jurisdiction.

Principle

The right to development must be fulfilled so as to equitably meet developmental and environmental needs of present and future generations.

Principle 4

In order to achieve sustainable development, environmental protection shall constitute an integral part of the development process and cannot be considered in isolation from it.

Principle

All States and all people shall cooperate in the essential task of eradicating poverty as an indispensable requirement for sustainable development, in order to decrease the disparities in standards of living and better meet the needs of the majority of the people of the world.

Principle

The special situation and needs of developing countries, particularly the least developed and those most environmentally vulnerable, shall be given special priority. International actions in the field of environment and development should also address the interests and needs of all countries.

(Continued)

(Continued)

Principle

States shall cooperate in a spirit of global partnership to conserve, protect and restore the health and integrity of the Earth's ecosystem. In view of the different contributions to global environmental degradation, States have common but differentiated responsibilities. The developed countries acknowledge the responsibility that they bear in the international pursuit of sustainable development in view of the pressures their societies place on the global environment and of the technologies and financial resources they command.

Principle

To achieve sustainable development and a higher quality of life for all people, States should reduce and eliminate unsustainable patterns of production and consumption and promote appropriate demographic policies.

Principle

States should cooperate to strengthen endogenous capacity-building for sustainable development by improving scientific understanding through exchanges of scientific and technological knowledge, and by enhancing the development, adaptation, diffusion and transfer of technologies, including new and innovative technologies.

Principle 10

Environmental issues are best handled with the participation of all concerned citizens, at the relevant level. At the national level, each individual shall have appropriate access to information concerning the environment that is held by public authorities, including information on hazardous materials and activities in their communities, and the opportunity to participate in decision-making processes. States shall facilitate and encourage public awareness and participation by making information widely available. Effective access to judicial and administrative proceedings including redress and remedy, shall be provided.

Principle

States shall enact effective environmental legislation. Environmental standards, management objectives and priorities should reflect the environmental and developmental context to which they apply. Standards applied by some countries may be inappropriate and of unwarranted economic and social cost to other countries, in particular developing countries.

Principle

States should cooperate to promote a supportive and open international economic system that would lead to economic growth and sustainable development in all countries, to better address the problems of environmental degradation. Trade policy measures for environmental purposes should not constitute a means of arbitrary or unjustifiable discrimination or a disguised restriction on international trade. Unilateral actions to deal with environmental challenges outside the jurisdiction of the importing country should be avoided. Environmental measures addressing transboundary or global environmental problems should, as far as possible, be based on an international consensus.

Principle

States shall develop national law regarding liability and compensation for the victims of pollution and other environmental damage. States shall also cooperate in an expeditious and more

(Continued)

(Continued)

determined manner to develop further international law regarding liability and compensation for adverse effects of environmental damage caused by activities within their jurisdiction or control to areas beyond their jurisdiction.

Principle 14

States should effectively cooperate to discourage or prevent the relocation and transfer to other States of any activities and substances that cause severe environmental degradation or are found to be harmful to human health.

Principle

In order to protect the environment, the precautionary approach shall be widely applied by States according to their capabilities. Where there are threats of serious or irreversible damage, lack of full scientific certainty shall not be used as a reason for postponing cost-effective measures to prevent environmental degradation.

Principle

National authorities should endeavour to promote the internalization of environmental costs and the use of economic instruments, taking into account the approach that the polluter should, in principle, bear the cost of pollution, with due regard to the public interest and without distorting international trade and investment.

Principle

Environmental impact assessment, as a national instrument, shall be undertaken for proposed activities that are likely to have a significant adverse impact on the environment and are subject to a decision of a competent national authority.

Principle

States shall immediately notify other States of any natural disasters or other emergencies that are likely to produce sudden harmful effects on the environment of those States. Every effort shall be made by the international community to help States so afflicted.

Principle

States shall provide prior and timely notification and relevant information to potentially affected States on activities that may have a significant adverse transboundary environmental effect and shall consult with those States at an early stage and in good faith.

Principle 20

Women have a vital role in environmental management and development. Their full participation is therefore essential to achieve sustainable development.

Principle

The creativity, ideals and courage of the youth of the world should be mobilized to forge a global partnership in order to achieve sustainable development and ensure a better future for all.

(Continued)

(Continued)

Principle

Indigenous people and their communities and other local communities have a vital role in environmental management and development because of their knowledge and traditional practices. States should recognize and duly support their identity, culture and interests and enable their effective participation in the achievement of sustainable development.

Principle

The environment and natural resources of people under oppression, domination and occupation shall be protected.

Principle 24

Warfare is inherently destructive of sustainable development. States shall therefore respect international law providing protection for the environment in times of armed conflict and cooperate in its further development, as necessary.

Principle

Peace, development and environmental protection are interdependent and indivisible.

Principle

States shall resolve all their environmental disputes peacefully and by appropriate means in accordance with the Charter of the United Nations.

Principle

States and people shall cooperate in good faith and in a spirit of partnership in the fulfilment of the principles embodied in this Declaration and in the further development of international law in the field of sustainable development.

In view of the impressive efforts put forward for the implementation of the programs of action as laid down in Agenda 21, it was naturally expected that the National Curriculum Framework for School Education brought out in 2000 would center around or focus on sustainable development. However, full-fledged education for sustainable development (ESD, which is different from sustainable development related education or SD-related education as will be discussed in detail in Chapter 9) or sustainable development as an emerging concern was not reflected in the document. Many aspects related to sustainable development, however, were spread all through the curriculum framework which could be comparable to SD-related education. For example, issues related to poverty, health, demography, population, and environment have been discussed, but without relating it to sustainable development. Nevertheless, this lapse was addressed to some extent in the documents published thereafter, including the Environmental Education in Schools—Syllabus for Environmental Education (2004) and the National Curriculum Framework 2005. These documents pointed out the importance and necessity of environmental education to facilitate the move toward sustainable development. However, focus remained on tackling environmental issues at different levels rather than highlighting all the components of sustainable development, that is, society, economy, and environment. Hence, a closer look revealed that the true essence of sustainable development was missing in these documents as well. But in the textbooks that were developed based on these documents, it was noted that sustainable development was included in some subject disciplines such as economics and geography. Though sustainable development was not clearly reflected in the environmental education syllabus of 2004 or the NCF-2005, several initiatives were undertaken by NGOs working in the field to promote sustainable practices in schools in different parts of the country.

Setting itself apart from other documents, the National Curriculum Framework for Teacher Education—Towards Preparing Professional and Humane Teacher 2009, however, briefly, yet precisely, emphasized the need to educate future generations through perspectives of gender equity, the perspectives that develop values for peace, respect the rights of all, respect and value work, and in the perspective of the present ecological crisis to promote equitable and sustainable development.[2]

JUST A MOMENT

Are you familiar with the concept of sustainable development? Has it been discussed satisfactorily in schools?

5.2 Implementation of EE in India

As discussed in the previous chapters, environmental education in India has gone through several changes and has evolved over the years to find a significant niche in different educational processes and curricula. The country has been trying to keep pace with the world in the field of environmental education and its efforts are now beginning to be visible. There is growing awareness among the population across the country as today environment-related studies are being carried out at all levels of education in schools and colleges. Its promotion is gradually becoming widespread, though the country still has a long way to go. A recent survey of the World Health Organization (WHO) that lists India among the top 10 most polluted countries in the world[3] is a reminder of the need to increasingly focus on environmental education. Though there are criticisms to this survey report, one cannot really deny the fact that the air in many cities of our country is indeed polluted beyond safe limits. More and more people, including young students, are increasingly becoming conscious of his environment and the need to protect it, which is encouraging. The number of environmentalists and NGOs contributing in the area of environmental protection and nature conservation is also multiplying and their contributions ever increasingly evident. Looking at the growing awareness among all sections of the society, it may be said that the country has made some progress in

---

[2] http://www.education.nic.in/Elementary/NCFTE-31.08.2009.pdf (accessed on 11 May 2010)
[3] The Weather Channel (http://in.weather.com/story/news/worlds-50-most-polluted-countries-20140513; http://www.abc.net.au/news/2014-05-08/10-countries-with-the-worlds-dirtiest-air/5438872 (accessed on 28 June 2015)

environmental education. In this section, we shall discuss how far environmental education has come to be what it is in India today and the present status of its implementation.

5.2.1 Intervention of the Hon'ble Supreme Court of India

To initiate our discussion, we may recall M.C. Mehta's writ petition No. 860/1991. For it was this petition which resulted in the Hon'ble Supreme Court order that has shaped the present status of implementation of environmental education in the country, to a large extent. It may be mentioned that NCERT was the respondent in the case representing all school systems of the country.

The previous chapter as well as in the discussions so far in this chapter suggest that India has made considerable efforts to incorporate environmental education in the school curriculum. However, the initiatives taken so far seemed to be too little and ineffective as far as ground reality is concerned. It was found lacking to tackle the fast deteriorating environment. Hence in 1991, M.C. Mehta filed a public interest litigation (PIL), stating that environment should be made a compulsory subject in schools and colleges in a graded system so that there would be a general growth of awareness. Based on which, the Hon'ble Court in its order dated 22 November 1991 stated,

> We accept on principle that through the medium of education awareness of the environment and its problems related to pollution should be taught as a compulsory subject...So far as education up to the college level is concerned, we would require every state government and every education board connected with education up to matriculation or even intermediate college to immediately take steps to enforce compulsory education on environment in a graded way. This should be done in such a manner that in the next academic year there would be compliance of this requirement.

Following the Hon'ble Supreme Court judgment, some steps were undertaken by states and other authorities concerned to comply with the court directions. Mehta, however, contended that the steps taken by many states and authorities were insufficient and not in conformity with the spirit and object of the court order. He submitted that the states and other authorities concerned should prescribe a suitable syllabus by way of a subject on environmental awareness, not only at the primary level of education but also in higher courses. He also submitted that in the absence of such uniform prescribed syllabus in educational institutions in various states different institutions were adopting different methods, some of which are only basic and which do not fulfill the requirements of the Hon'ble Court's directions. Based on this, the Hon'ble Supreme Court, on 18 December 2003, directed the NCERT, "to prepare a module syllabus to be taught at different grades and submit the same to this court by the next date of hearing so that we can consider the feasibility to introduce such syllabus uniformly throughout the country at different grades."

Based on the Hon'ble Supreme Court order of 18 December, NCERT, in 2004, came up with the syllabus "EE in schools," so that environmental education can be studied as a separate subject. The court order dated 22 April 2004 stated:

> M.C. Mehta, the petitioner in this petition, submits that the directions should also be given to train the teacher in the subject, but for the time being we do not intend issuing any direction on such request of Mehta. It will be considered at an appropriate time.

The Hon'ble Supreme Court also, in its order dated 13 July 2004, directed that the syllabus prepared by the NCERT for Class I to XII be adopted by every state in their respective schools. The order also stated, "NCERT is appointed as a nodal agency to supervise the implementation of this court order."

However, in 2005, when NCERT was given the task of developing a new curriculum framework, the group consisting of experts in the field of environmental education, Focus Group on Habitat and Learning, had a different opinion regarding the implementing environmental education as a separate subject. The group was concerned about adding to the curriculum load if environmental education was included as a separate subject. The group recommended that environmental education could best be done by infusing environment-related concepts at appropriate places in different subjects. Considering this, NCERT, representing schools in India, filed a supplementary affidavit dated 26 November 2007, wherein it mentioned, "The best way of accomplishing the order of the Supreme Court regarding the implementation of environmental education is to infuse the teaching of environmental education as a part of different disciplines while ensuring that adequate time is earmarked for pertinent activities." In its affidavit, NCERT also provided the details of how environmental education would be implemented in different classes. The orders of the Hon'ble Supreme Court as well as the contents of the affidavit submitted by the NCERT to the Hon'ble Supreme Court are important since failing to implement by all the concerned parties (states, UTs, different boards, NCERT, and so on.) as mentioned will amount to contempt of court.

JUST A MOMENT

Reflect on the intervention of the Hon'ble Supreme Court of India in the implementation of environmental education based on a PIL filed by Shri M.C. Mehta. You will appreciate how empowered citizens can impact the nation in a huge way.

5.2.2 Chronology of Important Events in EE in India

A chronology of some of the important events in the evolution of environmental education in India is presented in Table 5.1.

5.2.3 Present Status of EE in India

Environmental education is being implemented in India today in accordance with the details mentioned in the affidavit filed by NCERT in November 2007 and admitted by the Hon'ble Supreme Court in December 2010. Accordingly, environmental education is being imparted at different levels in schools in the following manner:

- Environmental education for Classes I and II: EE concerns and issues transacted through activities
- Environmental education for Classes III to V: Environmental education is imparted through a subject namely EVS (Environmental Studies)

Table 5.1	Chronology of Important Events in Environmental Education in India

Year	Event
1962	Article (51A) 'Fundamental Duties' of the Constitution was amended. Clause (g), thereof, requires every citizen to protect and improve the natural environment, including forests, lakes, rivers and wild life, and to have compassion for living creatures.
1975	The word Environmental Education was reflected in the first national curriculum framework for school education entitled 'Curriculum for the Ten-year School: A Framework.'
1986	The National Policy on Education was prepared which highlights the importance of protection of the environment and to create a consciousness of the environment which should inform teaching in schools and colleges in the entire educational process.
1988	A centrally sponsored scheme of Environmental Orientation to School Education was launched by the Ministry of Human Resource Development that will allow educational programs in schools to be fully harmonized with the local environmental situation and concerns.
1991	Writ petition (Civil) No. 860/1991was filed in the Hon'ble Supreme Court of India by M.C. Mehta with a petition to make environmental education a compulsory subject.
1991 (22 November)	The Hon'ble Supreme Court of India directed all educational institutions to teach environment and its problems related to pollution as a compulsory subject.
2003 (18 December)	The Hon'ble Supreme Court of India directed NCERT to prepare a module (model) syllabus.
2004	NCERT submitted the module syllabus to the Hon'ble Supreme Court entitled "Environmental Education in Schools: Syllabus for Environmental Education in Schools," in pursuance of the court's order dated 18 December 2003.
2004 (13 July)	The Hon'ble Supreme Court directed every state to adopt the syllabus prepared by NCERT for Class I to XII in their respective schools. The Hon'ble Supreme Court directed NCERT to be appointed as a nodal agency to supervise the implementation of the court's order.
2007 (26 November)	NCERT submitted a supplementary affidavit before the Hon'ble Supreme Court to review model syllabus in consonance with the NCF 2005 and presented the details of implementation of environmental education in schools.
2010 (3 December)	The Hon'ble Supreme Court admitted the affidavit filed by the NCERT. The Writ petition (Civil) 860/1990 is disposed of.

- Environmental education for Classes VI to X: Environmental education is imparted through the infusion approach
- Environmental education for Classes XI and XII: Environmental education is taught as a separate and compulsory project-based syllabus

5.2.3.1 Three-pronged Focus of EE

The National Curriculum Framework 2005 (NCF-2005) stated that:

> [T]he main focus of EE should be to expose students to the real-life world, natural and social, in which they live; to enable them to analyse, evaluate, and draw inferences about problems and concerns related to the environment; to add, where possible, to our understanding of environmental issues; and to promote positive environmental actions in order to facilitate the move towards sustainable development. To achieve these goals, the curriculum may be based on: (i) Learning about the environment (ii) Learning through the environment, and (iii) Learning for the environment.

This three-pronged approach of achieving the goals of environmental education, that is, learning 'about,' 'through,' and 'for' the environment follows the classification of environmental education by A.M. Lucas which is education 'about,' 'in,' and 'for' the environment. As we have seen the international scenario of implementation of environmental education, as discussed in Chapter 3, even in India the focus has been largely on the 'about' component, wherein only information is transmitted which enhances only the cognitive knowledge. The 'through' and 'for' components are yet to be seen to be considered in the school curriculum. As against what was envisaged in the NCF-2005, neither is there exposure to real-world situation nor are students provided opportunities to participate in resolution of environmental issues. In a recent study conducted at the national level to analyze the status of the biology curriculum at the higher secondary stage (Classes XI and XII) it was found that students are very rarely taken out of the four walls of their classroom as part of their teaching–learning process, contrary to what is expected to be a regular feature in the transaction of Biology curriculum (Shimray et al. 2013). This state of affairs indicates that meaningful environmental education is still a distant dream.

JUST A MOMENT

What do you think is the reason for the gap that exist between theory and practice in the implementation of environmental education?

5.2.3.2 Curricular Materials in EE

Following the infusion approach, environment-related topics and concerns have been infused at relevant places in all the textbooks developed by NCERT in the light of NCF-2005. While these are mostly information-based, relevant projects have also been incorporated at appropriate places in the textbooks. For Classes III to V, a separate textbook, namely, environmental studies, is in use. Besides these, NCERT also brought out other supplementary and complementary curricular materials such as model project books for Classes VI to XII and a teachers' handbook for project-based environmental education at the higher secondary stage. Many state boards have adopted or adapted these books, while others have developed theirs in a similar line. These positive developments suggest that adequate measures have been taken with regard to development of curricular materials.

Photo 5.1   Students and Teachers during a Nature Trail

Photo 5.2   Students Conveying the Message of Conservation through Folk Dance and Folk Lore of Assam

Photo Courtesy: WWF-India

Photo 5.3   A Campaign by the ESD Model School in Deepor Beel, Assam

Photo Courtesy: WWF-India

However, one might wonder about the situation in private schools which outnumber government or government-supported schools in the country. We know that, in most cases, these schools do not use the curricular materials developed by NCERT. These schools prescribe curricular materials developed by private publishers which may or may not reflect the philosophies of NCF-2005 with regard to environmental education. It is yet to be ascertained whether environment-related concerns have been infused sufficiently in such materials. For example, in spite of the recommendation of the NCF-2005 and an affidavit that for Classes III to V there would be a single subject environmental studies, it is found that many private schools still use two subjects—environmental studies (science) and environmental studies (social science). This suggests that there is lack of awareness about the interdisciplinary and holistic approach which is envisaged in the single subject approach which represents the basic philosophy of environmental education.

5.2.3.3 Assessment-related Concerns

NCERT committed in the affidavit submitted to the Supreme Court, dated 26 November 2007, that tests of environment-related concerns and components would be taken in the examination of the concerned subjects in which they have been infused. It also mentioned that all examination papers should compulsorily have questions pertaining to the environmental education component present in the text. It categorically mentioned that at the Class X-level examination, papers of different subjects should have compulsory questions on the concepts of environmental education and that 10 percent of the grand total of marks is earmarked for environmental education. The affidavit also mentioned that project work should receive enough importance in the evaluation which should be evaluated orally by an internal evaluator along with an external evaluator. Similarly, for the project-based syllabus at the higher secondary stage, the affidavit clearly mentioned how the core syllabus as well as the projects would be evaluated.

The affidavit also stated that CBSE and other state boards should ensure that appropriate measures are taken to implement them.[4] In spite of such details presented in the affidavit, it is yet to be ascertained how much of the court directions are being implemented in schools. Although there is no research study to back the claim, it is evident from interactions with teachers that the implementation falls much short of the expectations. There could be many reasons as to why it is not implemented. Is it because the affidavit submitted to the Supreme Court is not taken seriously by the boards? Is it because schools are not given strict instructions to follow the affidavit? Is it because schools are still not sure how exactly to go about as they have not been oriented to take up such task? One can only get the answers by exploring the reasons through intensive and extensive research.

5.2.3.4 Monitoring Implementation of EE

Monitoring the implementation of environmental education in schools in India is another matter of concern. Some of the reasons being the countless number of schools and educational institutions spread out in all corners of the country, including rural and remote places, and the absence of a systematic monitoring system. Strict monitoring is necessary not only to ensure implementation but also to find out the issues faced by different schools in the implementation and to look for ways to resolve such issues. Only then environmental education will be meaningfully implemented. The Supreme Court had in its order dated 13 July 2004 directed NCERT to be the nodal agency to monitor the implementation of environmental education in schools throughout the country.[5] As it has been contributing tremendously in the improvement of school education throughout the country, serious efforts by the NCERT will be very crucial to ensure effective monitoring of environmental education implementation which will be a huge challenge given the vastness of our country.

5.2.3.5 Implementation in States and Union Territories

Following the NCF-2005 recommendations and the environmental education-related curricular materials brought out by NCERT, different states and UTs are adapting or adopting the exercise undertaken by NCERT. As the affidavit submitted by NCERT was for the entire schools and school systems throughout the country, the methods of implementation are essentially in tune with those suggested by NCERT.

---

[4] http://ncert.nic.in/book_publishing/environ_edu/Affidavit.pdf (accessed on 4 July 2014)
[5] http://ncert.nic.in/book_publishing/environ_edu/13.07.pdf (accessed on 4 July 2014)

5.2.3.6 Barriers in Implementation

Despite the long history of environmental education in India, its formal introduction and implementation in the country's educational system is still at its nascent stage. Hence, it is difficult to say at this juncture whether environmental education has been successfully implemented in schools in India. A lot has been done, yet much remains to be done, especially through research in the area of environmental education to assess and analyze the existing status and to find out ways to overcome the shortcomings or limitations and loopholes. Since research in the area is wanting in India, we may take cue from researches undertaken in other countries at the international level. Most researchers admit that there is a problem in successful implementation of environmental education in schools owing to certain prevalent barriers. Ham and Sewing (1988 cited in Lane 2006; Bruyere et al. 2012, 330) categorized the most prevalent barriers into the following:

- Conceptual barriers: Lack of consensus about the scope and content of environmental education. Several misconceptions about environmental education help to promote its lack of a consistent identity. One such misconception is that environmental education is relevant only to science curricula.
- Logistical barriers: Perceived lack of time, funding, resources, suitable class sizes, and so on.
- Educational barriers: Teachers' misgivings about their own competence to conduct environmental education programs. Teachers with a poor background in a discipline may lack the personal interest or commitment to provide adequate instruction in that subject area.
- Attitudinal barriers: Teachers' attitudes toward environmental education and science instruction often are found to hinder environmental education implementation. The supposition is that if teachers do not have positive attitudes toward environmental education, very little instruction in this area will occur in the classroom (Lane 2006, 17–19).

Similarly, Ballantyne (1995 cited in Monde 2011, 20) clearly identifies problems with management of cross-disciplinary approaches or infusion and shortage of qualified and experienced environmental teacher educators as important barriers. While Scott (1996 cited in Monde 2011, 20) adds lack of practice in terms of working with students and schools and the lack of opportunity to deliver environmental education goals through preservice courses as the additional limits for implementation of environmental education, little effort is being put in amongst the in-service teachers to make-up for the gaps that exist in preservice courses. Many teachers have never been involved in in-service environmental education trainings which ultimately hampers its implementation (Filho and O'Loan 1996 and Ketlhoilwe 2007 cited in Monde 2011).

Of late, a barrier of a completely different kind has come to be recognized. This is related to the lack of clarity on the part of curriculum developers, educators, or practitioners as to whether they are implementing environmental education or ESD. The documents do not specify explicitly what is expected of the course. Since sustainable development is increasingly becoming popular, environmental education is considered to be redundant and it has become a trend to 'practice' ESD even without understanding what ESD is. But at the end of the day it so turns out that neither EE nor ESD is practiced in reality.

From the barriers mentioned above, one, some, or all of the barriers would invariably apply to teachers in India as well. Therefore, attempts to bring about successful implementation of environmental education should include adoption of measures to overcome such barriers. Of such barriers, one that stands out with regard to the implementation in India is related to the infusion approach which is prescribed by the curriculum framework. We have learned in Chapter 3 on EE approaches that infusion is not as simple as adding a few facts and information about environment-related concerns in different topics of different subjects. It involves an elaborate process of incorporating environmental concepts into existing subjects and understandings, as we now know, for its successful implementation. Therefore, the success of implementation of environmental education largely depends on how well the infusion approach is understood. But unfortunately, it has been observed that practicing teachers in India are invariably not aware of or familiar with the term 'infusion' or the 'infusion approach' of environmental education. This inadequacy could be due to lack of coherence between the curriculum framework developed for schools and the curriculum framework developed for preservice course or the in-service courses for teachers. As a result, there is no mention of infusion approach in all the professional development courses. We shall be discussing in detail about this issue in the ensuing chapters and especially in Chapter 8 when we discuss the issues concerning teacher education. Closely connected with the issue of infusion approach is the understanding that beyond Class V there is no more environmental education. Since the infusion approach is not discussed in the preservice courses or any other professional development courses, student-teachers or in-service teachers assume that environmental education is done only through EVS as a composite subject from Classes III to V. This is an issue which needs to be looked at very seriously. A study conducted recently amongst teacher educators from various District Institutes of Education and Training (DIETs) of the country revealed that much needs to be done to familiarize and strengthen educators on the infusion approach (Shimray 2015). Other important issues which hampers implementation of environmental education have also been listed by NCERT (1981, 56).

- The classroom teacher faces a problem in getting proper guidance to carry out some of the activities planned;
- Supplementary and reference materials are not easily available;
- The teacher does not get administrative support unless fellow teachers, headmasters, and supervisory staff are also properly oriented for the environmental education program;
- The teacher gets little time for proper planning of activities;
- The teacher loses interest in the new approach in the absence of regular follow-up action.
- The insistence on completion of the syllabus places too many constraints on teachers for them to be innovative.

These are only some of the practical barriers prevalent in schools throughout the country. There are many other barriers such as those relating to larger interest of the nation wherein environmental education might not be a priority, role of different stakeholders, lack of coordination and cooperation between different stakeholders, lack of accountability, and so on. Some of these issues are discussed in several sections of the book.

5.2.4 EE in Schools in India vis-à-vis USA

Earlier we have seen the status of implementation of environmental education in schools in India. After having a fair idea about what is happening in India one would naturally be curious to know what the status would be like in other countries, especially in the developed nations. For this purpose, a concise study was undertaken to compare the status of India with that of the USA. One might be tempted to think that all must be well in the USA and that comparing the two was unfair. However, there are areas where India is in an advantageous position for implementing environmental education more effectively. For example, in the USA every state develops its own curriculum, while in India we have a more uniform curriculum throughout the country. And when it comes to environmental education we have the Hon'ble Supreme Court's order and the affidavit which binds all the states and boards together. The detail of the study is provided in the Appendix. This will give readers some insight on how a developed nation like the USA is implementing environmental education.

Photo 5.4   The School Principal Participating with the Students in a Plantation Drive in Kanha, Madhya Pradesh

Photo Courtesy: WWF-India

Photo 5.5   Students Exploring in Beans Garden at Learning Gate, Florida, USA

JUST A MOMENT

Of all the barriers mentioned in the chapter, how would you rate 'attitude of teachers toward the environment'?

5.3 Practicability of Project-based Environmental Education in India

The fact that education is the key element in preventing and solving environmental problems (Makki, Khalick, and Boujaoude 2003; Oweini and Houri 2006; Taskin 2005; Tuncer, Ertepinar, Tekkaya, and Sungur 2005 cited in Genc 2015) has led to environmental education gaining prominence of late. In the previous chapters we have discussed quite elaborately the importance of 'doing' or 'participation' in order to do meaningful environmental education. Studies have also shown that environmental courses administered with teaching methods that encourage more active student engagement enhance students' environmental attitudes and conceptual comprehension (Leeming and Proter 1997; Cheong 2005 cited in Genc 2015). An often suggested activity toward this is getting students involved in meaningful projects, ultimately leading to resolution of environmental problems and issues. Should we distinguish between the two, an environmental problem is a situation in which something is at risk such as an endangered species, lack of clean air, and habitat destruction, whereas an environmental issue is more broad, and refers to the difference of opinion among people as to how the situation, that is, the environmental problem, should be managed (UNESCO 1991, 36). Numerous researchers have pointed out the importance of action or direct involvement of students in investigations (Disinger and Monroe 1994) and become problem-solvers so as to bring about quality environmental actions (Lahiry et al. 1988, 16; Lucas 1980; UNESCO 1980, iii, 15). The National Curriculum Framework 2005 (NCF-2005) is also a strong proponent of this approach. Besides, students also learn best about a situation in the situation (Tilbury 1997). Project-based learning has also been found to have a positive effect on students' environmental attitudes and, at the same time, students find this approach "beneficial, enhancing creativity, encouraging research, and providing permanent learning" (Genc 2015). This helps them to define environmental problems more clearly and take on more active tasks in the solution process. However, it has been found that teachers are apprehensive to move in this direction. It is unclear whether it is because they think the outcome is not worth the effort or because they are not convinced that it is practical. One of the reasons could be because it demands efforts and investments on the part of the teacher as compared to the easiest way of providing more cognitive knowledge. Tilbury (1997) observes that often such action-oriented activities could be related to controversial issues and hence teachers do not want to take the risk. We have mentioned earlier in Chapter 4 about the recommendation of NCF-2005 to include projects and activities in the implementation of environmental education. In this chapter we will discuss more elaborately the place of project-based EE in the present scenario in India and explore the possibilities and advantages of taking up such projects by providing the details of a pilot study that was undertaken.

5.3.1 Project-based EE in India

The NCF-2005 states that projects and activities will be the backbone of any scheme aimed at the effective implementation of environmental education in schools which should be as locale-specific as possible. It further says that in order to inculcate the desirable skills and competencies, it will be imperative to develop a basket of activities and projects that may vary in range in respect of their difficulty levels, coverage of skills, and parameters of environment, as well as the feasibility of carrying them out within the limitations of teacher competency, available resources, and time. The NCF-2005 also recommends the need to carve out separate time for projects and fieldwork from existing periods of SUPW, science, and other subjects, and develop tools and techniques for evaluation of projects and fieldwork. In addition, the task of developing project books along with other associated elements such as carving out separate time for projects and activities, assessment of projects, and so on, were also part of the activities committed in the affidavit that was submitted by the NCERT to the Hon'ble Supreme Court[6] as we had discussed earlier in the chapter.

---

[6] http://ncert.nic.in/book_publishing/environ_edu/Affidavit.pdf (accessed on 4 July 2014)

Photo 5.6   Vermicomposting in ESD Model School

Photo Courtesy: WWF-India

In the light of the above, the NCERT in 2009 developed project books for Class VI to X, entitled *Project Book in Environmental Education,* separately for each class. Subsequently, a project book for the higher secondary stage was also brought out by the NCERT in 2013. In order to connect the projects with the curriculum, the projects included were based on the concepts which were already discussed in the textbooks of different subjects. These projects were only exemplars and the methodologies provided in the project books were also only suggestive. Keeping in view the physical and cultural diversity of the country, it is envisaged that teachers and students can develop their own projects which are locally

Photo 5.7   Cleanliness Drive in Deshbhakta Tarun Ram Phukan M.E. School, Chakradeo (Deepor Beel)

Photo Courtesy: WWF-India

relevant to them. All concerned stakeholders such as state and central boards and other school systems were also informed about the project books. NCERT had even initiated orientation programs on the use of these project books at regional levels. Some states have translated or adapted the project books in their state language. For example, Mizoram has adapted in its state language with modifications in order to contextualize it. However, even five years after its development, it is uncertain as to how far these project books have reached the schools. Shome and Natarajan (2013) reported that such project books are neither known to all the schools nor are they implemented. The reason attributed by them is that the project books are not made mandatory. They did not, however, mention the details of their study. Here, we will not discuss further about the reach of the project books and the reasons for its reach to schools or for not reaching, for that matter. We will limit our attention to the practicability of the projects and how the possible barriers can be avoided or overcome. Though no scientific study has been undertaken to find out the issues facing the teachers and students in taking up such projects on environmental education, Shome and Natarajan (2013), in their article on project-based learning in general, pointed out issues such as lack of time on the part of teachers and lack of interest on the part of students and parents as the main barriers for project-based learning.

Keeping this in view, a pilot study was undertaken to figure out the realities existing in the schools, the possible barriers and difficulties in project-based environmental education, which could be academic or administrative in nature, so that appropriate measures can be worked out to tackle such issues. Since it is a pilot study, the experiences, observations, barriers, and possible suggestions provided will vary widely from place to place and project to project. Nevertheless, given the fact that school systems throughout the country follow a similar pattern in terms of periods and examination, the concerns in general will be comparable irrespective of the school or place.

JUST A MOMENT

How far in your opinion project-based EE will serve the goals of environmental education in general?

5.3.2 Pilot Study on Project-based EE

The following provides the details of the pilot study that was undertaken for one project. For the benefit of the teachers, the important points to be kept in mind at every step are provided as 'Note for teachers' in the box. The procedure which is followed in this project need not and should not be duplicated, but should be modified according to the need and requirement of the place where the study is conducted.

Class for which the study was conducted—Class X
Forming groups: The class was divided into groups consisting of at least three students. A group consisting of three students took up this project.

Note for teachers: It will be more meaningful if a group could include people from different communities or races. This will be environmental education in itself. Disinger and Monroe (1994) call it multicultural education wherein different social and ethnic groups work together to resolve environmental issues while Cole (2007) mentions the possible issues that may arise as a result of forming a group of mixed ethnicity.

Selecting topic: As mentioned earlier, the topics for the projects should be such that the concepts are already in the textbooks and are locally relevant. For this study, the topic Shifting Cultivation was chosen not only because this practice is rampant but also because this topic was a concept mentioned in the science textbook for Class X in the state. On the one hand, it is not ethical to simply do away with this age old practice of agriculture—besides there are no other plausible alternatives—and on the other hand it is also a known fact that changes that have taken place in the shifting cultivation practices contribute to global warming, loss of biodiversity, and loss of fertility of soil. This, therefore, is an important environmental issue that needs to be addressed.

> Note for teachers: The topic for the project should be related to some topics of the existing curriculum. Let the students come out with their choice of project and try to find out why they chose that particular project. If need be, modify the topic by discussing with the group.

Objective: To understand the patterns of shifting cultivation and the issues related to it.

> Note for teachers: Discuss with the group about the possible objectives of the project. It will be easier for the students if the objectives are made as specific as possible. This will give students directions as they carry out the project.

Methodology:

1. For their field study, the group identified a village located about 20 km from their school where shifting cultivation was practiced.

> Note for teachers: Field for the study should not be located very far from the school or from where the students reside. It should also be easily accessible. Problem-prone or conflict-prone locations should be avoided. This is not to be confused with the addressing of issues which are controversial or challenging. Environmental education prepares students to handle such issues and develop problem-solvers (UNESCO 1980, i). Hence, environmental education is sometimes referred to as problem-oriented teaching (UNESCO 1991, 36). Martha (1991 cited in Lane 2006; Monroe 2012) also emphasized the importance of dealing with controversial and challenging issues so as to make environmental education complete, that is, issue resolution. She attributes the lack of eagerness of educators for their learners to venture into the territory of controversial and challenging issues to be the cause of environmental education being perceived as a narrow version of what it actually is. Cole (2007, 35–36) also mentions of resolving controversial local environmental issues as part of environmental education.

2. A questionnaire was developed to obtain information on the following from 20 households:

   (i)   Since how many years they have practiced shifting (*jhum*) cultivation.
   (ii)   Whether there has been difference in the availability of land for shifting cultivation. If so the reason thereof.
   (iii) Whether there is any difference in the number of cycles in their grandparents and their parents' generation and now.

(iv)   Varieties of crops planted.
(v)   Whether there has been decrease or increase in productivity.
(vi)   Whether there has been increase or decrease in pests or plant diseases.
(vii)   Whether they use fertilizers or pesticides to increase productivity.
(viii) In what ways shifting cultivation benefit them.
(ix)   Whether they have other sources of livelihood.
(x)   Whether they can survive without practicing shifting cultivation.
(xi)   Whether they know about the negative impacts of shifting cultivation.

3. Information on the above was collected by the students over a couple of weeks through interaction with the farmers in the village.

Note for teachers: Developing a good questionnaire is very crucial for taking the study in the right direction. Students may find difficulty in obtaining the information for some questions. In such cases, the questionnaire needs to be modified accordingly. When different groups in the class work on different projects, the teacher will be required to carve out separate time or period so that the doubts and other issues related to the project faced by the students can be addressed.

Results: Students compiled the information they had obtained during their field study based on the questions. A simple analysis was done for each question so that they can summarize all the information question-wise. The students then prepared a report of their study.

Note for teachers: Students might need guidance on how to analyze their studies and come out with their reports.

Presentation in class: The group presented their study before the class besides sharing their experiences in the field study such as about transportations to reach the village, the socio-cultural aspects, technologies available, and so on. The group also responded to the queries raised by rest of the students in the class about their study.

Note for teachers: It might be necessary to intervene at times especially when other students might come up with irrelevant questions not with good intent but otherwise. The presentation should be divided amongst the group members so that every student of the group gets the opportunity to present. This will build their confidence in public speaking.

Discussion: It was the most important part of the study. After the presentation by the students further discussions followed. This was done to make sure that all the issues related to shifting cultivation were discussed. Students had only collected the data and did not get much out of it by themselves. For example, students had presented that they found the number of years for shifting cultivation cycle had reduced. So it was important to discuss the ecological implications of this reduction in the number of years in the cycle. It was also important to clarify some of the misconceptions regarding shifting cultivation. Shifting cultivation operates on a basic principle of:

> [A]lternation of short crop phases (usually one or two years of cropping) with phases of natural (or slightly modified) vegetational fallow...The key for the stability of the system, thus lies in retaining a minimum agricultural cycle length (length of the fallow period before the farmer returns to the same site for another cropping phase). It is during the fallow phase that soil fertility recovery occurs, which in turn determines economic yield. In the north-east Indian hill areas, where shifting agriculture is the major land use, a minimum of 10-year cycle was found to be necessary for its sustainability—for both economic efficiency and ecological efficiency, as evaluated through energy efficiency, and fertility sustainability..." (Ramakrishnan 2001, 85–89)

Some textbooks also give blanket statement that 'shifting cultivation must be completely banned' without discussing the circumstances under which this statement is applicable. Even the government appears to believe the views that shifting agriculture destroys the ecological balance and results in substantial soil erosion which subsequently leads to flooding of rivers and drying of hill springs (Gadgil and Guha 2000). However, this is not true under conditions of stable population growth and maintaining long fallow allowing sufficient time for the forest to rejuvenate and recuperate (Savyasachi 1986 in Gadgil and Guha 2000). In fact, shifting cultivation can be considered an eco-friendly method of cultivation since agricultural ecosystem functions such as nutrient cycling and pest population dynamics are controlled both through the complex cropping and the fallow phases. It is considered to be dangerous only because of the reduction in the average cycle length which has been found to be less than five years (Ramkrishnan 2001, 87). Similarly, discussions were also done on the trends of productivity and chemicals used, benefits of shifting cultivation to the farmers, other source of livelihood, and so on, by correlating it with their findings.

Before these discussions were undertaken in the class, the study did not make much sense to the students. But once they were able to relate to the findings of their study to the discussions that followed, students were able to understand shifting cultivation holistically. Not only the students who had conducted the study but the whole class benefited out of the study.

Note for teachers: This is one of the most crucial parts of the project. While the groups present their results and experiences, it is very important to discuss about the results they have obtained. Some of the points to be focused broadly in the discussion may include the following—(a) the scientific concept, (b) the social ramifications, (c) the economic issues.

Assessment: Assessment began from the time of selection of topics for the study till the presentation was over. Marks were given based on their overall performance.

> Note for teachers: Some of the areas for assessment may include clarity of the project, seriousness of the group throughout the project, compilation of the project, presentation of the project, and so on. But every group who completes the project should not be failed.

Outcomes: Students' environmental knowledge, here, shifting cultivation, increased, there were some impacts on their attitudes, they had good experience of learning and they will be able to influence others.

In spite of the issues teachers/students/school may face, project-based EE is definitely helpful for the students. It was observed in this pilot study that students were not only able to understand the connectivity of society, environment and economy but they also learned various process skills such as communication, comparison, analysis, design, interpret, relate, connect, reason, and organize. Monroe (1991 cited in Lane 2006, 16) listed the following skills necessary for problem-solving such as communications, group skills, leadership, creative thinking, and decision-making which students could learn through environmental education. Such a study conducted by the students themselves enables them to learn better. The most important outcome of project-based environmental education is that the learning that takes place is holistic and interdisciplinary in nature and thus is able to bring out the essence of environmental education.

One cannot imagine how much learning will take place if there were 10 groups of students in a class working on different projects.

> Note for teachers: The number of groups will not be less than 10 in a class and it might sometimes be difficult to handle the situation. It is for this reason separate time needs to be carved out for this activity. Since environmental problems and issues are not restricted to a specific discipline, it will be advisable to discuss with teachers from other disciplines about connectivity of the topic with their disciplines and get their inputs as well. This will promote interdisciplinarity of environmental education as we had discussed earlier under interdisciplinary approach. The whole activity will definitely be more time consuming compared to the chalk and talk method. However, at the end it will be worth it!

Follow-up actions: The National Curriculum Framework 2005 sums up environmental education as "Learning about the environment, learning in the environment and learning for the environment." We have also seen a similar definition of environmental education provided by Lucas (1972, 1980, 1980–1981 cited in Disinger 1997) in Chapter 1 wherein he defined it as "education 'about' the environment, education 'for' (the preservation of) the environment, education 'in' the environment." Through the discussions that followed, students were able to gather much information about shifting cultivation thus 'learning about the environment' is achieved. Through their personal field visits, students were able to understand the actual situation and thus 'learning in the environment' is achieved. Perhaps such experience has helped them build an attitude toward shifting cultivation. Hence the 'awareness,' 'knowledge,' 'attitude,' and 'skill' components of environmental education can be said to have been fulfilled. However, we have seen in the previous chapters that without action environmental education cannot be complete. This will at the same time help achieve the 'learning for the environment' goal. Therefore, this step of follow-up actions has been included as the concluding step of this project-based environmental education. The possible follow-up actions for this project were discussed such as educating the farmers about the various environmental impacts of shifting cultivation through small group meetings, through *nukkad natak* (street play), and so on, so that such practices can be sustained.

Note for teachers: Follow-up actions should be action-based and easily performed. It could be as simple as sensitizing people using word of mouth, posters, rallies, etc. or it could be cleaning up the locality or writing to the authorities highlighting the issues.

Photo 5.8   View of Vast Area under *Jhum*

Photo Courtesy: David Buhril

Photo 5.9   A Lady Harvesting Ginger from *Jhum* Field

Photo Courtesy: David Buhril

5.3.3 Why Did It Work?

Given the busy time table throughout the year, one may be curious to know what made this activity work. The key to its success was that the marks obtained by the students through this project were to be counted for their final board examination. The state board allots marks for internal assessment in science. The school administration agreed to reflect the marks obtained through this project as internal assessment marks. As a result of this, students took keen interest and worked seriously and sincerely for the completion and success of the project. This reminds us of the importance given to marks in the school systems. The craving for marks is clearly evident. Therefore, in the present circumstance, it is so important to link activities with marks if we want the activities to be taken up seriously and effectively. This was the strategy that was adopted for the pilot study and it worked.

However, for this to happen in every school, the role of the school administrators is very important. They should work out the plausible way with the teachers. For those schools which are under the umbrella of a bigger system such as Kendriya Vidyalaya, Navodaya Vidyalaya, Central Board of Secondary Education, and so on, the decision can be taken at the highest level and instructions passed on to every school. But passing on instructions does not guarantee that the activities will be undertaken. Teachers will be the key to the success of this activity. Or else this project-based environmental education will receive the same fate as other internal assessment activities where students are simply given marks based on 'nothing' or 'anything.'

Conclusion

The impact of initiatives undertaken in the area of environmental education at the international level is clearly visible in India. As a signatory to various international initiatives, it is expected that similar developments are taking place in other countries as well. This suggests that nations of the world need to meet regularly and not only chalk out ways for collective responsibilities but also share their resources and expertise to build each other up for the successful implementation of environmental education.

Implementation of environmental education in India has taken a proper shape. Beginning with a random and unsystematic manner of implementation till the 1990s, today, there is a clear mandate and objectives for implementation of environmental education throughout the country. However, there are barriers that have to be tackled and they are many. While in the chapter we have grouped such barriers under conceptual, logistical, educational, and attitudinal barriers, it cannot be contested that all such barriers stem from our marginalization of environmental education itself in the school curriculum and in teacher education. As a result, there is complete lack of coherence between the school curriculum and teacher-education courses in the area of environmental education. Unless such issues are fixed the barriers will remain.

As we implement environmental education we need to look for more effective ways of implementation so that its objectives are achieved. Project-based environmental education can be one such approach that can be successfully carried out in schools. As there is less and less interaction of students with their environment, such project-based environmental education will be a good opportunity to take them back to the real world and learn by themselves.

SUMMARY

- Changes and developments have been brought about in environmental education in India in tune with the developments taking place at the international level.
- Developments at the international level also led to the enactment of several environmental laws and effected even the amendment of the Constitution.
- Initiatives undertaken especially by IEEP have strengthened the implementation of environmental education through its various resource materials and training of personnel in India.

- The most recent global development is the evolution of environmental education in the shape of education for sustainable development (ESD) which is fast catching up in India as well.
- M.C. Mehta's PIL made a significant impact in the implementation of environmental education in India.
- At present in India, environmental education is implemented through the infusion approach throughout the country.

- Environmental education, more or less, have finally seeped into the school curriculum though meaningful implementation is yet to be seen.
- There exist several barriers in the successful implementation of EE—conceptual, logistical, educational and attitudinal barriers which could be related to issues of infusion approach, assessment or those related to teacher empowerment due to systemic issues.
- Working on projects is an opportunity for students to actually understand some of the environmental problems and issues around them. Project-based environmental education richly enhances learning.

- Learning that takes place through projects is holistic and students are able to relate their curriculum with what is actually happening around them, thus making sense of their curriculum. It provides opportunities where education or learning *about*, *in* and *for* the environment can be accomplished as students acquire the awareness, knowledge, skills, attitudes and opportunity to participate.
- As opposed to general views, project-based study is certainly doable and if linked with marks will motivate the students and teachers as they carry out the projects. The role of concerned government departments, the central and state boards, the school administration and the practicing teachers is important.

Exercises

1. How has the global scenario in environmental education impacted the trends in India? Elaborate your answer.
2. Which development at the international level in environmental education according to you has the most significant impact in the implementation of environmental education in India? Justify your answer.
3. Elaborate on the PIL filed in the Hon'ble Supreme Court of India related to environmental education.
4. How is environmental education implemented in India at present? Explain.
5. Enumerate on the recommendation of the National Curriculum Framework 2005 on the implementation of environmental education.
6. How effective is the implementation of environmental education in India at present?
7. What are the barriers in the successful implementation of environmental education in India? Elaborate your answer.
8. Should project-based environmental education be encouraged? Justify your answer.
9. How would project-based environmental education impact learning amongst students?
10. Elaborate on the possible barriers in the implementation of project-based environmental education in the schools in India.

References

Bruyere, B.L., Mark Wesson, and Tara Teel 2012."Incorporating Environmental Education into an Urban After-School Program in New York City." *International Journal of Environmental & Science Education* 7(2): 327–341.

Cole, A.G. 2007. "Expanding the Field: Revisiting Environmental Education Principles through Multidisciplinary Frameworks." *The Journal of Environmental Education* 38(2): 35–44.

Disinger, J.F. 1997. *Environmental Education's Definitional Problem*, Reprinted from: *ERIC Clearinghouse for Science, Mathematics and Environmental Education*. Information Bulletin No. 2, 1983. An Epilogue EE's Definitional Problem: 1997 Update. Available at: http://globalenvironmentaleducation.wikispaces.com/file/view/EE_Definitional_Problem.pdf (Accessed on 2 August 2014).

Disinger, John F. and Martha C. Monroe. 1994. *EE Toolbox—Workshop Resource Manual Defining Environmental Education*. Ann Arbor, MI: University of Michigan.

Gadgil, M. and R. Guha. 2000. *The Use and Abuse of Nature*, New Delhi: Oxford University Press.

GoI, Government of India. 1968. *National Policy on Education-1968*, Government of India.

—— 1986. *National Policy on Education-1986*, Government of India.

—— 2009. The National Green Tribunal Bill, 2009, Ministry of Environment, Forests and Climate Change, Government of India. Available at: http://envfor.nic.in/sites/default/files/division/national-green-tribunal-bill-2009.pdf (Accessed on 20 April 2015)

Ham, S. and D. Sewing. 1988. "Barriers to Environmental Education." *Journal of Environmental Education* 19(2): 17–24.

Lahiry, D., Savita Sinha, J.S. Gill, U. Mallik, and A.K. Mishra. 1988. *Environmental Education*: *A Process for Pre-service Teacher Training Curriculum Development*. UNESCO-UNEP International Environmental Education Programme Environmental Education Series No. 26, edited by Patricia R. Simpson, Harold Hungerford, and Trudi L. Volk. Paris: UNESCO.

Lane, J.F. 2006. *Environmental Education Implementation in Wisconsin*: *Conceptualizations and Practices*. Unpublished PhD Thesis: Department of Philosophy, University of Wisconsin-Madison. Available at: http://www.uwsp.edu/cnr-ap/wcee/Documents/JennieLaneDissertation.pdf (Accessed on 23 May 2014).

Lucas, A.M. 1980. "Science and environmental education: Pious Hopes, Self Praise and Disciplinary Chauvinism." *Studies in Science Education* 7(1): 1–26.

Monde, P.N. 2011. *Barriers to Successful Implementation of Environmental Education in Zambian High Schools*: *A Case Study of Selected High Schools of Central Province*. Unpublished PhD Thesis, University of Zambia. Available at: http://dspace.unza.zm:8080/xmlui/bitstream/handle/123456789/809/Monde.pdf?sequence=1 (Accessed on 15 April 2015).

Monroe, M.C. 2012. "The Co-evolution of ESD and EE." *Journal of Education for Sustainable Development* 6(1): 43–47.

NCERT, National Council of Educational Research and Training, 1981. *Environmental Education at the School Level*: *A Lead Paper*. New Delhi: NCERT.

—— 1988. *National Curriculum for Elementary and Secondary Education – A Framework (Revised Version) (1988)*. New Delhi: NCERT.

—— 2000. *National Curriculum Framework for School Education 2000*. New Delhi: NCERT.

—— 2005. *National Curriculum Framework-2005*. New Delhi: NCERT.

Shimray, C.V., S. Farkya, and S.L. Varte. 2013. *Study of Biology Curriculum at the Higher Secondary Stage: A Report (Unpublished)*. New Delhi: NCERT

—— 2015. *Meeting of DIET Functionaries to Assess the Status of D.El.Ed. Syllabus in the Context of Environmental Education—Report (Unpublished)*. New Delhi: NCERT.

Ramakrishnan, P.S. 2001. *Sustainable Agriculture in Ecology and Sustainable Development – Working with Knowledge Systems*. New Delhi: National Book Trust.

Shome, Saurav and Chitra Natarajan. 2013. "Ideas of and Attitudes Towards Projects and Changing Practices: Voices of Four Teachers." *Australian Journal of Teacher Education* 38(10): 64–81.

Tilbury, D. 1997. "Environmental Education (EE) A Head, Heart and Hand Approach to Learning about Environmental Problems." *New Horizons in Education* 38: 1–11.

UN, United Nations. 1993. *The Earth Summit—Agenda 21: The United Nations Program of Action from Rio*. Rio de Janeiro, Brazil

UNEP, United Nations Environmental Programme. 2005. *UNEP Strategy for Environmental Education and Training—A Strategy and Action Planning for the Decade 2005-2014*. Nairobi, Kenya: UNEP

UNESCO, United Nations Educational, Scientific and Cultural Organization. 1980. *Strategies for Developing an Environmental Education Curriculum*: *A Discussion Guide for UNESCO Training Workshops on Environmental Education*. Paris: UNESCO.

——. 1984. *Activities of the UNESCO-UNEP International Environmental Education Programme (1975-1983)*. Paris: UNESCO.

—— 1991. *Environmental Education for Our Common Future: A Handbook for Teachers in Europe Prepared by Faye Benedict on Behalf of the Norwegian National Commission for UNESCO*. Norwegian University Press: UNESCO.

Appendix

Environmental Education in the Schools of India and the United States of America

Introduction

By now we are, to some extent, familiar with the fundamentals of environmental education—from definition to implementations, to implications, to possibilities and directions for the future, especially with reference to India. It will be of interest to have an idea of the status of environmental education in other countries. Many countries including the United States (US), Australia, and Canada can be considered frontrunners in the area of environmental education. In order to have some understanding of the status in other countries, a general comparison of the status of environmental education in the schools in India and the United States is presented in this chapter. Necessary information related to the US was gathered through various approaches such as face-to-face interactions with experts, views collected through emails and telephonic conversations, interactions with practicing teachers and students, field visits to schools and centers promoting environmental education, presentations in conferences, workshops, classes in universities, books, journals, other reference materials, and websites of relevant organizations. Before we begin to compare the status of environmental education in the two countries, let us briefly discuss how environmental education has evolved in the US over the years. Evolution of environmental education in India has already been discussed in the previous chapters, especially in Chapters 4 and 5 and, hence, will not be repeated here.

The roots of environmental education in US can be traced back to as early as 1891 when Wilbur Jackman's *Nature Study for the Common Schools* launched a nature study movement which took students outdoors to explore an indivisible environment with an integrated academic approach. This was followed by the outdoor education theory by L.B. Sharp and Julian Smith during the 1920s, followed by the 'Dust Bowl' mentality of the 1930s which gave rise to conservation education. It was then in 1962 when Rachel Carson came out with her book *Silent Spring* which revolutionized the way ecosystem was understood. It brought to the knowledge of the common people how everything is connected to everything through examples of different pesticides that were indiscriminately used. Later, in 1970, US Congress passed the National Environmental Education Act of 1970 which led to the creation of an Office of Environmental Education in the US. This was followed by the establishment of various councils and bodies on environmental education. In 1990, the US Congress passed the National Environmental Education Act of 1990 which led to the creation of an Office of EE in the US Environment Protection Agency and conducting training programs for environmental educators. In most of the states, environmental education is implemented by integrating it in various subject areas. The latest No Child Left Inside Act of 2013 would focus on professional development to promote environmental education and focus on national environmental literacy for which every state will prepare their environmental literacy plans (ELP). Forty-eight states have developed or are in the process of developing the ELP[7] so as to effectively integrate environmental education into

---

[7] http://eelinked.naaee.net/n/elp (accessed on 12 August 2014)

the prekindergarten through Grade 12 curriculum and ensure that students graduate from high school environmentally literate.[8] Through environmental literacy it envisages that the capacity to perceive, understand, and interpret environmental systems will be enhanced and this will equip citizens to take appropriate action to maintain, restore, or improve the health of those interconnected systems.

Comparison of Status of Environmental Education in India and US

With the background as discussed above, let us now compare the status of environmental education in India and the US. The same is being presented under different heads.

I. Curriculum and Syllabus Development

In India there exist a single national curriculum framework and a common environmental education syllabus for different stages of school education. The National Curriculum Framework, 2005 recommended that environmental education be infused in all subject areas of all the classes. Accordingly, the NCERT adopted the infusion approach of environmental education in all its textbooks for all stages of school education. Yet it is observed that many states continue to implement environmental education as a separate subject especially at the Higher Secondary stage. The Project-Based syllabus developed for the Higher Secondary stage still awaits to be implemented. In spite of these lacunae, there is still a ray of hope for successful implementation of environmental education in India. This is because besides having a common national curriculum framework and a common environmental education syllabus, the teacher preparation programs are more or less uniform throughout the country. This suggests that if teachers are trained with a directed focus and the same is practiced in schools, then there is no reason environmental education cannot be implemented effectively.

While in the US, the curriculum and syllabus (standards) in different subject areas, including environmental education, are not uniform at the national level. The K-12 Guidelines for Learners on EE developed by the North American Association for Environmental Education (NAAEE) serves as the point of reference in the process of the development of curriculum and standards related to environmental education in every state in US. Most of the states do not have separate standards for environmental education, but instead integrate certain topics related to environmental education in different subject areas. Components of environmental education are integrated in different subject areas, especially in science under life science or living environment (or with different nomenclature in some states) up to the elementary level or the middle school and in the Advanced Placement Programs of Environmental Science (APES), biological science or biology and earth and space science in the high school level. But a wide range of difference exists in the way the contents reflecting environmental education are incorporated in the standards in different states. Besides science and environmental science, topics related to environmental education also find place in other subject areas such as social science, arts, health education, and so on, with much variation in different states. Hence, it is for the district in general and respective schools in particular to implement environmental education the way they think best suit their

---

[8] http://www.naaee.net/advocacy/ncli-update (accessed on 10 June 2015)

environment in terms of not only the physical and biological environment but also the infrastructures, facilities and expertise available.

Some of the states in US which have state environmental education standards include Wisconsin (environmental education), Kansas (environmental education),[9] Washington (integrated environmental and sustainability),[10] and Pennsylvania (environment and ecology). Besides being taught as a separate subject in the elementary level, Pennsylvania also incorporates environmental education in different subject areas such as science and social studies. Again at the high school level it is taught through some science, some social studies and there are separate environmental education courses offered to address the content area. Though Wisconsin and Kansas have developed their own environmental education standards, it is not taught as a separate subject but is integrated or infused into different subject areas throughout the curriculum. Same is the case with Washington.

II. Development of Curricular Materials (Printed or EE-Based)

The most commonly used material in the US related to environmental education includes the activity books developed under the national program such as Project Learning Tree, Project Wet, Project Wild, Wonders of Wetlands and Food, Land and People. Besides these, state specific materials are also available. These materials are not always developed by the concerned department of education, but in most cases by organizations or center for environmental education and other private publishers. State such as Pennsylvania has developed textbooks for the subject environment and ecology. Other supplementary materials which are developed by various farms, centers promoting environmental education, museums, and parks, are also available.

As far as India is concerned, the textbooks developed for different subject areas form the basic resource material available on environmental education. Nonetheless, additional materials on environmental education have also been developed which includes project books in environmental education for Classes VI to XII, teacher's handbook on environmental education for the higher secondary stage, other supplementary materials developed by non-governmental organizations such as Centre for Environment Education (CEE), The Energy and Resources Institute (TERI), and Centre for Science and Environment (CSE), to name some.

Electronic learning (e-learning) materials on environmental education are still not as popular as printed versions for learning amongst the students in India. Nevertheless a series of such materials have been developed by the, Central Institute of Educational Technology, NCERT, The Energy and Resources Institute and other organizations, most of which are theme-based focusing on certain environmental issues but not grade-specific or standard-specific.

As it is in India, and even in the US, not many e-learning materials have been developed on environmental education that are in sync with the school curriculum. Yet, there are umpteen number of environmental education-related e-materials and in contrast to India's situation, every student has no difficulty in accessing those materials because of the facilities available to use such materials in every school and in most homes.

---

[9] http://www.ksde.org/Portals/0/CSAS/Content%20Area%20%28F-L%29/History,%20Government,%20and%20 Social%20Studies/2013%20Kansas%20History%20Government%20Social%20Studies%20Standards.pdf (accessed on 16 July 2014)

[10] http://www.k12.wa.us/environmentsustainability/pubdocs/ESEStandards.pdf (accessed on 12 August 2014)

III. Practices in Schools and Outside

In India, implementation of environmental education in and outside schools exhibits a more or less uniform pattern in terms of practices in classrooms across the country which is quite expected due to the uniformity in the curriculum and syllabus and also the resource materials available for use. But, in the US its implementation presents a wide variation, not only in relation to the states but also within the state and between the schools in different districts. Without any exception, it is the school's prerogative to decide on the ways of implementation and this ultimately depends on the concerned teacher how well it is implemented. In the entire public school system of the United States, there are very few teachers who teach 'only' EE or ESD (Feinstein 2009, 37). As such, teacher's motivation, interest and expertise are key to successful implementation of environmental education, whether as a separate subject or as an integrated approach. It is also true that with the state formulated and state conducted assessments getting importance throughout the country, subject areas such as environmental education or topics related to it have been found to be increasingly neglected since it does not form part of the state assessments. According to a 2000 study conducted by the NAAEE and the Environmental Literacy Council (reported in Coyle 2005), 83 percent of elementary teachers and 44 percent of secondary teachers offer 'some' environmental education in their classrooms (Feinstein 2009, 37).

The use of the environment, that is, environment-based education—from the classroom environment, to the schoolyard, to local museums, nature centres, farms, and parks—has been on the rise in the schools across US ever since it has been found to be an effective means to achieve educational goals in general and environmental education goals in particular. It is observed that most of the schools, irrespective of the states, encourage teachers to take children out of school and engage them in outdoor learning and use the schoolyard as a resource and center for outdoor learning. Another way by which outdoor learning takes place is through service learning where students work closely with a community, identify their environmental problems, understand the problem, and work toward a solution along with the community people. The collaboration between schools and different centers promoting environmental education (nature centers, farms, museums, zoological and botanical gardens) is evident. Farm-based education is catching momentum especially in the north-eastern part of US. Learning which takes place in all these centers also form part of the regular school curriculum. Another trend that is becoming popular amongst environmental educators across the country is the more action-oriented project-based learning.

In India, outdoor learning is still a rare sight to be seen in schools. The reason for this can be partly attributed to the existing society itself which is against the idea of getting out of the classroom and dirtying one's hands in the course of studying the environment. Another possible barrier could be the class strength which averages to not less than 50 in many schools. It would be practically impossible for a single teacher to take such a class outdoor. The Government of India's initiative to encourage schools and its students to involve in activities to nurture the environment include setting up of Eco-clubs which is undertaken by the National Green Corps of the Ministry of Environment, Forests and Climate Change. More than 72,000 eco-clubs were established by the year 2004–2005. During financial year 2014–2015, a total of 92,310 Eco-clubs were supported by the

Ministry across the country.[11] Though the number may sound huge, it is far less than even 10 percent of the schools in India and the rate at which the number of eco-clubs increased in a decade is not very encouraging. Further it is interesting to find that the maximum number of schools targeted to be supported through this initiative by the end of the financial year 2013–2014 was just 10,00,000.[12] The target remained the same for the financial year 2014–2015.[13] A financial assistance @ ₹2,500 per annum is provided to every school to establish Eco-clubs for its various activities toward environmental preservation. Some of the activities commonly undertaken as part of eco-club include waste management, water harvesting, cleaning public places, planting of trees, visits to nature centers, and wildlife parks. Another program of the Government of India is the Environmental Orientation to School Education (EOSE). This program which was initiated by the Ministry of Human Resource Development provided funds to promote environmental education to various NGOs. EOSE is now managed and looked after by the National Council of Educational Research and Training.

Besides the eco-clubs which in most cases function in government schools, there are NGOs working invariably with private schools in the areas of water conservation, energy consumption, and so on. But such collaborations are limited to only a few hundreds of schools.

IV. Evaluation and Assessment

The methods adopted for evaluation and assessment on environmental education differs from state to state in India. We had mentioned in Chapter 5 about the suggested method of assessment as per the affidavit submitted to the Hon'ble Supreme Court of India. But with the infusion approach of environmental education it is almost impossible to assess EE separately. But definitely some of the topics on environmental education are assessed though it is difficult to ascertain the marks allotted for such topics. However, no studies are available to discuss further on this.

A similar trend is observed in the US school systems on assessment, in that there is no separate assessment for environmental education. Again, due to the integration of environmental education in different subject areas, it is difficult to find out the exact marks allotted to topics related to environmental education even when the subject forms part of the state assessment. Pennsylvania is an exception wherein environmental education, which is taught as Environment and Ecology (E&E), forms about 50 percent of the assessment in the subject of science (consisting of science, technology, E&E). In most of the states though this is not observed. However, there are several states which allot marks specifically for certain areas on environmental education such as life and environmental science standard (under the science standards) in Wisconsin in the state assessment test in science.[14]

As far as India is concerned, the affidavit submitted to the Hon'ble Supreme Court on implementation of environmental education in schools mentioned that all examination

---

[11] http://www.moef.nic.in/report/0506/Chap%2008.pdf (accessed on 4 July 2015)

[12] http://www.performance.gov.in/sites/default/files/document/rfd/rfd-2013-14/Syndicate1/ME%26F.pdf (accessed on 3 July 2015)

[13] http://www.moef.nic.in/sites/default/files/RFD-2014-15.pdf (accessed on 3 July 2015)

[14] http://standards.dpi.wi.gov/files/standards/pdf/envired.pdf (accessed on 12 August 2014)

papers should compulsorily have questions pertaining to the environmental education component present in the text. It also categorically mentioned that at the class X level, examination papers of different subjects should have compulsory questions on concepts of environmental education such that 10 percent of the grand total of marks are earmarked for environmental education. It is difficult to conclude whether the same is practiced since no studies in this direction has not been done.

V. Professional Development in Environmental Education

A study of the institutes of higher education running across US reveals that of the 825 (approximately) institutes about 50 institutes offer degree courses or concentrations in the Undergraduate, Graduate or Ph.D. in Environmental Education which makes up to about 6 percent of institutes. In addition to these, there are also a few institutes and organizations such as the Nova Southeastern University, Florida, and the Environmental Education and Training Partnership (EETAP) which offer online courses on environmental education. A survey conducted of teacher preparation programs nationwide showed that about half of the programs offered some form of environmental education (McKeown-Ice 2000 in Feinstein 2009, 37). In less than 15 percent of cases environmental education courses were compulsory, rather than optional, and about two-thirds of responding institutions ranked the effectiveness of their own environmental education preparation as 'poor' or 'adequate' rather than 'good' or 'excellent' (McKeown-Ice 2000 in Feinstein 2009, 37). A similar survey by Heimlich et al., four years later, found the situation largely unchanged (Heimlich et al. 2004 in Feinstein 2009, 37).

In some of the colleges of education, teaching methods in environmental education forms part of the methods of teaching science. For example, in the College of Education in the University of Florida, Environmental Education Methods and Materials is a course. But this is not true for all teacher-education programs in different states. There are a few states, such as Wisconsin, which make it a requirement that all teacher candidates who want to teach elementary school, secondary science, secondary social studies, or agriculture must have a 'background' (completed a specific course or has field experience) in environmental education in order to be certified. Each teacher-education program (32 at present in Wisconsin alone) meets this requirement in different ways. Pennsylvania also follows a similar pattern. Though at the elementary level, all subjects are taught by elementary certified teachers including environment and ecology, but at the high school level if the school district has a separate course for E&E then there is a certification they must have in agriculture, biology, earth and space science, environmental education or general science. There is also praxis test that are given for all subject areas including E&E. But in most of the states there is no essential qualification or special trainings required for teachers to teach topics related to environmental education. This means that all they need to possess is a Bachelor's degree in science to be a temporary teacher and an additional teacher certification to be a permanent teacher. As far as environmental science is concerned, since it is considered an 'integrated science,' teachers are required to be certified in chemistry, physics, biology or earth science. There are also special trainings available for Advanced Placement (AP) Environmental Science teachers. National Council for Accreditation of

Teacher Education (NCATE)[15] which is a professional quality control mechanism for teacher preparation, a coalition of 35 national education organizations representing teachers, teacher educators, subject-matter specialists and policy makers has approved the NAAEE Standards for the Initial Preparation of Environmental Educators.[16] This development could bring about better implementation of environmental education.

The in-service training programs include mainly workshops conducted on different activity books developed under the national programs such as PLT (Project Learning Tree), WET, WILD, Wonders of Wetlands, Food, Land and People. Besides these, each state also imparts trainings on the materials that have been specially designed and developed for the state. There are also other training programs, which by attending such programs the participants get credits in the process of obtaining higher degrees such as the summer teacher institute conducted by Earth Force.

The picture is altogether different in India. There are very few institutes which offer environmental education as a concentration at the tertiary level. Though the University Grants Commission, an umbrella body under which all universities functions (except for technical degrees) has provided a guideline and syllabus on Environmental Studies which is to be uniformly undertaken as a compulsory course in all the colleges throughout India, it is observed that most of the colleges ignore it or those which offers the course focus only on the 'science' part of it, thus rendering it as good as insignificant. The Indira Gandhi National Open University (a distant learning university) is in the process of including environmental education as one of the optional specialization areas in its MEd course. As for the existing colleges of education, teaching methods in environmental education is yet to find place in most institutes. In the Bachelor of elementary education course of Delhi University, there is a special focus on the pedagogy in environmental studies. In many other colleges and universities environmental education is discussed in some way or the other, the depth of which greatly varies, but not as a concentration or specialization area. Teaching methodology for infusion approach of environmental education is yet to find place in colleges of education. In the latest National Curriculum Framework for Teacher Education 2009 which was released in March 2010, UGC has proposed environmental education as one of the specialization areas in the M.Ed. course. Besides this, the Framework also re-emphasises the critical importance of environmental education at all levels including teacher education. As of now, there is no specific requirement or qualification for teachers to teach environment-related topics.

As far as professional development for in-service teachers is concerned, training programs specifically on environmental education have not been undertaken on a regular basis. Teacher training modules for different regions in India have already been developed by NCERT though. Besides NCERT, there are other NGOs working in the area of teacher training on environmental education at the local, state or national level. For example, The Energy and Resources Institute started organizing the national level Environment Educators' Conference in the year 2008 and is a regular activity of the

---

[15] NCATE has now been merged with Teacher Education Accreditation Council (TEAC) on 1 July 2013 into Council for the Accreditation of Educator Preparation (CAEP) as the new accrediting body for educator preparation. However, those colleges of education already accredited by NCATE or TEAC do not require fresh accreditation by CAEP.

[16] http://www.naaee.net/programs/certification (accessed on 12 August 2014)

institute. A Diploma in Environment Education course, an innovative program specially designed for in-service, is offered by the Institute of Environment Education and Research, Bharati Vidyapeeth University, Pune and is one of a kind for the country. Another program for in-service teachers, Green Teacher Diploma Program, a one year program is being provided from time to time by the Centre for Environment Education.

VI. Implementation of EE in the Schools in Diverse Regions

The position paper on Habitat and Learning of the National Curriculum Framework 2005 recommends that the focus for implementation of environmental education in different states should be locale specific, albeit in the context of a global vision. Many of the activities in the form of projects undertaken in the schools located in different states as part of the regular school curriculum or as part of eco-club are seen to be oriented toward their immediate local environment. The project books which have been developed to strengthen the implementation of environmental education in India clearly emphasize on activities and projects which are locally relevant environmental issues.

A similar trend is also observed in the schools in US. Activities undertaken are all closely connected with the students' immediate environment. This, perhaps, could be one of the reasons for the use of the terms such as environment-based education, place-based education, experiential education or experiential learning, farm-based education, service learning, or environment as an integrating context gaining popularity in different states.

VII. EE and Education for Sustainable Development (ESD)

In spite of ESD becoming more popular in many countries, superseding or replacing environmental education in many countries, in India and the US environmental education still remains to be dominantly practiced in the formal education system. However, in both the countries ESD is certainly gaining momentum. As a matter of fact, it is already widely practiced in the nonformal sectors in both the countries and is slowly, but surely making its presence felt in formal education sectors as well.

Conclusion

Elements of environmental education have been reflected in the education systems in both the countries since the 1930s. We might recall Gandhi's Basic Education introduced in 1937. However, environmental education as a discipline in the formal education system became established much later, in the 1960s in the US and in the 1970s in India. This suggests that environmental education was introduced in the formal education system almost simultaneously in the two countries. The only difference, a significant one at that, is that many of the pioneers of environmental education were professionals from the US. Much of the research leading to the evolution of environmental education globally can be credited to the studies undertaken in the US. Tremendous research has gone into and continues to be invested in various aspects of environmental education in the US. In fact, so many studies have been carried out on environmental education that abundant literature is available in every aspect. While in India, as we have seen in the preceding chapters, much need to be done in terms of research to strengthen implementation of environmental education.

However, in terms of implementation, similarities were observed in many of the aspects as discussed in the chapter. For example, not much of a difference was observed in the development of curricular materials or in terms of assessment. Assessment seems to be a matter of concern in both the countries. However, certain variations have been observed on curriculum and syllabus, professional development and practices in schools. For example, while there is no uniform curriculum in US schools, in India it is almost the same with the same model curriculum framework and the same core syllabus. US also have much established professional development courses as compared to India. The Standards for the Initial Preparation of Environmental Educators was approved by the NCATE in 2007, a professional quality control mechanism for teacher preparation. Successful teachers of this standard means that they possess the competencies necessary to help all P-12 students become environmentally literate citizens. Even in terms of practices in schools, schools in the US appear to exhibit more of 'education in and through the environment' practices while this is not common in schools in India. When practiced it is mostly limited to the few students who are part of the eco-clubs set up in schools. While flexibility seems to be more prevalent in US school curriculum, India can take advantage of its limitations. For example, the model syllabi for school education as well as teacher-education courses are same in India. If enough care is taken during the development of such syllabi to incorporate environmental education appropriately and adequately, then it is most likely that whatever is reflected in the syllabus with regard to environmental education will be implemented throughout the country. Another striking similarity between the two countries is that, in terms of implementation of ESD, it is yet to catch up in both the countries since environmental education is still part and parcel of formal education system.

These discussions suggest that there are scopes for improvements in the implementation of environmental education in both the countries, which may be more so in India beginning with serious research in different areas of environmental education. In spite of the many issues that exist in its education system, India is at a much advantageous position to effectively implement environmental education in its school because of the fact that it has the same model curriculum and the syllabus is almost uniform throughout the country. Besides, the teacher preparation courses are also similar throughout the country. As a result of these, teachers can be trained accordingly, and the same can be implemented in the schools throughout the country to achieve the desired outcome.

Further Reading

CEE, Centre for Environment Education. 2007. Environmental Education in the Indian School System, Status Report, Ahmedabad: CEE.

Disinger, John F. 1983. Environmental Education's Definitional Problems, ERIC Clearinghouse for Science, Mathematics and Environmental Education Information Bulletin, 2. Columbus, OH: ERIC/SMEAC.

———— 1993. "Environment in the K-12 Curriculum: An Overview." In Environmental Education Teacher Resource Handbook, A Practical Guide for K-12 Environmental Education, edited by Richard J. Wilke, 23-43. New York: Kraus International Publications

Disinger, John F. and Martha C. Monroe. 1994. EE Toolbox – Workshop Resource Manual Defining Environmental Education, Ann Arbor, MI: University of Michigan, National Consortium for Environmental Education and Training.

Feinstein, Noah. 2009. Education for Sustainable Development in the United States of America: A Report Submitted to the International Alliance of Leading Education Institutes, University of Wisconsin-Madison School of Education.

Genc, Murat. 2015. "The Project-based Learning Approach in Environmental Education." *International Research in Geographical and Environmental Education* 24(2): 105–117.

Lahiry, D., Savita Sinha, J.S. Gill, U. Mallik, and A.K. Mishra. 1988. UNESCO-UNEP International Environmental Education Programme Environmental Education Series 26, Environmental Education: A Process for Pre-service Teacher Training Curriculum Development. Paris: UNESCO.

Lane, J.F. (2006). Environmental Education Implementation in Wisconsin: Conceptualizations and Practices., Unpublished PhD Thesis: Department of Philosophy, A dissertation submitted in partial fulfillment of the requirements of the degree of Doctor of Philosophy (Curriculum and Instruction) at the University of Wisconsin-Madison. Available at: http://www.uwsp.edu/cnr-ap/wcee/Documents/JennieLaneDissertation.pdf (Accessed on 23 May 2014).

McCrea, Edward J. 2006. Roots of Environmental Education: How the Past Supports the Future, Environmental Education & Training Partnership. University of Wisconsin-Stevens Point, College of Natural Resources, Stevens Point, Wisconsin.

McKeown, R., C.A. Hopkins, R. Rizzi and M. Chrystalbridge. 2002. Education for Sustainable Development Toolkit. Energy, Environment and Resources Center, University of Tennessee, Tennese. Available at: http://www.esdtoolkit.org/esd_toolkit_v2.pdf (Accessed on 8 August 2014).

Monroe, Martha C, Elaine Andrews, and Kelly Biedenweg. 2007. "A Framework for Environmental Education Strategies." *Applied Environmental Education and Communications* 6: 205–216.

NAAEE 2004a. *Environmental Education Materials: Guidelines for Excellence*. Washington, D.C: NAAEE.

———— 2004b. *Excellence in Environmental Education: Guidelines for Learning (Pre K-12)*. Washington D.C: NAAEE.

———— 2004c. *Guidelines for the Preparation and Professional Development of Environmental Educators*. Washington D.C: NAAEE.

NCERT, National Council of Educational Research and Training, 2001a. *Environmental Orientation to School Education, A Training Module for Eastern Region*. New Delhi: NCERT.

———— 2001b. *Environmental Orientation to School Education, A Training Module for Northern Region*. New Delhi: NCERT.

———— 2001c. *Environmental Orientation to School Education, A Training Module for Southern Region*. New Delhi: NCERT.

———— 2001d. *Environmental Orientation to School Education, A Training Module for Western Region*. New Delhi: NCERT.

———— 2004. *Environmental Education in Schools, Syllabus for Environmental Education in Schools*. New Delhi: NCERT.

———— 2009. *Project Book in Environmental Education for Class VI, VII, VIII, IX and X*. New Delhi: NCERT.

———— 2011. *Teachers' Handbook on Environmental Education for the Higher Secondary Stage*. New Delhi: NCERT.

———— 2013. *Project Book in Environmental Education for the Higher Secondary Stage*. New Delhi: NCERT.

Wilson, Jeanette Randall and Martha C. Monroe. 2005. "Biodiversity Curriculum that Supports Education Reform." *Applied Environmental Education and Communication* 4: 125–138.

Acknowledgments

Most of the information for this study was gathered during the course of the author's Fulbright Fellowship in the School of Forest Resources and Conservation, University of Florida, United States of America during 2009. The information was updated for the purpose of this book accordingly. The author would like to specially thank the United States–India Educational Foundation, India; the Bureau of Educational and Cultural Affairs, United States for the fellowship; and the University of Florida to be the host institute for the fellowship tenure.

Worth a Thought!

It is often presumed that providing information and facts about the environment is all that it takes to bring about pro-environmental behavior and action. Contrary to this assumption, if teaching about the environment is limited to providing environmental facts, its contribution to bring about pro-environmental behavior or action will be as good as nil. Behavioral change takes into account numerous factors and requires elaborate discussion.

Chapter Overview

Environmental education can be said to be meaningful only if it brings about certain pro-environmental behavior. Anything short of this will render the effort worthless. An attempt has been made to bring out the various factors and variables that contribute to fostering responsible environmental behavior. Some models in this regard have been discussed here. The complexity on how the variables contribute to bring about behavioral change has also been highlighted. At the end of reading this chapter, it is envisaged that readers will obtain adequate understanding to:

- appreciate the importance of behavioral change and action for meaningful environmental education.
- explain the nonlinear relationship of knowledge-attitude-action.
- describe the various factors that contribute to behavioral change in responsible environmental behavior model.
- appreciate the complexity of behavioral change.
- explain how society/societal norms shape or influence behavior.
- describe the levels of activities necessary to bring about behavioral change.
- explain the significance of responsible environmental behavior model.
- practice some responsible environmental behavior in their daily life.

Introduction

So far we have discussed the goals and objectives of environmental education, the different approaches, its trends in India as well as globally, and also how it is dealt in our curriculum. However, all the efforts that we have put in will be meaningful only if we see some positive actions being taken, or observe some environmentally friendly patterns of behavior (not inherited but learned or imbibed) or, in other words, only if students display some kind of environmentally responsible behavior, or responsible environmental behavior (REB), or pro-environmental behavior. This brings us to the point that environmental education is all about promotion of REB (Bones 1994, 15; Disinger 1993, 35). Therefore, the importance of REB cannot be overemphasized. However, as important as it is, this aspect has not received much attention both in practice and research. In this light, several researchers including Lucas (1980a, 20–21; 1980b, 36), Gough (2013, 16) and others pointed out the importance of considering behavior change as the focus of environmental education practices and research. Some, however, argue that such a goal to bring about behavior change is overstated (Bob Jickling 1991 in Disinger and Monroe 1994). There has also been a lack of consensus amongst educators as to whether to teach explicitly for environmental action and it is because of this lack of consensus that this aspect has been brought into the formal curricula much later, after the introduction of environmental education itself (Disinger and Howe 1990, 15).

6.1 The Context of Responsible Environmental Behavior (REB)

Environmental education cannot be complete without 'action.' In other words, environmental education is not just 'knowing,' but environmental education will be complete only with 'doing,' which includes taking right choices. It may be reiterated that one of the goals of environmental education, as mentioned in the Tbilisi Conference on Environmental Education, is "to create new patterns of behavior of individuals, groups, and society as a whole toward the environment" (UNESCO-UNEP 1978). Whether an individual, a group, or a society has imbibed the new patterns of behavior will be known from the actions they take or the way they act while they are faced with different environmental situations. Hence, when we say 'new patterns of behavior' we essentially refer to the 'action' that a person undertakes. The importance of taking appropriate environmental actions so as to contribute meaningfully toward the betterment of the environment has also been highlighted in India's efforts to take environmental education forward. It may be cited that the syllabus for environmental education in schools had developed in pursuance of the Hon'ble Supreme Court's order and emphasized the importance of 'action' in environmental education wherein it says, "a value based, action oriented course of EE would lead from knowledge to feeling and finally to appropriate action" (NCERT 2004). The National Curriculum Framework 2005 (NCF-2005) further reiterates that the main focus of environmental education should be "to promote positive environmental actions" (NCERT 2005). However, it may be mentioned here that this 'creation of new pattern of behavior' is still considered debatable (Biedenweg et al. 2013) with regard to whether or not educators should be teaching for the purpose of changing the environmental behaviors of their students (Disinger 1993, 36). This is not surprising, especially looking at the earlier understanding of responsible environmental behavior which was authoritative in that environmentally responsible behaviors were considered to be those endorsed by professional resource managers and/or those championed by environmental advocates. Environmental educators were expected to teach students what those behaviors were and how to achieve them (Disinger 2009). It is argued that it is not right to inform the students about a particular pattern of behavior which, in many instances, could be biased and derived from the selfish motive of the educator and could turn out to be damaging and dangerous to the environment and do more harm than good in the long run. Volk (1993 cited in Disinger 2009), therefore, pointed out the necessity of including ecological knowledge, environmental sensitivity, knowledge of issues, investigation skills, citizenship skills, and feeling of effectiveness as part of the definition of environmentally responsible behavior. But the authoritative responsible environmental behavior mentioned earlier should not be confused with the new pattern of behavior discussed later, which is the outcome of an impartial and democratic process and is not influenced by insincere motive. It is not about promoting specific behavior changes, but those behavior changes which the students exhibit of their own as a result of their informed choices. In fact, environmental educators should emphasize the maintenance of neutrality in their environmental education-related endeavors.

In order to achieve this goal of environmental education—appropriate action or behavior—several aspects were laid down in the Belgrade Charter, Tbilisi Conference, and the Habitat and Learning Position Paper of the NCF-2005. These can be broadly categorized under awareness, knowledge, attitude, and skill and opportunity to be actively involved in working toward resolution of environmental problems. It was envisaged that if these aspects were taken care of, appropriate environmental action or behavior would ensue. Whether this supposition works or not, or how it works, will be discussed elaborately in this chapter.

As we shall see in the ensuing discussions, irrespective of what the environmental issue is about, in general, there are several factors which contribute to such pro-environmental behavior or REB. But how each factor contributes toward the process is difficult to be explicitly explained. In fact, it will not be possible to precisely quantify the factors that would bring about REB. In this chapter, we will discuss broadly what it takes to trigger appropriate actions or behave in an environmentally responsible manner.

> ## JUST A MOMENT
>
> Recall some pro-environmental behaviors which you think were prescribed to you by your teachers, while in school.

6.2 Traditional Thinking of REB

Based on the traditional thinking in the field of environmental education, it is envisaged that by making social groups and individuals aware of environmental issues and problems, and by imparting adequate knowledge about these issues and problems, appropriate actions or behaviors would follow suit. In other words, it is assumed that if students are properly taught *about* the environment, they will subsequently behave in an

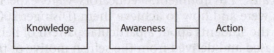

Figure 6.1   Traditional Thinking of Responsible Environmental Behavior: Model I

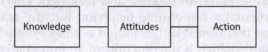

Figure 6.2   Traditional Thinking of Responsible Environmental Behavior: Model II

environmentally responsible manner and engage in pro-environmental actions (Disinger 1993, 35; Disinger 2009; Disinger and Howe 1990, 15). Two models related to such traditional thinking are presented here: First, wherein it was assumed that if human beings are made more knowledgeable, they will, in turn, become more aware of the environment and its problems and, thus, be more motivated to act toward the environment in more responsible ways (Fig. 6.1). Second, a model proposed by Ramsey and Rickson (1977 cited in Hungerford and Volk 1990) wherein it was envisaged that increased knowledge would lead to favorable attitudes, which in turn would lead to actions promoting better environmental quality. In other words, it was assumed that more knowledge will lead to more awareness, more awareness will bring about attitudinal change, and this will ultimately lead to taking appropriate action or behavior (Fig. 6.2).

The two figures provide linear models for appropriate environmental action or behavior. In both cases, knowledge may surely lead to awareness or attitudinal change. However, just because a person is aware about environmental problems, or has the right attitude toward the environment or environmental problems, it does not necessary lead to action. In fact, many researches that have been undertaken in this field do not find the linear relationships provided earlier to be valid. Instead, studies reveal that there are numerous other variables that are at play simultaneously for bringing about appropriate action or behavior. Nevertheless, gaining environmental insights (the ability to understand and appraise the society's effects on the ecosystem) and environmental attitude (defined as all positive or negative attitudes and thoughts of individuals regarding environmentally beneficial behaviors, such as fears, resentments, uneasiness, values, and readiness to solve environmental problems) contribute and influence behavior toward the environment (Genc 2015).

6.3 Responsible Environmental Behavior: What Decides?

To begin our discussion, let us consider the following questions: What makes us do the way that we do? What is that, that influences us most? How do we decide how to do? Do we even think that we 'decide' on the many things that we do every day? These are very relevant questions to ask when it comes to pro-environmental behavior. As a matter of fact, for every decision that we make—as big as buying a new house or as small as buying fruits—our actions are always associated with reasons, that we may be or may not be even conscious about. In such cases, we use information that is stored in our memory, based on previous experiences. A number of studies have been done on what affects our decision-making capacity or how people change their behavior. For example, Daniel Kahneman and Amos Tversky—two psychologists who developed a series of insightful experiments to test decision-making processes—found that decision-making could be affected, based on stored information, belief on initial fact, inappropriate use of logic and probability, and uncertainty (Kibert et al. 2012, 214–217). Social theorist Everett Rogers provides five successive steps that an individual goes through when changing behavior: Knowledge (People must first become aware of the potential action, behavior, technology, or idea), persuasion (People form an attitude on how the innovation is presented to them—relevant and meaningful context), decision (People decide whether they wish to adopt or reject the change after they perceive the change to be good or bad), implementation (People engage in the actual activity), and confirmation (People seek additional information to confirm whether their decision was right. Supportive information helps them to be firmly established in the change) (251–53). Rachel and Stephen Kaplan's Reasonable Person Model is another model which is about reasonableness in decision-making—in situations where the information is insufficient or excessive, or not understandable, or where a person lacks the skills to take actions, people are not able to take reasonable decisions (258). Umpteen studies have been undertaken to understand the criteria of decision-making in general and pro-environmental behavior in specific. One model in particular is being discussed more elaborately here in this chapter.

JUST A MOMENT

Do you think the existing school curriculum encourages students to inculcate environmentally responsible behavior?

6.4 Responsible Environmental Behavior Model

The REB model proposed by Hines et al. (1986/87) and Hungerford and Volk (1990) has been considered to discuss in detail the variables that can contribute to bring about pro-environmental behavior. Some modifications have been made by adding few more variables as we shall see further. An attempt has been made to present the model in a simplified manner. Figure 6.3 provides the detail of the model that is being discussed.

The model presented in Figure 6.3 shows that REB results from 'intention to act.' Intention to act does not occur naturally but is influenced by factors such as 'cognitive' and 'personality factors.' Cognitive factors include variables such as 'knowledge of issues,' 'knowledge of action strategies,' and 'action skills.' Certain situational factors may counteract or strengthen these variables. For example, if students have no access to a school this will counteract to the cognitive factor. Because in such cases students will not

Figure 6.3   Model of Responsible Environmental Behavior

Situational factors—counteract or strenghten variables (e.g. No access to school counteracts)

Situational factors— social settings (public places such as airports), status symbol (cycling by celebrities or public transport ride by politicians), benefits

Knowledge of issues

Knowledge of action strategies

Action skills

* Cognitive factors and Personality factors can cause some Intention to Act separately. However, they can also influence each other and their combined influence will strengthen the Intention to Act.

Cognitive factors *

INTENTION TO ACT

RESPONSIBLE ENVIRONMENTAL BEHAVIOR (REB)

NO INTENTION YET ACT

Triggering factors

Personality factors *

Investment for the action (e.g. choices present)

Impact of issue on individual

Visibility of the result of action

Complexity of action skills

Benefits— savings/ incentive

Law, legislation, etc. (e.g. pollution check)

Benefits may be out of:
(i) Savings (energy, water bills, etc.)
(ii) Incentives (cash, bonus, marks, etc.)
also called Behavioral Intervention Strategies.

Attitudes (toward the environment and toward taking action)

Locus of control (whether they think they can influence or not)

Personality responsibility (toward the environent and toward the issue)

Situational factors—counteract or strengthen variables (e.g. financial constraints forcing a person to cut trees for firewood counteracts. Society protecting forests strengthens)

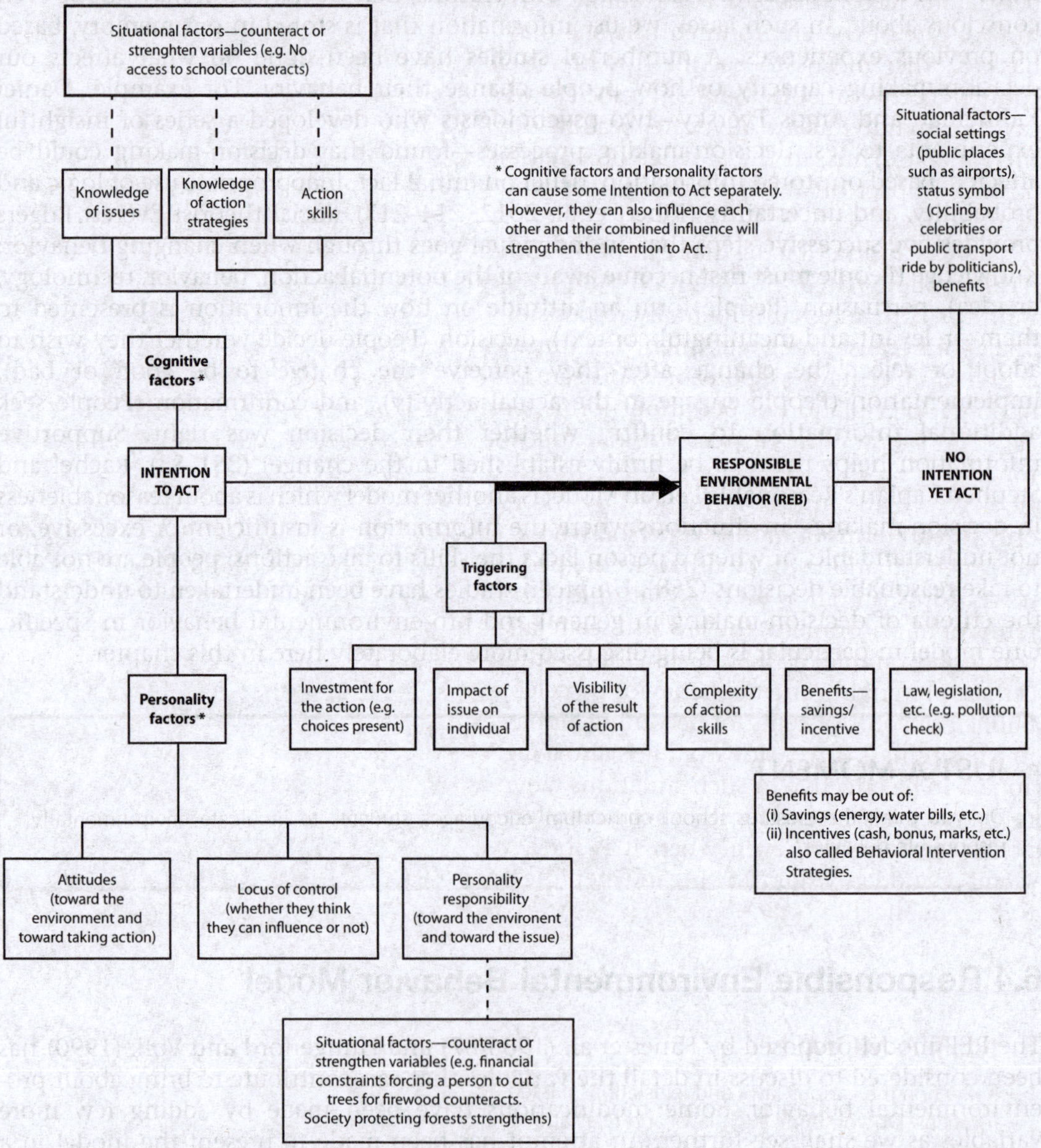

Source: Modified from Hines et al. (1986/87) and Hungerford and Volk (1990)

be able to gain knowledge about environmental issues, nor will they have knowledge of possible action strategies and action skills. This, in turn, will have a negative impact on the intention to act which will ultimately reduce the chances to exhibit REB.

Personality factors include variables such as 'attitudes' (toward the environment and toward taking action), 'locus of control' (whether they think they can influence or not), and 'personal responsibility' (toward the environment and toward the issue). As in the case of cognitive factors, some situational factors can counteract or strengthen the personality factor variables. For example, even if a person feels the personal responsibility to take care of the environment, he/she may still cut down trees for firewood if he/she has no other means to get fuel for fire. Hence, in this case, financial constraint can counteract the variable. While in a society which believes in protecting forests, it will be easy for an individual to advocate for judicious use of firewood. This situation strengthens the variable. Thus, in the absence of situations which counteract the variables, there is positive impact on the intention to act which ultimately will increase the chances to exhibit REB.

There is another factor that can bring about REB in spite of 'lack of intention' which has been designated 'no intention yet act.' In such cases, the person does not actually want to act in an environmentally responsible way, but he/she does so to save his public image or because the government has imposed some law which compels the person to act environmentally responsible. For example, the punishment (fine or imprisonment) imposed for violation of pollution norms, burning solid waste, and leaves in the open, clearing or uprooting of trees without following norms, discharging untreated water in water bodies, and so on, more often than not, influences a person to act responsibly. However, this is further influenced by the nature of punishment. If the punishment is only fine in terms of money, a person who is wealthy will care little about abiding by the law. Such situation will be unfair to the people who are not financially sound and hence it will turn into an issue of social injustice. However, if the punishment imposed is in terms of imprisonment, the law will seem fair to both the rich and the poor. Another very common example of REB, in spite of no intention to act, is the phony public display of certain pro-environmental behavior by celebrities or public figures such as taking ride in public transport systems, or becoming ambassadors for wildlife protection, or taking part in a cleanliness drive. However, it is also a fact that REB, in spite of lack of intention, also appear to be effective in such situations when a person who is idolized or is considered a role model sets a trend for REB. For example, it is never easy to shell out money from ones pocket as donation, even when it is for a very good social cause. However, donation seems to suddenly start flowing in when the person making the call for donation happens to be a public idol or an icon.

JUST A MOMENT

Reflect on the various laws and legislations passed by the government toward protection of the environment. Do you think such laws and legislations have been effective?

6.4.1 Complexity of Responsible Environmental Behavior

While it is evident that awareness and knowledge of environmental issues and concerns are imperative to build environmental attitudes, almost always following a linear pattern, the situation is not as linear and becomes much more complex when it comes to attitudes translating into a behavior or action (Kopnina 2014). Lucas (1980a, 1980 b), in his analysis of literature devoted to environmental education, found no strong evidence in support of the view that attitudes leads to appropriate behaviors or actions. He also found disparity in what a person believes 'people' ought to do and the same person's attitudes to the same question, and how a person's active concern for environmental issues dissipates when the costs include personal sacrifice. The question is, how 'strong' should an attitude be so that it is translated into action. Keeping this in view, Lucas suggested that environmental educators might instead concentrate on the direct modification of behavior rather than on intervention at the attitude level, which is matter of debate.

The complexity of REB is such that, even if all the variables of the cognitive and personality factors are favorable or positive, there are other factors, which we have collectively called 'triggering factors' here (this term has been used for convenience) that greatly affect REB. These factors include investment for the action (i.e., how much an individual has to invest to take the action, what are the choices present, and so on. For example, an air conditioner which is more energy efficient but costlier versus one which is less energy efficient but cheaper), impact of issue on individual (i.e., how much the issue has direct relevance on the individual. For example, dumping solid waste in the drain will impact an individual directly which will most likely trigger REB), visibility of the result of action (i.e., whether an individual will be able to see the positive result of his action immediately. For example, one will not be able to see the result even if he gets pollution check of his vehicle and hence he is not likely to readily exhibit REB), complexity of action skills (i.e., how difficult or inconvenient it will be to take the action. For example, it will be difficult to take toxic waste to the assigned place for discarding if the place is located far away from one's locality and hence that will act as a deterrent to REB), benefits–savings/incentive, (benefits may be from (a) savings (energy, water bills) and (b) incentives (cash, bonus, marks) also called behavioral intervention strategies.

JUST A MOMENT

What according to you is the biggest challenge in the process of taking environmentally responsible action?

6.4.2 Categorization of Variables

Hungerford and Volk (1990) distinguished the various factors which affect REB under different categories such as 'entry-level variables' (which include the pre-requisite variables that would enhance a person's decision-making such as environmental sensitivity, basic knowledge of ecology, and so on), 'ownership variables' (which include variables which make environmental issues personal to the individual such as in-depth knowledge of issues, personal investment in an issue, and so on), and 'empowerment variables' (which include those variables which make an individual feel empowered or sense of competence to help resolve environmental issues such as knowledge of and skill in using environmental action strategies, locus of control, and intention to act). Chawla and Cushing (2007), in 'education for strategic environmental' behavior, placed nature activities that an individual goes through during childhood and youth under the 'entry-level variables' since such activities predispose an individual to take an interest in nature, which enhances the possibility of the person to later work for its protection. Role models of children such as parents, other family members, and teachers who show an interest in nature are also included under this variable. Education programs and membership in environmental clubs and organizations where an individual gains increased knowledge about environmental issues and learns environmental action skills are included under 'ownership' and 'empowerment variables.' They maintain that a sense of competence, at an individual level as well as collectively, is the foundation of action and, hence, it is considered as a strong ingredient in the 'empowerment variable.' An individual can develop such a sense of competence in many ways—observing the success of others, seeing the processes other people use to achieve their goals, assessing their own competence in comparison, being surrounded by role models who are very persuasive (Bandura 1982; Schunk et al. 1987 cited in Chawla and Cushing 2007), verbal encouragement, one's own experience of tasting success (Bandura 1997 cited in Chawla and Cushing 2007), opportunities to work for social and environmental change, and so on.

JUST A MOMENT

Do you think the government is committed enough to bring about pro-environmental behavior amongst its citizens? How do you think the government should tackle this issue or is it the responsibility of the citizens?

6.4.3 Other Factors/Variables

There are many other factors or variables that have not been mentioned here which contribute to or promote REB. For example, social marketing techniques such as understanding the motivations of the audience, removing real and perceived barriers to change, establishing social commitments, avoiding approaches that can trigger unwanted reactions and persuasion, also could be significant areas for promotion of environmentally responsible behavior (Disinger and Monroe 1994). The mindset of the society is another factor that has not been accounted for in the model. How society looks at the people who exhibit REB in their daily lives or those who have no concern for it, can also be a very important factor. In a society which does not commonly exhibit or encourage REB or which have no regard for people with REB, it is most likely that the situation is going to worsen. Whereas, in a society which commonly exhibits or encourages REB or which has high regard for people with REB, it is most likely that even individuals who otherwise do not exhibit REB are most likely to change their environmental behavior so as to blend with the society. Bamberg and Möser (2007) mention various studies which indicate that pro-environmental behavior could be pro-socially motivated, in the sense that they are hugely influenced by social norms, or could be guided by a rational evaluation of behavioral consequences in terms of rewards and punishments, in the sense that a person behaves in a certain way so as to be rewarded or in order to avoid punishment.

It is important to understand that any of the factors on its own does not bring about REB. For example, educational research does not support the optimistic assumption that acquisition of information and skills will lead to positive changes in social behavior (Stapp 1970 cited in Disinger 1983; Disinger and Monroe 1994, 9). It is also possible that some of the variables may not be relevant in the years to come. For example, at present, legislature helps to in controling environmental quality a certain extent, which may not be necessary in the future if environmental education makes a meaningful impact in the society. Disinger and Monroe (1994) mention that environmental education can influence lifestyle choices and the students will be able to decide how to consider the environmental impact in their choices of electrical appliances, tools, gadgets, modes of transportation, and so on.

JUST A MOMENT

Make a list of ten pro-environmental behaviors that you can inculcate in your daily life. While you practice these behaviors pay attention to the barriers that prevent you from doing them.

6.5 Different Levels of Activities for Behavioral Change

Several studies have come up with other details related to the categories of variables that contribute to behavior (Hungerford and Volk, 1990). A hierarchical approach involving the following four levels of activities was put forward by Hungerford (1987, 28–29; Disinger and Monroe 1994, 7).

1. Ecological concepts: This goal level attempts to provide the learner with the ecological knowledge that will permit him/her to make ecologically sound decisions with respect to environmental issues. This knowledge would include, but not be limited to, such concepts as individuals and populations, limiting factors, biogeochemical cycling, abiotic influences, homeostasis, and succession. Other educators may add companion goals in political, economic, psychological, and social concepts.
2. Conceptual awareness: This goal level attempts to develop a conceptual awareness of how individual and collective behaviors influence the relationship between quality of life and quality of environment, as well as how human behaviors result in issues that must be resolved through investigation, evaluation, decision-making, and action by citizens.
3. Issue investigation and evaluation: This goal level attempts to develop the knowledge and skills needed to permit learners to investigate environmental issues and evaluate alternative solutions for resolving these issues. It also provides opportunities for students to investigate and evaluate real-world issues.

4. Environmental action skills—training and application: This goal level attempts to develop those skills needed for learners to take positive environmental action for the purpose of resolving or helping to resolve environment-related issues. It also involves the development of action plans by students and provides them with the opportunity to implement those plans, if they desire.

Research studies have indicated that behavioral change will occur only if students are thoroughly exposed to all the four goal levels (Disinger and Monroe 1994, 7; Hungerford 1987, 28–29).

However, at the end, there is no model which is foolproof. It will also be local-specific depending upon the environmental settings. Due to the number of variables that interact and influence each other to ultimately bring about REB, it is difficult to determine and specify which factors are the most important or the least important. As Sobel (2008, 145) says, "Just because children know that burning fuel creates carbon dioxide and that this is bad for the planet, they do not necessarily develop ecologically responsible buying patterns. Increased knowledge and a change in attitude do not necessarily translate into different behavior. It's more complicated than that." Nevertheless, we can never go wrong in saying that every variable contributes in some way or the other. But any and all of these will have some impact only if we give ourselves some time to pause and consciously decide on every decision we make, however small or big it may be.

There are several success stories regarding behavioral change which have been exhibited by students throughout India. One such example would be regarding the burning of firecrackers. Of late, it has been observed that an increasing number of students have stopped burning firecrackers or reduced the use of it during festive seasons. Besides the dangers associated playing with it, firecrackers are known to increase air pollution drastically. Such behavioral change amongst the students is highly appreciated and encouraging when it comes to dealing with environmental issues. It will be worth finding out what encouraged or led to such behavioral change so that similar strategies can be applied to other environmental issues such as consumerism, use of vehicles, and waste management.

JUST A MOMENT

Can you remember certain pro-environmental decisions that you or your family had taken consciously? Reflect on what motivated you to take the decision.

6.6 Significance of REB Model

The discussion on the REB model gives us a fair idea on how it works. We saw that there are numerous variables at play, each of which contributes toward REB. However, even when all the variables are favorable, it may not guarantee REB, indicating the complexity of how REB can be influenced. In spite of this uncertainty, the model definitely is significant as it provides a broad framework under which REB operates. This understanding of the impacts and importance of each variable will help policy makers and practitioners to identify the areas where they should focus while implementing environmental education. It will help them identify where the barriers are.

While trying to address any environmental issue, practitioners may begin by considering all the variables as mentioned in the model. They can also specifically focus on certain specific variables, as they can pick and choose depending on the requirements. For example, in the present trend of implementation of environmental education in the schools in India, it appears that the focus is largely on the cognitive factors, invariably on the 'knowledge of issues' component, and to some extent on the 'knowledge of action strategies' component. Adequate action skills are not provided, nor are opportunities given to apply the action skills. Hence in this case, focus can be now on strengthening action skills by providing opportunities to participate in actual resolution of environmental issues. The model is not only useful in the teaching–learning process for students but the same can be and must be used for teacher preparation. The reason is that only when teachers themselves are familiar with the model through participation will they be able to implement it successfully in their curriculum.

The model can not only guide the policy makers in the area of formal education but also inform other government departments on their roles. Funders can also refer to the model to identify where (in which area) to put their money and resources. Researchers can also take up in-depth research on specific variables, based on requirement. This will be especially useful in India's context since for successful implementation of environmental education we will have to bank on the findings of such research which as of now is pretty much lacking.

Conclusion

The more we have worked in the area of behavioral change, the more we have found out its complexities. There are many variables that work simultaneously or otherwise. Yet, we know that without a pro-environmental behavior we can never see the positive impact on the environment. Given this situation, all we can do is to try to address as many variables as possible. Though in this chapter we have seen that having the right attitude does not guarantee responsible environmental behavior, however, we can almost be guaranteed that without the right attitude responsible environmental behavior cannot take place.

It is indeed fascinating to think how a certain variable can so dominantly control our mind in our decision-making while at other times the same variable does not have any impact whatsoever in the decision we make. Since it is a human mind that is at play, a bit of each of these—experience, knowledge, emotion, feelings, social acceptability, and social status—all play an important role in all such actions. It appears that, in India, much of the factors are all controlled by social acceptability. We buy a certain house, a certain car, a certain furniture, or a certain gadget many a times because it reveals our social status. If this be the case, then addressing this aspect becomes a priority in our efforts to bring about responsible environmental behavior.

SUMMARY

- Taking action—environmentally responsible behavior, or pro-environmental behavior, or responsible environmental behavior—leading to environmental problem-solving is the ultimate goal of environmental education.
- Right action or environmentally responsible behavior does not come naturally to an individual.
- Numerous variables contribute in the process to bring about REB.

- Due to the complexity that is involved in bringing about REB, it is not possible to quantify or list the variables that will bring about REB. The impact of the variables for different environmental issues will also vary.
- The sum of all the variables do not add up to the product, that is, environmentally responsible behavior.
- There is no foolproof REB model which can work for all situations and issues at all places at all times.

Exercises

1. Should pro-environmental behavior be prescribed? Justify your answer with examples.
2. Why is it said that environmental education can only be meaningful if certain environmentally responsible behaviors are exhibited?
3. Will possessing environmental knowledge bring about positive environmental action? Elaborate your answer.
4. Explain in brief the responsible environmental behavior model discussed in the chapter.
5. How do society or societal norms influence behavior? Explain.
6. Explain the variables that contribute to intention to act.
7. Under what circumstances one tends to exhibit pro-environmental behavior in spite of having no intention to act?
8. How does locus of control contribute in intention to act?
9. How does cognitive factor contribute in intention to act?
10. Do you think rewards and incentives are important to bring about environmentally responsible action? Justify your answer with examples.

References

Bamberg, S. and G. Möser. 2007. "Twenty years after Hines, Hungerford, and Tomera: A New Meta-analysis of Psycho-social Determinants of Pro-environment Behaviour." *Journal of Environmental Psychology* 27: 14–25.

Biedenweg, K., M.C. Monroe and D.J. Wojcik. 2013. "Foundations of Environmental Education." In *Across the Spectrum: Resources for Environmental Educators*, edited by Martha C. Monroe and Marianne E. Krasny, 9-28. Washington, DC: North American Association for Environmental Education (NAAEE).

Bones, David. 1994. *EE Toolbox: Getting Started—A Guide to Bringing Environmental Education Into Your Classroom*, Ann Arbor: MI: University of Michigan.

Chawla, Louise and D.F. Cushing. 2007. "Education for Strategic Environmental Behavior." *Environmental Education Research* 13(4): 437–452.

Disinger, J.F. 1983. *Environmental Education's Definitional Problems*. ERIC Clearinghouse for Science, Mathematics and Environmental Education Information Bulletin, 2. Columbus, OH: ERIC/SMEAC. Available at: http://

globalenvironmentaleducation.wikispaces.com/file/view/EE_Definitional_Problem.pdf (Accessed on 5 April 2015).

Disinger, J.F. 1993. "Environment in the K–12 Curriculum: An Overview." In *Environmental Education – Teacher Resource Handbook*, edited by Richard J. Wilke, 23–43 New York: Kraus International Publications.

Disinger, J.F. 2009. "The Purposes of Environmental Education: Perspectives of Teachers, Governmental Agencies, NGOs, Professional Societies, and Advocacy Groups." In *Environmental Education and Advocacy*: *Changing Perspectives of Ecology and Education*, edited by Edward A. Johnson and Michael J. Mappin, 137–158. Cambridge: Cambridge University Press Available at: http://books.google.co.in/books?id=ac2M9upsf5 4C&pg=PA154&lpg=PA154&dq=should+schools+have+specific+roles+in+teaching+values?+john+f+disinge r&source=bl&ots=_jJykxLhG9&sig=DWdL16A5XOedV68GQaogETaVmYc&hl=en&sa=X&ei=kY8iVPThLcjlu QTk6YKoCQ&ved=0CB4Q6AEwAA#v=onepage&q=should%20schools%20have%20specific%20roles%20 in%20teaching%20values%3F%20john%20f%20disinger&f=true (Accessed on 25 September 2014).

Disinger, J.F. and R.W. Howe. 1990. *Trends and Issues Related to the Preparation of Teachers for Environmental Education*. Environmental Education Information Report. ERIC Clearinghouse for Science, Mathematics, and Environmental Education Information Report. Available at: http://files.eric.ed.gov/fulltext/ED335233.pdf (Accessed on 15 April 2015).

Disinger, J.F. and M.C. Monroe. 1994. *EE Toolbox – Workshop Resource Manual, Defining Environmental Education*. Ann Arbor, MI: University of Michigan, National Consortium for Environmental Education and Training.

Genc, Murat. 2015. "The Project-based Learning Approach in Environmental Education." *International Research in Geographical and Environmental Education* 24(2): 105–117.

Gough, Annette. 2013. "Emergence of Environmental Education Research: A 'History' of the Field." In *International Handbook of Research on Environmental Education*, edited by Robert B. Stevenson, Michael Brody, Justin Dillon, and Arjen E.J. Wals, 9–12. New York: Routledge. Available at: https://books.google.co.in/boo ks?id=efMxqII6FtwC&printsec=frontcover&dq=Gough,+Annette+(2013).+%E2%80%9CEmergence+of+Env ironmental+Education+Research:+A+%E2%80%9CHistory%E2%80%9D+of+the+Field.%E2%80%9D+In+R obert+B.+Stevenson,+Michael+Brody,+Justin+Dillon,+Arjen+E.J.+Wals,+Eds.+International+Handbook+of+ Research+on+Environmental+Education,+Routledge,+pp.9-12.&hl=en&sa=X&ved=0CCIQ6AEwAWoVChM Iitah5dGOyQIVkgiOCh1n6w_W#v=onepage&q&f=false (Accessed on 14 November 2015).

Hines, J.M., H.R. Hungerford, and A.N. Tomera. 1986/87. "Analysis and Synthesis of Research on Responsible Environmental Behavior: A Meta-analysis." *Journal of Environmental Education* 18(2): 1–8.

Hungerford, H.R. 1987. "Environmental Education and Student Behaviors in Trends and Issues." In *Environmental Education*: *EE in School Curricula*, edited by John F. Disinger, 25–38. Reports of a Symposium and a Survey. Environmental Education Information Reports. ERIC Clearinghouse for Science, Mathematics, and Environmental Education, NAAEE, Ohio, Available at: http://files.eric.ed.gov/fulltext/ED292608.pdf (Accessed on 16 April 2015).

Hungerford, H.R. and T.L. Volk. 1990. "Changing Behavior through Environmental Education." *Journal of Environmental Education* 21(3): 8–21. Available at: http://www.cbtrust.org/atf/cf/%7BEB2A714E-8219-45E8-8C3D-50EBE1847CB8%7D/Changing%20learner%20behavior%20-%20H%20and%20V.pdf (Accessed on 5 August 2015).

Kibert, C.J., M.C. Monroe, A.L. Peterson, R.R. Plate, and L.P. Thiele. 2012. *Working Toward Sustainability–Ethical Decision Making in a Technological World*. New York: John Wiley & Sons.

Kopnina, H. 2014. "Future Scenarios and Environmental Education." *The Journal of Environmental Education* 45(4): 217–231.

Lucas, A.M. 1980a. "Science and Environmental Education: Pious Hopes, Self Praise and Disciplinary Chauvinism." *Studies in Science Education* 7(1): 1–26.

Lucas, A.M. 1980b. "The Role of Science Education in Education for the Environment." *Journal of Environmental Education* 12(2): 33–37.

NCERT, National Council of Educational Research and Training, 2004. *Environmental Education in Schools— Syllabus for Environmental Education in Schools Submitted to the Hon'ble Supreme Court of India in Pursuance of its Order Dated 18th December 2003*. New Delhi: NCERT.

——— 2005. *National Curriculum Framework-2005*. New Delhi: NCERT.

Sobel, D. 2008. *Childhood and Nature—Design Principles for Educators*, 144–146. Portland, ME: Stenhouse Publishers.

UNESCO-UNEP, United Nations Educational, Scientific and Cultural Organization-United Nations Environment Programme. 1978. "The Tibilisi Declaration." *Connect, UNESCO–UNEP Environmental Education Newsletter* III(1): 1–8.

Multi-perspectives of Environmental Education

Worth a Thought!

The term 'environment' is understood by many educators in the narrow sense of nature consisting of plants, animals, and their physical environment such as air, water, and soil. Due to this partial or limited understanding of the term, the goal of environmental education by such practitioners is limited to teaching the 'science' of plants, animals, and the physical environment in isolation. There is nothing environmental education in such teaching practices.

Chapter Overview

The chapter seeks to draw out the varied views of the term 'environment' and the implications and ramifications due to such variation in understanding. It further attempts to relate the inconsistencies in the understanding of the term with the way environmental education is understood and practiced. To this end, three different perspectives of environmental education that are prevalent globally amongst practitioners and educators are discussed here. An attempt has also been made to situate the perspective that is seen in India by looking at certain relevant documents. This chapter will facilitate the readers to:

- **recognize the differences in the understanding of the term 'environment.'**
- **explain the implications of the lack of clarity of the term 'environment.'**
- **explain the different perspectives of environmental education.**
- **differentiate the three perspectives of environmental education.**
- **explain the prevalent perspective of environmental education in India.**

Introduction

In Chapters 1 and 2 we had discussed in detail about the definition and nature of environmental education. We had seen that environmental education is interdisciplinary, holistic, and encompasses the environment in totality, that is, biophysical, social, cultural, and economic. Yet, most people, including many educators, understand environmental education to be confined within the boundary of natural science or biophysical environment. Many would not even include the man-made environment and restrict their definition of 'environment' to the natural environment only. This, perhaps, has led to the marginalization of environmental education itself in the education system. However, this is not surprising as we shall see in the following discussion that the problem with this is as old as environmental education itself, which never got completely resolved universally. Referring to the range of meaning associated with environmental education, Lucas (1980) had written, "[U]nless there is a clear change of perception, a developing consensus, a sense of unity and purpose, then environmental education will continue under a cloud of confusion."

In *Environmental Education's Definitional Problem,* Disinger (1983) quoted Hungerford et al. (1983) as:

> It is disconcerting (to say the least) for those involved in the implementation of environmental education goals to hear again the question: 'What is environmental education?'…We submit that environmental education does have a substantive structure that has evolved through the considerable efforts of many and that the framework has been documented formally in the literature. The question asked…has most certainly been answered. One would dare hope that this question could, at long last, be laid to rest…the field is quite definitely beyond the goal setting stage and into the business of implementation.

JUST A MOMENT!

Give a thought on how you conceive the term 'environment.'

However, after more than six decades of the first use of the term environmental education in 1948 (Disinger 1983), the same question seems to be still relevant and prevalent today, especially with the 'environment' component of environmental education. There are basic questions that have not been answered–whether the environment as is used in environmental education includes the entire biosphere or just the species, or whether it includes humans as part of an ecosystem, or does it include only 'nature' or 'wilderness,' or whether 'acculturated' human landscapes such as urban parks and gardens are to be considered 'natural environments' is still debated. Kopnina (2012) also mentions the inherent complexity and diversity of the use of the term 'environment' (what is and what is not included in it) wherein throughout the discussion 'environment' has been largely used to refer to the biophysical environment. According to the National Green Tribunal Bill of India the term 'environment' includes water, air, and land and the interrelationship which exists among and between water, air, and land and human beings, other living creatures, plants, micro-organism, and property.[1] The term 'environment' is also spoken of to include "social, personal, cultural, economic, political, and, of course, biological and physical environments" (Wenzel 1997). This lack of clarity on the confines of 'environment' has brought about obscurity or vagueness in the understanding of the term environmental education and, hence, impacts its implementation in a major way.

---

[1] http://envfor.nic.in/sites/default/files/division/national-green-tribunal-bill-2009.pdf (accessed on 20 April 2015)

This is found to have already impacted the understandings of the students. In one such study undertaken to find out what students conceive or consider the term 'environment' to be, it was found that most of the students consider only the components of nature (plants, animals, mountains, rivers, but excluding man or man-made environments) to be part of the environment (Shimray et al. 2014). Disinger and Howe (1990, 1) discusses of the two ways in which the definitions of 'environment' can be presented, one in which humans are integral part of the environment (i.e., humankind in environment, as one participating species), the other in which the environment is considered as the surroundings of humans (i.e., humankind and environment, humans being considered separately from environment, with 'environment' thus defined as 'everything else'). They maintain that the concept of 'environment' is also evolving with the increase in the scientific knowledge about the environment and the understanding of the interactions and interrelationships within the natural environment. This has broadened the original sense of the term 'environment' which was limited to the biological study of plants and their environments, in an ecological sense to considering the totalities of complex environmental interdependencies which encompasses the manmade physical environment and the political, economic, cultural, technological, social, and aesthetic environments, as well as the bio-physical natural environment (Disinger and Howe 1990). While Orr (2004) suggests, "all education is environmental education" implying that is to suggest that students relate to and understand about the environment depending on how and what is included or excluded while being taught. For example, a teacher of Economics may include environment (ecosystem) while teaching about our economic life or she may teach economic life in isolation. Both are environmental lesson, but the latter is not the correct approach. Liberty Hyde Bailey, noted botanist, writer, college administrator, educator, and proponent of nature study had sent out a warning in this regard way back in 1905. He rejected the use of the term "environmental education" in his writing because he thought it was "imprecise, theoretical, pompous, and would always need to be explained" (McCrea 2006). Rightly said, it still remains to be explained even today. Indeed it is worth asking what do we include in the 'environment,' because all the activities and initiatives that would be taken up by the practitioners of environmental education, would heavily depend on how one envisions 'environment' in the composite term environmental education.

From the earlier discussion the varied views about environmental education is clearly evident. This lack of clarity on the limits and boundaries has in a way paved the way for education for sustainable development (ESD) to make its entry into the system. Therefore, what is being attempted in this chapter is to group environmental education under three categories, each signifying a perspective of environmental education, depending on how the 'environment' component is viewed. It will also elaborately discuss which of the perspectives holds true in India by looking at how environmental education has been reflected in the important documents and curricular materials it had brought out related to education since the latter half of the 20th century.

JUST A MOMENT

Did you find your view on the term 'environment' comparable with any of those presented earlier?

7.1 Three Perspectives of Environmental Education

Based on a broad analysis of the different views as discussed earlier, environmental education can be placed under the following three perspectives.

7.1.1 Environmental Education Is All-inclusive

The first view is held by those who are of the opinion that environmental education includes a very broad area of studies which encompasses biophysical as well as social dimensions. According to this view, the environment is not just about the bio-physical environment or nature but also includes the social as well as cultural and traditional environments. Here, environment is spatial—anything (bio-physical or social) that is within a space. In their report on *Urban Environmental Education–Demonstration*, Glasser et al. (1972) clearly highlighted that "the environment is the totality of one's surroundings. It involves more than biological factors affected by problems like air pollution and solid wastes problems, it also includes social factors that affect problems like poverty and racism." Further in the same report they defined the environment as, "[E]verything surrounding you. Generally, it's a system of forces that knowingly or unknowingly affects you. Specifically it includes a range of social and biological problems." They included recreation, class differences, open spaces, crime, dirt, drugs, solid wastes, housing, overcrowding, pollution, building codes, the consumer and the market place, unemployment, and transportation as part of environmental education. Stapp and Cox (1974, 3) also listed ecosystem, population, economics and technology, environmental decisions and environmental ethics as the five major concepts to be included in environmental education and organized the activities under these themes. This indicated the all-inclusiveness of EE—biophysical environment, social and economic dimensions. This view of environmental education is not held by them alone. Environmental educators such as Disinger and Monroe (1994, 13) also included drug abuse, homelessness, and teen pregnancy as environmental issues to be dealt as part of environmental education.

In an attempt to clarify the meaning of the term environment, Lahiry et al. (1988, 26) includes all nonliving and living objects, happenings and forces—both natural and man-made—which influences the life of an organism. The man-made environment not only included man-made structures and technologies such as means of agricultural and industrial production, transport and communication, and so on, but also social activities and institutions such as the family, religion, education, the economy, and politics. Similarly, to humanists, environment is the place of existence, a habitat—with all its historical, cultural, political, economic, emotional, and other aspects as is reflected in place-based environmental education (Sauvé 2005).

What we could gather from these views, as presented by different professionals in the field, is that all issues, irrespective of whether environmental (in this context meaning biophysical), social or economic, exclusively or involving either two or all of it combined, should be part of environmental education. In a sense, this view intends to signify that environmental education has no specific boundary. However, though plausible, making environmental education too broad will do little service to our attempt to restore and conserve the biophysical environment which is undoubtedly the primary goal of environmental education. This is because, in trying to address all the aspects of environment, focus on restoration and conservation of the biophysical environment may not garner the attention that it demands.

To sum up, according to this view, environmental education is all-encompassing—biophysical or social (economic and cultural aspects included) in nature. However, both are interconnected and, hence, are to be looked at holistically. Under this category, examples that would be relevant in Indian context could include social issues such as dowry, female foeticide, child marriage, migration, child labor, caste systems, racial discrimination, illiteracy, and poverty, which may not have direct relevance with the biophysical environment, besides the many bio-physical issues such as those related to pollution, deforestation, wildlife, conservation, and energy.

JUST A MOMENT

Do you think including everything under environmental education is a good idea? If this becomes a reality, visualize how the school curriculum will be like.

7.1.2 Environmental Education Is Moderately Ecocentric

According to this view, environmental education focuses on addressing biophysical issues along with its inherent social and economic issues. This view is supported by the fact that environmental education itself became established as a follow up of the United Nations Conference on Human Environment held at Stockholm in 1972 which met to mainly discuss the issues of deteriorating environment resulting from degradation and pollution. The conference pointed out that man had transformed the environment so much that the balance of nature was changed, which would in turn be dangerous for the living species. The declaration of the conference proclaimed that it has become an imperative goal for mankind "to defend and improve the environment for present and future generations" (UNESCO-UNEP 1978). We may recall some of the landmark decisions that were taken at the international level, particularly the Belgrade Charter of 1975 and the Tbilisi Declaration of 1977.

The Belgrade Charter was framed keeping in view the unprecedented economic growth and technological progress which, while bringing benefits to many people, had also caused severe social and environmental consequences. It was a call to eradicate the basic causes of poverty, hunger, illiteracy, pollution, exploitation, and domination with an aim to improve the quality of life. The need for peaceful coexistence and cooperation was also emphasized. It specifically mentioned that environmental education should consider the environment in its totality—natural and man-made, ecological, political, economic, technological, social, legislative, cultural, and aesthetic. The Tbilisi Declaration voiced the same wherein it mentioned, "to foster clear awareness of, and concern about, economic, social, political and ecological interdependence in urban and rural areas" as one of its goals. Also, its guiding principles reiterated that environmental education should "consider the environment in its totality—natural and built, technological and social (economic, political, cultural-historical, moral, aesthetic)" (UNESCO-UNEP 1978).

Looking at this, we do not seem to see any difference in the views presented here and the views presented in the previous category, that is, both categories express the all-inclusiveness of environmental education. However, the following statement, which is the first recommendation of the Tbilisi Declaration, sets the two views apart. It mentioned:

> Whereas it is a fact that biological and physical features constitute the natural basis of the human environment, it's ethical, social, cultural, and economic dimensions also play their part in determining the lines of approach and the instruments whereby people may understand and make better use of natural resources in satisfying their needs.

This suggests that the 'totality' that is being talked about here is in relation to the factors (ethical, social, cultural, and economic) that are connected to the biophysical issues, and not just any issue. It does not include those factors which do not have direct relevance to biophysical issues. For example, it will be difficult and would be stretching too far to relate issues like dowry or caste system with biophysical issues. Hence, such social issues are not included in this category. On the other hand, social issues such as women walking miles to bring water are an inherent part of biophysical issues such as scarcity of potable water. Therefore, while addressing scarcity of water, the problems faced by women will naturally be taken care of. Let us take another example. We are aware that poverty leads to misuse and exploitation of resources—natural and man-made. Therefore, in order to conserve resources, we need to first address the issue of poverty. Hence, poverty, though considered to be a social issue, is included in this category.

Thus, the key difference between this and the previous category lies in the following: The former includes social or economic issues which do not have direct relevance to biophysical issues under environmental education. The latter includes only those social and economic issues which are connected to the biophysical issues.

From these we can conclude that issues related to bio-physical environment is the key concern. At the same time, it is also clear that the approach suggested for tackling such environmental issues was never solely for the conservation of bio-physical environment alone but a holistic one. Hence, for practitioners with this view, the focus of environmental education remains bio-physical issues, that is, bio-physical issues is the reason for environmental education based on this perspective. Social and other economic ramifications associated with such issues are considered accordingly. In short, it takes into consideration the environment (biophysical), society, and economy which are interconnected while dealing with environmental issues. For example, Monroe (2012) provided the interconnections of environmental, economic, cultural, political, and technological components of different issues and how each component needs to be understood to identify a reasonable solution. This, she did by citing an example frequently used by Stapp, one of the pioneers of environmental education. She writes,

> Stapp recounted frequently the example of schistosomiasis, a water-borne disease that affects people in many developing countries, to illustrate these interconnections. The parasitic worm's life cycle includes infecting snails, to which people are exposed when using reservoirs

and canals for bathing. Pathogens in human waste disposed of in the same waterways find their way into snails to complete their life cycles. The cost of pumping water to standpipes or building desirable latrines in rural nations is prohibitive, and the economic impact of people unable to work a full day is equally severe. Cultural norms around the use of water are important factors. The construction of dams for irrigation, particularly in Egypt, is recognised as one cause of the problem. Schistosomiasis is known as the second most socioeconomically devastating disease after malaria in Africa, Asia and South America. (Monroe 2012)

Although the primary goal is to tackle bio-physical environmental issue, as we saw in the example, systems perspective is what we look for in matters of environmental issues. Here are some more examples. In order to manage or regulate *jhum* cultivation, not only are the adverse impacts of *jhum* cultivation on the environment are considered, but other concerns which have direct relevance such as alternative sources of livelihood, vocational development, and so on, are taken into consideration. Similarly, when dealing with soil pollution due to excessive use of insecticides and fertilizers, other areas such as impacts on health, and short term and long term economic loss are also taken into account. Hence, though the initial and central focus may be biophysical in nature, the social as well as economic concerns inherent in it are essentially taken care of.

JUST A MOMENT

What is your opinion about this perspective of environmental education? Do you think this perspective best fit environmental education as it was initially envisaged?

7.1.3 Environmental Education Is Purely Ecocentric

Proponents of this view consist largely of those who are pro-ESD advocates. According to this view, environmental education presents a one-sided approach to environmental issues and it lacks the holistic approach to resolve the issue. They argue that since the focus of environmental education is on conservation of nature and natural resources, social and other related concerns are ignored. This is true to certain extent if the earlier focus of environmental education, such as during the 1970s and 1980s, is to be considered, which was concentrated on mitigating pollution and conserving natural resources. Further, they maintain that if at all environmental education took care of social and other related concerns, it was insignificant. This view was also clearly highlighted in the UNESCO International Implementation Scheme (2005) which, while referring to environmental education says, "While some attention was attached to the social and economic issues inherent in these environmental issues the focus was largely on addressing the ecological impact of ever increasing unrestricted development." The proponents of this view are of the opinion that issue resolutions as demonstrated by environmental education are biased toward the bio-physical environment (i.e., more ecocentric) and not in favor of society at large.

Looking at the actual situation of how environmental education is practiced, the observations stated earlier may be true in many instances. However, if we look at the roots of environmental education, such viewpoints hold no ground. We will recall that social concerns have always been part of the debate and deliberations, even in the past, while addressing environmental issues. For example, in the Stockholm conference in 1972, Indira Gandhi, the then Prime Minister of India had made a statement, "Poverty is the worst form of pollution," keeping in view the concerns of the developing country (Strong 1999). The statement may not be very appealing to many at the first instance. However, when it is dissected and expanded the real meaning of the statement can be understood. It is a fact that due to poverty there is often increased exploitation and misuse of natural and man-made resources. Poverty-associated problems also include littering, improper waste disposal, lack of proper sanitation, and so on, which lead to increased pollution of soil, water, and air. When the statement was made, there were staggering populations of people under poverty in developing countries like India. Therefore, it was suggested that if we want to preserve our environment, it was important to first address the issue of poverty. Doing this meant indirectly working toward the preservation of the environment. Also, Tang Ke, leader of the Chinese delegation to the same conference had stated, "We hold that of all things in the world, people are the most precious" (Clarke and Timberlake 1982 cited in UNEP 2002, 2).

The earlier supposition (that environmental education does not address social and economic issues), coupled with fragmentary or non-holistic practices of environmental education by practitioners, fortified the view that environmental education is ecocentric in its approach. This ultimately led to the birth of the concept of ESD, which is considered to be holistic and more inclusive, encompassing the three dimensions of sustainable development—environment, society, and economy while resolving any issue. ESD could be done either through sustainable development related education, which include peace education, global education, development education, HIV and AIDS education, citizenship education, and so on, or through full-fledged ESD, which essentially requires the integration of all the three dimensions (UNESCO 2009), as we shall see in detail in Chapter 9. How similar or different environmental education and ESD are will also be discussed in more detail in that chapter.

JUST A MOMENT

Is it appropriate to say that environmental education is only concerned about the biophysical environment?

7.2 The Perspectives in India's Context

Having discussed three different perspectives concerning environmental education observed globally, we will now try to look for and arrive at the perspective which is prevalent in India. Do we adhere to a particular perspective or are all the three perspectives common. To do this, we will have to look at the developments that have taken place in the past four or five decades. In 1976 the Constitution was amended by incorporating an article (51A) with the heading 'Fundamental Duties.' Clause (g), thereof, requires every citizen to protect and improve the natural environment, including forests, lakes, rivers, and wild life, and to have compassion for living creatures. This was done to promote living in harmony with nature. Soon after the Stockholm conference of 1972 on human environment, the Water Pollution Control Act of 1974 came into the statute book. The Air Pollution Control Act came in 1981 and finally came the Environment Protection Act of 1986. The fact that these acts find mention in the 22 November 1991 order of the Hon'ble Supreme Court of India in the environmental education case, as discussed in the previous chapters, also suggested that the focus has been largely on bio-physical environment.[2]

Although environmental education was part of the curriculum since the 1970s, the bio-physical environment was definitely the focus. In fact, the NCERT (1981, 3) mentioned that since 1975 it has taken up environmental education as its priority area. For instance, it mentions textbooks for the social sciences such as geography where topics such as renewable and non-renewable resources of the country and conservation and afforestation as policy and practice have been discussed at length. However, the document clearly agrees that the strongest emphasis on evolving concepts of environmental education has been made in various generations of science textbooks developed by the NCERT. The document further provides some details of the topics that were included in the textbooks developed during different generations (NCERT 1981, 4–9).

The textbooks in biology published in 1967 had stressed population explosion, food problem, conservation, food chain and food webs, and the biosphere.

The next generation of biology textbooks, published in 1973, brought in elements of nature study, conservation, population, and general ecological principles into a comprehensive approach to environmental awareness.

The 1975–1980 generation of textbooks for lower classes had an emphasis on learning through environment with the objective of making the learner familiar with social and biophysical environments. While for the middle, secondary and higher secondary levels the topics that featured included, human dependence on nature, adaptability of animals and man to their environments, population, ecological succession and eco-crisis, and population and conservation as well as community health.

Based on the document, the focus of environmental education appears to be more on the biophysical dimension and less on the socio-economic aspects.

The National Policy on Education, 1986 mentioned the protection of the environment, such as forests, rivers, lakes, and wild life, as one of the values to be promoted through the common core.[3] This recommendation of the policy was based on Article 51-A(g) of the Constitution of India as discussed earlier. It also mentioned the paramount need to create a consciousness of the environment through teaching in schools and college. In the light of this 1986 policy, the 1988 curriculum framework highlighted protection of the environment and conservation of nature. Special emphasis was given on maintaining

---

[2] http://ncert.nic.in/book_publishing/environ_edu/22.11.pdf (accessed on 4 July 2014)
[3] http://www.ncert.nic.in/oth_anoun/Policy_1986_eng.pdf (accessed on 14 July 2014)

ecological balance. It included topics such as air, water, soil, conservation of natural resources, energy, fuel, biosphere, man and his environment, pollution, land, climate and resources, human response in environment, urbanization, poverty, indicators of economic development, food problems, new technologies in agriculture, and so on. (For details refer to Chapter 4, Appendices 3 and 5; NCERT 1995, 8–15.) Yet again, the topics reflected that the focus was definitely on bio-physical issues. However, there is ample scope to discuss the social and economic dimensions of such biophysical issues. Hence, whether such practice of environmental education can be considered to be holistic depends purely on how the teacher transacts the topics in the classroom.

More recently, in the 2000 curriculum framework (National Curriculum Framework for School Education 2000; NCERT 2000), a more balanced approach of environmental education was adopted wherein one of the objectives of education was "to help to generate and promote among the learners understanding of the environment in its totality both natural and social, and their interactive processes, the environmental problems and the ways and means to preserve the environment." It reaffirmed the provisions of Article 51-A(g) of the Indian Constitution which lays down that it is the duty of every citizen to improve and protect the environment and the need to integrate the same in the school curriculum. Again, the focus was on the conservation of bio-physical environment. Similarly, in the 2005 curriculum framework (National Curriculum Framework 2005; NCERT 2005), though environmental education was to facilitate the move toward sustainable development, the focus was again on biophysical environment such as water pollution, sustainable agriculture, and so on.

Most importantly, we may recall the famous environmental education PIL of 1991. Not many will disagree that environmental education in India became evidently recognized only after the Hon'ble Supreme Court had passed an order in 1991 to make environmental education compulsory in all stages of school education. It is noteworthy to mention that this petition itself was filed keeping in view the increasing issues related to environmental pollution, which again is biophysical in nature.

The document "Environmental Education in Schools—Syllabus for Environmental Education in Schools, Submitted to the Hon'ble Supreme Court of India in Pursuance of its Order Dated 18th December 2003" (NCERT 2004; refer to Chapter 5 for detail), besides the bio-physical environmental concerns, had clearly pointed out that environmental education should be an instrument for inculcating healthy personal and social attitudes toward environment and development for which a focus on the social environment is necessary. However the same is not reflected in the stage-wise syllabus which was provided in the document. Of the many content areas provided for each class only a handful were social in nature such as human rights, fundamental duties and value education, women and child welfare. The rest are all bio-physical in nature.

One thing strongly emerges from the discussion: there is no clarity on what the term 'environment' includes or excludes and, therefore, no clarity on what environmental education encompasses. However, considering the above, it would be appropriate to say that we have been, at best, implementing environmental education with a focus on biophysical issues and, to some extent, its inherent social and economic issues. All the curricular materials developed during different times showed that environmental (here, biophysical) topics have been adequately incorporated. As mentioned earlier, whether only biophysical aspects are considered or all the dimensions of environmental education such as biophysical, social, and economic aspects are addressed depends more or less on how the teacher transacts the topics.

JUST A MOMENT

Reflect on the ways of implementation of environmental education in India and try to identify some of its drawbacks.

Conclusion

How we understand environmental education in general and 'environment' in particular has an influence on how we practice environmental education. We have seen the differing views of the professionals and practitioners about the meaning of the terms. This lack of clarity has brought about the misconceptions on environmental education itself, which has also paved way for the introduction of other forms of education such as education for sustainable development. The different perspectives of environmental education based on such views can be categorized into three: (a) environmental education is all encompassing, (b) environmental education is moderately ecocentric, and (c) environmental education is purely ecocentric. Each view has a message of its own. If we look closely at these perspectives, one thing is clear, that is, the fundamental difference is based on the biophysical environment. How much importance is given to this component, categorizes the three. Each category will serve a good purpose. However, with the increasing damage that is meted out to the environment, which in turn has become a threat for the existence of humankind, a perspective with a little more inclination toward the biophysical environment may be the need of the hour. This could bring about some hope in the restoration and conservation of the already degraded biophysical environment.

With regard to India, clarity on the meaning of the terms is more important. This is because the country is huge and the population of the country is equally overwhelming. Besides, the health of the environment plays an important role in defining the health and economy of the people. Such clarity in the understanding of the terms will benefit India much more than any other country. This is because the model curriculum for the school and teacher-education courses is the same for the whole country. Once understood clearly by the practitioners, environmental education will be implemented more effectively.

Therefore, defining the boundaries for the terms 'environment' and 'environmental education' appear to be the foremost task that should be taken up for effective implementation of environmental education. This would greatly help practitioners in the implementation of environmental education in the long run. Most of all, it will give environmental education its much needed 'identity.'

SUMMARY

- There is a need to clearly define the terms environmental education or 'environment' so that practitioners are able to take up environmental education meaningfully.
- Different views exist amongst different professionals and practitioners on what is included under 'environment' and what is excluded. Based on differing views and practices, the different perspectives of environmental education can be categorized into three, such as (a) environmental education is all encompassing, (b) environmental education is moderately ecocentric and, (c) environmental education is purely ecocentric.
- Lack of clarity brought about the misconceptions on environmental education has paved way for the introduction of other forms of education such as education for sustainable development.
- In India, there is not much clarity on what it includes in environmental education and what it excludes. However, the focus seems to be largely on the biophysical dimension.

- Boundaries, will have to be drawn in two aspects—drawing boundary for 'environment' in the term environmental education and drawing boundary for the term 'environmental education' itself.
- One of the ways of defining boundary could be to say that 'environment' includes everything around us by defining the boundary in terms of space. While also clearly spelling out that when we say 'environmental education' the overall focus is to preserve and conserve the biophysical environment by maintaining utmost care with respect to the socio-economic aspects associated with it.
- Another way of defining boundary is to say that 'environment' includes everything around us and hence environmental education includes education in any aspect of such environment. This will include anything and everything related to social, economic or biophysical environment wherein there is no specific emphasis on any one aspect.
- Defining boundaries will give environmental education its 'identity.'

Exercises

1. Mention some of the contentions and debates regarding the term 'environment' in the chapter.
2. Do you think it is important to clearly define the term 'environment' in order to successfully implement environmental education? Justify your answer.
3. What are the different perspectives of environmental education? Briefly differentiate these perspectives.
4. Which perspective of environmental education do you think should be promoted? Justify your answer.
5. Why is there so much inconsistency in the understanding of environmental education? Explain.
6. If environmental education is all-encompassing, what are the possible drawbacks?
7. Give some examples which suggest that environmental education in India seems to be focusing more on the biophysical aspects.
8. What would you suggest so that environmental education can be implemented more meaningfully and effectively?
9. What do you think should be the appropriate way to define the term 'environment'?
10. Defining boundaries is essential for environmental education. Justify the statement.

References

Disinger, J.F. 1983. *Environmental Education's Definitional Problem*. ERIC Information Bulletin No. 2, Columbus, OH: ERIC Science, Mathematics, and Environmental Education Clearinghouse. Available at: http://globalenvironmentaleducation.wikispaces.com/file/view/EE_Definitional_Problem.pdf (Accessed on 5 April 2015).

Disinger, J.F. and R.W. Howe. 1990. *Trends and Issues Related to the Preparation of Teachers for Environmental Education*. Environmental Education Information Report ERIC Clearinghouse for Science, Mathematics, and Environmental Education Information Report. ED335233. Columbus, OH: ERIC/SMEAC. Available at: http://files.eric.ed.gov/fulltext/ED335233.pdf (Accessed on 15 April 2015).

Disinger, J.F. and M.C. Monroe. 1994. *EE Toolbox—Workshop Resource Manual Defining Environmental Education*. Ann Arbor, MI: University of Michigan, National Consortium for Environmental Education and Training.

Glasser, R., B. William Stapp, and J. James Swan. 1972. *Urban Environmental Education—Demonstration*. Final Report. Michigan University, School of Natural Resources, Ann Arbor, Michigan.

Kopnina, H. 2012. "Education for Sustainable Development (ESD): The Turn Away from 'Environment' in Environmental Education?" *Environmental Education Research* 18(5): 699–717.

Lahiry, D., Savita Sinha, J.S. Gill, U. Mallik, and A.K. Mishra. 1988. *UNESCO–UNEP International Environmental Education Programme Environmental Education Series 26, Environmental Education: A Process for Pre-service Teacher Training Curriculum Development*, edited by Patricia R. Simpson, Harold Hungerford, and Trudi L. Volk. Paris: UNESCO.

Lucas, A.M. 1980. "Science and Environmental Education: Pious Hopes, Self Praise and Disciplinary Chauvinism." *Studies in Science Education* 7(1): 1–26.

McCrea, E. J. 2006. *The Roots of Environmental Education: How the Past Supports the Present*. Environmental Education and Training Partnership. Wisconsin: EETAP. Available at: http://cms.eetap.org/repository/moderncms_documents/History.Final.20060315.1.1.pdf (Accessed on 19 July 2015).

Monroe, M.C. 2012. "The Co-Evolution of ESD and EE." *Journal of Education for Sustainable Development* 6(1): 43–47.

NCERT, National Council of Educational Research and Training. 1981. *Environmental Education and NCERT*. New Delhi: NCERT.

——— 1995. *Environmental Education in the School Curriculum developed by the NCERT*. New Delhi: NCERT.

——— 2000. *The National Curriculum Framework for School Education*. New Delhi: NCERT.

——— 2004. *Environmental Education in Schools–Syllabus for Environmental Education in Schools Submitted to the Hon'ble Supreme Court of India in Pursuance of its Order Dated 18th December 2003*. New Delhi: NCERT.

——— 2005. *The National Curriculum Framework 2005*. New Delhi: NCERT.

Orr, D.W. (1994) 2004. *What is Education For? In Earth in Mind: On Education, Environment and the Human Prospect*. 10th anniversary edition, 7–15. Washington: Island Press.

Sauvé, Lucie. 2005. "Currents in Environmental Education: Mapping a Complex and Evolving Pedagogical Field." *Canadian Journal of Environmental Education* 10(Spring): 11–37.

Shimray, C.V., A.N. Hoshi, and R. Sasidhar. 2014. "Preliminary Study of Environmental Awareness of Students with Implementation of Environmental Education in Schools in India." *School Science* 52(2). New Delhi: NCERT.

Stapp, W.B. and D.A. Cox. 1974. *Environmental Education Activities Manual*. Dexter, MI: Thomson–Shore. Available at: http://files.eric.ed.gov/fulltext/ED119947.pdf (Accessed on 5 June 2015).

Strong, M.F. 1999. *Hunger, Poverty, Population and Environment*. The Hunger Project Millennium Lecture, 7 April 1999. The Hunger Project, Madras, India. Available at: http://www.grida.no/geo/GEO/Geo-1-021.htm (Accessed on 15 November 2015).

UNEP, United Nations Environment Programme. 2002. *Integrating Environment and Development: 1972-2002, Global Environment Outlook 3—Past, Present and Future Perspectives, London, Earthscan*. London: UNEP. Available at: http://www.unep.org/geo/GEO3/english/pdfs/chapter1.pdf (Accessed on 15 November 2015).

UNESCO, United Nations Educational, Scientific and Cultural Organization. 2009. *Learning for a Sustainable World: Review of Contexts and Structures for Education for Sustainable Development*. United Nations Decade of Education for Sustainable Development (DESD, 2005-2014). Paris: UNESCO.

UNESCO-UNEP, United Nations Educational, Scientific and Cultural Organization-United Nations Environment Programme. 1978. "Tbilisi Declaration." *Connect, UNESCO–UNEP Environmental Education Newsletter* III(1): 1–8.

Wenzel, Eberhard. 1997. "Environment, Development and Health: Ideological Metaphors of Post-traditional Societies?" *Health Education Research–Theory & Practice* 12(4): 403–418. Available at: https://www.researchgate.net/publication/249278804_Health_environment_and_education (Accessed on 11 June 2015).

Chapter	Teacher Empowerment in
8	Environmental Education:
	A Concern

Worth a Thought!

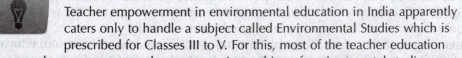

Teacher empowerment in environmental education in India apparently caters only to handle a subject called Environmental Studies which is prescribed for Classes III to V. For this, most of the teacher education courses have a separate pedagogy paper in teaching of environmental studies. However, how teachers are to transact environmental education from Class VI onwards is not reflected adequately in any of the existing teacher education courses.

Chapter Overview

The chapter brings out the importance of teacher preparation in environmental education. It discusses the basic contents that should be included in all teacher empowerment courses in environmental education. The existing scenario of teacher preparation in the area of environmental education in the country in general is presented by comparing a preservice course as implemented in some institutes. The disparity in the existing preservice programs has also been discussed here. It specifically attempts to bring out some of the issues related to teacher education in the area of environmental education in India and suggests some measures to address such issues. At the end of reading this chapter, it is envisaged that readers will be sufficiently equipped to:

- explain the status of environmental education in teacher-education courses in India.
- justify the importance of including environmental education in teacher-education courses.
- describe the contents for environmental education that should be reflected in any teacher-education course.
- explain the barriers that hinders popularization of environmental education in teacher-education courses.
- analyse the existing teacher-education courses vis-à-vis environmental education.
- explain the issues and suggest solutions related to preservice teacher-education courses with respect to environmental education.
- explain the issues and suggest solutions related to in-service teacher-education courses with respect to environmental education.
- identify the issues related to teacher educators in the area of environmental education.

Introduction

In the previous chapters we have discussed how environmental education has evolved over the years. We have also discussed how the same is being reflected in the policy documents and national curriculum frameworks and, ultimately, in the school curriculum. We have also discussed the Hon'ble Supreme Court's intervention in the implementation of environmental education in India. Together, it shaped environmental education to the form it is today in India. In this chapter we will focus on how these changes in the school curriculum or the Hon'ble Court's intervention have brought about the necessary changes in professional development courses for teachers—both preservice and in-service. In this discussion, emphasis will be given to preservice course, namely, Bachelor of Education (B.Ed.) course, and to some extent on in-service programs. We will also touch upon some of the issues concerning teacher educators as well.

Teacher empowerment must form an integral part of any reform in school education. NCERT (2005) states "the hope of revitalising school education in India, via an idealistic or ideologically driven attempt at revising curriculum will probably meet with little success, if the central agency of the teacher remains unrecognised." Teachers form the key factor in all educational development and hence they need to be professionally equipped. Some statistics as mentioned in National Curriculum Framework for Teacher Education (NCFTE) 2009 (NCTE 2009, 5) related to professional development is provided in Box 8.1. The message is loud and clear that teacher education is vital for the successful implementation of 'reformed' curriculum. However, in spite of the recognition of the importance of professional preparation of teachers for qualitative improvement of

---

BOX 8.1

Some Statistics Related to Professional Development

The number of courses offered at different stages—pre-primary, elementary and secondary—face-to-face and distance modes of teacher education; programs of M.Ed., face-to-face and distance modes, C.P.Ed., B.P.Ed., and M.P.Ed. have increased from 3,489 courses in 3,199 institutions in March 2004 to a whopping 14,428 courses in 11,861 institutions in March 2009. The student intake has likewise increased from 274,072 to 1,096,673 during this period. This expansion has taken a heavy toll on quality parameters of infrastructural provision, faculty qualification, learning resources, and student profile.

Till December 2009, as many as 31 Institutes of Advanced Studies in Education (IASEs) and 104 Colleges of Teacher Education (CTEs) were sanctioned and all of these were functional. Of the 599 districts in the country, District Institutes of Education and Training (DIETs) were set up in 571 districts, of which only 529 are functional. Thus, 42 DIETs are yet to become functional. The main problem facing DIETs is nonavailability of qualified faculty. Presently, the faculty appointed does not possess qualifications or experience in elementary teacher education. A good number of CTEs face faculty shortage and poor library facilities, and spend more time on initial teacher education while research, development, and innovative activities are yet to take concrete shape. The same is the case with IASEs. The capacity of both CTEs and IASEs in performing their mandated roles has recently come under serious scrutiny.

education since the 1960s,[1] very few concrete steps have been taken in the last three decades to operationlize this (NCERT 2006). Chattopadhyaya Commission also notes, "[I]f school teachers are expected to bring about a revolution in their approach to teaching...that same revolution must precede and find a place in the Colleges of education" (NCERT 2006). However, teacher-education programs continue to train teachers to 'adjust' to the needs of an education system in which education is seen as the transmission of information and learning reproduced from textbooks. The reforms in the school education programs are not being reflected in such programs. With these recommendations and observations made by different committees and commissions at the backdrop, we will see whether these have any implications for teacher-education programs in environmental education.

JUST A MOMENT

Reflect on how seriously teacher preparation and empowerment programs are taken by the student-teachers or practicing teachers. What impact will this have in the teaching–learning process?

8.1 Teacher Preparation in Environmental Education

Teacher preparation in environmental education is a non-negotiable component to realize the goals and objectives laid down in the curriculum. Its importance cannot be overemphasized. As it is with other disciplinary subject, the key to successful environmental education in the classroom is the teacher—if teachers do not have the knowledge, skills, or commitment to "environmentalize their curriculum, it is unlikely that environmentally literate students will be produced" (Wilke 1985, 1 cited in Heimlich and Smith 2004; Tilbury 1997). Environmental literacy, here, does not mean having content knowledge about environmental issues. It refers to having the required knowledge, attitude, motivation, commitment, and skills to take informed decisions concerning the environment and its various issues. The prospective teachers, therefore, need to be environmentally sensitive individuals, who volunteer to solve environmental problems and develop positive environmental attitudes. Then only will they be able to educate their students in a similar vein (Genc 2015).

Teacher preparation is more so required in environmental education since it is comparatively a new focus which requires specific awareness, knowledge, and skills, along with an outlook which might not have been developed in the rest of the educational career of the student-teachers or the in-service teachers (Lahiry et al. 1988; Tilbury 1992 cited in Heimlich and Smith 2004, 15). It is not possible to expect teachers without the expertise to transmit environmental ideas to students in a manner that will stimulate the students to think holistically, regionally, and globally about the environment, rather than treating each topic as an isolated, discrete entity (Taylor 1988 cited in Heimlich and

---

[1] Kothari Commission, 1964-66 in http://www.teindia.nic.in/Files/Reports/CCR/KC/KC_V1.pdf (accessed on 16 April 2015)

Smith 2004, 15). A study conducted by Plevyak et al. (2001) on the level of teacher preparation and the implementation of environmental education found a significant correlation between the levels of exposure of teachers to environmental education topics in the preservice preparation and their confidence about teaching environmental education and a greater understanding of what is involved in integrating environmental education into the curriculum. The study also found a higher rate of implementation of environmental education amongst teachers who had higher levels of exposure to environmental education such as participation in some preservice environmental organizations, workshops, or programs, and so on.

Tilbury (1997) suggested that professional development in environmental education is needed for the following purpose:

1. to learn about the purpose and goals of environmental education;
2. to find out how the different approaches such as education 'about,' 'in,' and 'for' approach (or the head, heart, and hand approach) contribute toward the achievement of environmental education goals;
3. to explore how the 'about,' 'in,' and 'for' dimensions can be integrated into the curriculum in practice.

We have mentioned in the previous chapters, more specifically in Chapter 3, about the issues with implementation of environmental education such as an incomplete or fragmentary way of approaching environmental education. We have seen that information-based education 'about' environment is found to be the most convenient and common way of doing environmental education. A major factor for such practice is attributed to lack of teacher education and professional development (Fien and Ferreira 1997; Lahiry et al. 1988). Without undergoing the basic course or training in environmental education, teachers do not completely understand the philosophies behind it and very few understand the purpose of EE. Studies have shown that teachers, in most cases, conceive environmental education as a body of knowledge rather than a learning process (Hawkins 1987 cited in Tilbury 1997). Hence their objective of environmental education is limited to providing content knowledge on environmental topics and issues such as personal hygiene and environmental sanitation, water and air pollution, energy, material resources, forestry, climate and weather, populations, and so on. Neither are they concerned about helping students inculcate environmental attitudes or providing opportunities to participate in the resolution of environmental issues nor are they equipped to do so. It will not be, therefore, possible to implement environmental education meaningfully in schools unless teachers obtain adequate training. Not only is orientation of teachers essential, but intensive teacher education is a must for successful implementation of environmental education if we want to do away with the existing fragmented approaches of traditional education (Lahiry et al. 1988, 17).

However, this realization that teacher training and professional development is necessary for meaningful implementation of environmental education is not recent; it is as old as the concept of environmental education itself. For example, the Tbilisi Declaration in 1977 had clearly mentioned the steps to be taken regarding teacher preparation and professional development (UNESCO 1978, 35–36). The same is reproduced in Box 8.2.

BOX

Tbilisi Declaration on Teacher Preparation and Professional Development

Training of Personnel

Recommendation No

The Conference,

Considering the need for all teachers to understand the importance of environmental emphasis in their teaching,

Recommends to Member States

- that environmental sciences and environmental education be included in curricula for pre-service teacher education;
- that the staffs of teacher-education institutions be assisted in this respect; and
- that teachers should get appropriate environmental training relating to the area, either urban or rural, where they are going to work.

Recommendation No

The Conference,

Considering that the importance of in-service training is underlined by the fact that a great majority of present-day teachers were graduated from teacher-training colleges at a time when environmental education was largely neglected and thus did not receive sufficient education in environmental issues and the methodology of environmental education,

Recommends to Member States

- that they take the necessary steps to make in-service training of teachers in environmental education available for all who need it;
- that the implementation and development of in-service training, including practical training, in environmental education be made in close co-operation with professional organizations of teachers, both at the international and national levels;
- that in-service training take account of the area, either urban or rural, where the teachers are working;

Recommends to UNESCO

To promote the dissemination of ideas, programmes, and instructional material relevant to the promotion of in-service training in environmental education.

JUST A MOMENT

Do you think a teacher will be able to handle environmental education without adequate training?

8.1.1 Barriers in the Popularization of EE in Teacher Preparation

In spite of all the reasons discussed earlier on the need for teacher preparation in environmental education, what is being observed in reality is far from what is expected.

There is a tremendous lack of environmental education courses at both the tertiary level and in preservice teacher education. Very few institutes are known to offer environmental education at the tertiary level. Several reasons have been put forth which act as barrier in the popularization of environmental education in preservice courses. This may be due to:

1. Confusion in the terms of environmental education and environmental studies even amongst the community of teacher educators (Harde 1982 cited in Monde 2011; Filho and O'Loan 1996 cited in Heimlich and Smith 2004).
2. Environmental education being limited by being placed in science as its disciplinary home (Disinger and Howe 1990).
3. Most educators and decision makers about education consider environmental education to be a fringe activity (Briceno and Pitt 1988 in Heimlich and Smith 2004).
4. Within the curriculum of teacher preservice programs, environmental education must compete for time and space with many subjects and a series of interdisciplinary topics (Filho and O'Loan 1996 cited in Heimlich and Smith 2004).

Besides these reasons, Heimlich and Smith (2004, 17) point out several philosophic barriers for the inclusion of environmental education into preservice programs such as:

1. the structure of preservice education limits environmental education;
2. the philosophic ways in which preservice teachers are taught—disciplinarily, content (not outcome) focused—and the models of instruction they receive do not demonstrate integration, multi- or trans-disciplinary education;
3. environmental education is not identified as such in those courses where it *is* taught;
4. the desire for incorporation of environmental education by the institution as evidenced by the inclusion of qualified EE teacher instructors (i.e., institutional interest);
5. time in the classroom; and
6. few opportunities to incorporate environmental education into practice for students in teacher preparation programs.

Ballantyne (1995 cited in Monde 2011, 20) clearly identifies problems with management of cross-disciplinary approaches or infusion and shortage of qualified and experienced environmental teacher educators as important barriers. While Scott (1996 cited in Monde 2011, 20) adds lack of practice in terms of working with students and schools and the lack of opportunity to deliver environmental education goals through preservice courses as the additional limits for implementation of environmental education.

NCERT (1981, 55–56) had also identified teacher preparation as a barrier in the effective implementation of environmental education, going to the extent of labeling it as the 'greatest hurdle.' The issues with regard to noneffective implementation is not restricted to countries where environmental education is yet to catch momentum, but it is seen even in countries like the United States of America where the reason is attributed to lack of emphasis in preservice training in environmental education (Feinstein 2009, 36). The situation, however, is found to be improving as the current teacher preparation programs offer some form of environmental education (McKeown-Ice 2000 cited in Feinstein 2009, 37).

8.1.2 Course Content in EE for Teacher Preparation

Wilke et al. (1987) suggest three ways in which teacher preparation programs could incorporate environmental education, such as a specific course in environmental education methods, infusion into existing courses and additional courses in the curriculum which deal with foundational components. However, these are not alternate ways to incorporate environmental education: all the three are essential for effective implementation. This is because teachers or prospective teachers need to have foundational knowledge about environmental education, then he/she would need to learn about the methods and pedagogy to teach environmental education and finally through infusion into other courses he/she will be able to learn about infusion which he/she would apply in her classroom.

In *Strategies for Developing an Environmental Education Curriculum*, UNESCO (1980) provided guidelines for teacher preparation in environmental education which is reproduced in Box 8.3. Looking at the guidelines and considering the purpose of professional development in environmental education as mentioned earlier, four basic

---

BOX

Guidelines for Teacher Preparation in EE (UNESCO 1980)

Teacher preparation in environmental education should…

1. focus on and reflect the many-faceted and interdisciplinary nature of environmental education. In so doing, teachers should be provided with opportunities to acquire and apply the knowledge, skills, and attitudes inherent in environmental education. At the very minimum, this preparation should include:
   - basic training in ecology.
   - field and/or laboratory experiences for teachers in the area of environmental science.
   - knowledge of environmental issues and problems of resource management.
   - competencies in environmental problem identification, investigation, evaluation, and citizenship action.
   - opportunities to develop value clarification skills and knowledge of the roles of human values in environmental issues.
2. provide instruction and experience with environmental education multidisciplinary (infusion) models curriculum as well as instructional activities and methods similar to those they might utilize in their own classrooms.
3. provide for an opportunity for preservice teachers to experience a multidisciplinary or infusion model in their own training, that is, be a receiver in a tertiary infusion model of environmental education.
4. provide instruction on the philosophy and goals of environmental education and the nature of interdisciplinary and multidisciplinary (infused) environmental education curricula. Further, teachers should be trained in the implementation of these models.
5. provide specific training–particularly at the elementary level–in the use of environmental education content as a vehicle for teaching basic general education skills, e.g., in language arts, reading, and mathematics.
6. provide opportunities for teachers to develop skills in identifying, inventorying, and evaluating local resources for use in environmental education.

essential elements can be identified so as to be included in all training programs in environmental education—preservice and in-service. These elements are: (a) purpose and goals of environmental education, (b) functional knowledge of environmental sciences or how natural systems work, (c) educational methods and professional skills including value clarification and action oriented abilities, and (d) exposure to actual situations in which learners can further strengthen their reservoir of skills. The latter three elements are further discussed in *Environmental Education: A Process for Pre-service Teacher Training Curriculum Development* (Lahiry et al. 1988). The same elements are true for professional development of practicing teacher educators or to-be-teacher educators and practicing teachers and to-be-teachers. This is because, to be able to implement environmental education successfully in schools, practicing teachers should be equipped with the necessary skills; and to equip practicing teachers or to-be-teachers, teacher educators need to master such skills themselves. There are many instances where programs for preparation of teacher educators do not adequately incorporate environmental education. Besides this, due to shortage of trained teacher educators in environmental education, these teacher educators, though lack the expertise, are engaged in professional development of teachers in EE. Therefore, professional development in environmental education for such teacher educators is also a must. In preparing a scheme for preservice teacher training, Stapp (1975 cited in Lahiry et al. 1988, 19) grouped the competencies required of a teacher into the following levels:

1. Environmental science competencies comprising (a) Ecological foundations, (b) Economic foundations, and (c) Human ecosystem foundations.
2. Educational competencies comprising (a) psychological foundations, and (b) educational foundations.
3. Environmental educational skills comprising (a) problem-solving, (b) handling of values and controversial issues, and (c) use of materials and local situations pertaining to the environment.
4. Methods of teaching environmental education comprising (a) aims and objectives, (b) environmental education methods and techniques, (c) resources for learning and group dynamics, (d) curriculum design, and (e) field work and environmental ethics. (Lahiry et al., 1988, 19)

Standards for the Initial Preparation of Environmental Educators of the NCATE which was prepared by the NAAEE (2007), included the following standards in the course:

1. Nature of Environmental Education and Environmental Literacy
2. Environmental Literacy of Candidates
3. Learning Theories and Knowledge of Learners
4. Curriculum: Standards and Integration
5. Instructional Planning and Practice
6. Assessment
7. Professional Growth in Environmental Education

As part of the Environmental Literacy of candidates, this NAAEE document mentions that a candidate should demonstrate in-depth knowledge of the following topics: earth as a physical system, including processes that shape the Earth; changes of matter; energy and its transformations; living systems, including organisms, populations, and communities; heredity and evolution; systems and connections; flow of matter and energy; interface of environment and society, including consumerism, uses of land, ecosystem alteration, energy and resource consumption, and human population growth; and roles that social, economic, political, and cultural systems play in issues such as resource depletion, environmental degradation, and sustainability.

Whether presented in the form of basic elements, competencies, or standards, what is important to note here is that teacher training programs necessitates careful planning by ensuring that every dimension, as discussed earlier, is addressed. The duration of the programs or the depth of dealing each component may vary, depending upon the prior experiences and qualifications of the teachers. For example, a teacher/student-teacher who has been trained in biological science may not require much time to understand how ecological or natural systems functions. However, it is important that every aspirant teacher has a basic understanding of how ecological or natural systems functions: simply put, functional knowledge of environmental science is a must for all. This requirement for content knowledge has also been clearly emphasized in the *Report of the High-Powered Commission on Teacher Education Constituted by the Hon'ble Supreme Court of India,* GoI (2012). Professionals in the field have recommended different sets of course content. For example, Hungerford et al. (1994) listed the following:

The Global Nature of Environmental Issues: the phenomenon called 'entropy,' an introductory overview of critical global issues including: population, land use management, world hunger, energy resources, rain forest management, water resources, pollution, and wildlife management.

Population: population dynamics, relationships between population, pollution, resource use, technology, sustainable development, and health; the concept of a sustainable world population, human population control, variables conflicting with population control, critical issues to be resolved.

Land Use Management: land use in developed and developing nations, the role of parks, wilderness, and wildlife refuges; urbanization and urban growth, zoning, problems in the urban environment, strip mining and reclamation, the relationships between population and land use management from a sustainable development perspective.

World Hunger: the relationships between food supplies and world hunger, relationships between population size and hunger, problems associated with various agricultural systems, benefits of various agricultural systems, problems associated with cultivating more land and increasing crop yields, problems associated with pesticide usage, the critical nature of soil erosion, and the limits to sustainable fisheries.

Energy Resources: types of energy resources, how man has applied various energy resources, benefits and problems associated with technology and energy production, the limits to fossil fuels, alternatives to fossil fuels and attendant problems, the role of solar energy in all its forms, developing a regional and global energy plan.

The Tropical Rain Forest: distribution, ecological impact of the rain forest, economics of preservation vs. development, the rain forest as species habitat, development and extinction, management problems and the potential for resolving these problems.

Water Resources: worldwide supply, the role of water in issues associated with sustainable development, distribution and use of water, issues associated with water including soil salinization, use of fossil water supplies, water diversion, surface water pollution, groundwater pollution, and dams.

Air and Noise Pollution: types of pollution, effects of smog and other forms of air pollution, acid rain and its consequences, noise and its effects on human beings, regional issues associated with air and noise pollution.

Wildlife Management: the ecological role and benefits of wildlife, endangered species, habitat destruction, over-utilization, extinction, the need for preserving gene pools, feral animal problems, protection and management of game and nongame species, regional issues associated with wildlife (including fisheries management).

Economics, Politics, and Environmental Ethics: national and international costs associated with environmental degradation, costs of resolving problems/issues, future costs if improvements are not made, the role of politics in environmental decision-making including sustainable development, using the political process for initiating change, components of an environmental ethic, the need for appropriate life styles, influencing change at the local/regional levels.

While Ballard and Pandya (1990 cited in Disinger and Howe 1990, 13–15) included the following as contents:

A. Natural Systems

1. General
(a) Environment   (b) Earth   (c) Biosphere

2. Abiotic Components
(a) Energy   (b) Atmosphere   (c) Land and Soil   (d) Water

3. Biotic Components
(a) Plant   (b) Animal

4. Processes
(a) Weather and Climate (b) Biogeochemical Cycles (c) Evolution and Extinction

5. Biological Systems
(a) Ecosystems   (b) Food Chains and Webs   (c) Community
(d) Population   (e) Habitat and Niche

B. Resources

1. Natural Resources
(a) General   (b) Distribution and Consumption
(c) Management and Conservation   (d) Sustainable Development

2. Abiotic Resources
(a) Energy and Minerals (b) Water   (c) Land and Soil

3. Biotic Resources
(a) Forests   (b) Wildlife and Fisheries (c) Biodiversity

4. Degradation of Resource Base
(a) Limits to Systems   (b) Pollution

C. Human Systems

1. Humans and Environment
(a) Humans as Part of Environment   (b) Human Adaptation to Environment
(c) Human Influence on Environment   (d) Population Factors

2. Technological Systems
(a) Agriculture   (b) Settlements   (c) Manufacturing and Technology

3. Social Systems
(a) Economic Systems   (b) Sociopolitical Systems   (c) Culture and Religion

4. Environmental Awareness and protection
(a) Values and Ethics
(b) Education and Communication
(c) Participation/Voluntary Action
(d) Legislation and Enforcement

As we can see, most of the contents recommended in the two sets are overlapping. Both present the basic environmental knowledge required to be attained. However, keeping in view the current status of our environment and the prevalent issues of the day, it is pertinent to specifically include some present-day issues in the list. These include global warming and climate change, ozone layer depletion, consumerism, carbon footprint, toxic chemicals in food and appliances, natural and human-made disaster management, *El Nino*, *La Nina*, and so on. Today we have recognized that most of ecological or environmental crisis that we see have direct link with our modern values and behavior patterns and hence topics such as environmental ethics should also find adequate space. With almost all environmental issues, if not all, linked to economy, it will be appropriate to include a topic on environmental economics in the course.

When it comes to how best prospective teachers can learn, Kilinc (2010 cited in Genc 2015) suggested the project-based learning approach for environmental education programs since it enhance prospective teachers' environmental knowledge, attitudes, and behaviors. Hence, teacher preparation courses need to carefully incorporate such an approach. Even short-term project tasks are adequate for prospective teachers to attempt solving real social problems (e.g., garbage, water supply and sewers, abandoned land, erosion, paper recycling, turtle protection) (Cheong 2005 cited in Genc 2015).

Besides providing the basic essential elements during initial preparation of teachers, another concern facing teacher education programs pertains to the approach/model of environmental education that is to be followed in the curriculum. For example, in India, the existing school curriculum mandates that environmental education be taught as an infusion approach. It is, therefore, essential that teachers are equipped in handling such approach. The pros and cons of two models, interdisciplinary (separate subject) and multidisciplinary (infusion), have been discussed elaborately in Chapter 3. However, when it comes to actual classroom situations, infusion model can pose a problem compared to interdisciplinary model. Hence, all teacher training programs, both in-service and preservice, should adequately address this aspect for effective implementation of environmental education in schools. There are several other areas that need to be taken care, such as details of teacher preparation for the early childhood, primary or secondary stage, strategies that can be adopted, evaluation of different teacher training programs, and so on. However, the details of such concerns are beyond the purview of this book and hence are not discussed here further.

JUST A MOMENT

Assess you own understanding regarding different environmental topics. Do you think you have sufficient knowledge to explain it holistically?

8.2 Teacher Preparation in EE in India: Preservice

The preservice teacher-education course aims at a complete development of the student-teacher, particularly in knowledge and skills, in individual care of the learner, and in methods and evaluation designed to facilitate learning. The Yashpal Committee Report (1993 cited in NCERT 2006) on 'learning without burden' attributed the cause for unsatisfactory quality of learning in schools to inadequate programs of teacher preparation. It highlighted the need to restructure the content of the program to ensure its relevance to the changing needs of school education.

Preservice courses are expected to cater to the current curricular concerns of school education. Any inadequacies and lapses in the preservice courses can in no way be compensated by any in-service program, however well-structured it may be. It is often seen that new focuses of learning or specific concerns are brought forth every time a new national curriculum framework for school education is brought out. For example, the NCF-2005 talks about infusion approach or infusion model to achieve the objectives of environmental education through the school curriculum. This is specific and needs special emphasis in the teacher education courses. However, it is quite alarming to find that in the National Curriculum Framework for Teacher Education 2009 developed by the apex body for teacher education in the country, NCTE, environmental education itself is not reflected adequately, not to mention of the aspect of infusion approach. Hence, looking at the syllabi of the courses universities offer across the nation for preservice teachers, it is no more a surprise to see that courses on environmental education are rarely offered, and when offered, it is almost always optional. And even when offered, infusion approach is hardly discussed[2] (NCERT 2012).

By now, we are aware of the complexities surrounding the inclusion of environmental education in school education in general and infusion approach of environmental education in particular, and to understand the approach one needs to go through a systematically and meticulously designed course, as already discussed in Chapter 3. With this situation prevailing in the country one can so easily situate the status of environmental education in school education. However, the syllabus being prepared by

---

[2] http://cie.du.ac.in/academics/bed/BED_SYLLABUS_2010_COURSE_WISE.htm (accessed on 23 May 2014); http://ignou.ac.in/userfiles/Prospectus%20BED%202014%20English.pdf (accessed on 23 May 2014)

the NCTE (mentioned to be in draft form) does have some scopes for infusion. Yet again, there is no mention of the goals and objectives of environmental education in the syllabus and hence it is unclear how one would infuse what.[3]

8.2.1 Comparative Study of B.Ed. Syllabus

A cursory comparative study of B.Ed. syllabi was done to find out how far environmental education is reflected in the syllabi of B.Ed. courses in general. For this, the syllabus of one-year bachelor of education course of Delhi University, one-year bachelor of education (secondary) program of the NCTE and the two-year bachelor of education syllabus of the NCERT (2012) were analysed considering some aspects including goals and objectives, and nature and scope, theory, pedagogy, alignment with the NCF, environmental education through projects and activities, and participation in resolution of environmental issues in the context of environmental education. These three syllabi, however, are not representative of the syllabi of all the universities of the country. The result of the study is being summarized in Table 8.1.

Table 8.1   Comparative Study of B.Ed. Syllabus

S. No.	Context	National Council for Teacher Education (NCTE)	National Council of Educational Research and Training (NCERT)	University of Delhi (DU)
1.	Goals and objectives and Nature and Scope of EE	Not defined	Not defined	Not defined
2.	Theory on EE	A: Foundations of Education A1: Education and Development Unit 1: Education for national development: Education for sustainable development; Role of education in ensuring sustainable development A3: Contemporary concerns and issues in secondary education Unit 4: Peace education Unit 5: Education for conservation of environment	Group C: Developing Teacher Sensibilities Section II: Experiences for Social and Environmental Sensitivity – Gender issues in education; Education for peace; Issues of conservation and environmental regeneration; Addressing special needs in classrooms	Part A: Theory Unit V: Compulsory Elective: Gender, School and Society; Education for the children with special needs; Peace education

(Continued)

(Continued)

S. No.	Context	National Council for Teacher Education (NCTE)	National Council of Educational Research and Training (NCERT)	University of Delhi (DU)
3.	Pedagogy courses on EE	No specific course but can be taken up under the Foundation of Education section.	No specific course but can be taken up under the Development of Teacher Sensibilities section.	Only in relation with teaching of Environmental Studies.
4.	Alignment with NCF 2005 (Infusion approach)	Infusion approach not given emphasis. The only section where there is scope to discuss infusion approach is in "Explore the school curriculum for integrating environmental concerns."	Infused in different pedagogy courses such as social sciences, biological sciences, physical sciences, etc. but infusion approach not discussed.	Infused in different pedagogy courses such as social sciences, biological sciences, physical sciences, etc. but infusion approach not discussed.
5.	EE through projects and activities	Scopes exist but not clearly defined.	In general scopes exist but not clearly defined; projects could have been suggested as topics on Developing Teacher Sensibilities such as gender, peace, environmental conservation, etc. are discussed.	Scopes exist but not defined in relation to EE.
6.	Participation in actual resolution of environmental issues	No scope	No scope	No scope

As it has been mentioned, the result does not represent or depict the status prevalent in all the universities. Nevertheless, however crude the methodology of the study might have been, it does signify or indicate a few interesting results which could be generalized for all the syllabi considered in this analysis. For example, the result shows that while environmental education has been reflected in some ways, there are aspects that need to be addressed and there are scopes for improvement in others. Such as, in all the three syllabi, the goals and objectives, and nature and scope of environmental education are not reflected. Without clearly defined goals and objectives, and nature and scope, it is not likely that rest of the content of the course will be able to meaningfully deliver the concerns of environmental education. This trend is not unexpected since clear instruction or information on how to incorporate environmental education is not provided in the model curriculum for B.Ed. program laid down by the University Grants Commission[4] or the syllabus prepared by the NCTE (mentioned to be in draft form).[5] This needs serious intervention. Then there are issues of infusion approach which have been discussed earlier. This has not found place in the syllabi. NCF-2005 mentions that projects and activities will form the backbone of environmental education. However, even this has not been clearly spelt out in the syllabi. Nevertheless, environmental concerns have been taken into consideration in all the syllabi to some extent. The study also reveals that the syllabi are biased toward theory given the fact that projects and activities have not been emphasized. We have also discussed a great deal about opportunities to participate in the resolution of environmental issues in teacher training programs. This is essential for achieving one of environmental education's goals of preparing problem-solvers. For this, teacher training programs need to inculcate problem-solving skills through actual involvement in issues. Environmental education will only be meaningful when this aspect is fulfilled. However, this is found to be completely missing from the syllabi under study. Besides this study, teachers have cited the noninclusion of topics related to infusion of environmental education in different subjects in the D.Ed. and B.Ed. courses as the reason for their inability to effectively implement environmental education in classroom (CEE 1999, 31).

At the same time it was also found that the manner in which environmental education is represented in all the three syllabi appear to be different. While the syllabus of NCTE and NCERT took special care to incorporate concerns related to bio-physical environment (e.g., conservation of environment) in the theory portion, this is found missing in the DU syllabus. DU includes a full-fledged pedagogy course for EVS, which is found wanting in the NCTE and NCERT syllabus. However, this exclusion of pedagogy course in EVS in the NCTE syllabus is because the NCTE syllabus purely caters to teaching at the secondary level and EVS is dealt in the D.El.Ed. course. On the other hand, besides the secondary stage, DU B.Ed. course also caters to the primary stage as well. The same could be true for the syllabus developed by the NCERT.

As mentioned earlier, the analysis of syllabi presented above do not have the same course duration. While the NCERT syllabus is for a two-year course, the NCTE and DU syllabi are for a one-year course. This disparity in the course duration will not remain an issue anymore since the government has decided that B.Ed. course throughout the country will hence forth be of a uniform duration of two years and the same has been implemented beginning the academic year 2015–2016. However, the lacunae that is found in the syllabi with respect to environmental education does not have much to do with the course duration. It reflects more of a deliberate marginalization, and treatment of environmental education as insignificant. This is evident from the fact that even the recently brought out two-year B.Ed. curriculum by NCTE (2015) does not discuss environmental education except for mentioning EVS as a composite area of study at the primary stage that integrates science, social science, and environmental education. Another section where environmental education has found some relevance in this curriculum is where there is mention that, "in the pedagogy course on science may include environment based projects to address concerns of a particular village/city or a community." It remains to be seen how this idea of environmental education will be deciphered and taken forward by the teacher educators and put into practice in the course.

---

[4] http://www.ugc.ac.in/oldpdf/modelcurriculum/edu.pdf (accessed on 27 July 2014)
[5] http://www.ncte-india.org/BED.pdf (accessed on 1 February 2016)

Looking at the gaps that exist in the syllabi of different institutions, it would be appropriate if a core syllabus is prepared with clear instructions for syllabus developers in different institutes. With this in place, specific concerns such as environmental education, or other concerns that are new, will find place in the syllabus of every institute. As for EE, syllabus developers may not have to spend much time to incorporate it. A paragraph or two could be incorporated with a clear outline on 'what,' 'why,' and 'how' of Environmental education will make a difference. A slight environmentally oriented thought while framing the syllabi might just be required.

Interestingly, unlike the three syllabi discussed earlier, the credit-based B.Ed. syllabus of the University of Pune is very encouraging with regard to environmental education.[6] A good amount of content on environment-related topics find place in the syllabus. Elective courses such as education for sustainable development, and environment education and disaster management have also been included. Under the core courses, foundations of education, environment education and disaster management has been included as one of the optional electives along with introduction to educational research, inclusive education and education for sustainable development. The concept, nature and scope of environmental education clearly form part of the course. The course also provides ample opportunities to enrich environmental content knowledge. Another important feature of this syllabus is that student-teachers will observe four lessons of other student-teachers on lessons related to value education or environmental education and every student-teacher is also required to take an innovative lesson in the same which carries one credit. Though the effort to include environmental education in the course itself is appreciated, this syllabus is also not without its limitations. There exist some genuine concerns. For example, the elective is optional and it carries only 2.5 credits of the total 75 credits for the complete course. Thus, the maximum credits available for environmental education is only 3.5 of the total 75 credits. Besides, there is no mention about the pedagogy of environmental education in the syllabus. Also, the scope for participation in the resolution of environmental issues does not seem to find place in the course. These are basic essential elements that are missing in the course.

JUST A MOMENT

What do you think should be done so that all B.Ed. programs throughout the country should uniformly reflect environmental education?

8.2.2 Duration of Preservice Courses

Until the academic session 2014–2015, the duration of a preservice B.Ed. course was either one year (as was practiced in most institutes) or two years, depending on the institution a person attends. One can only wonder how could such a disparity could be allowed to carry on for years for the same degree course. Thankfully, an order was issued

[6] http://www.unipune.ac.in/Syllabi_PDF/revised_2014/education/B_Ed_Syllabus_2014_Final_30-6-14.pdf (accessed 3 October 2014)

to offer B.Ed. course in all institutes throughout the country as a two-year course beginning the academic session 2015–2016. This decision will be important keeping in view the implementation of environmental education. A two-year B.Ed. course will be more conducive to accommodate and implement environmental education. The competition for slots to include environmental education in a one-year course in the time table with the "more important topics" will not exist anymore. Environmental education can be taken up more meaningfully with sufficient time allotted for it. The National Curriculum Framework for Teacher Education 2009 also suggested the need to structurally transform the one-year course to a two-year course to strengthen both in theory and practice (NCTE 2009, 10–11). Environmental education components need to be incorporated appropriately and adequately while these structural changes are being undertaken in the course. Such major changes do not occur frequently, and once a course is set in place it will run for years, if not decades. It is, therefore, very crucial for the curriculum developers for teacher education to realize the importance of allocating an appropriate and adequate space for environmental education during the process of modifying of the course. Failure to take care of this will be a set-back for environmental education, the impact of which will be felt for years throughout the country in school education. We will then have to wait for another major change to take place in the curriculum framework for teacher education and that will be too heavy a price to pay.

Similarly, the duration for other preservice courses, such as D.El.Ed. (Diploma in Elementary Education), B.El.Ed. (Bachelor in Elementary Education), and so on, may also be modified accordingly so as to accommodate environmental education without compromising the existing course content.

8.3 Teacher Preparation in EE in India: In-service

The lack of adequate preservice training opportunities in environmental education means that there are very few on-the-job teachers who have received environment-focused instruction, either pedagogical or content-specific (Disinger and Howe 1990, 19). The situation was understandable during the 1990s since environmental education was still new then. But nothing much has changed even today and hence the imperative need for in-service environmental education programs.

In-service teacher education programs in general will serve the following purposes: One, it will update the teacher on the new trends and practices. Two, it will prepare the teacher to be able to meet the requirements of teaching–learning in accordance with the changes in the curriculum framework for schools as well as for teacher education. Three, those who have not undergone any kind of preservice course in environmental education, as is not uncommon in several parts of the country, will benefit the most in all areas of in-service professional development.

In the earlier discussions, we saw that preservice courses do not give much emphasis to environmental education in general and hence they do not reflect infusion approach of environmental education adequately. It is not surprising that practicing teachers are, invariably, not aware or familiar with the philosophies, goals, and practices related to environmental education and their understanding about 'infusion' or 'infusion approach' is limited to the literal meaning of the word. And so, whether the teachers know what and where environmental education has been infused and how it is to be transacted becomes irrelevant. At present, things do not look very bright for environmental education in preservice courses. Though not impossible, it might take some time, a few years, for environmental education to be reflected in such courses. While this transformation is taking place in the preservice sector, there are avenues for 'damage control' in the in-service sector. Most education committees and commissions have acknowledged the potential for radical shifts in the school practices and programs via effective in-service education programs. The Education Commission (1964–1966) strongly recommended that: (a) large scale programs for in-service education of teachers should be organized by universities, and teacher organizations at all levels should enable every teacher to receive at least two or three months of in-service education for every five years of service, (b) continuing in-service education should be based on research inputs, (c) training institutions should work on a 12-month basis and organize in-service training programs, such as refresher courses, seminars, workshops, and summer institutes.

In-service programs need to be paid equal attention as preservice courses, if not more, since these teachers will not be going back to attend another preservice course, unless it is made mandatory for the post/position he/she holds if he/she has not undergone such course earlier. The Acharya Ramamurthi Review Committee (1990 in NCERT 2006) explicitly stated that, "in-service and refresher courses should be related to the specific needs of the teachers. In-service education should take due care of the future needs of teacher growth; evaluation and follow up should be part of the scheme."

Far from what has been recommended, there are just a few in-service teacher programs being offered in the country in environmental education. Mention may be made of the Green Teacher Diploma, a distance education program for in-service teachers offered occasionally by Centre for Environment Education (CEE) and Commonwealth of Learning (COL) Vancouver, Canada. There are no other regular programs, short-term or long-term, provided in environmental education. The needs of the teachers which were not addressed by the preservice course remain unaddressed due to lack of such programs. Feedback obtained from the nodal officers in environmental education of different states and UTs suggest that specific training or orientation in environmental education is required for the teachers. Most of them suggested a one-week program (Shimray et al. 2014). Similar feedback on the need for capacity building in the area of environmental education was also obtained during the course of interaction with teachers teaching in DIETs in different parts of the country (Shimray 2015).

There are some institutes which offer an in-service B.Ed. course through distance mode such as the two-year B.Ed. degree by Maulana Azad National Urdu University for in-service graduate teachers[7]; Indira Gandhi National Open University (IGNOU)[8]; and Annamalai University. But such courses do not incorporate environmental education adequately.

The NCFTE 2009, however, mentions that systems are in place for imparting in-service trainings which are provided by institutes of advanced studies in education in chosen institutions and university departments of education, district institutes of education and training in each district, and SCERTs in states. It also mentions the continuous in-service teacher-education program which requires each teacher to receive 20 days of training every year under the *Sarva Shiksha Abhiyan* (SSA) (NCTE 2009, 63). It is to be seen as to how much of environmental education components have been incorporated in such programs.

---

[7] http://www.manuu.ac.in/admissions/Bed_prospectus2014-15.pdf (accessed on 23 May 2014)
[8] http://ignou.ac.in/userfiles/Prospectus%20BED%202014%20English.pdf (accessed on 23 May 2014)

Photo 8.1   Teacher Educators Engaged in an Activity during a Training Program

Photo 8.2   Teacher Educators from DIET Engaged in an Activity during a Training Program

JUST A MOMENT

Reflect on the issues related to in-service programs in environmental education. Is it even feasible to train every in-service teacher?

8.3.1 Possibilities for In-service Teacher Empowerment

There are other possibilities to include environmental education in the training/ orientation/refresher courses provided by different school systems such as Kendriya Vidyalaya Sangathan, Jawahar Navodaya Vidyalaya, Delhi Public School, DAV Schools, and so on, which conduct such programs for their teachers on an almost regular basis. Another possibility to include environmental education is in the training programs organized as part of the Government's initiative such as those conducted under SSA and *Rashtriya Madhyamik Shiksha Abhiyan* (RMSA). However, in all these efforts one may bear in mind that it has been very difficult to follow the cascade model wherein a set of people are trained, who in turn train another set, and so on. Since environmental education is comparatively new to the teaching community, instead of focusing on cascade model, it will be appropriate if the maximum possible numbers of teachers are directly exposed to the training programs conducted by the well-trained educators. This will also avoid possible dilution and ineffectiveness that could occur at every level of the cascade. This, of course, is going to be a very ambitious task and would require tremendous commitment by the government, huge funding, enormous human resource, and so on, to take the task ahead.

Though it will be challenging, mechanisms could still be worked out to train in-service teachers in government/local body schools. A more serious concern is regarding the large chunk of para-teachers and teachers in private schools where certificates or degrees are not mandatory nor are there in-service training programs in place. We know that the number of such teachers far exceeds those in government schools.

8.3.2 Some Systemic Issues

Motivation comes with confidence, confidence comes with training, and trainees are motivated by benefits and incentives—though not necessarily in that sequence. However one thing is definite: teachers need motivation to make their class EE-oriented. With the work load that teachers have, most of the time their focus is on 'completing' the course. Moreover, the school administration and parents expect teachers to give 'results' in the form of marks. Why then would teachers follow the more elaborate and sometimes challenging route by considering environmental education? They would obviously go for 'note' and 'rote' method by which students can still score marks, and score very high at that. But if the government is ready to part with some of their exchequer, considering a mandatory certification program in environmental education with accompanying incentive for in-service teachers will be a step in the right direction.

8.4 Teacher Preparation in EE in India: Teacher Educators

Another area of concern related to teacher education is the lack of adequate professionally qualified teacher educators in environmental education. The issue with teacher educators is not only with environmental education, though. The situation is the same for teacher educators in general as NCFTE 2009 (NCTE 2009, 75) points out that:

> The need and importance of professionally trained teacher educators has been underscored in statements on educational policy, time and again, but the situation on the ground remains a matter of concern; there is a considerable shortage of properly qualified and professionally trained teacher educators at all stages of education and especially at the elementary stage. The shortage refers both to the inadequacy of required numbers as well as to mismatch in the qualifications of teacher educators and their job requirements.

In a similar line, NCERT (2006) states, "There are also no established mechanisms to create a professional cadre of teacher educators, especially at pre-primary and the elementary stage. Most teacher educators, training pre-primary and elementary school teachers for example, are themselves trained in secondary education." Needless to say, the situation is worse when it comes to environmental education. There are no specific courses in higher education institutions which prepare qualified teacher educators in environmental education who would be capable of teaching the preservice or in-service courses. In a study undertaken recently amongst teacher educators from various district institutes of education and research of the country, more than half of the respondents mentioned that environmental education or related topics are taught by educators who have had no specific education or training in the area (Shimray 2015). This is quite alarming. All the respondents suggested the urgency to build the capacities of teacher educators in EE.

Therefore, the problem is, how do we prepare such huge numbers of teacher educators to cater to the need of the whole nation? Who would provide them such courses or training? Do we have enough professionals to train them all? Wouldn't it be appropriate to look outward (trainers from other countries) for such academic support? Is the government ready to take up such an important step? The issue at hand is not even about the course content for training teacher educators but is about coming up with a mechanism to set up such courses. The newly launched nationally sponsored scheme—*Rashtriya Uchchatar Shiksha Abhiyan* (RUSA), National Higher Education Mission—by the Government of India in 2013 would be the right platform to address concerns related to teacher educators. Crores of rupees will be spent each year on capacity-building which is one of the goals of RUSA. It would be worth investing a portion of the budget in capacity building of teacher educators in the area of EE. For this to happen, either the government/concerned body of the government or some concerned teacher educators/institutes have to work out a plan strategically and ensure its implementation. Without a deliberate effort, the capacity building of teacher educators in the area of environmental education will not happen naturally. These are some of the many issues related to the area of teacher educators. In that sense we have a long way to go when it comes to professional development of teacher educators in EE.

JUST A MOMENT

When sufficient courses are not available in environmental education, it is possible to have sufficient teacher educators to cater to the needs?

8.5 Changing Names

Another concern that has come in the way of effective implementation of environmental education is about the change in focus and the change in names. Since the past decade, education for sustainable development (ESD) has gained popularity. While this should not have interfered in the implementation of environmental education but rather strengthened it, since the goals of EE and ESD are practically similar (UNESCO 2009, p. 31), unfortunately, what we find is that ESD or sustainable development (SD) has overshadowed environmental education, at least in documents. This is evident even in the NCFTE 2009 document which substantially covered SD while the term environmental education did not find even a mention. One might say that ESD or SD will ultimately take care of EE. Ideally it should. But we need to be reminded of the fact that environmental education did not get the focus it deserved even decades after it was introduced in the 1970s. For decades we have not succeeded in informing teachers what environmental education is and now that the focus has suddenly shifted to ESD or SD one can only keep guessing how many decades it would take us to really implement it in letter and spirit. The details about ESD are discussed in the next chapter.

Conclusion

We have seen that in spite of all the efforts that have been put into environmental education, serious issues exist in the area of teacher empowerment, including the teacher educators, which need immediate attention. Environmental education has not been adequately reflected in the syllabi of preservice courses. Some of the reasons could be that the curriculum developers missed out the topic deliberately, or could not find adequate space and time to incorporate such topics, or did not understand the importance of environmental education. There could be many other reasons, but what is clear from this is that the courses need to be of adequate duration so that there is no room to make excuses for its noninclusion. The issues with in-service courses are also no less. But we know that without empowering teachers it is impossible to expect any positive result in the implementation of environmental education in schools. Indeed, in a huge nation like ours where there are more than seventy lakh school teachers (71, 81, 692) teaching at primary to higher secondary schools,[9] it is not going to be easy to think of professional development for each one of them. In this scenario, one might think that it will be too ambitious to think of working out a model for professional development

---

[9] http://www.aises.nic.in/surveyoutputs (accessed on 7 July 2014).

in environmental education when even after decades a proper system could not be worked out for teacher education in general. But looking at the gravity of environmental issues that is spiraling out of our control, we are left with no choice but to work out a suitable model for professional development in environmental education—preservice and in-service.

Keeping this in view, there is an urgent need to review the syllabi of the existing professional development courses. Some of the suggestions that might be considered in such exercise are discussed below.

Preservice Courses

1. Inclusion of environmental education as one of the compulsory papers: Preservice courses such as B.El.Ed. and B.Ed. consist of many compulsory papers which invariably include philosophy of education, basic concepts in education, and emerging areas. In such papers environment-related education is mentioned only as passing statements. The issue is not so much with the primary stages because most of the courses offer environmental studies. The problem begins from upper primary stage when the infusion approach or model of environmental education is being followed. We have also mentioned that environmental education is kept only as one of the optional papers in B.Ed. course. And environmental education not being a popular option, student-teachers graduate from such courses with no clear understanding of what environmental education is. In order to avoid this, it is important to include environmental education as one of the compulsory papers or at the least it can be part of a compulsory paper. NCERT (1981) had also brought forth this idea of introducing a compulsory paper in environmental education.
2. As far as pedagogy of environmental education is concerned, there can be two ways of addressing the concern—by having a separate paper on pedagogy of environmental education or by clearly highlighting how environmental education should be reflected in the pedagogy of different curricular subjects.
3. To foster quality assurance and sustenance, the National Assessment and Accreditation Council (NAAC) need to ensure that environmental education is taken as one of the components in its process of quality assessment.

In-service Courses

1. In-service professional development courses in environmental education which is recognized by competent authorities need to be prepared. The government needs to formulate some ways to ensure that every teacher undergoes such course. An incentive to those who complete such course would enhance participation.
2. Routine in-service training programs for different subjects conducted at the national level, state level or by different school system need to include environmental education adequately in all such programs.
3. Distance Education Council (DEC) need to ensure that environmental education component is seriously considered in its in-service teacher education under the Open and Distance Learning (ODL) mode.

Training of Teacher Educators

The most neglected, yet the most important of all professional development programs is that of the teacher educators who teach preservice courses. Most of the teacher educators have not been trained in the area of environmental education. This is not surprising since, as mentioned earlier, environmental education is not compulsory in preservice professional development courses. Moreover there is no mechanism in place for them for professional development in environmental education. It is therefore essential to empower these teacher educators with the emerging trends in the area of EE. The tasks sound enormous. However it is workable. The following provides a simple way of organizing a short-term training program (which could be for five days) for teacher educators in DIET. There are approximately 630 districts in India. The number of DIETs set up till December 2009 is 571, of which only 529 are functional. Two teacher educators from each DIET can be trained to be master trainers who would in turn train other faculty members. These master trainers can also be utilized to provide trainings to teachers working in schools located in the district.

Stakeholders need to wake up and take appropriate measures so that teacher preparation and empowerment in environmental education is seriously taken up. Or, as with the 1991 order from the Hon'ble Supreme Court of India to make environmental education compulsory in all stages of education throughout the country, do we wait for another order from the Hon'ble Court to make this aspect (teacher preparation and empowerment) compulsory for all preservice and in-service teachers?

SUMMARY

- Serious issues exist in the area of teacher empowerment, including the teacher educators, in environmental education.
- Environmental education is not adequately reflected in the syllabi of preservice courses. Even when environmental education is included under the elective papers, it is kept an optional paper.
- Infusion approach of environmental education does not appear in any of the existing preservice or in-service professional development courses.
- Appropriate duration for various preservice courses need to be worked out to ensure that environmental education is highlighted sufficiently in the courses.
- There are also issues with in-service courses regarding environmental education. No system is in place to regularly provide training to in-service teachers in environmental education.
- There is no mechanism for the professional development of teacher educators, many of whom themselves have not received sufficient training in the area of environmental education.
- The existing mass training programs organized through *Sarva Siksha Abhiyan* and the *Rashtriya Madhyamik Siksha Abhiyan* for different subjects can be used as a platform to train in-service teachers in environmental education throughout the country.
- In-service training programs organized by Kendriya Vidyalaya Sangathan, Jawahar Navodaya Vidyalaya Samiti, and so on, may accommodate some sessions on environmental education.
- Lack of clarity on what exactly is being implemented—environmental education, sustainable development, education for sustainable development, and so on—is becoming an issue in the implementation of environmental education.

Exercises

1. Do you think teacher preparation programs reflect the importance of environmental education adequately? Justify your answer.
2. What are the barriers that hinder the popularization of environmental education in teacher preparation programs?
3. What are the broad areas that you think should be covered in a typical environmental education course in preservice program?
4. Content knowledge on fundamental environmental topics is essential for all student-teachers or in-service teachers. Do you agree with this statement? Justify your answer.
5. Is the present practice of keeping environmental education or related course as an optional elective paper in the preservice program sensible? Elaborate your answer.
6. Will the recent decision to make B.Ed. program throughout the country a two-year course make any difference in the implementation of environmental education? Explain how.
7. Which approach do you think should be followed to provide training to in-service teachers throughout the country in the area of environmental education?
8. Why is it important to have sufficient teacher educators who are trained in the area of environmental education?
9. Suggest some measures so that environmental education receives more importance in preservice programs.
10. Suggest some measures so that practicing teachers will be motivated to incorporate environmental concerns in their classroom transactions.

References

CEE, Centre for Environment Education. 1999. *Environmental Orientation to School Education—A Programme of Ministry of Human Resource Development: A Documentation of the Scheme and Some Projects under the Scheme*, edited by Meena Raghunathan and Mamata Pandya. Ahmedabad: CEE

Disinger, J.F. and R.W. Howe. 1990. *Trends and Issues Related to the Preparation of Teachers for Environmental Education*. Environmental Education Information Report. Columbus, OH: ERIC Clearinghouse for Science, Mathematics, and Environmental Education. Available at: http://files.eric.ed.gov/fulltext/ED335233.pdf (Accessed on 15 April 2015).

Feinstein, Noah. 2009. *Education for Sustainable Development in the United States of America: A Report Submitted to the International Alliance of Leading Education Institutes*, University of Wisconsin-Madison.

Fien, John and Jo-Anne Ferreira. 1997. "Environmental Education in Australia–A Review." *International Research in Geographical and Environmental Education* 6(3): 234–259, Channel View Books/Multi-Lingual Matters Ltd. Available at: https://www.academia.edu/8161935/Environmental_Education_in_Australia_-_A_Review. (Accessed on 28 September 2014).

Genc, Murat 2015. "The Project-based Learning Approach in Environmental Education." *International Research in Geographical and Environmental Education* 24(2): 105–117.

GoI, Government of India. 2012. *Vision of Teacher Education in India: Quality and Regulatory Perspective, Report of the High-Powered Commission on Teacher Education Constituted by the Hon'ble Supreme Court of India*. Ministry of Human Resource Development, Department of School Education and Literacy, New Delhi.

Heimlich, J.E. and L. B. Smith. 2004. *Preservice Environmental Education: What Do We Know?* A Report to World Wildlife Fund, US: Office of Environmental Education. Ohio State University Extension, Columbus, Ohio. Available at: http://eelink.net/eetap/tidesrpt.pdf (Accessed on 14 April 2015).

Hungerford, H.R., T.L.Volk, W.J. Bluhm, B.G. Dixon, T.J. Marcinkowski, and A.P.C. Sia. 1994. *An Environmental Education Approach to the Training of Elementary Teachers: A Teacher Education Programme (Revised), A Discussion Guide for UNESCO Training Seminars on Environmental Education*. UNESCO-UNEP International Environmental Education Programme, Environmental Education Series 27. Paris: INESCO.

Lahiry, D., Savita Sinha, J.S. Gill, U. Mallik, A.K. Mishra. 1988. *Environmental Education: A Process for Pre-service Teacher Training Curriculum Development*. UNESCO-UNEP International Environmental Education Programme Environmental Education Series No. 26, edited by Patricia R. Simpson, Harold Hungerford, and Trudi L. Volk. Paris: UNESCO.

Monde, P.N. 2011 *Barriers to Successful Implementation of Environmental Education in Zambian High Schools: A Case Study of Selected High Schools of Central Province*. PhD Thesis: University of Zambia, 19. Available at: http://dspace.unza.zm:8080/xmlui/bitstream/handle/123456789/809/Monde.pdf?sequence=1 (Accessed on 15 April 2015).

NAAEE, North American Association for Environmental Education. 2007. National Council for Accreditation of Teacher Education (NCATE) *Standards for the Initial Preparation of Environmental Educators*, Washington, DC: NAAEE. Available at: http://www.ncate.org/LinkClick.aspx?fileticket=Fm%2FqA4uarLk%3D&tabid=676 (Accessed on 3 October 2014).

NCERT, National Council of Educational Research and Training. 1981. *Environmental Education at the School Level: A Lead Paper*. New Delhi: NCERT.

—— 2005. *National Curriculum Framework 2005*. New Delhi: NCERT.

—— 2006. *Position Paper of the National Focus Group on Teacher Education for Curriculum Renewal*. New Delhi: NCERT.

—— 2012. *Syllabus for Two-year Bachelor of Education (B.Ed.)*. New Delhi: NCERT.

NCTE, National Council for Teacher Education. 2009. *National Curriculum Framework for Teacher Education 2009*. New Delhi: NCTE.

—— 2015 *Curriculum Framework: Two-year B.Ed. Programme*. New Delhi: NCTE. Available at: http://ncte-india.org/Curriculum%20Framework/B.Ed%20Curriculum.pdf (Accessed on 8 June 2015).

Plevyak, L.H., M. Bendixen-Noe, J. Henderson, R.E. Roth, and Richard Wilke. 2001. "Level of Teacher Preparation and Implementation of EE: Mandated and Non-Mandated EE Teacher Preparation States." *The Journal of Environmental Education* 32(2): 28–36.

Shimray, C.V., A.N. Hoshi, and R. Sasidhar. 2014. *Monitoring the Implementation of Environmental Education in Schools in States and UTs in Compliance with the Hon'ble Supreme Court's Order: Meeting of Nodal Officers—A Report (Unpublished)*. New Delhi: NCERT.

Shimray, C.V. 2015. *Meeting of DIET Functionaries to Assess the Status of D.El.Ed. Syllabus in the Context of Environmental Education—Report (Unpublished)*. New Delhi: NCERT.

Tilbury, D. 1997. "Environmental Education (EE) A Head, Heart and Hand Approach to Learning about Environmental Problems." *New Horizons in Education* 38:1–11.

UNESCO, United Nations Educational, Scientific and Cultural Organization. 1978. *Intergovernmental Conference on Environmental Education*, Tbilisi, 14–26 October 1977, Final Report, Paris.

—— 1980. *Strategies for Developing an Environmental Education Curriculum: A Discussion Guide for UNESCO Training Workshops on Environmental Education*. Paris: UNESCO.

—— 2009. *Learning for a Sustainable World: Review of Contexts and Structures for Education for Sustainable Development*. United Nations Decade of Education for Sustainable Development (DESD, 2005–2014). Paris: UNESCO.

Wilke, R.J., R.B. Peyton, and H.R. Hungerford. 1987. *Strategies for the Training of Teachers in Environmental Education*. Environmental Education Series 25. Division of Science, Technical and Environmental Education. Paris: UNESCO-UNEP.

Education for Sustainable Development: Departure from Environmental Education

Worth a Thought!

The concept to integrate social, economic, and environmental concerns holistically did not originate from the Brundtland Commission Report—*Our Common Future*—which popularized the concept of sustainable development. Such concerns were already reflected in the Belgrade Charter (1975) and Tbilisi Declaration (1977) on environmental education.

Chapter Overview

The chapter discusses quite at length about the origin and nature of education for sustainable development and thereafter about the Decade of Education for Sustainable Development (DESD) and the Global Action Programme as a follow-up. It then discusses on the types of sustainability education by trying to clarify the difference between sustainable development related education and full-fledged education for sustainable development. Attempts have been made to bring out the difference, or similarities for that matter, between education for sustainable development and environmental education. Further, it discusses whether environmental education should be continued alongside education for sustainable development. Discusses on some of the ramifications that can be expected with the implementation of education for sustainable development have also been included. This chapter will facilitate the readers to:

- **explain the origin of education for sustainable development.**
- **describe the characteristics of education for sustainable development.**
- **list the thrust areas of education for sustainable development.**
- **explain the dimensions of education for sustainable development.**
- **explain the impact of decade of education for sustainable development.**
- **explain the role of Global Action Programme.**
- **describe the types of sustainability education.**
- **differentiate SD-related education and education for sustainable development.**

- analyze the differences and similarities between education for sustainable development and environmental education.
- justify the need for environmental education alongside education for sustainable development.
- explain the ramifications of implementation of education for sustainable development.

Introduction

In the previous chapters some discussions have gone into how Education for Sustainable Development (ESD) apparently came about. ESD is fundamentally about values, with respect at the center: respect for others, including those of present and future generations, for difference and diversity, for the environment, for the resources of the planet we inhabit (UNESCO 2006). Since the Rio Conference in 1992, ESD gained enormous popularity. It has almost replaced environmental education in the process of implementation in many countries. To a lay person ESD might sound like a totally new concept which could tackle all sustainability issues which environmental education has not been able to address. In this context, it is important to understand what exactly ESD is, how did it originate, what is the DESD, what happens after DESD, and so on. The types of sustainability education will also be elaborately discussed in the chapter. It will also attempt to find out how ESD is similar to or different from environmental education. This chapter will discuss the departure of ESD from environmental education and also focus on some of the possible implications it could bring about while addressing environmental issues. Will ESD be able to give enough emphasis to tackle the ever-increasing biophysical environmental issues? If so, will there still be a need to continue with environmental education? These are the concerns which the chapter will try to touch upon.

JUST A MOMENT!

Of all the technological advances the world has made, what has intrigued you the most and what has disappointed you the most?

9.1 Education for Sustainable Development (ESD)

9.1.1 Genesis

The roots of ESD can be traced back to the history of two distinct areas of interest of the United Nations—(a) education and (b) sustainable development.

9.1.1.1 Education

Irina Bokova, Director-General of UNESCO in 2012 had said, "Education is the most powerful path to sustainability. Economic and technological solutions, political regulations or financial incentives are not enough. We need a fundamental change in the way we think and act" (UNESCO 2014a).

In terms of education the root of ESD goes back to the Declaration of Human Rights in 1948 which states, "Everyone has the right to education." The Convention on the Right of the Child (CRC) adopted by the United Nations General Assembly in 1989 reinforced this right to education by declaring that primary education should be compulsory and available free to all. The CRC further mentions that children may not be excluded from any right—including education—based on race, sex, disability, economic status.

Following this, in 1990, the Jomtien Declaration on Education for All (EFA) declared, "Basic education should be provided to all children, youth and adults. To this end, basic education services of quality should be expanded and consistent measures must be taken to reduce disparities." The declaration also made efforts to address the issue of gender disparity prevalent in the world by pointing out that utmost priority must be given to ensure access to, and improve the quality of, education for girls and women, and to remove every obstacle that hampers their active participation. It further added that all gender stereotyping in education should be eliminated.

Furthermore, international development targets (IDT), a set of goals selected from the series of UN conferences held in the 1990s, includes "by 2015, children everywhere, boys and girls alike, will be able to complete a full course of primary schooling."[1]

Another very significant event in the area of education—The World Education Forum—took place in Dakar, Senegal in 2000 (UNESCO 2000). The Dakar Framework for Action adopted during this Forum lists six important educational goals which include: "Improving all aspects of the quality of education so that recognized and measurable learning outcomes are achieved, especially, in literacy, numeracy and essential life skills." Meanwhile, in the UN Millennium Summit (2000) held in New York, world leaders committed to achieve the Millennium Development Goals (MDGs) by 2015. Of the many goals the MDGs seek to address, the ones on education are: "Achieve universal primary education," "Promote gender equality and empower women," and "Ensure environmental sustainability." Furthermore, the United Nations General Assembly (UNGA) declared 2003–2012 to be the United Nations Literacy Decade (UNLD) to support collective efforts to achieve the goals of Education for All (EFA) by 2015. It is evident from the above that the importance of education for all has been addressed by the United Nations repeatedly over its entire history (UNESCO 2005) with the momentum catching up markedly since the late 1980s.

> ## JUST A MOMENT
>
> Much emphasis seems to have been given in order to make education available to all. Do you think what is happening on the ground is in tune with the efforts that have been put into by the whole world?

---

[1] http://siteresources.worldbank.org/INTPOVERTY/Resources/WDR/stiglitz/Hanmer.pdf (accessed on 20 July 2015)

9.1.1.2 Sustainable Development

Sustainable development has its roots in United Nations history in the environmental movement which goes back several decades (UNESCO 2005). In this long journey, mention may be made of the 1968 UNESCO Conference on Biodiversity and the landmark 1972 United Nations Conference on the Human Environment in Stockholm, Sweden which led to the establishing of many environmental protection agencies and the United Nations Environment Programme (UNEP) besides many environmental ministries and non-governmental organizations (NGOs) working to conserve the planet's resources. Due to unprecedented growth and development taking place, especially beginning the second half of the 20th century, nations realized the urgency to tackle the issues collaboratively rather than adopting national approaches and solutions. Following the Stockholm conference, UNESCO came out with the Belgrade Charter and the Tbilisi Declaration (for details refer Chapter 1). Though holistic approach was envisaged, it was observed that while some attention was attached to the social and economic issues inherent in these environmental issues, the focus was largely on addressing the ecological impact of ever increasing unrestricted development. The global community acknowledged the pressing need to explore the inter relationships between the environment and natural resources, and socio-economic issues of poverty and underdevelopment. It was increasingly realized that unless such issues are addressed the environment will be subjected to ever more degradation. This formed the basis for the United Nations to hunt for a more encompassing strategy which would address both the needs of the society as well as the environment. The search finally ended with the report of the World Commission on Environment and Development or the Brundtland Commission Report (named after the head of the Commission)—*Our Common Future*—that came out in 1987 (UN 1987). Based on this report, sustainable development was endorsed by the United Nations as an overarching framework or construct for future development policy at all levels of government. It defined sustainable development as "development that meets the needs of the present without compromising the ability of future generations to meet their own needs." This definition is with reference to the capacity of the natural environment. It implies that development which is essential to satisfy human needs and improve the quality of life should occur in such a way that the capacity of the natural environment to meet present and future needs is not compromised. Though sustainable development began to be used extensively ever since the Brundtland Commission Report, references on the concept of sustainable development have also been indicated prior to this (Tortajada 2005). Several other definitions related to sustainable development have also been used by different professionals and researchers based on different context (Pezzey 1992). Some of them are provided in Box 9.1.

Following this development, a parallel concept of education to support sustainable development was visualized by the United Nations which finally materialized in the form of Chapter 36 of Agenda 21, 'Promoting Education, Public Awareness, and Training.' UNESCO was appointed to be the Task Manager for this chapter. This effort to promote education for sustainable development was further strengthened by embedding education as an enabling or implementation strategy in each of the 40 chapters of Agenda 21 (refer Chapter 5) which was adopted by the participating nations in the Earth Summit held in Rio de Janeiro in 1992 (UN 1992). To further this initiative of identifying education to be

BOX

References to Sustainable Development

Porritt (1984)—Director, U.K. Friends of the Earth

"All economic growth in the future must be sustainable: that is to say, "it must operate within and not beyond the finite limits of the planet."

Repetto (1985)—Economist, World Resources Institute

1. "The core of the idea of sustainability, then, is the concept that current decisions should not impair the prospects for maintaining or improving future living standards... This implies that our economic systems should be managed so that we live off the dividend of our resources, maintaining and improving the asset base. This principle also has much in common with the ideal concept of income that accountants seek to determine: the greatest amount that can be consumed in the current period without reducing prospects for consumption in the future."

2. "This does not mean that sustainable development demands the preservation of the current stock of natural resources or any particular mix of human, physical and natural assets. As development proceeds, the composition of the underlying asset base changes."

Tolba (1987)—Executive Director, U.N. Environmental Programme

1. "[Sustainable development] has become an article of faith, a shibboleth: often used but little explained. Does it amount to a strategy? Does it apply only to renewable resources?
What does the term actually mean? In broad terms the concept of sustainable development encompasses:

   (1) help for the very poor because they are left with no option other than to destroy their environment;
   (2) the idea of self-reliant development, within natural resource constraints;
   (3) the idea of cost-effective development using different economic criteria to the traditional approach; that is to say development should not degrade environmental quality, nor should it reduce productivity in the long run;
   (4) the great issues of health control, appropriate technologies, food self-reliance, clean water and shelter for all;
   (5) the notion that people-centered initiatives are needed; human beings, in other words, are the resources in the concept."

Turner (1988)—Academic Economist

"[I]n this [sustainable development] mode...conservation becomes the sole basis for defining a criterion with which to judge the desirability of alternative allocations of natural resources."

Source: Pezzey (1992)

inseparable from achieving sustainable development, it was in the Johannesburg World Summit on Sustainable Development (WSSD) in 2002 that the year 2005–2014 was proposed as the Decade of Education for Sustainable Development (DESD) (UNESCO, 2005). Milestones leading to ESD, and thence to DESD is provided in Table 9.1.

Table 9.1   Milestones in ESD

Year	Event
1968	**UNESCO Conference on Biodiversity** UNESCO organized the first intergovernmental conference to reconcile environment and development. It led to UNESCO's Man and the Biosphere (MAB) Programme. It was a significant step in the process that led to the United Nations Conference on the Human Environment. As a follow-up of this conference, the United Nations Environment Programme (UNEP) was established.
1972	**United Nations Conference on the Human Environment held in Stockholm, Sweden** Led to the establishing of many environmental protection agencies and the United Nations Environment Programme (UNEP) besides many environmental ministries and non-governmental organizations (NGOs) working to conserve the planet's resources
1987	**'Our Common Future'** (Report of the World Commission on Environment and Development, also known as the Brundtland Report) published. It defined sustainable development as "development that meets the needs of the present without compromising the ability of future generations to meet their own needs."
1992	**United Nations Conference on Environment and Development (UNCED) - Rio Earth Summit held in Rio de Janeiro, Brazil** Agenda 21 and the Rio Declaration on Environment and Development were adopted by 178 governments. Agenda 21 is a global action program for sustainable development. UNESCO was designated Task Manager of Chapter 36 of Agenda 21 on education, training and public awareness, as well as Chapter 35 on Science for sustainable development.
2002	**World Summit on Sustainable Development (Johannesburg Summit, Rio+10) held in Johannesburg, South Africa** Member States and global stakeholders reviewed the outcomes of the 1992 Earth Summit and made recommendations for future actions including recommendations to the UN General Assembly to consider adopting a Decade of Education for Sustainable Development, starting in 2005.
2002	**57th session, UN General Assembly held in New York** Adopted resolution 57/254 that declared the period between 2005 and 2014 as the United Nations Decade of Education for Sustainable Development (UNDESD) and designated UNESCO as lead agency.
2005	**United Nations Decade of Education for Sustainable Development (2005–2014)** Officially launched at UN Headquarters in New York.
2009	**UNESCO's mid-DESD World Conference on Education for Sustainable Development held in Bonn, Germany** The Bonn Declaration provided the international community with an action plan on ESD and outlined steps for implementing the remainder of the DESD. To guide its work, UNESCO developed a UNESCO Strategy for the Second Half of the UN Decade of Education for Sustainable Development.

(Continued)

(Continued)

Year	Event
2009	**First DESD Global Monitoring and Evaluation Report**
	Completion of the first phase of the DESD monitoring and evaluation process: 2007–2009 provided a review of contexts and structures for ESD.
2012	**UN Conference on Sustainable Development (Rio+20), Rio de Janeiro, Brazil**
	The Rio+20 outcome document, *The Future We Want*, contained commitments made to education as important for a green economy, for work and social protection, and for training for sustainability.
	Member States resolved to 'promote education for sustainable development and to integrate sustainable development more actively into education beyond the DESD.'
	Tbilisi+35 commemorates 35 years of global educational efforts toward a sustainable world
	An Intergovernmental Conference (Tbilisi+35) in Tbilisi, Georgia brought together delegates from all over the world to carry forward the global appeal for environmental education as a means for sustainable development.
	Second DESD Global Monitoring and Evaluation Report
	Completion of the second phase of the DESD monitoring and evaluation process: 2009–2012 provided a review of processes and learning for ESD.
2013	**37th session, UNESCO General Conference, Paris**
	Adopted 37 C/Resolution 12, which endorsed the Global Action Programme (GAP) on ESD as the follow-up to the DESD.
2014	ESD included as a target in the **Muscat Agreement** adopted at the Global Education For All Meeting (GEM) and in the proposal for **Sustainable Development Goals** (SDGs) adopted by the Open Working Group (OWG).
	UNESCO World Conference on Education for Sustainable Development, Aichi-Nagoya, Japan
	Learning Today for a Sustainable Future Conference has the following four objectives: (a) celebrating a decade of action; (b) reorienting education to build a better future for all; (c) accelerating action for sustainable development; and (d) setting the agenda for ESD beyond 2014. The Conference marks the end of the DESD, celebrating its achievements and launches the Global Action Programme on ESD.
	Final Global Monitoring and Evaluation Report
	Completion of the third and final phase of the DESD global monitoring and evaluation process: 2005–2014. This focuses on the impacts and outcomes of the DESD.

JUST A MOMENT

The concept of sustainable development is sweet to the ears. Are you convinced about the feasibility of this concept?

9.2 What Is Education for Sustainable Development?

ESD is "an emerging but dynamic concept that encompasses a new vision of education that seeks to empower people of all ages to assume responsibility for creating and enjoying a sustainable future" (UNESCO 2002, 5). It empowers everyone to make informed decisions for environmental integrity, economic viability and a just society for present and future generations, while respecting cultural diversity (UNESCO 2014a). Further, "it is not so much education about sustainable development but education for sustainable development" (Pigozzi 2003).

9.2.1 Key Characteristics of ESD

Education for sustainable development:

- is based on the principles and values that underlie sustainable development;
- deals with the well-being of all three realms of sustainability—environment, society and economy;
- promotes life-long learning;
- is locally relevant and culturally appropriate;
- is based on local needs, perceptions and conditions, but acknowledges that fulfiling local needs often has international effects and consequences;
- engages formal, nonformal and informal education;
- accommodates the evolving nature of the concept of sustainability;
- addresses content, taking into account context, global issues and local priorities;
- builds civil capacity for community-based decision-making, social tolerance, environmental stewardship, adaptable workforce, and quality of life;
- is interdisciplinary. No one discipline can claim ESD for its own, but all disciplines can contribute to ESD;
- uses a variety of pedagogical techniques that promote participatory learning and higher-order thinking skills.

These essential characteristics of ESD can be implemented in myriad ways, so that the resulting ESD program reflects the unique environmental, social and economic conditions of each locality (UNESCO 2005).

9.2.2 Four Major Thrusts of ESD

Chapter 36 of Agenda 21 identified four major thrusts of education to support a sustainable future (UNESCO 2005).

- **Improving access to quality basic education:** The first priority of ESD is improving the access to and quality of basic education since the content and years of basic education differ greatly around the world. This recognition of the need for quality basic education sets ESD apart from other educational efforts such as environmental education or population education (McKeown et al. 2002). Retention is another area that is a priority. In this process, basic education must be reoriented to address sustainability and expanded to include critical-thinking skills, skills to organize and interpret data and information, and skills to formulate questions. Skill development to analyze local issues and lifestyle choices that do not erode the natural resource base or impinge on the social equity and justice of their neighbors should also be part of basic education. Such quality basic education alone can bring about sustainable societies.

- **Reorienting existing education programs:** Creating sustainable societies is at the heart of sustainable development. This can only be achieved by reorienting the content and relevance of education. ESD identifies questioning, rethinking, and revising education from pre-school through university to include more principles, knowledge, skills, perspectives and values related to sustainability in each of the three realms—environment, society, and economy. It envisages achieving this through a holistic and interdisciplinary context, engaging society at large, but carried out by individual nations in a locally relevant and culturally appropriate manner.

- **Developing public understanding and awareness of sustainability:** To make progress toward more sustainable societies requires a population that is aware of the goals of sustainability and has the knowledge and the skills to contribute toward those goals. A knowledgeable citizenry supports a more sustainable society in several ways—supporting government policy related to resource management and civic conduct, supporting measures related to sustainable development and politicians who introduce and support enlightened legislation, by becoming knowledgeable consumers taking into account environmental responsibility and sustainable business practices, and helping communities and governments enact sustainability measures and move toward more sustainable societies.

- **Providing training:** All sectors—including business, industry, higher education, governments, NGOs, and community organizations—should be encouraged to train their leaders in sustainability issues such as environmental management, equity policies, etc., and to provide training to their workers in sustainable practices. There needs to be collaboration between those in the formal education and nonformal education sector such as nature centers, NGOs, public health educators and agricultural extension agents, etc.

The following seven strategies were identified for ESD:

1. Vision-building and advocacy
2. Consultation and ownership
3. Partnership and networks
4. Capacity-building and training
5. Research and innovation
6. Use of information and communication technology (ICT)
7. Monitoring and evaluation

9.2.3 Dimensions of ESD

Based on its characteristics, thrust areas and strategies, the focus of the implementation of ESD can be placed under the following four dimensions.

- **Learning content:** Integrating critical issues, such as climate change, biodiversity, disaster risk reduction (DRR), and sustainable consumption and production (SCP), and others into the curriculum.
- **Pedagogy and learning environments:** Designing teaching and learning in an interactive, learner-centered way that enables exploratory, action-oriented and transformative learning. Rethinking learning environments—physical as well as virtual and online—to inspire learners to act for sustainability.
- **Learning outcomes:** Stimulating learning and promoting core competencies, such as critical and systemic thinking, collaborative decision-making, and taking responsibility for present and future generations.
- **Societal transformation:** Empowering learners of any age, in any education setting, to transform themselves and the society they live in.
  - Enabling a transition to greener economies and societies.
    - Equipping learners with skills for 'green jobs.'
    - Motivating people to adopt sustainable lifestyles.
  - Empowering people to be 'global citizens' who engage and assume active roles, both locally and globally, to face and to resolve global challenges and ultimately to become proactive contributors to creating a more just, peaceful, tolerant, inclusive, secure, and sustainable world (UNESCO 2014b).

9.3 Decade of Education for Sustainable Development (DESD)—2005 to 2014

UNESCO was identified as the lead UN agency for DESD. The overall goal of the DESD is to integrate the principles, values, and practices of sustainable development into all aspects of education and learning (UNESCO 2005). Some of its key goals are provided in Table 9.2.

9.3.1 Relationship of DESD with Other International Initiatives

As discussed earlier under the sub-heading Genesis, DESD shares several concerns with other international initiatives such as MDGs, EFA, and UNLD. The common objectives shared by these are:

- A concern to improve the quality of life: all of them aim to reduce poverty and improve health;
- The promotion of human rights: all of them see education as a right, and they aim to increase the equality of women and men, as well as advance the human rights of all, particularly minorities and other marginalized communities;

Table 9.2 Key Goals of the DESD	
Promoting ESD	ESD is about engaging and empowering people in sustainable development. The former seeks people's commitment to sustainable development; the latter gives people the power to make decisions and bring changes.
Introducing lifelong learning perspectives	All possible spaces of learning—formal, nonformal and informal—with a lifelong learning perspective should be considered.
Promoting quality education and learning	Quality education and learning are a requirement in our current system. Teacher training and educators' retraining are important components.
Seeking new governmental structures and support	Governments are playing a very important role in the DESD's success. At governmental level, policies, strategies and action plans in ESD need to be established. The first half of the DESD focuses on this particular goal.
Engaging stakeholders (including those not already involved)	The DESD not only should engage stakeholders who are currently working toward ESD objectives but also those stakeholders who are less aware about sustainable development issues.

Source: Mulà and Tilbury (2009)

- A commitment to education: all believe that education is a key to development, as a way of enabling people to fulfill their potential and take increasing control over decisions that affect them. The MDGs and DESD focus on broader purposes beyond education, whereas the purposes of EFA and UNLD are about making sure that basic education, and literacy within that, is available to all;
- Primary education: all four recognize that primary education plays an important foundational role in development;
- The participation of everyone in education and development: all of the initiatives call not only for governmental engagement but also the active involvement of organizations, civil society, the private sector, communities and individuals (UNESCO 2007).

Hence the International Implementation Scheme for UNDESD framed by UNESCO reflects the initiatives to promote education, not only those concerning ESD but all other global initiatives as well (UNESCO 2014a).

While the DESD shares common ground with the other international initiatives, it differs from them by the very virtue of its mission in that while other initiatives ensure the right to education for all and address the needs of all learners, and especially those who are excluded from access to quality basic education, the DESD stresses the need and relevance of education for sustainable development for all, within and beyond the formal sphere of education. Besides, the outreach of the DESD is broader than the other initiatives as it not only tackles education but also addresses the way we live, and our attitudes and values that impact the sustainability of not just our societies but our planet (UNESCO 2007).

9.3.2 Impact of DESD

The 2014 Global Monitoring and Evaluation Report, *Shaping the Future We Want–UN Decade of Education for Sustainable Development (2005-2014),* brought out the outcomes of 10 years of work around the world to advance education as a critical tool for moving societies toward sustainability. It also provides insights on the impact of the call for a UN Decade of Education for Sustainable Development (DESD) on all levels and areas of education, and it charts the major lessons that will inform future work. It lays down 10 key findings and trends that have emerged which will guide ESD into the future:

ESD, an enabler for sustainable development	ESD is galvanizing pedagogical innovation
1. Education systems are addressing sustainability issues	6. Whole-institution approaches help practice ESD
2. Sustainable development agendas and education agendas are converging	7. ESD facilitates interactive, learner-driven pedagogies
Importance of stakeholder engagement for ESD	**ESD has spread across all levels and areas of education**
3. Political leadership has proven instrumental	8. ESD is being integrated into formal education
4. Multi-stakeholder partnerships are particularly effective	9. Nonformal and informal ESD is increasing
5. Local commitments are growing	10. Technical and vocational education and training advances sustainable development

Source: UNESCO (2014a)

At the end of the DESD, the report said, a solid foundation has been laid for ESD being achieved by raising awareness, influencing policies, and generating significant numbers of good practice projects in all areas and levels of education and learning. However several challenges have also been identified in the report. For example,

1. While much has been done to advance the ethos and values of ESD, a full integration of ESD into education systems has yet to take place in most countries.
2. It mentions the need for further alignment of education and sustainable development sectors.
3. Major work remains to ensure full policy coherence between the education sector and the sustainable development sector.
4. ESD is not integrated coherently across relevant sectorial or sub-sectorial policies.
5. ESD implementation requires enhanced capacities among policy-makers, curriculum developers, school leaders, assessment experts and, most importantly, teachers (UNESCO 2014a).

JUST A MOMENT

Can you think of any significant effort made in the education system following the declaration of the Decade of Education for Sustainable Development?

9.4 Global Action Programme (GAP)

The Global Action Programme on Education for Sustainable Development, as follow-up to the United Nations Decade of Education for Sustainable Development after 2014, was developed by UNESCO and it was endorsed by the UNESCO General Conference in 2013. GAP was launched at the World Conference on Education for Sustainable Development in Aichi-Nagoya, Japan in November 2014 and adopted by the Member States as part of the Aichi-Nagoya Declaration on Education for Sustainable Development (Box 9.2). It may be mentioned that ESD is one of the seventeen sustainable development goals (SDGs) listed by United Nations envisaged to be achieved by 2030.

BOX

Aichi Nagoya Declaration on Education for Sustainable Development

We, the participants of the UNESCO World Conference on Education for Sustainable Development held in Aichi-Nagoya, Japan, from 10 to 12 November 2014, adopt this Declaration and call for urgent action to further strengthen and scale up Education for Sustainable Development (ESD), in order to enable current generations to meet their needs while allowing future generations to meet their own, with a balanced and integrated approach regarding the economic, social and environmental dimensions of sustainable development. This Declaration recognizes that people are at the center of sustainable development and builds on the achievements of the United Nations (UN) Decade of ESD (2005-2014); the deliberations of the UNESCO World Conference on ESD in Aichi-Nagoya; and the Stakeholder Meetings held in Okayama, Japan, from 4 to 8 November 2014, namely, UNESCO ASPnet International ESD events, the UNESCO ESD Youth Conference, the Global Regional Centres of Expertise Conference, and other relevant events and consultation processes, including regional ministerial meetings. We express our sincere gratitude to the Government of Japan for hosting the UNESCO World Conference on ESD.

1. **CELEBRATING** the significant achievements made by the UN Decade of ESD (2005-2014), in particular, in putting ESD higher on national and international agendas, advancing policy, improving the conceptual understanding of ESD, and generating substantive good practice amongst a wide range of stakeholders,

2. **EXPRESSING** our appreciation to many governments, UN entities, non-governmental organizations, all types of educational institutions and setups, educators and learners in schools, communities and workplaces, youth, the scientific community, academia and other stakeholders who have actively committed to and participated in the implementation of the UN Decade of ESD, and to UNESCO for the leadership role it has played as lead agency of the Decade,

(Continued)

(Continued)

3. **RECALING** the international commitment to further promoting ESD that was included in the outcome document of the 2012 UN Conference on Sustainable Development (Rio+20), *The Future We Want,*

4. **NOTING** that the Global Action Programme (GAP) on ESD, endorsed by the 37th session of the General Conference of UNESCO as a follow up to the Decade of ESD and a concrete contribution to the post-2015 agenda, aims at generating and scaling up ESD actions in all levels and areas of education, training and learning,

5. **REAFFIRMING** ESD as a vital means of implementation for sustainable development, as recognized in intergovernmental agreements on climate change (Article 6 of the UN Framework Convention on Climate Change and its Doha work program), biodiversity (Article 13 of the Convention on Biological Diversity and its work programs and related decisions), disaster risk reduction (Hyogo Framework for Action 2005–2015), sustainable consumption and production (Sustainable Lifestyles and Education Programme of the 10-Year Framework of Programmes on Sustainable Consumption and Production 2012–2021), and children's rights (Articles 24[2], 28 and 29 of the UN Convention on the Rights of the Child), among many others,

6. **WELCOMING** the growing international recognition of ESD as an integral and transformative element of inclusive quality education and lifelong learning and an enabler for sustainable development, as demonstrated by the inclusion of ESD as a target in the Muscat Agreement adopted at the 2014 Global Education For All Meeting and in the proposal for Sustainable Development Goals (SDGs) by the Open Working Group of the UN General Assembly on SDGs,

7. **RECOGNISING** the establishment of the UNESCO-Japan Prize on ESD approved by the Executive Board of UNESCO at its 195th session,

We, the participants,

8. **EMPHASIZE** the potential of ESD to empower learners to transform themselves and the society they live in by developing knowledge, skills, attitudes, competences and values required for addressing global citizenship and local contextual challenges of the present and the future, such as critical and systemic thinking, analytical problem-solving, creativity, working collaboratively and making decisions in the face of uncertainty, and understanding of the interconnectedness of global challenges and responsibilities emanating from such awareness,

9. **STRESS** that ESD is an opportunity and a responsibility that should engage both developed and developing countries in intensifying efforts for poverty eradication, reduction of inequalities, environmental protection and economic growth, with a view to promoting equitable, more sustainable economies and societies benefiting all countries, especially those most vulnerable such as Small Island Developing States and Least Developed Countries,

10. **UNDERSCORE** that the implementation of ESD should fully take into consideration local, national, regional and global contexts, as well as the contribution of culture to sustainable development and the need for respecting peace, non-violence, cultural diversity, local and traditional knowledge and indigenous wisdom and practices, and universal principles such as human rights, gender equality, democracy, and social justice,

11. **APPRECIATE** the commitments to ESD expressed by all concerned stakeholders through their specific contributions to the GAP Launch Commitments,

(Continued)

(Continued)

12. **COMMIT** ourselves to building and maintaining the momentum of the launching of the GAP, in its five Priority Action Areas for ESD, namely policy support, whole-institution approaches, educators, youth, and local communities, through inclusive quality education and lifelong learning via formal, non-formal and informal settings,

13. **CALL UPON** all concerned stakeholders, including governments and their affiliated institutions and networks, civil society organizations and groups, the private sector, media, the academic and research community, and education and training institutions and centres as well as UN entities, bilateral and multilateral development agencies and other types of intergovernmental organizations at all levels, to: (a) set specific goals, (b) develop, support and implement activities, (c) create platforms for sharing experiences (including ICT-based platforms), and (d) strengthen monitoring and evaluation approaches in the five Priority Action Areas of the GAP in a synergistic manner,

14. **URGE** all concerned stakeholders, in particular Ministries of Education and all ministries involved with ESD, higher education institutions and the scientific and other knowledge communities to engage in collaborative and transformative knowledge production, dissemination and utilization, and promotion of innovation across sectoral and disciplinary boundaries at the science-policy-ESD practice interface to enrich decision-making and capacity building for sustainable development with emphasis on involving and respecting youth as key stakeholders,

15. **INVITE** governments of UNESCO Member States to make further efforts to:

    a) Review the purposes and values that underpin education, assess the extent to which education policy and curricula are achieving the goals of ESD; reinforce the integration of ESD into education, training, and sustainable development policies, with a special attention paid to system-wide and holistic approaches and multi-stakeholder cooperation and partnerships between actors of the education sector, private sector, civil society and those working in the various areas of sustainable development; and ensure the education, training and professional development of teachers and other educators to successfully integrate ESD into teaching and learning;

    b) Allocate and mobilize substantial resources to translate policies into actions, especially building necessary institutional capacities for both formal and non-formal education and learning at national and sub-national levels along the five Priority Actions Areas of the GAP; and

    c) Reflect and strengthen ESD in the post-2015 agenda and its follow-up processes, ensuring, first, that ESD is maintained as a target in the education goal and also integrated in SDGs as a cross-cutting theme; and, second, that the outcomes of the 2014 World Conference on ESD are taken into consideration at the World Education Forum 2015 to be held in Incheon, Republic of Korea from 19 to 22 May 2015,

16. **REQUEST** UNESCO's Director-General to continue to:

    a) Provide global leadership, support policy synergy, and facilitate communication for ESD, in cooperation with governments, other UN entities, development partners, private sector and civil society, within the framework of the UNESCO Roadmap to Implement the GAP;

    b) Harness partnerships and mobilize networks including the UNESCO ASPnet, UNESCO Chairs, Centres under the auspices of UNESCO, the World Network of Biosphere Reserves and World Heritage Sites, as well as UNESCO Clubs and Associations; and

    c) Advocate the importance of ensuring adequate resources including funding for ESD.

9.4.1 Goals and Objectives

The GAP contributes to achieving the vision put forward by the Decade of ESD: "a world where everybody has the opportunity to benefit from education and learn the values, behavior and lifestyles required for a sustainable future and for positive societal transformation."

The overarching goal of the GAP is "to generate and scale up action in all levels and areas of education and learning to accelerate progress towards sustainable development."

The GAP will deploy a two-fold approach to multiply and to scale up ESD action: (a) integrating sustainable development into education and (b) integrating education into sustainable development. Corresponding to this overall approach, the program has the following two objectives.

- to reorient education and learning so that everyone has the opportunity to acquire the knowledge, skills, values, and attitudes that empower them to contribute to sustainable development.
- to strengthen education and learning in all agendas, programs, and activities that promote sustainable development (UNESCO 2014b).

9.4.2 Priority Areas of GAP

To enable strategic focus and foster stakeholder commitment, the GAP has identified five priority action areas to advance the ESD agenda.

1. **Advancing policy:** Mainstream ESD into both education and sustainable development policies, to create an enabling environment for ESD and to bring about systemic change
2. **Transforming learning and training environments:** Integrate sustainability principles into education and training settings
3. **Building capacities of educators and trainers:** Increase the capacities of educators and trainers to more effectively deliver ESD
4. **Empowering and mobilizing youth:** Multiply ESD actions among youth
5. **Accelerating sustainable solutions at local level:** At community level, scale up ESD programs and multi-stakeholder ESD networks (UNESCO 2014b).

9.5 Types of Sustainability Education

As brilliant as the concept of ESD may sound, it is not without limitations and ambiguities. There exists lack of clarity on whether Education for Sustainable Development as a concept is different from any practice of education 'for'/'leading to' sustainable development. If they are different, how does it affect in our efforts toward sustainable development or sustainability in the education process. We will explore some aspects of this in the following discussions.

UNESCO (2009) identifies two types of sustainability education. They are:

1. SD-related education ('adjectival' educations), which include peace education, global education, development education, HIV and AIDS education, citizenship education, and intercultural education, human rights education, as well as long-existing educations such as environmental education and health education, and so on. The list of such SD-related education will be numerous and each of these types of SD-related education will invariably contribute to one of the dimensions of SD.
2. Full-fledged ESD which essentially requires the integration of all the dimensions of SD: environmental, social (cultural dimension included), and economic. UNESCO (2014b) also clearly mentions the integrated, balanced, and holistic approach to environmental, social, and economic pillars of sustainable development in ESD. The key here is 'integration' and therefore any issue discussed under this will always include the environmental, social and economic aspects.

However, it has also been clarified that SD-related education and ESD cannot be totally separated since the broader the interpretation of these particular SD-related educations, the more they resemble ESD (UNESCO 2009, 28).

In this context, it might be appropriate to elaborate on how SD-related education continues to remain as SD-related education and when the same becomes ESD-like. Let us take for example, health education. As long as the focus of health education is on 'health' by concentrating on topics such as how to eat healthy, how to live healthy, how to take preventive measures from diseases, how to prevent the spread of diseases, first aid, and so on, then such health education is considered SD-related education. To maintain a sustainable society, this aspect definitely counts but here, health education is done in isolation. However, when the discussion is broadened to include its environmental dimensions such as pollution of air, water, soil, solid wastes, scarcity of potable water, and economic dimensions related to health—such as inability to procure nutritious food, maintain healthy surroundings (such as inability to afford smokeless *chulha* or inability to construct toilet) or inability to avail basic medical facility due to poverty, and even other social issues such as alcoholism leading to health and other problems—then we can say that it has taken the form of ESD, because now all the dimensions of ESD—environment, society, and economy—are in the purview of health education and is done holistically. In such a situation, there will be an integration of all the dimensions and each will impact the course of action of the other. And finally, what is being seen to be practiced in ESD is an integration of all the three dimensions, often reinforcing the other while also accepting a 'compromised' stand many a times. However, every issue related to SD-related education cannot take the form of ESD. Discrimination based on race or caste or disability, for example, is purely a social issue and it will be difficult to give it the form of ESD. Another example is of the natural extinction of flora and fauna, many of which occur even before we could identify them or even know that they exist (not to be confused with the increased rate of extinction due to exploitation of nature by man). This phenomenon is purely environmental in nature and hence can only fall in the purview of SD-related education.

An important point to be noted here is, though every SD-related education contributes in some way to ESD, the sum of all SD-related education does not give rise to ESD.

Similarly, every sustainable action with respect to environment, society, or economy, contributes in some way to sustainability or sustainable development. However, the sum of all sustainable actions carried out independently of other parts does not give rise to sustainable development of a whole. In sustainability or sustainable development, integration of the three dimensions is essential while addressing issues. To illustrate this view more explicitly, let us consider sustainability or sustainable development as a coat. As mentioned earlier, SD-related actions do contribute in some way in the process of sustainability or SD. However, since the different actions are not correlated or linked with other sustainable development actions, what we obtain is a weird-looking coat which is disproportionate in every respect, as shown in Figure 9.1. For example, environmental education, health education, population education, gender education, and so on, taken up independently in isolation will give rise to such situation. While in Figure 9.2 we see that all the pieces have been arranged in proportion to the other parts thus giving a perfect shape to the coat. This represents a situation wherein during the process of taking up a specific SD-related education, all dimensions of sustainability are addressed holistically. That means, it has taken the form of ESD. However, all the types of SD-related education are not necessarily linked directly with each other as arranged in the figure and their placement in the coat does not indicate their functional proximity in reality. Nor does the shape and size of each patch which indicates a specific SD-related education in the figure represent the proportion of its relative role in sustainability. The figure has been used only for the purpose of illustrating the concept so as to differentiate between SD-related educations and ESD.

Figure 9.1   SD-related Educations Done in Isolation

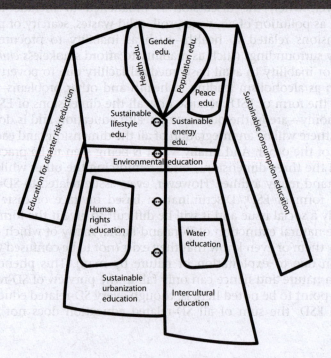

Figure 9.2 SD-related Educations Taking the Form of ESD

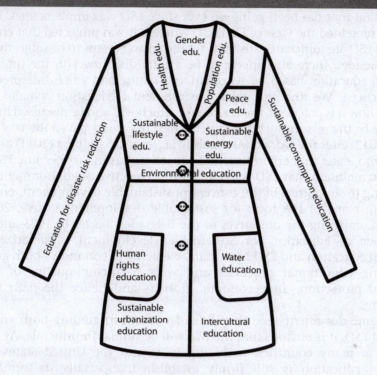

In the figure, only some SD-related education has been mentioned. Besides these, there are many other forms of SD-related education.

Interestingly, UNESCO also included environmental education, which is considered to be the base for ESD, under the SD-related education. However, at the same time, it also acceded that the relationship of ESD with environmental education is more striking compared to other SD-related education signifying the conceptual proximity of the two. This is because the founding documents of both environmental education and ESD are practically the same. The Tbilisi Declaration was the founding document for environmental education while for ESD it was Chapter 36 of Agenda 21—education, public awareness, and training—for which the Tbilisi Declaration provided the fundamental principles for the proposals in the Chapter 36 document. Therefore, labeling environmental education as SD-related education is not as much to do with the nature of environmental education but more so to fortify the identity, existence, and relevance of ESD.

JUST A MOMENT

Reflect on any one issue prevalent in your neighborhood and try to relate the issue in terms of social, environmental and economic aspects.

9.6 Is EE Very Different from ESD?

This is a question that has been going on ever since ESD was implemented. In the earlier discussion we presented the view of UNESCO wherein it was projected that environmental education and ESD are sufficiently distinct. Yet the answer seems to be subjective as we shall discuss here. Besides, there also appear to be a total disconnect in the interpretation of environmental education based on its origin and nature and when interpreted based on how it is practiced. We find that what environmental education actually is, is totally different from how it is practiced, the reasons for which will also be discussed in this section. Whatever may be the reason, such indistinctiveness has surely paved the way for ESD.

Kopnina (2012) cites the work of Arlemalm-Hagser and Sandberg (2011) and Eilam and Trop (2010) who argue that environmental education has in fact become ESD. There are also those who maintain that ESD is a dominant perspective of environmental education while according to supporters of the concept of sustainable development, environmental education is just one of the tools for sustainable development (Sauve, 2005). Gough (2006), while comparing the objectives of the Belgrade Charter of 1975 and the United Nations Decade of Education for Sustainable Development, summarizes that both environmental education and ESD have many elements in common—both are concerned with reforming educational processes and with balancing quality of human life, environmental protection, and economic growth—and hence the path for both are essentially same.

With the same document (i.e., the Tbilisi Declaration) guiding both environmental education and ESD, it is obvious that the two will be similar in principle. As such, it is no surprise that in many countries, including India and the United States of America, environmental education is still firmly established, especially in formal education systems. However, ESD is slowly catching up in such countries and other countries have gone ahead with various variants of sustainability education such as education for sustainability, sustainability education or education for sustainable development. This parallel existence and development of environmental education and ESD has given rise to questions about the relationship between the two and the call for distinctions by some or for convergence by others. Toward this confusion, pro-ESD proponents claim that ESD is intended to build on the lessons of environmental education and not to simply perpetuate environmental education under another name. They maintain that SD-related educations, including environmental education, continue to contribute to ESD in terms of content and pedagogy.

UNESCO (2005, 26) mentions of programs initiated under the United Nations Environment Programme (UNEP), of which environmental education was a major initiative, as: "while some attention was attached to the social and economic issues inherent in these environmental issues the focus was largely on addressing the ecological impact of ever increasing unrestricted development." This view is also shared by many others. For example, McKeown et al. (2002) argue that equal attention is not focused on the social and economic strands in environmental education. These observations, however, did not imply that the concept of environmental education itself was flawed or lacking holistic approach. All that they indicate is that there were drawbacks in the implementation. As a matter of fact, it would be nonsensical for one to contest that environmental education was incomplete since all the guiding documents of environmental education clearly talk about its holistic and interdisciplinary nature. We may recall the first guiding principle of environmental education programs of the Belgrade Charter which states, "Environmental education should consider the environment in its totality—natural and man-made, ecological, political, economic, technological, social, legislative, cultural and esthetic" (UNESCO–UNEP 1976). Similarly, the Tbilisi Declaration characterizes environmental education as "interdisciplinary and holistic in nature and application" with one of its goals being "to foster clear awareness of, and concern about, economic, social, political and ecological interdependence in urban and rural areas." Further, the guiding principle of the Tbilisi Declaration states that "EE should consider the environment in its totality—natural and built, technological and social (economic, political, cultural-historical, moral, esthetic)" (UNESCO–UNEP 1978). The Belgrade Charter or the Tbilisi Declaration does not signal even a slightest indication that social and economic dimensions should be kept secondary or given lesser importance. The fact that environmental education presents a holistic view is reiterated by many professionals in the field such as Jenkins (1994, 606 cited in Gough 2008) who argues that "environmental education exposes with particular clarity the complex interactions among social, economic, personal and other value positions associated with almost any environmental issue." In the light of these discussions and arguments, we may come to an agreement that environmental education is indeed holistic in approach and if it is felt that equal attention is not focused on the social and economic aspects then it has to do with implementation. This can be supplemented by studies undertaken by many researchers. For example, Braus and Wood (1993) observed that educators continue to link environmental education exclusively with science education in spite of the fact that environmental education is interdisciplinary in nature and that it requires the understanding of economics, math, geography, ethics, politics, and other subjects. As a result of this, the focus turn out to be on providing scientific content knowledge, leaving little space for discussion on social and economic issues.

Therefore, the issue with environmental education is to be attributed to implementation. Environmental education 'done right' serves the objectives of ESD equally well. However, instead of holistically approaching environmental education, practitioners have been implementing environmental education according to their convenience; many a times they did not have a choice. The reasons for such undesirable deviation from what is expected could be many—lack of government support, method of dealing with environmental issues were more confrontational and skills were provided accordingly—and hence environmental education apparently became less interdisciplinary; skills to communicate with officials, understand environmental issues, persuade, lobby, and boycott became part of the curriculum; challenging and controversial issues which are at the core of environmental education were dropped; and, most importantly, environmental education became more focused on teaching science-based information about ecosystems and conservation (Monroe 2012). An altogether different meaning of environmental education was, therefore, presented to the world. These ultimately resulted in the need to explore for a more encompassing, broader, and more-inclusive alternative which was eventually discovered in the concept of ESD. With the 'three pillars—society, environment and economy'—clearly defined in ESD, it is envisaged that practitioners will naturally consider all the 'pillars' when dealing with any issue or topic. But this will be easier said than done. Many factors will come into play such as level of training of the practitioners, motivation factors, monitoring factors, political pressure, and so on. Having seen what environmental education went through during the past more than three decades, it is now feared that ESD could also see the same fate unless special measures are kept in place.

In the light of our earlier discussions, the practical difference between environmental education and ESD, if they are indeed different or considered to be different, might be summed up in the following words: In environmental education, the 'environment' component is still not clearly defined while in ESD 'environment,' as one of its pillars, is explicitly about the biophysical environment. Further, in environmental education, issue identification invariably begins with biophysical problems. It then considers the holistic approach to resolve the issue. For example, degradation of soil due to use of chemical fertilizers is a biophysical issue for which productivity of the farmland, and poverty of the farmers and their social life also form important concerns which are taken in account while resolving it,. With ESD, issue identification has no boundary. It may begin with biophysical environmental problem, social problem, or economic problem but the holistic approach to resolve the issue remains the same as in environmental education. Hence, productivity of the farm due to use of fertilizers (economic in nature), poverty of farmers and their social life (social in nature), or degradation of soil due to use of chemical fertilizers (environmental or biophysical in nature) can all be associated with ESD. However, the above view might be contested by many environmental educators who also consider social problems for issue identification as mentioned in Chapter 7 (Glasser et al. 1972; Stapp and Cox 1974). If this view be accepted, then there will be practically no difference between environmental education and ESD.

JUST A MOMENT

Don't you think too much emphasis is given to the names such as EE or ESD when in reality we have not been able to implement either of the two in our classrooms?

9.7 Do Away with EE?

Another matter of debate arises with the wide endorsement of ESD. Where does environmental education stand in the context of ESD? Does focusing on full-fledged ESD mean doing away with SD-related education including environmental education? Like other SD-related educations, the fate of environmental education will be settled with this. A plausible answer to this could be, rather than doing away, synergies need to be created between ESD and other SD-related educations, which should mutually support rather than compete with each other. With the root of ESD established in EE (UNESCO 2009), we might as well retain environmental education viewing it as indispensable to achieving the broader goal of ESD (Jenkins and Jenkins 2005) as 'environment' represents one of the three 'pillars of sustainable development' (UNESCO 2006, 14) or as one of the three spheres of sustainability (UNESCO 2005, 28). Besides, it has also been established that EE and ESD are complementary to each other (McKeown and Hopkins 2003; Monroe 2012).

Though we now know that ESD would address both the needs of the society and the environment, we need not do away with environmental education. The reason is, environmental education, whether practiced with a focus on biophysical environment or with equal emphasis on the biophysical, social, or economic aspects, it would only strengthen ESD and ultimately in our move toward sustainable development. Further, the Brundtland Commission Report—*Our Common Future*—based on which the whole concept of sustainable development became popular, itself encourages the implementation of environmental education as it says in Chapter 4: "Environmental education should be included in and should run throughout the other disciplines of the formal education curriculum at all levels—to foster a sense of responsibility for the state of the environment and to teach students how to monitor, protect, and improve it."

Besides, environmental education continues to receive enormous attention even after the concept of sustainable development or ESD became established globally. For example, the role of environmental education for sustainable development was widely recognized at the World Summit on Sustainable Development (Boojh 2003). Similarly other conferences on environmental education remain to be conducted with the same vigor and purpose, though sustainable development became an unavoidable suffix in all such endeavors. Mention may be made of the Fourth International Conference on Environmental Education Toward a Sustainable Future which was held in Ahmedabad, India which looked into the current status of environmental education and its development to meet the challenges of sustainability and the objectives of the DESD and an Intergovernmental Conference (Tbilisi+35) which commemorates 35 years of global educational efforts toward a sustainable world was held in 2012 during which the delegates carried forward the global appeal for environmental education as a means for sustainable development (UNESCO 2014).

We can suffice from the above discussions that whether we practice and profess ESD only or ESD and environmental education is not the issue. As Monroe (2012) writes,

> We need quality education that prepares people to understand multiple views; to listen and communicate with others; to vision and evaluate options; to collect, synthesise and understand data; to learn how others have balanced contentious elements of an issue; and to be able to adopt actions. Both environmental education and ESD have the potential to provide exactly that.

9.8 Ramifications of Implementation of ESD

Professionals have been raising concerns about the possible fallout of implementing ESD if practitioners are not cautious. This is because, nature, in the notion of sustainable development, is conceived as a resource and reflects anthropomorphic and even economic motives (Bonnett 2004a, 2004b; Sauve 1999 cited in Hadzigeorgiou and Skoumios 2013). The ramifications of implementation of ESD could be many. Here we shall look into a few of those.

(i) ESD is more issue-based, or challenge-based, or problem-based while environmental education is an approach to learning environmental concepts and is not limited to issues and problems. This whole approach to learning may entirely be neglected with the implementation of ESD. As a result deeper understanding of environmental concepts may not occur in schools. Practitioners are most likely to superficially deal with the environment components in ESD.

(ii) Another concern of implementation of ESD is that the pluralistic perspectives of ESD might not be truly democratic as the discourse on sustainable development is dominated by the perspectives of the political and corporate elites. Considering the power of political or corporate elites and the glaring influence of industrial capitalism in shaping the discourse on development, with its clear emphasis on human welfare, the chances for the students to develop ecocentric values is far from certain. But what is most likely is that the environment could be considered nothing more than a resource to be exploited in the name of development. Keeping in view the influence of the corporatists it is feared that such perspectives may find way in the school in the form of hidden curriculum and further encourage development and discourage ecocentrism.

(iii) The pluralistic perspective of ESD will not be able to address the real-world problems arising as a result of continuing exploitation of the environment that need urgent attention (Bonnett 2013 and Fien 2000 cited in Kopnina 2014).

(iv) Professionals and researchers have voiced their concerns on the increased focus on social issues as a result of implementation of ESD. This is because in such issues which involve both the environment and the society, our natural tendency would be to first attempt to alleviate the concern of the society. Invariably we will find our decisions always biased and inclined toward the society. As a result, environmental concerns take secondary place.

In the situation the world is in today, any education toward sustainability is welcome and ESD is definitely one such approach that will cater toward this end. But, it will also be worthwhile to specially ponder on the serious damage it has done to its environment and to look for ways for its restoration as well as for prevention of further damage. In this context, apprehensions have been raised especially on the nature of ESD and its pluralistic views. There are concerns that suggest that ESD presents a radical change of focus from prioritizing environmental protection which is the essence of environmental education and gravitate toward mostly social issues, which may or may not be related to environment. As Kopnina (2012) in *Education for sustainable development (ESD): the turn away from 'environment' in environmental education* argues:

> [R]ecent ESD debate does not fully realize the problematic nature of economic development for the ecological health of the biosphere. Pluralistic perspectives on ESD can lead practitioners into an essentially anthropocentric paradigm which can be counter-productive to the effort of fostering environmentally concerned citizenry.

There is also a concern that the pluralistic anthropocentric orientation in ESD will weaken our moral obligation toward non human species. In line with this view, Kopnina (2014) supports education for deep ecology so that the intrinsic value of non human species is recognized and argues that ecocentric educators need to advocate by being the 'voice' of these non human species so that they are protected. Interestingly, the Hon'ble Supreme Court of India, in its judgment dated 15th April 2013 in Centre for Environment

Law, WWF-I Vs. Union of India and Others (I.A. No. 100 in Writ Petition (Civil) No. 337 of 1995 (I.A. No. 3452 in WP(C) No. 202 of 1995), had also reiterated that sustainable development is anthropocentric with little concern for the rights of other species on earth and hence suggested a move toward ecocentrism which is nature-centered, where humans are part of nature and non humans have intrinsic value.

This is especially true in terms of environmental justice. Environmental justice refers to equitable distribution of environmental goods such as natural resources, clean air, water, and so on, among human populations as well as between species. This can be broadly grouped into anthropocentric environmental justice and ecological justice. The issue here is that, in both the cases, man has to stand up to raise concerns. While anthropocentric environmental justice has its own issues (such as an economically weaker section of the society having to bear the adverse impacts of environmental issues for example, industrial waste, while not receiving proportionate good out of it), when it comes to priority between anthropocentric environmental justice and ecological justice, it is most likely that the former will prevail. In the process of unprecedented development and growth of population with increasing demand for resources, it is but expected that ecological justice will not find enough space and place as part of human priorities. That is, the ecocentric perspectives will not be addressed adequately, if not neglected entirely. This will lead to a situation which will do more harm to the already deteriorating environment which will, in turn, ultimately impact human life.

This suggests that conscious and deliberate efforts need to be taken while implementing ESD so that ecological justice is given equal priority. A huge responsibility rests on the practitioners and educators so that ESD is implemented fairly and justly without any biases. It must be remembered that human life can only be sustained when the ecosystem is sustained and not the other way round. The ecosystem can exist *sans* man!

JUST A MOMENT

Reflect on the nature of human beings and analyze how far the environment is safe in our hands?

Conclusion

The concept of Education for Sustainable Development (ESD) has indeed become very popular. However, when it comes to its implementation, there still appears to be lack of clarity. ESD covers such a vast area that it might appear that there would be no issue with implementation. In fact, hardly any topic under the sun can be beyond the purview of ESD. But this feature itself seems to have become a disadvantage to it. The idea that education should be aimed at bringing about sustainable development is yet to be understood by practitioners in relation to their curriculum; how they should do it is a whole different issue to be addressed. While ESD itself is a unique approach to education, there are also other forms of sustainable development related education. These two broad categories of education focused at bringing about sustainable development—ESD and SD-related education—will have to be clearly interpreted for the sake of practitioners.

While proponents of ESD might claim that environmental education is ecocentric and that social and economic concerns are not taken care of through environmental education, there are valid concerns that ESD could sideline the concerns related to the biophysical environment. Many are of the opinion that ESD is anthropocentric and that ecological justice may not be done with the implementation of ESD. If this is true, the dangers to human life and survival of humankind will be at a greater risk than ever, the inconvenient truth which humans fail to seriously consider.

One might sometimes wonder if it has been really worth debating whether environmental education is better or ESD should be the way. Many, probably, might have also wasted years in their effort to transit from environmental education to the in vogue ESD and many will still struggle in their attempt to transition, not doing any good to either in the process.

SUMMARY

- ESD came about to cater to the two broad areas of interest of the United Nations–Education and Sustainable Development.
- ESD is envisaged to contribute toward other initiatives of the United Nations such as the Education for All, the Millennium Development Goals, or the UN Decade of Literacy.
- To further the implementation of ESD, 2005–2014 was declared by the UN as the Decade of Education for Sustainable Development (DESD).
- The Global Action Programme (GAP) was initiated to take forward the vision of DESD. GAP is envisaged to generate and scale up action in all levels and areas of education and learning to accelerate progress toward sustainable development.
- Sustainability education is not limited to ESD but is also done through different forms of education which are collectively called SD-related education.
- ESD and environmental education are fundamentally similar as both environmental education and ESD share the same footing in the document Tbilisi Declaration of 1977. And that both environmental education and ESD will lead to the same result that we strive for – sustainable future.
- Due to inconsistencies in the implementation, environmental education is thought to be more ecocentric while giving little importance to social and economic issues and hence the need for a more encompassing concept was felt which ESD was believed to provide.
- Many are of the opinion that ESD is anthropocentric and that ecological justice may not be done with the implementation of ESD.

Exercises

1. Explain how education for sustainable development came into being.
2. What are the thrust areas of education for sustainable development? How can formal education contribute in addressing these thrust areas?
3. Why did the United Nations declare 2005–2014 as the Decade of Education for Sustainable Development? How far this Decade helped in achieving the goals of education for sustainable development?

4. How will Global Action Programme take forward the initiatives of DESD? Explain.
5. Do you think sustainable development is an ideal but abstract concept? Or do you think it is achievable? Justify your answer.
6. Is environmental education different from education for sustainable development? Explain.
7. What difference will it make if environmental education is implemented but not education for sustainable development?
8. When education for sustainable development is already practiced, should there be environmental education along with it? Elaborate your answer.
9. Why is it felt that implementation of education for sustainable development might not address environmental concerns? Explain.
10. Do you think education for sustainable development is the answer to our prevalent environmental, social and economic problems? Justify your answer.

References

Boojh, Ram. 2003. "Is a Sustainable World Possible?—The WSSD: An NGO Report." *Connect, UNESCO International Science, Technology & Environmental Education Newsletter* XXVIII (1–2): 7–9.

Braus, J.A. and D. Wood. 1993. *Environmental Education in the Schools: Creating a Programme That Works!* Manual M0044. Washington, DC: Peace Corps Information Collection and Exchange.

Gough, Annette. 2006. "A Long, Winding (and Rocky) Road to Environmental Education for Sustainability in 2006." *Australian Journal of Environmental Education* 22(1): 71–76. Available at: http://www.aaee.org.au/docs/AJEE/Volume%2022-1%20(2006)%20(A%20Long%20%20Winding%20(and%20Rocky)%20Road%20to%20Environmental%20Education%20for%20Sustainability%20in%202006).pdf (Accessed on 28 September 2014).

——— 2008. "Towards More Effective Learning for Sustainability: Reconceptualising Science Education." *Transnational Curriculum Inquiry* 5(1):32–50. Available at: http://nitinat.library.ubc.ca/ojs/index.php/tci (Accessed on 5 June 2014).

Hadzigeorgiou, Y and M. Skoumios. 2013. "The Development of Environmental Awareness Through School Science: Problems and Possibilities." *International Journal of Environmental & Science Education* 8: 405–426.

Kopnina, H. 2012. "Education for Sustainable Development (ESD): the Turn Away from 'Environment' in Environmental Education?" *Environmental Education Research* 18(5): 699–717. Available at: https://www.academia.edu/807510/Education_for_Sustainable_Development_ESD_The_turn_away_from_environment_in_environmental_education (Accessed on 28 September 2014).

Kopnina, H. 2014. "Future Scenarios and Environmental Education." *The Journal of Environmental Education* 45(4): 217–231.

McKeown, R. and Hopkins, C.A. 2003. "EE ≠ ESD: Diffusing the Worry." *Environmental Education Research* 9(1): 117–28.

McKeown, R., C.A. Hopkins, R. Rizzi, and M. Chrystalbridge. 2002. *Education for Sustainable Development Toolkit.* Knoxville, TN: University of Tennessee. Available at: http://www.esdtoolkit.org/esd_toolkit_v2.pdf (Accessed on 8 August 2014).

Monroe, M.C. 2012. "The Co-evolution of ESD and EE." *Journal of Education for Sustainable Development* 6(1): 43–47.

Mulà, Ingrid and Daniella Tilbury. 2009. "A United Nations Decade of Education for Sustainable Development (2005–2014)—What Difference will it Make?" *Journal of Education for Sustainable Development* 3(1): 87–97.

Pezzey, John. 1992. *Sustainable Development Concepts–An Economic Analysis.* World Bank Environment Paper No. 2. Appendix 1. Washington, DC.

Pigozzi, M.J. 2003. "UNESCO and the International Decade of Education for Sustainable Development (2005-2015)." *Connect, UNESCO International Science, Technology & Environmental Education Newsletter,* XXVIII(1–2): 1–7.

Sauvé, Lucie. 2005. "Currents in Environmental Education: Mapping a Complex and Evolving Pedagogical Field." *Canadian Journal of Environmental Education* 10, (Spring): 11–37. Available at: http://cjee.lakeheadu.ca/index.php/cjee/article/view/175/9 (Accessed on 28 September 2014).

Tortajada, Cecilia. 2005. "Sustainable Development (SD): A Critical Assessment of Past and Present Views." In *Appraising Sustainable Development—Water Management and Environmental Challenges*, edited by Asit K. Biswas and Cecilia Tortajada, 1–17. New Delhi: Oxford University Press.

UN, United Nations. 1987. *Report of the World Commission on Environment and Development: Our Common Future.* New York: UN.

——— 1992. *Agenda 21: Programme of Action for Sustainable Development Earth Summit.* United Nations Conference on Environment and Development (UNCED), Rio de Janeiro, 3–14 June 1992. New York: UN.

UNESCO, United Nations Educational, Scientific and Cultural Organization. 2000. *The Dakar Framework for Action Education for All: Meeting our Collective Commitments.* Paris: UNESCO.

——— 2002. *Education for Sustainability – From Rio to Johannesburg: Lessons Learnt from a Decade of Commitment.* Paris: UNESCO.

——— 2005. *UNDESD International Implementation Scheme.* Paris: UNESCO.

——— 2006. *Framework for the UNDESD International Implementation Scheme.* Paris: UNESCO.

——— 2007. *The UN Decade of Education for Sustainable Development (DESD 2005–2014)—The First Two Years.* Paris: UNESCO.

——— 2009. *Learning for a Sustainable World: Review of Contexts and Structures for Education for Sustainable Development.* United Nations Decade of Education for Sustainable Development (DESD, 2005-2014), Paris, UNESCO.

——— 2014a. *Shaping the Future We Want – UN Decade of Education for Sustainable Development (2005–2014) Final Report.* Paris: UNESCO.

——— 2014b. *Roadmap for Implementing the Global Action Programme on Education for Sustainable Development.* Paris: UNESCO.

Way Forward

Worth a Thought

We have a constitution that strongly favors environmental education.
We also have the National Policy on Education, 1986 that supports and
promotes the ideas contained in the constitution and other contemporary
environmental issues. To top it up we have the Hon'ble Supreme Court's order that
mandates environmental education to be taught as a compulsory subject. Yet, we have
not been able to make a visible impact in environmental education in India. Is it about
time we look for another route to tread?

Chapter Overview

In spite of all efforts put in by different agencies, government and non-governmental, the
outcome of implementation of environmental education in the country is far from satisfactory.
Looking at the ineffectiveness of the present status of implementation of environmental
education in India, this section of the book attempts to work out a comprehensive roadmap
for its implementation in India. Implementation of environmental education will require the
contribution of different stakeholders—governmental and non-governmental. Their
contribution has been enormous and will remain wanted, and this aspect has been provided
in the chapter in brief. Any such attempt to improve the implementation of environmental
education can only happen with rigorous research in different aspects concerning
environmental education. Keeping this in view, some possible areas for research have also
been provided here. It is envisaged that this chapter will facilitate readers to:

- appreciate the contribution of different stakeholders in the implementation of
  environmental education in India
- justify the importance of the contribution of different stakeholders in the
  implementation of environmental education in India
- identify the need of a new roadmap for implementation of environmental
  education in India
- explain the different components as envisaged in the new roadmap
- justify the importance of each component as envisaged in the new roadmap
- identify the areas for research in environmental education

Introduction

From the various chapters that we have gone through in this book we now understand the status of implementation of environmental education in school, the barriers in the implementation, and the issues related to teacher education and many other relevant areas as well. Successful implementation will require taking into consideration various elements and putting each one of them in place. The elements could include the policy documents, different stakeholders, training, research, and so on. Concerns put forth in the policy documents or the curriculum framework need to be in sync with the efforts made in professional development courses and in the teaching–learning process in the classrooms. The collective efforts of different stakeholders, including the non-governmental organizations, are key to the successful implementation of environmental education. One organization or institute with its all-out efforts cannot make environmental education work. For example, even if teacher-education institutes give the best of trainings, but the school syllabus or routine does not give space for teachers to apply their experiences, then nothing can be achieved. Similarly, even if the school syllabus and routine provides opportunities to implement environmental education, if the teachers are not trained in the area, then there will be no result. Hence, implementation in patches will do no good. What we need now is concerted efforts to work simultaneously to make environmental education work. To effectively deal with the issues and for successful implementation, systems need to be in place. For a system, which may be as big as a nation or as small as a school, it is necessary to have a plan for implementation if we have set some goals before us.

Besides government agencies, other major contributors in the implementation of environmental education in India are those in the non-governmental sectors and institutes of higher education. The role of these organizations and institutes cannot be overemphasized. They will continue to play an important role in the future as well and, hence, they have been prominently featured in the proposed roadmap which will be discussed in the chapter. Therefore, before discussing the roadmap a brief description of major agencies—governmental and non-governmental—in environmental education has been provided to highlight and understand the contributions they have made so far in strengthening environmental education in India.

Notwithstanding the many issues en route its implementation, we can acknowledge the fact that environmental education as a discipline or as an approach to education has now seeped into the education systems world over, including India. The problem related to its implementation is not limited to India but is seen to be prevalent even in the most developed nations. It will be impossible to find out what exactly was not done right or suggest measures to address the issues facing rest of the world. However, there definitely seems to be a ray of hope when it comes to India. The reason being, there are issues related to the organization and functioning of different systems which have not been given much attention up till now. Addressing these could possibly help us make some headway in the implementation of environmental education with more impact. Some feasible modalities for doing this are suggested in this concluding chapter. Whether India will continue implementing environmental education or whether it wants to switch over to ESD model, the same strategy, which is presented in this chapter, can be adopted.

In spite of the many issues related to the implementation of environmental education in India, very little studies have been undertaken to look into the reasons and suggest the means to overcome the barriers which could be related to curricular materials, pedagogy, administrative issues, issues related to policies, and so on. Such studies are necessary to provide inputs for improving the system. In view of the importance of research, the chapter reiterates the role of research and also discusses some specific areas for focus, even as research has been mentioned as one of the important areas in the road map for implementation of environmental education in India. This will guide the stakeholders and researchers to identify the areas to take up appropriate studies.

10.1 Brief Description of the Roles and Contributions of Stakeholders

Undoubtedly, hundreds of agencies throughout the country have contributed in the implementation of environmental education in India. The contributions of these agencies have been portrayed to be even more crucial in the proposed roadmap. It is, therefore, imperative to understand the nature of contributions of these agencies. In the following, a brief description of the activities of some prominent agencies—both governmental and non-governmental—is provided. However, this in no way undermines the contributions of the many other agencies not mentioned here but have otherwise made tremendous contributions and are solicited to continue in their endeavor.

JUST A MOMENT

Can you think of some stakeholders who are responsible for the implementation of environmental education in your state/UT?

10.1.1 Government Agencies

10.1.1.1 Ministry of Environment and Forests (MoEF) (Recently Renamed as Ministry of Environment, Forests and Climate Change, i.e., MoEF&CC)

Various initiatives have been taken up by MoEF&CC for the promotion of environmental education both in formal and nonformal sector of which is the Environmental Education, Awareness and Training (EEAT)—a flagship scheme of the Ministry for enhancing the understanding of people at all levels about the relationship between human beings and the environment and for developing capabilities/skills to improve and protect the environment. The objectives of this scheme are being realized through the implementation of the following programs:

(i) National Environment Awareness Campaign (NEAC): Through this program, it creates environmental awareness at the national level by providing nominal financial assistance to NGOs, schools, colleges, universities, research institutes, women and youth organizations, army units, government departments, and so on, from over the country for conducting awareness-raising and action oriented activities. Thirty four Regional Resource Agencies (RRAs) appointed by the Ministry are involved in conducting, supervising and monitoring the NEAC activities. During NEAC 2013–2014, 11,754 organizations participated from across the country.

(ii) National Green Corps (NGC): This scheme is operated through eco clubs established in schools. As of today, there are about 100,000 eco clubs established across the country, making it one of the largest conservation networks. A monetary support of ₹2,500 is provided to each school per annum. The program has a unique partnership between the MoEF&CC and the state government agencies, along with the dedicated NGOs working in the field of environmental education. Recognizing the fact that children can be catalysts in promoting a mass movement about the ensemble of the environmental issues, this scheme envisages that inculcation of environment-friendly attitudes and behavioral patterns amongst them could make a significant difference to the long term efforts for protection of environment. As a result, children can trigger a chain reaction, making a difference at the local and community level, which in due course can lead to awareness at village, city, state, country, and global level.

(iii) Seminars/Symposia/Workshops/Conference: This program provides a forum to professionals, scientists, environmentalists, and other groups of the society to share knowledge and experience on various aspects of environment. Under this programs, financial assistance is provided to universities, academic institutions/colleges, NGOs, government departments and so on, to create mass environment awareness for the organization of seminars/symposia/workshops/conferences on identified thrust areas related to the environment, or any emerging area impinging on technology and innovation with regard to the environment which can be taken up at the state, national, or international level.

(vi) Other awareness programs, such as vacation programs, quiz/essay/debate/poster/slogan competitions, training programs and so on, which are outside the purview of aforementioned programs. Different stakeholders such as NGOs and other organizations may propose such awareness activities.

MoEF&CC has also listed three centers of excellence devoted for environmental education. They are:

1. Centre for Environment Education (CEE), Ahmedabad: Activities of CEE will be discussed in more detail later in the chapter.
2. CPR Environmental Education Centre (CPREEC), Chennai: Activities of CPREEC will be discussed in more detail later in the chapter.
3. Centre for Animals and Environment, CARTMAN, Bengaluru: The main objective of the project is to study the mutual dependence and inter relationship between the animals (livestock) and the environment (plant life) and initiate steps to preserve environment and to improve the health and welfare of animals by making them more productive. Another activity envisaged is to eliminate pollution of environment caused by city-based abattoirs by providing alternate locations where animals are

born and reared. This would also result in development of rural areas by retaining the value added in the process in villages and nearby towns.

Other centers of excellence of MoEF&CC include:

- Center of Excellence in Environmental Economics
- Foundation for Revitalization of Local Health Traditions
- Center for Ecological Sciences
- Center for Environmental Management of Degraded Ecosystem
- Center for Mining Environment
- Salim Ali Center for Ornithology and Natural History
- Tropical Botanic Garden and Research Institute

10.1.1.2 Ministry of Human Resource Development (MHRD)

Besides working through institutions under the ministry such as NCERT, CBSE, NVS, KVS, and so on, the ministry has also taken specific programs to promote environmental education. One such program it had initiated was the scheme of Environmental Orientation to School Education (EOSE) in 1988 (GoI 1988). This scheme was introduced in the light of the National Policy on Education, 1986 (revised in 1992) which stated that protection of the environment being a value must form an integral part of curriculum at all stages of education and also highlighted the need to create a consciousness of the environment. The rationale of this scheme was:

> [O]ne set of syllabi and textbooks are used in a State whereas the environmental conditions and environmental concerns vary from one region of the State to the other...It has, therefore, been decided to take up a centrally sponsored scheme of Environmental Orientation to School Education which will allow educational programmes in the schools to be fully harmonized with the local environmental situation and concerns.

The centrally sponsored scheme was proposed to be implemented through the education departments in the states/UTs and the voluntary agencies having expertise and interest in environmental education. It was proposed that the scheme would assist the voluntary organizations for taking up programs for increasing awareness about environmental issues and for taking up activities for improving environment. Some of the activities suggested under the scheme were adoption of monuments for upkeep and maintenance, preparation of informative brochures, and so on; nature study; study of ecological problems of a village, educating people on the hazards of environmental pollution, advocating construction of sanitary toilets, and participation in the conservation efforts of the community; preparation of textbooks/instructional materials, and so on. Though the scheme could not be implemented through the education departments of states/UTs as proposed, the ministry appointed three organizations as the nodal agency for implementation of the scheme. They were Centre for Environment Education, Ahmedabad; C.P.R. Environmental Education Centre, Chennai; and Uttarakhand Seva Nidhi, Almora (CEE 1999; Sonowal 2009).

However, EOSE scheme is no more implemented as was laid down in the initial implementation framework. It has now taken a different form in that the scheme has been transferred to NCERT and is no more implemented through the nodal agencies.

MHRD must now try to make the most of the massive training/orientation programs organized for in-service teachers such as those conducted under the SSA or the RMSA umbrella. Since it has not been possible to train teachers separately for environmental education so far, due to administrative or other reasons, MHRD must tap these nation-wide programs by keeping special sessions for environmental education in all such programs, if not come out with special training/orientation programs only for environmental education.

Besides, MHRD may consider initiating a scheme wherein teachers who completes a diploma or certification course in environmental education are provided some kind of incentives. For this, an appropriate course may be developed and the same may be provided through nodal institutions.

10.1.1.3 National Council of Educational Research and Training (NCERT), State Council of Educational Research and Training (SCERT)/State Institute of Education (SIE)/State Institute of Educational Research and Training (SIERT), National Council for Teacher Education (NCTE), University Grants Commission (UGC)

NCERT's role in this task is undoubtedly enormous, being the apex body for school education in the country. Beginning with its role in preparing the national curriculum framework, development of curricular materials, training programs it organizes for pre-service and in-service, and so on, to its role in policy making as an advisory body, it has a huge responsibility at hand. The challenges that will be associated with each activity that it undertakes will be tremendous. How prepared it is to overcome such challenges is a matter of concern. If environmental education is a priority in the country, then it becomes the NCERT's responsibility to see to it that same is reflected in all its activities. For that, first and foremost, it should see that it has requisite experts in the area of environmental education to ensure effective implementation. We had discussed in the previous chapters, especially in Chapter 5, how the NCERT has contributed so far in the implementation of environmental education. Besides considering environmental education in the curriculum as a contemporary area as part of its routine activity of curriculum revision, it is also legally binding on the part of the NCERT to ensure its implementation in all the schools throughout the country, as we had seen in the Hon'ble Supreme Court's order. Hence, how the NCERT highlights environmental education through the curriculum framework or through the curricular materials it develops will be an indicator to gauge the success of the implementation of environmental education in the country. This is because, states and UTs adopt or adapt the curriculum framework developed by NCERT and they have to abide by the instructions that are given to them with regard to environmental education, in compliance with the Hon'ble Supreme Court's order. NCERT also has to ensure that the state and UT functionaries are equipped to implement environmental education in their states and UTs. At the state level, the SCERT/SIE/SIERT or its parallel body will be responsible for taking up similar activities as NCERT.

The NCTE has the challenge of bringing out a curriculum framework for teacher preparation to meet the challenges in the area of environmental education reflected in the curriculum framework for schools and in the development of appropriate curricula for preservice and in-service courses so that environmental education is given adequate space and time. It is high time NCTE considers including environmental education as one of the compulsory papers in all its courses, instead of the optional paper it offers in some of its preservice courses. The UGC has similar role in bringing out an appropriate model curriculum for the teacher preparation courses besides introducing courses related to environmental education at the tertiary level. While we have seen in the previous chapters about the disconnect in the school curriculum and the teacher education courses we know that how these organizations reflect environmental education in their activities will go a long way in the implementation of environmental education.

10.1.1.4 Central and State Boards and School Systems

The role of central boards such as the Central Board of Secondary Education (CBSE), Council for the Indian School Certificate Examinations (CISCE), and other state boards are crucial for the success of implementation of environmental education. Their contribution could be through curricular materials, training, examination, and so on. Besides, school systems such as Kendriya Vidyalaya Sangathan and Navodaya Vidyalaya Samiti also can play an important role in this process. They can ensure that their teachers get sufficient training in the area of environmental education and consider environmental education as an important component of their training programs.

10.1.2 Non-governmental Organizations and Other Institutes

10.1.2.1 Centre for Environment Education (CEE)

CEE is another organization whose contribution has been immense in the area of environmental education, both in the formal and nonformal sector. It is committed to ensuring that due recognition is given to the role of environmental education in the promotion of sustainable development. CEE develops innovative programs and educational material, and builds capacity in the field of education and communication for sustainable development. As a center of excellence of the MoEF, it provides technical support to the nodal agency in implementing the National Green Corps program in 15 states and 2 union territories. Mention may be made of its popular program "Paryavaran Mitra Programme," a nationwide ESD school programs.[1] As a nodal agency for the Environmental Orientation to School Education Scheme of the MHRD, CEE had taken up several projects through its various centers located in different parts of the country and through collaboration with other NGOs. The projects included, (a) development of locale-specific print material, (b) audio-visuals, (c) capacity building through training programs/workshops, (d) training/camps, (e) adaptation and translation of existing environmental education materials (CEE 1999).

10.1.2.2 Centre for Science and Environment (CSE)

CSE is a non-governmental research and advocacy organization that researches, lobbies for, and communicates the urgency of development that is both sustainable and equitable. Its environment education unit targets the future inheritors of this earth and

---

[1] http://www.ceeindia.org/cee/history.html (accessed 29 July 2014)

tomorrow's planners and administrators by bringing out quality resource material and programs for school, college, and university students as well as environment educators and parents to bring about awareness about our environment. The Green Schools Program is a practical tool for environmental education that involves teachers and students in assessing the environmental performance of their own school.[2]

10.1.2.3 C.P.R. Environmental Education Centre (CPREEC)

With a mission to increase awareness and knowledge of key target groups (school children, local communities, woman, and so on) about the various aspects of environment, CPREEC has been a pioneer in environmental education efforts in South India and has conducted a variety of programs to spread awareness and interest among the masses.[3] Some of its activities include developing curricular materials, imparting training to teachers in different states on how to integrate environmental education into the school curriculum, and framing curriculum for environmental education in schools at the state and national level. CPREEC is also a center of excellence of the MoEF.

10.1.2.4 Institute of Environment Education and Research, Bharati Vidyapeeth University, Pune

The Institute of Environment Education and Research, Bharati Vidyapeeth University (BVIEER) is a unique educational and research institution. It is probably the only post-graduate environment science center in the country to have a large extension division that implements school environmental education programs. BVIEER began its environmental education programs in 1995 with three-day workshops conducted for teachers of the Bharati Vidyapeeth schools, numbering more than a hundred spread over western Maharashtra. The same year it initiated the School Environment Education Programme (SEEP) with a focus on capacity building of teachers in environmental education, giving special emphasis on 'infusion approach' so that teachers are equipped to incorporate environmental education in the existing curricula. BVIEER thereby developed a manual for teachers using the 'infusion approach'—a first for India. This 200-page manual in English and Marathi was closely linked to the textbooks of Maharashtra and provided suggestions for activities, games, ideas for field visits, and school projects. It contained basic information on natural resources, biodiversity, nonconventional energy, and pollution. This task was significant because it was done at a time when most environmental-education activities where through nature clubs which were optional and seen as 'extracurricular' or 'nonserious.'

To further its efforts to integrate environmental education into the school curricula, BVIEER initiated a school environment education program within urban schools of the city of Pune and rural schools in the Mawal and Mulshi regions of the Western Ghats, with funding from the Confederation of Indian Industries and Tata Power Company,

---

[2] http://www.cseindia.org/node/252 (accessed on 29 July 2014)
[3] http://www.cpreec.org/ (accessed on 29 July 2014)

respectively. The school program that was evolved includes developing a set of modules using various interactive methods focusing on activity based learning that were implemented in the schools by the trained teachers with assistance from educators of the BVIEER. This program culminates into an academic year-end environment fair for all the students involved in the program, wherein schools and teachers not only display the action projects they have implemented but also participate in a host of competitive events.

Over the last fifteen years, BVIEER has implemented this model in more than 600 schools in Pune and Ahmednagar districts of Maharashtra as well as in schools in Madhya Pradesh and Uttar Pradesh with the support of various funders and by maintaining close cooperation with the state education departments. The program implemented in the new schools today has a strong linkage to community environment action.

In 1998, BVIEER was assigned the task to review the status of environmental infusion in the school curriculum and suggest strategies for the same. This mammoth task involved analyzing 1,848 textbooks from all the states of India. This in-depth study provided interesting insights into the present status of environmental information in school textbooks, as well as the mode of delivery of environmental concepts in schools. Following the textbook analysis, the Ministry of Environment and Forests selected eight states for rewriting of textbooks taking into consideration the suggestions from the BVIEER study.

In its bid to improve textbooks, BVIEER also conducts workshops specifically targeted at orienting textbook writers across India to infuse concepts related to sustainable development into their textbooks. It has provided training to textbooks writers from 33 states, who were deputed by the respective State Council of Educational Research and Training (SCERT).

BVIEER also contributed to the development of the existing undergraduate environmental studies curriculum as mandated by the Hon'ble Supreme Court. The course is implemented across the country. It also provides a diploma course for in-service teachers in environmental education and a master's degree course in education for sustainable development.

The BVIEER has been appointed as the resource agency for Maharashtra for the National Green Corps program of the Ministry of Environment and Forests, Government of India, since 2002 till date. This program reaches out to 9,050 schools and involves 457, 500 students across the state of Maharashtra. Through this program, it provides training to teachers across the states and supports the program with educational material in the form of innovative low-cost posters that communicate project ideas to be implemented in schools. It has also initiated a 'gray to green school' concept that involves rating the green level of the school through specific projects and measureable indicators, through the medium of well-designed posters.

The distinctive characteristics of the BVIEER are its wide mandate of teaching, research, and extension. It has worked in the field of environmental policy-building and furthered academic excellence through various collaborations with international universities and organizations. The notable achievements of the institute include its projects and programs that have led to influencing policy and implementation of environmental education at the school and college level and infusion of sustainability issues in school textbooks across India along with strategies for protected area management.

10.1.2.5 The Energy and Resources Institute (TERI)

With a vision to creating innovative solutions for a sustainable future, TERI has also been working in the area of environmental education through various activities such as providing training, developing relevant materials, and working on specific projects to create awareness, as well as capacity building activities in different parts of the country for students, teachers, school communities, and the society at large on different issues, and so on. The Environment Educators' Conference for practicing teachers that is held annually is one such program.[4]

10.1.2.6 Toxics Link

Toxics Link is a Delhi-based environmental NGO (with a nodal office in Kolkata), dedicated to bringing toxics-related information into the public domain, both relating to struggles and problems at the grassroots as well as global information to the local levels. Toxics Link also engages in ground work, especially in areas of municipal, hazardous, and medical waste management and food safety among others. Working in networks, utilizing community outreach and education, policy analysis, research, training, and program development, they work at the state and central levels to help create solutions, which are driven by the needs of people. Through persistent campaigns, the organization has been able to make a strong awareness among the public and stakeholders about toxicity and pollution. It also contributes in policy making by directing concerned people through interaction about pro-people and environment-friendly policies.[5]

10.1.2.7 Uttarakhand Seva Nidhi Paryavaran Shiksha Sansthan (USNPSS) or Uttarakhand Environmental Education Centre (UEEC)

Initially appointed as a nodal agency by the Department of Education, MHRD to undertake locale-specific environmental education programs both in rural schools and villages in the hill districts of Uttarakhand, USNPSS is now a full-fledged organization handling all the environmental activities of the organization. USNPSS supports the educational activities of rural schools, NGOs and community-based organizations by organizing training programs and discussion meetings, supplying teaching/learning materials, village and school visits for on-the-spot guidance and problem-solving, and providing honoraria to preschool teachers and small project grants. Besides its many other contributions, with the cooperation of the state's department of education, USNPSS has designed and introduced environmental education course focused on village land rehabilitation and sustainable management into the regular school curriculum in Classes 6, 7, and 8.

10.1.2.8 World Wide Fund for Nature–India (WWF-India)

Education has been an integral part of WWFs global activities since the very beginning. Through its environmental education program, which began in 1969, WWF-India's vision has been to inform, inspire, and empower India's children and youth to take

---

[4] http://www.teriin.org/our-work (accessed on 29 July 2014)
[5] http://toxicslink.org/?q=profile (accessed on 04 May 2015)

action for a healthy planet. The organization has been working to build an environmentally aware generation through both formal and nonformal approaches in education. With a wide range of programs meant for teachers, students, and policy makers, WWF-India has always endeavored to use creative and participatory ways of reaching out to its varied audiences.

Through the Nature Clubs of India, which set the tone for the Eco Clubs, The Wild Wisdom Quiz, the National Nature Camps Program, and many other activities, WWF-India has been engaging school children in myriads of exciting ways for nature conservation and environmental awareness. The 'Aqua Symphony' drew participation from school bands who composed original songs on water conservation and came together to win the prize for the best song on World Wetland Day.

The Wild Wisdom, which started in 2008, is India's only national and Asia's biggest wildlife quiz. The objective of the quiz is to raise awareness about Indian flora and fauna in India and inculcate a sense of pride amongst students about India's rich natural heritage. So far, more than 65,000 students have participated in the quiz.

In the formal realm, WWF-India has been working to embed ESD in the entire educational framework of the country through a four pronged approach. This approach includes policy intervention, training national and state educational authorities on ESD, creating resource material for teachers and students, and developing ESD model schools.

The organization has adopted 12 schools near the protected forest areas in Assam, Chhattisgarh, Madhya Pradesh, and West Bengal to demonstrate the practical implementation of the ESD approach to the government and community members. The schools have been created as models using the 'whole school approach,' which works to develop the schools holistically in five areas that include: school estate, pupils, teaching and learning, communities, and monitoring and evaluation. WWF-India has also trained over 3,000 master trainers from 95 District Institutes for Education and Training and 4 State Councils for Education Research and Training to build their capacity in ESD.

The backbone of all these programs has been the rich and varied educational resource material that has been created through books, audio-visuals, and manuals in English, Hindi, and many other local languages of India. WWF-India had recently developed a handbook in Locally Relevant Themes (LORET), a portfolio of local curricula to guide teachers in individual schools that will also inspire teachers elsewhere. This pedagogical tool integrates issues of sustainable development into subject teaching and connects this teaching to nonformal education that targets key developmental issues in the local community and, at the same time, satisfies the demands of the national curricula. The team is now working to disseminate these resources among teachers and students by creating a central web-based interactive platform.

JUST A MOMENT

Reflect on the roles of different stakeholders who have been contributing in the implementation of environmental education in India.

Photo 10.1   Wild Wisdom National Level Quiz When the Winners from all 17 Cities Came Together in Delhi. October 2014

Photo Courtesy: WWF-India

Photo 10.2   Community Members Being Trained to Create Fuel Briquettes Out of Waste in Sunderbans, West Bengal

Photo Courtesy: WWF-India

Photo 10.3   Fisheries Business Started by Community Members in Kanha after Receiving the Small-Scale Business Trainings from WWF-India

Photo Courtesy: WWF-India

10.2 Road Map for Implementation of EE in India

This chapter provides a broad road map or blue print for action in the form of a flow chart for the implementation of environmental education in India (Fig. 10.1). It elucidates how different agencies working at different levels can contribute individually as a body as well as collaboratively and collectively, or how their nature of collaboration can be. The flow chart is self-explanatory and detailings have been avoided.

The flow chart presents various activities which can be grouped under the following heads—(a) administrative and academic set-ups, (b) development of curriculum and curricular materials, (c) training, (d) research, (e) monitoring, (f) evaluation, (g) networking, (h) implementation, and (i) web portal. Each of these is explained briefly as follows.

Figure 10.1   Road Map for the Implementation of Environmental Education in India

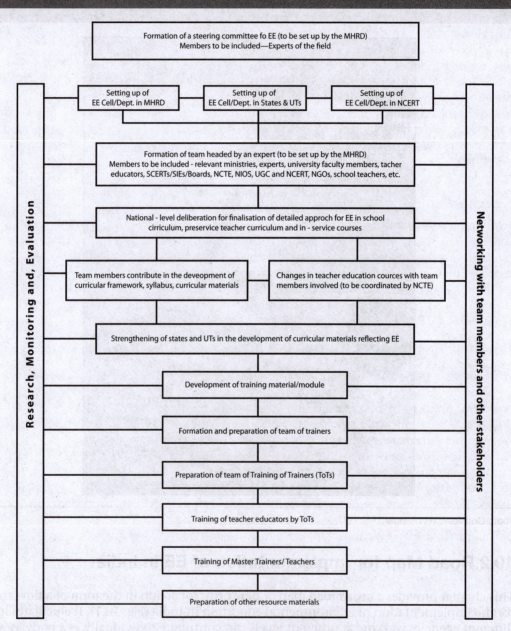

Formation of a steering committee fo EE (to be set up by the MHRD)
Members to be included—Experts of the field

Setting up of
EE Cell/Dept. in MHRD

Setting up of
EE Cell/Dept. in States & UTs

Setting up of
EE Cell/Dept. in NCERT

Formation of team headed by an expert (to be set up by the MHRD)
Members to be included - relevant ministries, experts, university faculty members, tacher
educators, SCERTs/SIEs/Boards, NCTE, NIOS, UGC and NCERT, NGOs, school teachers, etc.

National - level deliberation for finalisation of detailed approch for EE in school
cirriculum, preservice teacher curriculum and in - service courses

Team members contribute in the deveopment of
curricular framework, syllabus, curricular materials

Changes in teacher education cources with team
members involved (to be coordinated by NCTE)

Strengthening of states and UTs in the development of curricular materials reflecting EE

Development of training material/module

Formation and preparation of team of trainers

Preparation of team of Training of Trainers (ToTs)

Training of teacher educators by ToTs

Training of Master Trainers/ Teachers

Preparation of other resource materials

Creation of national web portal to upload all the activities - research studies, monitoring
and evaluation reports, materails developed, activities of different partners, etc.

Research, Monitoring and, Evaluation

Networking with team members and other stakeholders

All programmes to be coordinated by NCERT unless otherwise specified

10.2.1 Administrative and Academic Set-ups

One of the most important factors that hinder the implementation of environmental education can be attributed to lack of appropriate administrative and academic set-ups. Environmental education has not been taken seriously by organizations and institutes working in the area of school education and hence in most cases, it is not reflected in their organizational set-ups. For example, the NCERT, which is the apex body in school education for the country till date, has been managing with a make-shift arrangement to look after all concerns related to environmental education. The situation in other institutes is expected to be no better. Hence, the first task to begin implementation of environmental education would be to remedy this issue. The first step in this direction would be to set up a steering committee for EE by the MHRD consisting of members who are experts in the field. This committee would guide the MHRD in its implementation of environmental education. This will be followed by the setting up of cells/departments in relevant bodies such as the MHRD, SCERTs/SIEs/Boards, NCTE, UGC and NCERT. These cells/departments will be manned by requisite numbers of administrative staff and academicians. This should not be a make-shift arrangement but a permanent structure. A team will also be formed by the MHRD at the national level, to be headed by an expert. Members may include concerned people from the relevant ministries, university faculty members, teacher educators, SCERTs/SIEs/Board, NCTE, NIOS, UGC, NCERT, NGOs, and school teachers. This team will be instrumental in taking up all academic tasks.

10.2.2 Development of Curriculum and Curricular Materials

This is another very crucial step in the implementation of environmental education. What we want to achieve through our school curriculum, with respect to environmental education, needs to first be worked out—that is, defining goals. Based on this, the teacher-education curriculum will be prepared. But, we have seen that school curriculum suggest a few things while teacher-education courses do not reflect such suggestions at all. For example, the National Curriculum Framework, 2005 recommended that environmental education should be taught in an infusion model, but the same is not considered in the teacher education courses. First, environmental education is not reflected in the compulsory courses. Besides, there is no mention of infusion approach in the optional courses as well. The reason for such discrepancies is that school curriculum and teacher-education curriculum (preservice courses) are developed independently of each other and, hence, there is no coherence in the two. Therefore, measures must be taken so that these activities occur simultaneously so that concerns of both can be considered and sorted out. While this could tackle issues related to preservice courses, measures also need to be taken for the courses for in-service programs. This is necessary since most of the in-service teachers have not received any training in environmental education.

Development of curricular material is another very important activity that requires special attention. If environmental education is to be infused in different subject areas, it is very important that the teachers should be able to identify what has been infused, where it has been infused, and how it has been infused. These should be clearly reflected in the curricular materials. The material should be such that teachers should be able to make use of it to achieve the goals of environmental education. Hence, experts in environmental education should be involved in all the developmental activities of curricular materials for different subject areas. Appropriate materials for preservice and in-service courses should also be prepared accordingly.

10.2.3 Training

This will form the backbone of the whole process in the implementation of environmental education. The stronger and durable the trainings, the better the implementation. Training will be at different levels and depths. It will be necessarily include the following steps: (a) development of training modules for each level; (b) preparation of a team of trainers; (c) training of trainers (ToTs); (d) training of teacher educators by ToTs; (e) training of master trainers/in-service teachers.

10.2.4 Research

This is another indispensable component in the implementation of environmental education. Research will regularly provide feedback on the status of implementation. It will also suggest ways to improve implementation at every step. This can be taken up by any of the stakeholders, as mentioned in the plan of implementation. The results of such a study should be shared on a common platform which can be accessed by all.

10.2.5 Monitoring

Strict monitoring will ensure that all the stakeholders are serious in the implementation of environmental education. The Hon'ble Supreme Court had directed the NCERT to monitor the implementation of environmental education throughout the country. Strategies need to be worked out so that monitoring is effective. Regular assessment of the monitoring report should also be conducted which could be done annually or biannual. This will enable timely action to fix issues in the process of implementation.

10.2.6 Evaluation

Evaluation of the activities undertaken should form an important component of the implementation strategy. Besides research and monitoring, meetings of all the stakeholders should be organized at regular intervals so that each stakeholder is aware of the latest status of implementation. This will also bring about transparency in the functioning of different stakeholders. State level or national level seminars, workshops and conferences should also be organized regularly which will provide inputs toward improvement of the strategies.

10.2.7 Networking

In a huge country like India, successful implementation of environmental education or any plan or program for that matter will depend heavily on how well the networking is done. This appears to have been one of the drawbacks in the implementation of environmental education in India. There is no dearth of organizations, mostly non-governmental though, working for the environment throughout the country, yet so little impact is seen in terms of success. There is no mechanism to share each others' works and success stories. In the present scheme of implementation being proposed, we can see the involvement of several organizations, institutes, departments, ministries, state bodies, school systems, and so on, each functioning as an important part of a larger body. Without systematic networking, it is impossible to expect that each of these will be able to contribute meaningfully. A system needs to be in place so that there is constant coordination and cooperation between all the parts that will enable the body as a whole to be effective and productive. Stray initiatives, however good it may be, cannot have any visible impact. Only when such initiatives are shared and collectively implemented, then only will it make the efforts worthwhile.

Perhaps it is this lack of networking that is the reason for the present sorry state of affairs in environmental education where there is complete lack of coherence between what is proposed in the school curriculum and what is being implemented in the professional development courses and also by the different school systems and boards of school education. As a result of these, the actual classroom practices do not reflect any elements of environmental education.

10.2.8 Implementation

Implementation of the proposed strategies needs to be coordinated by an agency. As represented in the flow chart, the NCERT, being the apex body in school education, is found to be most appropriate to be the nodal agency for the whole exercise and coordinate all the programs, except wherever specified. It will network and collaborate with all stakeholders in all the matters concerning the implementation of environmental education in the formal education system and should also be answerable for the lapses. Besides the NCERT, all stakeholders should also be made accountable for their respective share of activities.

10.2.9 Web Portal for EE

It is often not possible to share every material with all the stakeholders or it might happen inadvertently. To avoid such a situation, it is important that a website is created so that all relevant documents, materials, and reports can be uploaded. A space can be created for all the stakeholders to update their activities by uploading on the proposed website. This site can not only be accessed by the stakeholders but is open for access for viewing online to all, the only difference being that the stakeholders will be able to modify the contents. This website can also be used for many other activities such as alerting about upcoming events in environmental education, other relevant information, and so on.

JUST A MOMENT

Look at the proposed road map and try to examine the different components in the plan and its feasibility.

10.3 Areas for Research in Environmental Education in India

Research is the foundation or basis on which any idea or thought stands. It is fundamental for taking any field or area of study forward or for improving upon any existing situations and practices. Excellence and qualitative improvement in the teaching–learning can be brought about by policy makers, teacher educators and practicing school teachers by utilizing the findings of educational research. Policy documents are guided by research findings. So also is the curriculum—pedagogy, syllabus, teaching–learning materials, and so on. However, research in the area of environmental education is few and far between. As is evident from the previous chapters, environmental education is no more a very new field in India. But it is also true that the field has not progressed with time. Not much has been done to improve pedagogy in schools and professional development programs or to ensure implementation at the grassroots level. At the same time, no data base or research findings are available based on which necessary changes can be brought about. Qualitative as well as quantitative research remains the answer to improve the prevailing situation. Evidence-based practices such as those that "has been implemented and evaluated, and there is evidence of some kind, based on data that have been systematically collected and analyzed, and are available for public inspection, to support the view that it achieves all (or atleast some) of its intended outcomes" (Evidence-based Practice in Science Education Research Network, 2003 cited in Lucas 2008) or "the use of practices, interventions, and treatments which have been proven, through scientifically based research, to be effective in improving outcomes for individuals when the practice is implemented with fidelity" (CDE 2011) need to be promoted. However, such practices may be implemented under specific conditions and in the context of some specific content and generalization may not be possible due to diversity in cultures, and hence the focus of research should also be to explore ways how evidence-based practices "can be sustained, identify the conditions which would have to be met to make it possible, and explore its strengths and limitations as a strategy for improving practice" (Evidence-based Practice in Science Education Research Network 2003 cited in Lucas 2008). Keeping in view the importance of research in strengthening environmental education in India, this chapter will focus on some of the areas where researchers in environmental education can focus on. The same is discussed under different heads based on their relevance to school education.

JUST A MOMENT

How far do you think research can improve the implementation of environmental education in India?

10.3.1 Trends and Practices

It is said that nothing in this world is static—change is the norm. This is also true with academic subjects and areas. It is evolving. It is therefore important to understand how environmental education is evolving in different parts of the world; what causes it to move to certain direction; and how and why different countries are implementing environmental education the way they are implementing. This could be called micro-evolution since the changes will not be drastic but mostly contextual/local-specific. Researchers can also look into the more drastic changes taking place in the area of EE which could be called macro-evolution. For example, environmental education has its roots in nature study, conservation education, and so on, and some are of the opinion that environmental education has now evolved into ESD. Given this trend, what is the form environmental education going to take in the near future would be an important area of research.

10.3.2 Policy Documents

We know that implementation of any philosophy or area or concern begins with the same being reflected in the policy documents. In matters related to education, we have the National Policy on Education documents which are again formulated based on the recommendations of various committees and commissions. Then there are the national curriculum frameworks for schools and teacher education. Based on these documents states/UTs come out with an adapted version for their state/UT. In this regard, research can focus on how environmental education is reflected in such documents and how the same can be better incorporated. These tasks go through an elaborate process which is worth researching. Findings of such studies can be feeders in the development of such documents.

10.3.3 Curricular Materials

The syllabus, textbooks, and other complementary and supplementary books developed from time to time by different states, UTs, boards, private publishers, and so on, demands serious research. Comparative analysis of all the syllabi may be conducted with respect to environmental education. It is also necessary to find out the age-appropriateness of the concepts provided for different classes. Similarly, textbooks and other curricular books can be analyzed to find out how environmental concepts have been discussed. At the same time, ways for improvement can also be suggested through such studies. Results obtained from such studies can be made available to concerned state, UT, board, publisher, and so on. Another important area that demands serious research is the prevalence of the use of two textbooks in environmental studies for Classes III to V, as we saw in Chapter 5, which is against the recommendation of NCF-2005 as well as the affidavit submitted by the NCERT representing all schools of the country and is also against the philosophy of environmental education itself. Studies need to be undertaken to find out the implications of such practices.

10.3.4 Pedagogy

The pedagogy adopted by teachers in classrooms for different subjects is another area where research need to be focused. This can be considered the most important aspect for research since it involves the actual implementation of environmental education. The success of implementation of environmental education is heavily dependent on this aspect. Studies in this regard will bring out the barriers teacher encounter in the process of implementation which could be due to academic, administrative or many other issues. Based on this, appropriate measures can be taken up to overcome such barriers.

10.3.5 Information and Communications Technology (ICT)

The application of ICT in the teaching–learning process is gaining momentum in all disciplines. The use and abuse of technologies is well known in general. Even in the area of environmental education one is often tempted to entirely focus on ICT due to its convenience, attractiveness, and hassle-free nature, since one need not get exposed to the hot sun, biting cold, polluted air, stinking locality, and so on. Though ICT can be used to address some aspects of environmental education such as providing information, enriching knowledge, collecting and sharing data, and so on, it cannot entirely replace hands-on activities and field-based tasks. Hence, to what extent and in which areas ICT can be and should be used in environmental education has become a serious concern. It is therefore essential to find out the possibilities and limits of use of ICT in the implementation of environmental education.

10.3.6 Impact of Implementation

Regular study needs to be undertaken so as to find out how far the goals and objectives of environmental education are achieved. This will help us find out the gaps and problems in different states and UTs, and the interventions required and work for possible solutions of the same. Impact of implementation of environmental education in terms of behavioral change would form an important area of research. This can be done in terms of the programs initiated by the Government. For example, Eco-club, a program initiated by the MoEF&CC under the National Green Corps has been running for decades in over one lakh schools. Evaluation of this program, on whether students who are part of such clubs exhibit some change in their attitude and behavior during their involvement in such activities or whether such experiences produce lasting effect, would give us some idea on the effectiveness of the program, and the same can be used for further improvement of the program.

10.3.7 Functioning in States and UTs

States and UTs are the ones who are actually going to implement environmental education. For this, it is essential that they have a system set-up for the same. This is not only in terms of administrative set-up but also academically. It is therefore imperative to find out the situation in the states and UTs—is there any system in place to ensure implementation or promote EE; if not, what are the issues and limitations or what are the possible ways to address the same.

10.3.8 Assessment and Evaluation

This is a very important area for research. We had already mentioned in earlier chapters about the importance of linking environmental education with 'scores.' Though it will be challenging, it is important to study the existing assessment pattern of environmental education by different boards and also to formulate assessment methods which are practical. The challenge will lie in coming out with an appropriate assessment measures for different subjects as infusion approach of environmental education is followed in the country.

10.3.9 Professional Development

This is another area that researchers can focus on. Unless teachers are empowered, environmental education will never see the light of day. Despite UGC's core curriculum for teacher-education courses, like the B.Ed. course, there is so much disparity in the syllabi of teacher-education courses throughout the country. It is evident that there is little focus on environmental education. Researchers may find out how best environmental education can be reflected in the syllabi of such courses without adding additional burden to the student–teacher. Another area that researchers can explore is the duration of preservice courses. It is unclear whether the duration of the courses is based on research findings. One might wonder why the duration for the same course could be different. For example, while majority offered a one-year B.Ed. course, some offered the same course for two years. And what is more surprising is that this went on years after years, till recently, when it was decided that the course would be offered by all as a two-year course. The basis of such fixing of duration can be looked into in the context of environmental education. Researchers can also look more closely at the integrated courses such as B.Sc.Ed. (Bachelor in Science Education) (bachelor in Science Education) or M.Sc.Ed. (Master in Science Education)—are they really integrated or are two separate courses offered simultaneously so as to call integrated course? Besides, the effectiveness of other professional development courses such as B.El.Ed. (Bachelor in Elementary Education), D.El.Ed. (Diploma in Elementary Education), D.Ed. (Diploma in Education), and so on, or the effectiveness of open and distance learning can also be studied. Researchers can also focus their study in the in-service courses in environmental education. What exists, what works, what doesn't work, and why it doesn't work, are some of the areas they can look out for. It can even be on the qualifications of teacher educators at present and what should be the essential qualification for different professional development courses to be an environmental educator.

10.3.10 Roles of Institutions

Roles and functions of organizations such as NCERT, NCTE, UGC, CBSE, and other boards are very crucial in the implementation of EE. While NCERT formulates the curriculum for school education, NCTE does it for the teachers. UGC directs colleges and universities, CBSE directs schools under it, and other boards and institutes direct schools under their jurisdiction to implement them. Hence, each body has its specific role. Any lapse on the part of any one of them is going to impact the implementation of EE. Besides, being specific in the nature of their roles, these institutions cannot work in isolation. They need to take into consideration what the rest are doing. Hence, coordination and consultation with each other will be the mantra for effective delivery of their functions. How do they collaborate, what is the nature of their collaboration, how effective is their collaboration, and so on, will form important areas for research.

10.3.11 Government Agencies

School education is looked after the by MHRD. It is therefore very important that this ministry has a very strong environmental education base. The success of implementation of environmental education, or failure for that matter, will to a large extend depend on how strong and serious this ministry is about environmental education. Its organizational set-up in the context of environmental education, its mode of instruction or functioning with states and other national bodies, and so on, will form an important area of research. Environmental education, by virtue of its name, has also been a 'commodity' of MoEF&CC. Whether MHRD and MoEF&CC work in the area of environmental education independent of each other, or whether there are some areas where they work together, and so on, is another important area for research. The effectiveness of the different programs and activities undertaken, and the materials developed by MoEF&CC as mentioned earlier, can also form a good area of research.

10.3.12 Non-governmental Organizations (NGOs)

The role of NGOs in the implementation of environmental education has been instrumental and will remain very crucial. Their contribution has been enormous. Many NGOs have adopted schools in different places and are working with them while others collaborate with schools in different ways. However, it has not been possible to assess how far their contribution has been, whether they are getting enough support from the government, whether they collaborate with other educational bodies, what are the activities they take up in schools, what the barriers are in their functioning, and so on. All these areas can be looked into by researchers.

Conclusion

Implementation of environmental education successfully in a huge and populous country like India will indeed require extraordinary efforts. While the country makes all possible efforts to ensure that every child till the age of 14 receives free and compulsory education through its universalization of primary and secondary education programs, to press for implementation of environmental education somewhat seem to be a little overambitious. Besides, there are other disciplines which are considered more important. Yet, we are also aware that so much depends upon the health of the environment. There is so much at stake if we fail to take appropriate and timely measures to take care of our environment. Given this situation, a well-thought of way of implementation needs to be worked out, wherein the role of each stakeholder is clearly defined. The proposed road map has tried to clearly identify the role of each stakeholder. Laxity on the part of any one of the stakeholders and the proposed activities in the road map will affect the effectiveness of rest of the stakeholders, which will ultimately render all the efforts to naught.

Research is certainly one area where India needs to focus and promote. It is research findings that will guide policy makers, curriculum developers, educators, practitioners, and so on, to take environmental education where it should be headed. Therefore, in order to strengthen environmental education in the country, it is inevitable that researchers in colleges, universities, education institutes, and NGOs working in the area of environmental education are encouraged to take up serious research. In the chapter, the focus was only on some possible areas for research. It will be much broader and deeper as researchers begin to explore. Many other areas of greater importance will unravel. Meaningful research studies can be taken up in research leading to Ph.D. or postdoctoral research, which basically will form a long term research. In that case, it can also be taken up in parts by students as part of project assignments during their teacher development course or as part of their masters or M.Phil. dissertations. There are various other ways to work at it. Dissemination of research findings will also be instrumental in taking environmental education forward. It will be a good idea to set up an online portal where thesis, dissertations, reports, research articles, other relevant results, and so on, in the area of environmental education can be posted which can be utilized by other researchers or stakeholders.

SUMMARY

- A road map proposed for implementation of environmental education in India has been provided.
- There are six broad areas that have to be taken into consideration for successful implementation of environmental education in the country, such as administrative set-up, development of curriculum and curricular materials, training, research, monitoring, and evaluation.
- Different agencies and stakeholders, such as the state functionaries, different school systems, boards, institutes, non-governmental organizations, policy making bodies, and so on, have been instrumental in the implementation of environmental education in India and their contribution will continue to be very significant to take environmental education forward.

- The lacunae in the system such as issues of infusion approach, assessment, monitoring, teacher empowerment, and so on, could be due to lack of coordination, collaboration, and networking between these organizations.
- Research findings will guide policy makers, curriculum developers, educators, practitioners, and so on, so as to take environmental education in the right direction. However, there is little evidence of research undertaken in India in the area of environmental education.
- Since sufficient data is not available in India so as to refer to implement appropriate measure, it will have to look outward and tap on the research undertaken in other countries where environmental education has received tremendous attention in terms of research.

Exercises

1. Why do we need to have a road map for implementation of environmental education in India?
2. Contributions of different stakeholders—governmental and non-governmental—are essential for the successful implementation of environmental education in India. Justify the statement.

3. Do you think the Ministry of Human Resource Development has done enough in the area of environmental education? Elaborate your answer.
4. Explain the basic areas in the proposed roadmap.
5. How important are the roles of NGOs in the implementation of environmental education in India?
6. How is training proposed to be undertaken in the proposed roadmap?
7. Do you think it is appropriate to assign NCERT as the nodal agency to look after the overall implementation of environmental education in the schools in India? Justify your answer.
8. Why is networking between different stakeholders in environmental education important?
9. Only research can help improve implementation of environmental education in India. Do you agree with the statement? Justify.
10. Research in which area of environmental education should be given priority at present and why?

References

CDE, Colorado Department of Education. 2011. *Fast Facts, Evidence-Based Practice*. Denver, CO: CDE. Available at: http://www.cde.state.co.us/sites/default/files/documents/cdesped/download/pdf/ff-ebp_mh_intro.pdf (Accessed on 18 November 2014).

CEE, Centre for Environment Education. 1999. *Environmental Orientation to School Education—A Programme of Ministry of Human Resource Development: A Documentation of the Scheme and Some Projects under the Scheme*, edited by Meena Raghunathan and Mamata Pandya. Ahmedabad: CEE.

GoI, Government of India. 1988. *Scheme of Environmental Orientation to School Education*, Ministry of Human Resource Development, Department of Education, Government of India, New Delhi.

Lucas, A.M. 2008. "Evidence-based Practice and the De-professionalization of Practitioners." *Studies in Science Education* 44(1): 83–91.

Sonowal, C.J. 009. "Environmental Education in Schools: The Indian Scenario." *Journal of Human Ecology* 28(1): 15–36.

Afterword

In the present day, using the word 'environment' as a prefix or suffix has become the trendiest thing to do in all public speeches and discourses. While we have 'used' and 'abused' the 'environment' beyond repair physically, we have not spared to replicate its exploitation in our words as well. Should it be the policy makers, economists, bureaucrats, educationists, personalities in the field of arts, culture and literature, and so on, none seem to have spared. The word is 'sexy' and so it 'sells'! We are all aware of the amount of money that is pumped-in in the name of environment which is staggering. But do we really mean what we say as we talk so much about the environment? Has it done any good to the environment? Hardly. Reality says it all!

Isn't it about time we now 'do' something for the environment? But where do we start? More importantly, how do we deal with it in our school curriculum? Toward this, efforts are being made and the buzz word seems to be 'climate change' and of course, a very important one at that. The importance is clearly evident with the United Nations Secretary General terming climate change to be 'the major overriding environmental issue of our time' and 'the single greatest challenge facing environmental regulators.' Climate change is largely manifested as a result of global warming which is contributed to a great extent by human activities especially in the form of greenhouse gas emissions such as carbon dioxide, methane, nitrous oxide, and so on. No doubt, the rise in global air temperature at the present rate is going to affect, in fact, it has already affected, the economy, agricultural production, weather pattern throughout the world, health and safety, security, and many other dimensions, putting the survival of human race itself at risk. And we have put in all our 'energy' to address this issue by focusing on energy use—how to reduce emissions of greenhouse gases, how to tap renewable sources of energy such as wind and solar energy, and everything else related to energy. That's all fine and good. We definitely must focus on that. But there are issues related to this which are two-fold. First, there are issues concerning our approach as we try to address climate change, global warming in particular. Second, there is a lopsided emphasis on climate change, as if environmental education is all about climate change and climate change is all that matters in environmental education.

Let us assume that we (the whole world) have succeeded in our efforts to rely only on renewable sources of energy for all means of transportation. Should that mean that we can now buy as many vehicles as we want or can effort? Should that be the end of environmental problems related to greenhouse gas emissions? The manner in which focus has been given to global warming by trying to address vehicular emission issue is likely to backfire in our attempt to address environmental issues as a whole. This is because environmental issues are much more complex than they appear. Unfortunately, the cause (emissions)—effect (global warming)—solution (renewable energy) sequence of events is what is presented to students while explaining global warming, one of the climatic changes. This is not only simplification, but it is trivialization of the understanding about global warming. Besides these events, there are other factors which need to be taken into consideration. It is very important that students are able to link their consumption pattern of food products, their modes of transportation, their energy consumption, their lifestyle in terms of clothing, housing, and so on, with emissions. They need to know that the clothes factories which release greenhouse gases manufacture clothes because there is demand. So the more we buy, the more the factories are going to manufacture. The same is true with processed food where it requires a lot of resources to preserve, pack, and transport them to distant places, consuming a lot of fuel in the process. If the demand for processed food decreases, the production of the same will also reduce automatically and thereby reducing the use of fuel. The same is also true with our vehicles. We talk so much about vehicular exhaust that we hold it as the culprit for global warming to a large extent. Even if we use clean and green fuel to run the vehicles, we still have to use a lot of resources, including energy, in the manufacture of vehicles. These 'unaccounted' causes of environmental issues in general, and global warming in particular, need to be emphasized in the school curriculum.

The argument here is that we fail to focus on the source where the problem actually started. The point source of global warming is not vehicular pollution which releases greenhouse gases. It all started during the construction of the manufacturing units for different parts of motor vehicles, and then during the manufacturing process of the vehicles which are the cause of pollution. We might not be even aware that pollutions from factories, in fact, are aggravated because we have no control over our purchase tendency. If we can afford it, we simply purchase it, irrespective of whether we need it or not, thereby contributing in more production leading to more pollution. Ships and cargoes transport food commodities and releasing greenhouse gases in the process, all because we love consuming processed foods and any other foods from other far off states or countries. At this point, one might say that that is how economy functions and that the more our purchasing capacity increases the more a nation is considered to economically develop. But 'at the cost of what' deserves an explanation. These topics should form the basis for discussion while talking about global warming.

Besides, a lopsided emphasis on climate change is clearly evident in environmental education which is sending out a wrong signal about our approach to environmental education. However, some might argue that the curriculum needs to specially include climate change due to the urgency to tackle it. But the fact is, environmental education was not introduced to tackle climate change, but for environmental issues in general. More importantly, environmental education is an approach to education as a whole and is not issue-specific. Focusing on climate change alone will do much harm to the environment since there are many other environmental issues, besides climate change, that would be neglected.

Having said that, we are yet to arrive at the ultimate source of all the environmental problems and issues that are prevalent today. Looking closely, we will realize that it all begins with our attitude, our value system, and our ethics. As long as we think that it is alright to buy as many cars as we can afford; as long as we think that it is alright to buy imported foods instead of buying local foods, as long as we have money; as long as we think it is alright to change our electronic gadgets as often as possible; as long as we think it is alright to waste domestic energy, as long as we are able to pay the bills; as long as we think that it is alright to convert agricultural lands into housing complexes in the name of development; as long as ... and the list goes on. Unless we change our attitudes and our way of thinking, all our efforts to address climate change or any environmental problem for that matter can never bear fruit and sustainable development will remain a distant dream. Though one may rightly argue that such an attitude does not guarantee the resolution of environmental problems (we have discussed on 'attitude' at several places in the book), however, it definitely guarantees that without it there can be no resolution. It is based on the simple logic that unless we think right we cannot act right. And the education system has a huge role to play in shaping this 'attitude' aspect of young minds.

While we set ambitious goals at the 'big' global level meetings to curb the emission of greenhouse gases or ozone layer depleting gases, efforts to address attitudinal problems at individual level, which is more realistic, should not be undermined. In fact, this should receive priority if we are looking for a solution that will sustain. It is possible to achieve such efforts, not at the so-called meetings of the mighty and powerful people of the world but within the lowly classrooms of schools. It is in this context that if at all we want to achieve anything in our efforts to tackle environmental problems, it has to begin in schools.

Till date, it appears that our attempts have only been top-down, wherein decisions are taken at the highest international level and the instructions are passed down. When instructions are passed down, however true or good it may be, there is no sense of belongingness or lack of excitement to act. However, when the approach is bottom-up, there tends to be an increasing surge in our sense of responsibility to take an appropriate action. A person is more motivated in a situation where she wants to act because she knows and has the right attitude, and not because somebody else is instructing her to do so. For example, the instruction 'I will use public transport as much as possible because I want to reduce pollution' will work better than 'Use public transport as much as possible because that will reduce pollution.' The issue facing us is not so much about climate change or any other environmental problem per se, but it is to do with our mindset, our attitude, and our value system. Therefore, the topical treatment that we have been applying so far is only skin deep and cannot be an answer for a long-term solution. We need to look for something that heals from within, which in our context is changing our mindset through the course of education.

Education systems in general, and school education in particular, will be instrumental in tackling environmental problems effectively, whether those at the top accept this or deny. Those of us in the education system may have to go out of our way so that environmental education is given its due importance in the curriculum. Unfortunately, 'environment' has become a public property which is nurtured by none. And hence, we might as well adopt it and make it an integral part of our education system sincerely and provide all the care it needs by educating our students. We, as educators, have a huge responsibility on our shoulders. We may take the challenge forward as an educator concerned for the environment or, as has been a practice, brush the responsibility aside like an escapist, blaming the curriculum developers for not incorporating the concern enough in the syllabus. We should know that curriculum developers may never incorporate environmental concerns adequately in the curriculum because there are other subjects which are considered 'more important.' In this situation, what we can do is to look beyond the prescribed syllabus, employ our innovative ideas, and work out the curriculum accordingly to address environmental concerns wherever relevant and possible. Should we take the easy route which is ritualistic and conventional or should we take the more challenging and inspiring route to do our bit to integrate environmental concerns meaningfully in our curriculum? It will definitely be a challenge since educators have a larger task at hand to complete the course and comply with the administration in various other tasks as well. On top of that, educators have to satisfy the school and parents with 'good results.' Yet, we also know that we are best placed to nurture students to become environmentally conscious citizens. We might not get all the support we need and might also have a convincing list to shy away from this noble endeavour. Even so, let our conscience lead us...

Index

Acharya Ramamurthi Review Committee, 208
Aichi-Nagoya Declaration on ESD, 229–231

Basic Education Movement, 82
behavioural intervention strategies, 170
Belgrade Charter, 181
  and Tbilisi Conference, 121
Brundtland Commission Report, 123

Centre for Environment Education (CEE), 208
Chattopadhyaya Commission, 193
Commonwealth of Learning (COL), 208
Convention on the Right of the Child (CRC), 219
Currents in STSE Education
  Mapping a Complex Field, 40 Years
    currents, 40
curricular materials
  in environmental education (EE), 263
curriculum framework, 127

Dakar Framework for Action, 219
Decade of Education for Sustainable
    Development (DESD), 123, 218, 226
  impact of, 228
  international initiatives, 226, 227
  key goals, 227
disciplinary areas, nature of, 32, 34
  boundary, 34
  social science, 33
  subjects, 33
District Institute of Education and Training
    (DIETs), 214

Earth Summit, 123
education for all (EFA)
  goals of, 219
  Jomtien Declaration, 219
education for sustainable development (ESD),
    25, 179, 212, 218, 241
  Aichi-Nagoya Declaration, 229–231
  define, 224
  dimensions, 226
  education, 219

genesis, 218
key characteristics, 224
milestone, 222, 223
ramifications implementation of, 239–241
sustainable development, 220
thrusts, 224, 225
entropy, 199
environment, 178
environmental concerns
  as global issue, 32
environmental education (EE), 11, 45, 179, 212
  definitional problem John F. Disinger, 178
  environmental science
    Carter and Simmons statement, 46
    concern of, 45
    Davis argument, 46
    relationship between, 46
  environmental science and environmental
      studies
    implementation/practice, 48
    relationship, 48, 49, 51
  environmental studies
    characterization of, 46
    Davis indication, 48
    Nash argument, 46
ESD, 23, 236–239
Hon'ble Supreme Court of India,
    intervention, 129
important events, chronology of, 25, 26
in schools India vis-à-vis USA, 138
nature of, 35, 37
  activities, 35
  Caldwell statement, 36
  Disinger and Monroe statement, 36
  environmental values development,
      emphasis on, 35
  feature, 38
  holistic approach, 37
  situations, 35, 36
  skills development, 36
perspectives, 180–183
  bio-physical issue, 181, 182
roots of, 12

STS education
    application/design, 40
    characterization of EE, 39
    currents, 40
    difference between, 40
    Hadzigeorgiou and Skoumios indications,
        41
    Harms view, 39
    historical, 40
    implementation strategies, lack of, 41
    limitations of STS, 40
    logical reasoning, 40
    Lucas review, 38
    movement, 38
    Pedretti and Nazir indication, 40
    Science Education by Jim Gallagher, 38
    socioculture context, 40
    socio-ecojustice, 40
    theory and practice, gaps between, 39
    truth revealed, 39
    value-centred, 40
    words by Rubba, 39
    trends
        India vis-à-vis global initiatives, 119–123, 128
environmental issues
    dealing with, 27
    emergence of, 9
    International Conference on Environmental
        Education, 9
    International Environmental Education
        Workshop, 9
environmental problems
    areas, deal with, 47
    issue of depletion, presented as, 35
environmental science and environmental
        studies
    importance of, 46
    interchangeable terms, used as, 47

functioning in states and UTs, 264

Global Action Programme (GAP), 229
    goals and objectives, 232
    priority areas, 232

impact of implementation, 264
implementation of EE, 266
India
    environmental education (EE)
        areas for research, 262–264, 266

assessment and evaluation, 264
    implementation, 128
    status, 130
functioning in states and UTs, 264
impact of implementation, 264
information and communications
        technology (ICT), 264
non-governmental organizations (NGOs),
        266
    pedagogy, 263
    policy documents, 263
    professional development, 265
    roles of institution, 265
Indian Education Commission—Education &
        National Development, 84
    aim of, 84
    Kothari Commission, known as
        recommendations, 84
information and communications technology
        (ICT), 264
    application, 264
infusion/multidisciplinary approach, 66
    advantages, 67
    EE infusion, all subjects into, 66
    Hungerford et al. views on, 66
    meaning, 66
    model, 66
    Monroe (1991) and Engleson suggestions,
        68
    Monroe and Cappaert views on, 67
    Monroe recommended activities, 67
    National Council of Educational Research
        and Training (NCERT), material by, 68
    support by professional environmental
        educators, 67
International Conference on Environmental
        Education, 9
international development targets (IDT), 219
International Environmental Education
        Programme (IEEP), 17, 121
    activities in India, 122
    first phase, 18
        goals of EE, 21
        guiding principles of EE, 22
        objectives of EE, 21
    phases of, 17
    second phase, 22
    third phase, 23
International Environmental Education
        Workshop, 121

International Union for Conservation of Nature (IUCN), 119, 120
Ishwarbhai Patel Review Committee (1977), 92

Johannesburg World Summit on Sustainable Development in 2002, 123

Millennium Development Goals (MDGs), 219
Ministry of Environment, Forests and Climate Change (MoEF&CC), 266
Ministry of Human Resource Development (MHRD), 266

National Council for Accreditation of Teacher Education (NCATE), 198
National Council of Educational Research and Training (NCERT), 92, 129, 130
National Curriculum for Elementary and Secondary Education—A Framework, 122
National Curriculum Framework 2005 (NCF-2005), 97, 122, 132
  curriculum recommended by
  science, 99
  social science, 99, 100
  work and education, 100
National Curriculum Framework for School Education, 92, 122, 127
 'Frontline Curriculum', 93
 'world of work', 93
  classes covered, 94, 95
  subjects covered, 93
National Curriculum Framework for Teacher Education (NCFTE), 192
National Curriculum Framework for Teacher Education—Towards Preparing Professional and Humane Teacher 2009, 122
National Green Tribunal Act, 2009, 121
National Policy on Education, 89
  Education Commission recommendations
  environmental issues, exclusion from, 85
  statement of, 89
  thrust of, 89
  work experience, related to, 90
National Policy on Education (NPE-86 document), 90
natural science
  limitations of, 33

next generation science standards (NGSS)
  science education approach
  major concern about, 44
non-governmental organizations (NGOs), 220, 266
North American Association for Environmental Education (NAAEE), 198, 199

pedagogy, 263
policy documents, 263
professional development, 265
project-based environmental education in India, 140, 142, 149, 150
  pilot study, 143, 144, 146, 147
  practicability, 139

responsible environmental behaviour (REB), 166, 172
  cognitive factors, 168
  complexity of, 169, 170
  intention to act, 168
  lack of intention, 169
  mindset of, 171
  models, 167, 168
  personality factors, 168
  significance of, 173
  traditional thinking
  models, 166
  variables, categorization, 170, 171
Rio Declaration on Environment and Development, 123, 126, 127
roles of institution, 265

science education, converging with EE
  Gough view about, 45
  possibilities and limitations, 42–44
  questions arises on, 43
  reasons for, 42
  review of literature by Lucas, 43
  categories of, 44
  Fensham and May, view of, 44
  McMichael and Strom's suggestion, 43
science–technology–society (STS)
  and socio-scientific issues (SSI), 40
Secondary Education Commission, 83
  recommendations, 83, 84
  general science, 84
  social science, 83
social science
  aim of, 34

considered as, 34
  normative responsibility, 34
social studies educators, 39
stakeholders, 214
Stockholm Conference, 120
  UNESCO, 220
sustainability education (SE)
  types of, 232–235
sustainable development (SD), 212, 220
  references, 221

Tbilisi Conference, 121
Tbilisi Declaration, 34, 181
  components to be addressed as, 35
  EE characterization as, 34
  in 1977, 194
teacher empowerment, 192
teacher preparation
  environmental education (EE), 193, 194
    barriers, 195, 196
    comparative studies of B.Ed. syllabus, 203–206
    course content, 197–201
    guidelines, 197
    in India, 211
    in-service in India, 207, 208, 210

preservice in India, 202, 206, 207
  systemic issues, 210

UN Decade of Education for Sustainable
  Development (UNDESD), 25
United Nations conference
  on human environment organized in
    Stockholm in 1972, 120
United Nations Environment Programme
  (UNEP), 121, 220

Water Pollution Control Act of 1974, 120
Wilbur Jackman's *Nature Study for the Common
  Schools*, 14
Working Group (1984) and the National Policy
  on Education Review Committees
  (1990), 92
Working Group Report (1987), 90
World Commission on Environment and
  Development or the Brundtland
  Commission Report, 220
World Summit on Sustainable Development
  (WSSD), 25

Yashpal Committee Report, 202